# A BIBLIOGRAPHY
## OF
## JAMES WHITCOMB RILEY

JAMES WHITCOMB RILEY, 1902

PORTRAIT BY THEODORE CLEMENT STEELE, IN THE EAGLE CREST LIBRARY

*Reproduced through the courtesy of The Bobbs-Merrill Company*

# A BIBLIOGRAPHY OF

# James Whitcomb Riley

BY *ANTHONY J. RUSSO* AND

*DOROTHY R. RUSSO*

INDIANA HISTORICAL SOCIETY

INDIANAPOLIS · 1944

PRIVATELY PRINTED FOR THE INDIANA HISTORICAL SOCIETY

BY THE LAKESIDE PRESS, R. R. DONNELLEY & SONS COMPANY

CHICAGO, ILLINOIS, U. S. A.

TO JOSIAH K. LILLY JR.,
WHOSE INTEREST HAS MADE POSSIBLE
THE PREPARATION OF THIS BOOK

# Preface

~~~~~~~~~~~~~~~~~~~~~~~~~~~~~~~~~~~~~~~~~~~~~~~~~~~

THIS BIBLIOGRAPHY is the result of a grant to the Indiana Historical Society by the Lilly Endowment, Inc. It is hoped that it will prove useful to collectors of first editions, to librarians and to research workers in the field of American literature. Throughout the whole process of gathering information and of sifting and arranging it, the chief aim has been accuracy combined with clarity. The terminology is that of customary usage and the form according to bibliographical practice. The first division of the bibliography might have had its three parts amalgamated but, in order to give a well-proportioned picture of Riley's published works, it seemed best to separate the ephemeral pieces, and the books by other authors with contributions by Riley, from his own commercially published books. Reprint editions have been split into three sections: books, sheet music, collected works. Poems attributed to Riley but not established as his work have been treated in a separate group. Rileyana is divided into one section of books containing material about Riley, and another of magazines; both are selective. The list of first lines does not include those indexed in the *Biographical Edition* (1913). The list of periodicals immediately preceding the general index deals only with first appearances of Riley's writings in magazines or newspapers.

Riley's first book was a joint enterprise between the author and George C. Hitt, business manager of the *Indianapolis Journal*. No publisher saw a chance for profit in "*The Old Swimmin'-Hole,*" *and 'Leven More Poems*, but in July of 1883,

Riley saw his book in print, thanks to the interest and aid of his good friend. On a hot summer day, fifty-six years later, Mr. Hitt opened a trunk in his apartment and showed the compilers of this bibliography the old journal in which he had kept records of the transaction. All honor is due Mr. Hitt for his loyalty and assistance when it was needed.

Later in 1883 an Indianapolis firm, Merrill, Meigs & Company, undertook a second printing of the book (oddly, both this and Bowen-Merrill's printing in 1886, carry the statement "Second Edition"). So far as we can learn, it was Merrill, Meigs & Company's first entry into the field of miscellaneous publishing; they had been issuing law books only. In 1885 the firm was consolidated with Bowen-Stewart & Company and became The Bowen-Merrill Company. Lee Burns, who was with The Bowen-Merrill Company at that time, recalls taking corrected proof sheets from Riley as fast as the author returned them, and delivering them to Carlon & Hollenbeck, Indianapolis, who printed and bound the books, a thousand copies at a time. As the demand for Riley's works increased, this small local bindery could not handle the quantity production and a Chicago firm, A. J. Cox & Company, was called upon to bind them. Theirs is the familiar parti-colored cloth of the Riley books of the 1890's, a two-toned green combination of smooth cloth, or tan and maroon combination of twilled cloth. They also used the red cloth with extra gilt-stamped spine, which made a pleasing binding for Riley's poems. About 1898 The Bowen-Merrill Company shifted their printing and binding to Brooklyn, New York, to Braunworth, Munn & Barber, later Braunworth & Company. On January 19, 1903, The Bowen-Merrill Company became The Bobbs-Merrill Company (see the *Indianapolis Sentinel*, January 25, 1903). The firm continued to publish Riley's books, but with other publishing houses coming into the picture too.

Publication prices are taken from the United States Catalog and from advertisements in national journals. In the Indianapolis newspapers the books were frequently offered at cut prices.

Wherever any poem or prose sketch makes a first appearance in a Riley book, that book is collated in the "First Editions" section, with previous printings of the first edition material noted. If published previously in more than one newspaper, magazine, piece of ephemera, or book by some other author, only the first appearance in each form is listed. The *Biographical Edition* (1913) is the standard of comparison and we have noted variations in titles between first Riley book appearance, previous printings and *Biographical Edition*. The latter contains much first edition material itself and is collated.

The Indianapolis newspapers to which Riley contributed so copiously have been made available to us and we have examined them as carefully as possible in the hope of making the record complete and accurate. In the Kokomo Public Library there are mutilations in the file of the *Kokomo Dispatch* but the dates of two Riley poems that appeared therein are duly authenticated. The issues of the *Kokomo Tribune* have been carefully preserved by the publishers, and the same is true of the *Hancock Democrat* at Greenfield, although some issues of the latter have been tampered with. We have failed so far in our quest for files of the *Greenfield Commercial*, *News* and *Republican* to which Riley undoubtedly contributed his earliest work. William Ross Hartpence in his *Early Recollections of James Whitcomb Riley* (1902) tells of Riley's poems in the *Greenfield News*, and Marcus Dickey and Edmund H. Eitel in their works on Riley mention other appearances of his writings in the above-mentioned newspapers, but further research is at a standstill until they are unearthed and made available.

It is known that Riley wrote a great deal for the *Anderson Democrat* from April through August, 1877, but the file of these

issues found by Mr. Eitel in 1913 in the County Recorder's
Office in the Madison County Court House (as described in the
*Indianapolis Star*, September 14, 1913) cannot now be located.
Dates for much of the Riley material in the *Anderson Democrat*
have been supplied from the occasional issues saved by friends
of the author and from clippings in various scrapbooks. It is
hoped that some day the original records will appear and be
housed in a library accessible to research workers with a serious
purpose.

All too frequently people have preserved newspaper or
magazine clippings without any identification, or with incor-
rect identification. Many of these have been traced to their true
source, some have had to be ignored. At least two letters have
been printed in newspapers and apparently not elsewhere, but
we cannot establish the place or date: one was written by Riley
to Mary Alicia Owen on November 22, 1892, the other to John
Habberton on June 19, 1901.

We have one issue of the *Mooresville Enterprise*, 1873, which
contains a Riley letter, but have not located other Mooresville
papers of this period. Early in his career Riley may have contributed to the *Peoria (Illinois) Call* but no file of it has yet been
searched.

Often there has appeared in a newspaper, magazine or book,
a Riley poem which, to judge by its title, has had no previous
printing. Earlier publications under different titles may, however, be located through the index of first lines in the *Biographical Edition* or the supplemental list in this bibliography, pp.
263–274. No attempt has been made to note all the changes of
titles in such reprintings but a few examples may be mentioned
here: "The Smitten Purist" was in the *Indianapolis News*,
October 8, 1915, as "To Any Smith"; "Your Height Is Ours"
was published in *The Book Buyer*, April, 1897, as "To Richard
Henry Stoddard"; "Hymn Exultant" appeared in the *Reader*

*Magazine,*\* May, 1905, as "Easter" (not the same as his uncollected poem, "Easter," that appeared in an advertisement for The When); "What Little Saul Got for Christmas" ("What Little Saul Got, Christmas") was reprinted from *The Cosmopolitan* in the *Indianapolis News*, December 6, 1904, as "What Santa Claus Got Christmas"; "While the Musician Played" was reprinted in the *White House Hand-Book of Oratory* (1899) as "A Dream," a title under which Riley wrote several poems; "Decoration Day on the Place" appeared in *Spanish-American War Songs* (1898) as "On Every Soldier's Grave."

A problem arises in cases where part of a published poem has been reprinted under a new title without any accompanying statement regarding source. If the part is from the middle or latter portion, the first line index is no help. Only familiarity with the text of Riley's poems makes identification possible. Among examples noted but not mentioned in the text of his bibliography are the following: part of "A Child's Home—Long Ago" appeared in the *Saturday Herald* (*Indianapolis*), August 10, 1878, as "The Old Cabin"; the fourth stanza of "Old Man's Nursery Rhyme" was reprinted in *The Reader*, March, 1907, as "Rabbit Huntin' "; part of "The Silent Victors" appeared in *The Reader*, June, 1905, as "Memorial Day"; one of the untitled lyrics in "The Flying Islands of the Night" was published in *The Reader*, December, 1907, as "The Song of the Lonely Gnome."

The titles of poems were often changed between their printings in successive Riley books, varying from changes in articles, punctuation or spelling, to such alterations as the following: "A Tale of the Airly Days" to "The Airly Days"; "Fame" to

---

\**The Reader*, a magazine containing many selections from Riley, some original contributions and some not, offers some difficulty in regard to its title. Sometimes published as *The Reader*, sometimes *The Reader Magazine*, its running title, cover title and index vary. Therefore it may be mentioned in passing that under either title the same publication is meant.

"And This Is Fame"; "My White Bread" to "Eatin' My White Braid"; "Noon," or "A Noon Interval," to "A Midday in Midsummer"; "We Are Not Always Glad When We Smile" to "Not Always Glad When We Smile"; "O, Her Beauty" to "Oh, Her Beauty"; "The Old Man" (the poem without the prose) to "Salutation—To Benj. F. Johnson"; "Craqueodoom" to "Spirk Troll-Derisive." Other examples are noted in the text of this bibliography.

The fact that Riley wrote and rewrote his poems until each couplet was a polished thought, phrased in simple words or the dialect he used so well, means that his manuscripts exist in numerous drafts, with changes in both text and title. A study of revisions would be a separate work. It is important to check at least first lines to determine whether or not a manuscript represents an unpublished work. In the Riley Home at Greenfield, Indiana, there is an autograph album belonging to Lizzie Harris, containing a poem, "To Lizzie." It was later collected as "Lines for an Album." Booth Tarkington has a letter written by Riley to his sister, Mrs. Ovid Butler Jameson, which includes a poem, "A Midsummer Siesta." The only printed appearance of this poem is in the *Indianapolis Journal*, May 21, 1881, under the title, "Cream for Two." The original manuscript title of "God's Mercy" was, apparently, "New Years"; a facsimile of it has been found mounted in two sets of the *Elizabeth Marine Riley Edition* of Riley's works.

It is outside the realm of this bibliography to study closely the revisions in the poems once published. We have, however, considered that by extending "An Old Sweetheart of Mine" and "Out to Old Aunt Mary's," and issuing them as separate books in 1902 and 1904, Riley made the poems new. Other important revisions are mentioned in the text of this bibliography.

Riley apparently wrote more than one draft of his letters as well as his poems. In *The Youth of James Whitcomb Riley* by

Marcus Dickey (1919), p. 318, there appears a letter addressed
to Henry Wadsworth Longfellow, dated November 20, 1876,
for an answer to which, Mr. Dickey states, Riley endured ten
days' suspense. Actually the letter received then by Longfellow
(and answered promptly by him) was dated November 27,
1876, and differs in text. The second letter which Riley wrote to
Longfellow, on September 2, 1878, also differs slightly from the
one printed on p. 325 of the above-mentioned book. Evidently
Mr. Dickey saw earlier drafts of the letters. Through the kindness
of Henry Wadsworth Longfellow Dana we know their final form.

The metamorphosis of Riley's handwriting is a fascinating
study. To those who are familiar only with the engraving-like
script which he perfected in the 1880's, his earlier letters and
manuscripts appear to be in the handwriting of a different
person. Only in his signature is there any similarity. Probably
his annoyance over typographical errors, combined with a
meticulous attention to detail, made him practice long and
painstakingly until he had evolved a form of writing that was
both legible and exquisite. His manuscripts exist in three states:
early, in quite poor handwriting; intermediate, with character-
istics of both early and late; late, crystallized script.

Riley used a number of pseudonyms. They are noted in this
bibliography in the list of periodicals containing first appearances (pp. 277–309). The only one carried over into his books
is familiar to most people, "Benj. F. Johnson" or "Benj. F.
Johnson of Boone." However, neither *"The Old Swimmin'-Hole"*
(1883) or *Neghborly Poems* (1891) are pseudonymous publications; his real name appears also. Other pseudonyms used by
Riley were: "Edyrn," "Jay Whit," "John C. Walker," "Doc
Marigold," "Harrison Driley" (a combination of Lee O. Harris
and James Whitcomb Riley). In letters he often signed himself
"Jamesy O'Riley" and "Jamesy O'Reilly," or let his fancy have
free rein, his signatures varying according to his mood of the

moment. The story of the poem written by Riley and initialed "E. A. P." is told briefly in the discussion of "Leonainie" (p. 147). One poem, "Lord Bacon," in its first newspaper appearance was ascribed by Riley to his business manager, Amos J. Walker. In October, 1905, comparatively late in his career, three Riley poems appeared under the pseudonym, "John Challing" (see "Imitations of Three Southern Singers," later "Some Imitations").

In December, 1890, "The When" store in Indianapolis began a series of advertisements that appeared at intervals until February, 1892. These were printed in the form of an open book entitled, "Old Mother When's Nursery Rhymes." The jingles were unsigned but undoubtedly Riley was their author. Later many of them appeared with only minor changes in *Armazindy* (1894), one in *Morning* (1907), one in the *Memorial Edition*, Vol. 9 (1916); possibly others were rewritten and used also in his books. Today one wonders why there was any secrecy regarding them, but Riley probably enjoyed both writing them and mystifying Indianapolis. Many other unsigned writings in local newspapers have a James Whitcomb Riley flavor and quite possibly were written by him, but without proof or competent evidence we have not listed them as his. On December 25, 1895, he wrote to Lee O. Harris and mentioned that he had a poem in "today's Journal," also an editorial that made his soul "blush to the roots of its hair." The poem to which he referred was "A Dream of Christmas." Certainly neither of the Christmas articles on the editorial page of this issue need have embarrassed him, so probably he meant the brief one concerning an explosion in a Greenfield candy factory.

It is possible that Riley's poems have been translated into foreign languages and published abroad. That offers an interesting field for future investigation, when the libraries of Europe are freed from wartime restrictions.

In 1879 or 1880, Riley and Mary Hartwell Catherwood planned a joint book which was to be entitled "The Whittleford Letters." This never materialized, nor did Riley participate in a book jointly with Mrs. Frances Hodgson Burnett as indicated by a newspaper in the '90's.

Occasionally the poetry of James Riley has been confused with that of James Whitcomb Riley. In the *Readers' Guide* and in some library card catalogues the James Riley records have crept into the James Whitcomb Riley category. Except that James Riley is said to have been born in Ireland in 1848 and to have had three books published in Boston, we have little data regarding him.

As the fame of James Whitcomb Riley spread beyond his native state, his poetry was used in unnumbered ways. Selections have appeared in an amazing number of anthologies, and in American Braille. Barclay Walker wrote a play, "At Griggsby's Station" (based on "Griggsby's Station"), with musical settings of several Riley poems, which was produced by the Holden Players at the Colonial Theatre in Indianapolis in May, 1913. "An Old Sweetheart of Mine" was dramatized by Robert McLaughlin and presented at English's, Indianapolis, the week of October 2, 1916. "Home Again," Robert McLaughlin's dramatization of Riley's early life and works, opened at the Playhouse, New York City, November 11, 1918. This play was copyrighted in 1918 under the title, "Home-Folks," and was published later as "Little Orphan Annie." Movies, too, have been built around Riley's poems. "A Hoosier Romance," with Colleen Moore, appeared at the Alhambra Theatre, Indianapolis, August, 1918. "The Old Swimmin' Hole," presenting Charles Ray, produced by Arthur Kane, was reviewed in the *Indianapolis News*, March 2, 1912.

In 1902 Riley was made Honorary Master of Arts by Yale; in 1903 Wabash College gave him the degree of Doctor of

Letters and in 1904 the University of Pennsylvania similarly
honored him; in 1907 Indiana University made him Doctor of
Laws. In 1911 he was elected to the American Academy of Arts
and Letters, and in 1912 was awarded the gold medal for poetry
by the National Institute of Arts and Letters (the first poet to
receive this medal). In October, 1911, the State Superintendent
of Public Instruction in Indiana proclaimed a "Riley Day" in
the schools in honor of his birthday on October 7, a date that is
still being celebrated. Books have been dedicated to him by
Joel Chandler Harris, Booth Tarkington, Bliss Carman, Madison Cawein, W. S. Blatchley and others. All kinds of things
have been named for him: a park, a hotel, a summer resort, a
carnation, a cigar, brands of food, a train and a ship, to mention
just a few. His famous "Little Orphan Annie" was used in a
comic strip by Harold Gray, syndicated and still appearing in
many newspapers.

Though neither a biographer nor a literary critic, a bibliographer inevitably becomes cognizant of his subject's personality.
The qualities of the man Riley that shine through his writings
are the essence of the truly great: love and sympathy for his
fellowmen, appreciation of nature and of simple virtues, capac-
ity for deep friendship, sensitive perception of the humor and
the pathos of life. As "The Hoosier Poet," Riley recorded life
in the Middle West, in a rural community, in the decade immediately preceding the Civil War, and historians might do well
to consult his works. Out of his poetry there emerges a pattern
of people, scenes and customs that rings true. He has brought
a message of hope and cheer to countless people. Because of all
these things it is possible that his work will live on in the hearts
of generations to come.

In no sense is this bibliography the work of the compilers
alone. It has benefited in full measure from the help of many
libraries and many individuals. The Indiana State Library has

furnished a rich store of Riley material, and the following members of its staff have played a special part in its progression: Esther U. McNitt (now deceased), Marguerite Anderson, Ennid Kirk, Hazel Hopper, Leona Tobey, Thelma Sullivan and Margaret Donnell. Caroline Dunn, Librarian of the Indiana Historical Society, William Henry Smith Memorial, has helped tremendously. In the Indianapolis Public Library aid was given by Luther L. Dickerson, Grace Kerr, Mary Gorgas, Mary Fishback, Marie Peters, Mary Wells and May Kane. Our great national institution, the Library of Congress, supplied many needed records and assistance in seeing the Riley material in Washington. We are grateful to John Earner, David C. Mearns and Richard S. Hill. The Copyright Office, too, has been most helpful. The list of other libraries that have helped is too long for inclusion here, but we are truly cognizant of the importance of the information secured from them.

To the publishers who have cooperated we wish to make public acknowledgement: Longmans, Green & Company, Ltd., of London; Charles Scribner's Sons, New York (through David A. Randall); Theodore Presser Company, Philadelphia. Indianapolis booksellers have also helped, as have I. R. Brussel of Brooklyn, New York, and Gabriel Engel, New York City. Both friendly interest and helpful information have come from the following persons: Mr. and Mrs. John F. Mitchell, Mr. and Mrs. Will Hough, Young E. Allison (II), Lee Burns, George C. Hitt, Frank G. Darlington, James B. Darlington, Emma M. Cox, Booth Tarkington, Elizabeth Trotter, John T. Jameson, Harriet Eitel Johnson, Blanche Stillson, Herman C. Wolff, Rev. Frederick R. Daries, Paul G. Henderson, Barton Currie, Mrs. Archie A. Mumma, W. B. Shrimplin, John A. Hayes, Mrs. Theodore M. Weiss, Anton Scherrer.

The committee of the Indiana Historical Society in charge of bibliographical work has given fine support every step of the way: Christopher B. Coleman, Benjamin D. Hitz, J. K. Lilly, Jr., Chairman. In addition Mr. Lilly threw open to us his fine collection in the Eagle Crest Library. If this bibliography succeeds in its purpose the fullest credit belongs to him. The services of Jacob Blanck throughout the year 1943 have helped see the work through to completion. Well-known as a bibliographer in the field of American first editions he has been a competent judge of the accuracy of our findings, and of aid in advising the best possible way of presenting collations of the Riley books. Alberta Morlock has served as assistant since the beginning of the research in 1939. Her careful checking of details has improved tremendously the quality of the whole.

By June 6, 1940, the date of the death of Anthony J. Russo, the most important part of the work was finished. Countless Riley books had been examined in the year's time and a plan prepared. In the fine, logical mind of Anthony J. Russo, sequences were clearly visioned and no amount of rechecking has proved him wrong in any of his findings. Some added material has, of course, come to light since 1940, but the points of issue stand as he determined them. His intelligence of rare order and his scholarship are memorialized in this bibliography.

D. R.

# Contents

# Illustrations

~~~~~~~~~~~~~~~~~~~~~~~~~~~~~~~~~

xxi

# FIRST EDITIONS

# Books

~~~~~~~~~~~~~~~~~~~~

## 1883

## "The Old Swimmin'-Hole"

"The | Old Swimmin'-Hole," | AND | 'Leven More Poems, | BY | BENJ. F. JOHNSON, OF BOONE. | [*rule*] | [JAMES WHITCOMB RILEY.] | [*rule*] | INDIANAPOLIS, IND.: | GEORGE C. HITT & CO. | 1883.

[Note: Printed in red. Brackets enclosing author's name appear on the title-page.]

COLLATION: [1]², [2–4]⁸, [5]². Leaf measures 6¼″ x 4⅝″, all edges untrimmed. The book is printed on cream-white laid paper with a scant inch between the horizontal wire marks.

PAGINATION: Blank, pp. [i-iv]; fly title, p. [1]; blank, p. [2]; title-page (inserted, hence not figured in pagination) with: *Copyrighted By James W. Riley* (no date) on verso; *Publishers' Note*, p. [3]; blank, p. [4]; *Preface*, p. [5]; blank, p. [6]; table of contents, p. [7]; blank, p. [8]; text, pp. [9]–50; blank, pp. [51–52].

ILLUSTRATIONS: None.

BINDING: Cream-colored vegetable parchment wrappers folded loosely over an inner wrapper of book paper which is pasted to spine. The front cover, printed in red, repeats the title-page. The book appeared in a dust wrapper of brown pulp paper with title printed in red between red double rules.

PUBLICATION DATE: July, 1883. The first reviews in the Indianapolis

3

newspapers appeared July 20, 1883.* The title was entered for copyright July 7, 1883. A copyright deposit copy is stamped received July 21, 1883.

NOTES: The book was first printed by Robert Clarke & Company, Cincinnati, Ohio, in an edition of 1,000 copies. Mr. Riley and Mr. George C. Hitt shared expenses of publication (the author being the & Co. on the title-page). In the end their profits amounted to $83.20 each, according to the journal kept by Mr. Hitt. His journal shows the distribution of the thousand copies to have been as follows: "Gifts to state press and elsewhere, 103; Riley took 28; sold at the *Journal* counting room (at retail price of 50c), 130; sold at local bookstores and elsewhere (at wholesale, 33⅓c), 739." The supply was exhausted within three months.

The second printing carries the statement *Second Edition* and was published by Merrill, Meigs & Company, Indianapolis, in the latter part of 1883†. A copyright deposit copy in the Library of Congress is stamped received October 1, 1883. All of the printed pages bear a rectangular red border rule, with the exception of the title-page. There are innumerable typographical changes throughout the book and alterations in punctuation and in spelling: p. 15, *chipmuck's* (*chipmunck's* in first printing); p. [17], *breth* (*breath* in first printing); p. 25, *natchural* (*natural* in first printing); etc. Pages 49–50 are on an inserted leaf, followed by two blank leaves.

The third printing, published by the Bowen-Merrill Company in 1886, carries the statement *Second Edition* (!) on the front wrapper and the title-page.

In 1895 the Bowen-Merrill Company issued a limited edition of 100 numbered and signed copies of *Neghborly Poems* under the title, "*The Old Swimmin'-Hole.*" The title-page carries the limitation notice and author's signature.

FACSIMILES: A number of facsimile reprints of the first printing have been issued, among them the following:

Facsimile, signed by the author, issued December 11, 1909, with an inserted leaf stating that it was presented to [members of] the Indiana

---

*In an unidentified newspaper clipping, it is stated that "the first copy of James Whitcomb Riley's first book . . . was bought, and is yet a prized possession of Captain William Smith King, of this city, who was then connected with the Indianapolis Daily Journal." According to the account, Riley inscribed the book and dated the inscription July 20, 1883.

†The publishers advertised *New Red-line Edition, Price .50,* in the *Indianapolis Journal,* November 10, 1883.

" The

Old Swimmin'-Hole,"

AND

'Leven More Poems,

BY

Benj. F. Johnson, of Boone.

[James Whitcomb Riley.]

INDIANAPOLIS, IND.:
GEORGE C. HITT & CO.
1883.

Society of Chicago with the compliments of The Bobbs-Merrill Company and the author.

Facsimile, possibly of the same printing, not signed by the author, with an inserted leaf bearing a Christmas greeting dated December 25, 1909.

Facsimile, issued in 1920 for Marshall Field & Company as a souvenir of their book fair, with a note regarding the facsimile on a preliminary leaf.

Facsimile, issued by The Bobbs-Merrill Company in November, 1929*. A preliminary leaf carries the statement *Facsimile Reprint* with copyright date of 1883 and renewal date of 1910.

Facsimile, used as a special edition by The Riley Old Home Society, 1937,† is apparently of the same printing as the one described immediately above; contains a 4-page insert relating to The Riley Old Home Society. The insert prints part of a letter written by Riley to a Greenfield high school girl in 1898. This letter is here stated to be unpublished, but it was written to Miss Helen Downing, December 12, 1898, and printed in the [Greenfield] *High School Budget*, June, 1899; also in *Harper's Monthly Magazine*, December, 1917, p. 4.

The following is a simple chart of the most readily distinguishable differences between the first and the facsimile editions:

| GENUINE | FACSIMILE |
|---|---|
| Title-page inserted | Title-page an integral part of the book |
| Sigs.: [1]², [2–4]⁸, [5]² | Sigs.: [1–4]⁸ |
| P. 41, stanza 4, line 1, *William* | P. 41, stanza 4, line 1, *W* lacking in *William* |
| Printed on laid paper with a scant inch between the horizontal wire marks | Copies occur on different types of laid paper in which the space between the horizontal wire marks varies from a full inch to an inch and a quarter |

This collection of poems has been reprinted many times under the title of "*The Old Swimmin'-Hole*"; also, with additions, as *Neghborly Poems, (q. v.)*.

---

*The *Indianapolis News*, November 9, 1929, reports publication of a facsimile edition by The Bobbs-Merrill Company "to celebrate the recent observance of the birthday of James Whitcomb Riley."

†See *Indianapolis Sunday Star*, October 8, 1937.

CONTENTS: 12 poems, all of which are here first collected. All had previously appeared in the *Indianapolis Journal* under the pseudonym, *Benj. F. Johnson.* This pseudonym was used for the first time on June 17, 1882, with the poem, "The Old Swimmin'-Hole." With the publication of the twelfth poem, "The Clover," September 16, 1882, the author's identity was revealed.

The Old Swimmin'-Hole   *Indianapolis Journal*, June 17, 1882

Thoughts fer the Discuraged Farmer   *Indianapolis Journal*, June 24, 1882 (With introductory letter: To the Editor . . .*)

A Summer's Day   *Indianapolis Journal*, July 1, 1882

A Hymb of Faith   *Indianapolis Journal*, July 8, 1882

Worter-melon Time   *Indianapolis Journal*, July 22, 1882

My Philosofy†   *Indianapolis Journal*, July 29, 1882 (with title: Mr. Johnson of Boone Philosophizes)

When the Frost Is on the Punkin   *Indianapolis Journal*, August 5, 1882

On the Death of Little Mahala Ashcraft   *Indianapolis Journal*, August 16, 1882 (with title: Lines on the Death of Little Mahala Ashcraft)

The Mulberry Tree   *Indianapolis Journal*, August 19, 1882

To My Old Neghbor, William Leachman   *Indianapolis Journal*, August 26, 1882 (with title: To My Old Friend and Neighbor(!), William Leachman. Title in *Biographical Edition:* To My Old Friend, William Leachman)

My Fiddle   *Indianapolis Journal*, September 2, 1882

The Clover   *Indianapolis Journal*, September 16, 1882

---

*Later incorporated in the preface to *Neghborly Poems* (1891).

†Part of "My Philosofy" appeared in *Judge*, December 14, 1889, under the title, "Just Do Your Best." It begins: "The signs is bad when folks commence"

# 1886

## *(Published 1885)*

# The Boss Girl

CHARACTER SKETCHES | [*rule*] | THE BOSS GIRL | A CHRISTMAS STORY | AND | OTHER SKETCHES | BY | JAMES WHITCOMB RILEY | AUTHOR OF "THE OLD SWIMMIN' HOLE," ETC. | INDIANAPOLIS | THE BOWEN-MERRILL CO | 1886

COLLATION: One unsigned leaf*, [1]⁸, 2–3⁸, [4]⁸, 5–6⁸, [7]⁸, 8–11⁸, [12]⁸, 13–14⁸, [15]⁸, 16⁸, 17⁴, one unsigned leaf*. Leaf measures 7⅛" x 5", all edges trimmed. The book is printed on white laid paper with ¾" between the horizontal wire marks.

PAGINATION: End paper, brown coated; fly leaf*(its conjugate pasted down under the lining paper); title-page, p. [1]; copyright notice in the name of James Whitcomb Riley, with date 1885, and imprint of *Carlon & Hollenbeck, | Printers And Binders, | Indianapolis.*, p. [2]; table of contents, p. 3; blank, p. [4]; half-title, p. [5]; proem, p. 6; text, pp. [7]–263; blank, p. [264]; fly leaf* (its conjugate pasted down under the lining paper); end paper.

ILLUSTRATIONS: None.

BINDING: Issued simultaneously in both cloth and pictorial wrappers. *Dark brown smooth cloth:* Front cover stamped in gilt: [*at top*] Character [*ornament*] | [*ornament*] Sketches | [*at foot*] JAMES WHITCOMB RILEY The cover is bordered by a blind-stamped rectangular triple rule. The spine is stamped: [*decorative rule*] | [*double rule*] | THE | BOSS GIRL | AND | OTHER | SKETCHES. | [*double rule*] | J. W. RILEY. | [*decorative rule*] All rules are blind-stamped, all lettering gilt-stamped. The back cover is blank except for blind-stamped rectangular triple rule border.

NOTE: One copy has been noted in a similar cloth but without the blind-stamped borders; the spine is wholly blank; the title and author's name are gilt-stamped on the front cover; the back cover is the same as the front but is blind-stamped.

---

*There are no fly leaves, front or back, in the only complete paper-bound copy so far located.

*Green pictorial wrappers:* Front cover printed in bluish-black ink as follows: THE | [*oval portrait*] BOSS GIRL [*oval portrait*] | A X-MAS STORY, AND | AN ADJUSTABLE LUNATIC | TOD | A REMARKABLE MAN | A NEST-EGG | TALE OF A SPIDER | MARY ALICE SMITH | ECCENTRIC MR. CLARK | THE BOY FROM ZEENY | THE OLD MAN | &c. &c. &c. | BY | JAMES WHIT-COMB RILEY | INDIANAPOLIS, IND: | THE BOWEN-MERRILL CO. 1886. The design shows the sun and its rays above a cloud bank; out of the lower right of the clouds a demon reaches down with a quill pen to fire a cannon formed of an ink bottle. Below the ink bottle cannon is printed: CHANDLER SC. INDPLS. The whole is within a rectangular single thin rule border. The spine reads as follows, vertically, running down: RILEY'S CHRISTMAS STORY, and OTHER SKETCHES. Price, 50 Cts. The back cover is identical with the front.

PUBLICATION DATE: December 19, 1885. Application for copyright was made December 18, 1885, and a copy was deposited for copyright December 26, 1885.

NOTES: The work is found in five distinct states, in both cloth and pictorial wrappers. The order of their appearance is as follows:

*State* 1: As collated. Available on the day of publication in both cloth and pictorial wrappers.

Copyright notice in the name of James Whitcomb Riley.
Page 9, line 5, exclamation point after the word *sir*!
Page 9, line 12, apostrophe in *comin'*
Page 82, last line, first words *Oh he'll be* present and in alignment.
No advertisements in back.

*State* 2: Printed on laid paper with 1¼" between the horizontal wire marks instead of ¾" as in the first state.

Copyright page as in State 1.
Page 9, line 5, exclamation point omitted after the word *sir*
Page 9, line 12, *g* replaces the apostrophe in *comin'*
Page 82, last line, first words *Oh he'll be*  missing.
No advertisements in back.

This state was issued in tan pebbled cloth wholly stamped in black. The front cover is stamped with the same design as that on the wrappered copies of State 1 but is bordered by a thick rule, single at the sides, double at top and bottom. The spine is stamped in black: [*ornamental rule*] | [*double rule*] | THE | BOSS GIRL | AND | OTHER | SKETCHES. | [*double rule*] | J. W. RILEY. | [*ornamental rule*] The back cover is unstamped. This state was also issued in the pictorial wrappers. In the cloth-bound copies CHANDLER SC. INDPLS. (at the lower right of

the front cover) appears only as a faint inkless trace. This is the "new edition" advertised as "published today" in the *Indianapolis News*, January 19, 1886.

*State* 3: Same as State 2 but has two leaves inserted at the back advertising the Bowen-Merrill edition (November, 1886) of *"The Old Swimmin'-Hole."* The first page of this advertisement is a reproduction

A boy was sent to bring him, but returned alone, to say that he had not been able to find any trace of him.

"Oh, he'll be here in time enough," said

A boy was sent to bring him, but returned alone, to say that he had not been able to find any trace of him.

here in time enough," said

A boy was sent to bring him, but returned alone, to say that he had not been able to find any trace of him.

"Oh, he'll he here in time enough," said

*The three states of p. 82 of* The Boss Girl

of the title-page, the second and third pages are pp. [13]–14 of the book; the fourth page is a *Publishers' Note* regarding publication.

In the cloth-bound copies the author's name on the spine is replaced by the statement *THIRD EDITION\**. In the wrappered copies the spine reads: RILEY'S SKETCHES. Price, 50 cents.

*State* 4: Verso of the title-page is changed. The Bowen-Merrill Company's name replaces J. W. Riley's as copyright claimant. The words *Stereotyped by Wanamaker & Marshall, Indianapolis*, now appear for the first time in addition to the printers' and binders' slug. On page 82, last

---

\*A copy has been noted in reddish-brown cloth, completely unstamped but for the lettering on the spine: THE | BOSS GIRL | AND | OTHER | SKETCHES | J. W. RILEY. This may be a publishers' trial binding or, possibly, a rebound copy.

line, the words *Oh he'll be* have been replaced but are not in perfect alignment (see illustration, p. 9 of this bibliography).

The advertisement for *"The Old Swimmin'-Hole"* is present as in State 3. Copies in wrappers have the spine lettered as in the first and second states except that the comma is omitted after *STORY* and *and* is in capitals, reading: RILEY'S CHRISTMAS STORY AND OTHER SKETCHES. Price, 50 Cts.

*State 5*: Same as State 4 but without the advertisement for *"The Old Swimmin'-Hole."* Two copies in this state have been noted in green cloth with the usual pictorial stamping on the front cover. All the edges are gilt. One of the copies is inscribed December 25, 1886, which suggets that copies in green cloth, all edges gilt, may have been so bound for the Christmas trade.

Examination of copies with contemporary inscriptions indicates beyond any doubt that copies without the advertisement followed copies with the advertisement.

NOTES (continued): Quite probably there will come to light copies of the first edition in variant bindings other than those noted. The copy in plain brown wrappers mentioned by Merle Johnson* has not been located. There is a possibility that the publishers stripped some of the paper-bound copies and issued them in cloth, but of this there is as yet no absolute evidence.

The publishers issued a prospectus dated November 23, 1885, in which it was stated that the book, "bound in stamped cloth and paper, with an artistic and unique cover, will be a handsome 12mo. of about 200 pages." Since the book, when published, contained 263 numbered pages, it is obvious that the prospectus was written before the book was set. Two days after publication of the book a notice from the Bowen-Merrill Company appeared in the *Indianapolis News* (December 21, 1885); "OH YES IT'S OUT—But not enough of them. We mean that new Book by James W. Riley entitled *The Boss Girl*. The only trouble is we can't get enough of them. The bindery can't turn them out fast enough to supply one-half the demand. We are doing our very best though and expect to fill all orders tomorrow or next day at latest. Of course, we are never satisfied so still say orders respectfully solicited. Cloth $1.00—paper 50c. Bowen-Merrill Co."

The publishers give us further enlightenment, just a week after publication, in the *Indianapolis News* (December 26, 1885): "The sale of Jas. Whitcomb Riley's new book, *The Boss Girl*, has exceeded all hope

*In *American First Editions*, 1929, 1932, 1936.

# ⊣THE BOSS GIRL⊢
## A CHRISTMAS STORY,
# AND OTHER SKETCHES.
—BY—
## JAMES WHITCOMB RILEY,
### AUTHOR OF "THE OLD SWIMMIN' HOLE."

It gives us much pleasure to announce that, on Dec: 1st, we will publish a new book, under the above title, by Indiana's favorite and now famous Poet, Author and Lecturer, James Whitcomb Riley. Those who have read Mr. Riley's "Old Swimmin' Hole," or revelled in the humor of his lectures, will be delighted with

## THE BOSS GIRL.

The book, bound in stamped cloth and paper, with an artistic and unique cover, will be a handsome 12mo. of about 200 pages, and will contain ten very interesting and pathetic character sketches.

Each story will be prefaced by a short poem, relevant to the subject.

This little book reveals the two-fold ability of the gifted author, who, though totally different in tone and style, reminds one of Edgar Allen Poe.

Mr. Riley's insight into life is marvelous, and his faithful presentation of it is as true as it is marvelous, and powerfully appeals to the heart.

We congratulate both ourselves and the people at large on the publication of this book, which, we feel, is assured of a hearty welcome and widely extended sale.

### Price, Cloth, $1.00. Paper, 50c.
Respectfully,
### THE BOWEN-MERRILL CO.,
#### Publishers, Booksellers and Importers,
16 and 18 West Washington Street,
INDIANAPOLIS, IND.

NOVEMBER 23, 1885.

and expectation. The first edition of 1,000 copies, which it was thought would last at least until another edition could be printed, went off with a whiz in less than a week, and the book is now entirely out of print. As the paper on which it is printed is of exceptional quality it has to be made especially for us, so it will be fully two weeks before this new edition can be published. Meantime we continue to solicit orders, but must ask purchasers to wait for the new edition, which will be sufficiently improved to compensate for the delay."

No further announcement is to be found until January 19, 1886, when the same newspaper carried the following publishers' advertisement, with the caption, *Again on the Wing:* "The new edition of James Whitcomb Riley's new book, *The Boss Girl* is published today. The cloth edition has been vastly improved in appearance and is now one of the handsomest $1.00 books published in the United States. The paper edition sells for 50c."

Note that the improvement, earlier promised, is here mentioned in the cloth-bound copies, not those in wrappers. What else could it have been but that "artistic and unique cover" promised in the prospectus, present in the paper-bound copies of the first edition, but for some reason not carried out on the cloth-bound copies? Quite probably the die was not ready in time and with publication delayed considerably past the December first date set for it, and with Christmas so near, the work was rushed out in the undecorated dark brown cloth.

Apparently the book went along in State 5 form until 1891, when the title was changed to *Sketches in Prose and Occasional Verses* (1891, *q. v.*) and the title of "The Boss Girl" was changed to "Jamesy." No material was added.

In 1897, as Vol. 2 of the *Homestead Edition*, the "occasional verses" were omitted and the title of the book became *Sketches in Prose*. Nothing new was added.

In 1905, *Sketches in Prose* reappeared in the *Greenfield Edition* (*q. v.*).

In 1913, the same prose sketches reappeared as *Eccentric Mr. Clark*, with rearrangement but no added material.

Mr. Booth Tarkington has given us the following statement* regarding his contribution to this work: "Sometimes he (Mr. Riley) would spend the greater part of an evening drawing with me and he went so far as to ask me for suggestions about the cover of his first 'full-size book.' It was to be a paper cover; and for it he'd designed an ink

---

*In a letter from Elizabeth Trotter, his amanuensis, March 14, 1941. The account is essentially the same as in his reminiscences, "As I Seem to Me," *The Saturday Evening Post*, August 2, 1941, p. 46.

bottle mounted as a cannon firing a charge that exploded into the words, THE BOSS GIRL. When he'd sketched the design, I drew upon the paper an imp flying downward from the top of the page and, with the point of a long quill pen applied to the touch-hole, firing the ink-bottle cannon. The idea pleased the poet; he made much of it and of me, and the book was printed with my imp upon the cover. Whenever he talked to me of *The Boss Girl* he spoke as if to a fellow-workman who'd had much to do with the book's creation and rightfully shared credit in its modest success. I glowed, but didn't swell. In all my relations with the good and true poet, mercy from on high vouchsafed that I should know my place."

CONTENTS: All of the poems and prose sketches herein contained are first appearances in a Riley book:

God Bless Us Every One  *Saturday Herald* (*Indianapolis*), July 26, 1879

The Boss Girl (prose)  *Indianapolis Journal*, December 29, 1878 (title in *Biographical Edition:* Jamesy)

Bells Jangled  *Saturday Herald* (*Indianapolis*), August 16, 1879 (with title: The Serenade)

An Adjustable Lunatic (prose; includes 2 poems: [The Dream of Death—"O gentle death, bow down and sip"] and [A Fantasy— "A fantasy that came to me"])  *Indianapolis Journal*, April 23, 1878

Little Tommy Smith  *Saturday Herald* (*Indianapolis*), July 19, 1879 (title in *Biographical Edition:* Tommy Smith)

Tod (prose)  *Indianapolis Journal*, April 3, 1879*.

Fame  *Earlhamite*, February, 1877; *Boston Evening Transcript*, June 26, 1882; *Indianapolis Journal*, September 30, 1882 (with title: A Descant on Fame)

A Remarkable Man (prose; includes 3 poems: [My Father's Halls— "My father's halls, so rich and rare"]; [The Harp of the Minstrel —"The harp of the minstrel has never a tone"]; and a passage in imitation of Shakespeare beginning: "Falstaff. I call him dog, forsooth, because he snarls")  *Indianapolis Journal*, February 16, 1877

Old-Fashioned Roses†  *Saturday Herald* (*Indianapolis*), June 14, 1879; *Locomotive Firemen's Monthly Magazine*, January, 1881

---

*See *Biographical Edition* (1913), Vol. 6, p. 399, for reference to an earlier newspaper appearance.

†See *Biographical Edition*, Vol. 2, p. 485, for introduction to the poem, used by Riley in recitations.

A Nest-Egg (prose)  *Indianapolis Journal*, June 3, 1882

The Beetle  *Kokomo Tribune*, August 16, 1879 (title in *Biographical Edition:* Dusk Song—The Beetle)

Tale of a Spider (prose; includes 3 poems: Ye Scholar; Death [Is Dead]—"And did you know our old friend Death is dead?"; and a sonnet without title beginning, "O, what strange tragedy is this of mine")  *Indianapolis Journal*, May 13, 1879

The Elf Child*  *Indianapolis Journal*, November 15, 1885 (title in *Biographical Edition:* Little Orphant Annie)

Where Is Mary Alice Smith? (prose)  *Indianapolis Journal*, September 30, 1882

The Ban  *Indianapolis Journal*, January 8, 1880 (with title: Opium)

Eccentric Mr. Clark (prose)  *Indianapolis Journal*, May 6, 1882

The Brook  *Indianapolis Journal*, February 4, 1882 (title in *Biographical Edition:* The Brook-Song)

"The Boy from Zeeny" (prose)  *Indianapolis Journal*, June 10, 1882 (with title: The Boy from Xenia)

The Orchard Lands of Long Ago  *Indianapolis Journal*, January 30, 1881; *The Humbler Poets* by Slason Thompson, (1886; pub. 1885?, see p. 169)

The Old Man (prose; includes poem of the same title)  *Indianapolis Journal*, February 20, 1884

---

*"The Elf Child" is herein named "Little Orphant Allie."

# 1888

*(Published 1887)*

# Afterwhiles

AFTERWHILES | BY | JAMES WHITCOMB RILEY | Indianapolis | BOWEN-MERRILL CO., PUBLISHERS | 1888

COLLATION: One unsigned leaf, [1]² (title-page inserted between these two leaves), two unsigned leaves (table of contents and a blank leaf), [2–11]⁸, one unsigned leaf. Leaf measures 7″ x 4⅜″, all edges trimmed, top edge gilt. Printed on white laid paper.

PAGINATION: End paper, white laid; fly leaf (its conjugate pasted down under the lining paper); fly title, p. [i]; list of books *By the Same Author*, p. [ii]; title-page (inserted), p. [iii]; copyright notice with date 1887, and *A. R. Baker* | *Electrotyper And Printer*, p. [iv]; dedication to Humboldt Riley, p. [v]; blank, p. [vi]; table of contents (inserted), pp. [vii–viii]; blank leaf (inserted), pp. [ix–x]; proem, pp. 1–3; blank, p. [4]; text, pp. 5–160; fly leaf (its conjugate pasted down under the lining paper); end paper.

ILLUSTRATIONS: None.

BINDING: Light tan boards with brown cloth shelfback. Front cover printed in brown: [*at top*] AFTERWHILES | [*at foot*] James Whitcomb Riley Spine stamped in gilt: AFTERWHILES | James | Whitcomb | Riley   Back cover blank.

PUBLICATION DATE: The title was entered for copyright November 1, 1887. The book was announced for sale in the *Indianapolis News* of November 25, 1887. The copyright deposit copy is stamped received December 24, 1887.

PUBLICATION PRICE: $1.25.

NOTES: The sheets exist in various states:
    *State* 1: As collated
           Table of contents set in upper and lower case
           Page 27, fourth line from the bottom, first word *And*
    *State* 2: Same as State 1 but p. 27, fourth line from the bottom, first word *Till*

*State* 3: Signatures: one unsigned leaf, [1]⁴, one unsigned leaf,
[2–11]⁸, one unsigned leaf
Table of contents reset in small capitals
*Fourth Thousand* stated on the title-page; subsequent
thousands similarly distinguished
Page 27 as in State 2

The bindings vary, the earliest being that described in the collation,
light tan boards, brown cloth shelfback. On the front cover the space
from the top of the *I* in *AFTERWHILES* to the bottom of the *m* in
*James* is 6⅛″. Earliest located presentation copies, given by the author
to his relatives and close friends, are in this state of binding; one of
them is dated December 8, 1887. For Riley's letter to Bill Nye, November
21, 1887, regarding this book, see *Letters of James Whitcomb Riley*
edited by William Lyon Phelps (1930), p. 78.

The cloth binding possibly did not appear until December 20,
1887. On that date the publishers announced in the *Indianapolis News*
that "the first edition of 1,000 copies didn't last a month" and described
a "second edition, now ready: 12mo, gilt top, $1.25. Holiday edition,
gilt top and fancy gilt sides, $1.75." The former copies are no doubt
those in brown twilled cloth with front cover stamped in black: AFTER-
WHILES | James Whitcomb Riley   The spine is stamped in gilt: AFTER-
WHILES | James | Whitcomb | Riley   A bandeau of vertical rules (with
horizontal rules, two above, one below), stamped in black, extends
across the top of the spine to the fore edge of the front cover. Back
cover blank. The copyright deposit copy, received in Washington
December 24, 1887, is in this state of binding, with sheets in the second
state.

The "Holiday edition" described in the advertisement of December
20th refers obviously to copies in illuminated boards with an all-
over design, extra gilt shelfback.

The fourth state of binding is similar to the first state but the space
on the front cover from the top of *I* in *AFTERWHILES* to the bottom
of the *m* in *James* is 6⅝″.

A later binding is cloth of various colors with lettering totally un-
like that of earlier states, and with a farm scene in a panel at the top of
the front cover.

In 1890 the book appeared with a portrait frontispiece, the first portrait of the author to appear in one of his books.

In 1898, as Vol. 3 of the *Homestead Edition*, the book had
the contents rearranged, four poems omitted and a number added.
Of the poems added, three made first appearance in a Riley book
(see p. 72).

CONTENTS: All of the poems herein are first appearances in a Riley book:

[Proem]   (Title in *Biographical Edition:* Afterwhiles)

Herr Weiser   *Indianapolis Journal*, August 24, 1884

The Beautiful City   *Indianapolis Journal*, June 30, 1883

Lockerbie Street*   *Indianapolis Journal*, July 12, 1880; *Life*, August 2, 1883

Das Krist Kindel   *Indianapolis Journal*, December 25, 1877 (with title: A Dream of Christmas)

Anselmo   *Indianapolis Journal*, October 18, 1884

A Home-Made Fairy Tale

The South Wind and the Sun   *Indianapolis Journal*, September 23, 1882

The Lost Kiss   *Indianapolis Journal*, December 2, 1879

The Sphinx   *Indianapolis Journal*, October 22, 1880

If I Knew What Poets Know   *New Castle Mercury*, December 7, 1876;† *Indianapolis Journal*, October 2, 1877

Ike Walton's Prayer   *Indianapolis Journal*, July 26, 1885

A Rough Sketch   *Indianapolis Journal*, April 30, 1880

Our Kind of a Man   *Indianapolis Journal*, March 5, 1884

The Harper   *Indianapolis Journal*, April 26, 1884

Old Aunt Mary's§   *Indianapolis Journal*, June 14, 1884; *The Elocutionist's Annual No. 13* (1885); (title in both same as in *Biographical Edition:* Out to Old Aunt Mary's)

Illileo   *Indianapolis Journal*, July 25, 1886

The King   *Indianapolis Journal*, November 2, 1884

A Bride   *Kokomo Tribune*, November 15, 1879 (with title: Tired)

The Dead Lover   (No previous publication noted save as last 3 stanzas of "In State" in *Indianapolis Journal*, May 17, 1884)

A Song ("There is ever a song somewhere, my dear")   *Indianapolis Journal*, April 5, 1884 (with title: Song)

When Bessie Died   *Indianapolis Journal*, September 14, 1884

The Shower   *Indianapolis Journal*, April 19, 1879

A Life-Lesson   *Indianapolis Journal*, July 25, 1880

A Scrawl   *Indianapolis Journal*, May 24, 1884

---

*This poem appeared in a pamphlet entitled, *Lockerbie Street Fair;* undated, probably *ca.* 1900.

†Not seen except as a clipping with manuscript note of date.

§See *Biographical Edition*, Vol. 3, p. 522, for introduction to the poem, used by Riley in recitations. See *Out to Old Aunt Mary's* (1904) for discussion of the poem's development.

Away* *Indianapolis Journal*, May 31, 1884

Who Bides His Time *Indianapolis Journal*, April 12, 1885

From the Headboard of a Grave in Paraguay *Indianapolis Journal*, September 21, 1884

Laughter Holding Both His Sides *Indianapolis Journal*, May 10, 1884

Pan *Saturday Herald (Indianapolis)*, July 5, 1879

Dusk *New Castle Mercury*, November 16, 1876 (with title: Evening. In *Biographical Edition* part of: Dead Leaves)

June ("O queenly month of indolent repose")

Silence *Sun (New York)*, April 11, 1880

Time *Indianapolis Journal*, November 29, 1880 (first stanza only, with title: A Mood); *Indianapolis Journal*, July 12, 1885 (second stanza only, with title: The Smell of Bruised Grass)

Sleep ("Thou drowsy god, whose blurred eyes, half awink") *Saturday Herald (Indianapolis)*, August 23, 1879

Her Hair *Indianapolis Journal*, April 14, 1883

Dearth *Earlhamite*, March, 1877; *Indianapolis Journal*, November 3, 1878

A Voice from the Farm

When She Comes Home *Century Magazine*, June, 1887; *Indianapolis Journal*, June 5, 1887

Art and Love *Indianapolis Journal*, April 26, 1885

Griggsby's Station *Indianapolis Journal*, May 17, 1885 (with title: Back Where They Used To Be); *Judge*, September 5, 1885 (with title: Back to Griggsby's)

Knee-Deep in June *Indianapolis Journal*, June 14, 1885 (with title: Long About Knee Deep in June)

When the Hearse Comes Back *Indianapolis Journal*, August 14, 1887

A Canary at the Farm *Indianapolis Journal*, September 21, 1884; *Judge*, March 13, 1886

A Liz-Town Humorist *Indianapolis Journal*, November 2, 1884

Kingry's Mill *Northwestern Miller*, Christmas, 1886; *Indianapolis Journal*, May 29, 1887

Joney *Indianapolis Journal*, June 7, 1885 (with title: Had a Hare-Lip)

Nothin' to Say *Century Magazine*, August, 1887; *Indianapolis Journal*, July 31, 1887

---

*The poem appeared on a white card 5¼″ x 3¼″, decorated with floral design and hair-line lavender border, published by Ernest Dudley, Boston—probably issued after 1900.

Like His Mother Used to Make   *Indianapolis Journal*, December 14, 1884; *The Humbler Poets* by Slason Thompson (1886; pub. 1885?, see p. 169)

The Train-Misser   *Indianapolis Journal*, December 20, 1885; *Judge*, January 30, 1886 (with title: Missed the Train Again)

Granny   *Indianapolis Journal*, May 10, 1885

Old October   *Indianapolis Journal*, October 24, 1886 (with title: Sompin' Strange about October)

Jim   *Indianapolis Journal*, September 26, 1886; *Judge*, November 6, 1886

A Tale of the Airly Days   *Indianapolis Journal*, March 7, 1886

To Robert Burns   *Indianapolis Journal*, January 27, 1880

A New Year's Time at Willards's *Indianapolis Journal*, January 1, 1885

The Town Karnteel   *Indianapolis Journal*, August 2, 1884 (part of prose sketch: A Wild Irishman)

Regardin' Terry Hut   *Indianapolis Journal*, February 28, 1886

Leedle Dutch Baby   *Saturday Herald* (*Indianapolis*), June 28, 1879 (with title: Lullaby)

Down on Wriggle Crick   *Indianapolis Journal*, March 8, 1885

When de Folks Is Gone   *Indianapolis Journal*, January 23, 1881

The Little Town o' Tailholt   *Saturday Herald* (*Indianapolis*), September 13, 1879

# 1888

# Old-Fashioned Roses

OLD-FASHIONED ROSES | BY | JAMES WHITCOMB RILEY | [*floret*] | LONDON | LONGMANS, GREEN, AND CO. | 1888 | All rights reserved

COLLATION: [A]⁶, B-I⁸, K⁸, L². Leaf measures 6¼″ x 3⅞″, top edge gilt, other edges untrimmed. The book is printed on white laid paper watermarked *I D & Co.*

PAGINATION: End paper, white laid; blank leaf, pp. [i–ii]; fly title, p. [iii]; printers' slug: *Printed By* | *Spottiswoode And Co., New-Street Square* | *London*, p. [iv]; title-page, p. [v]; blank, p. [vi]; dedication, p. [vii]; blank, p. [viii]; table of contents, pp. viii–ix (should be ix–xi); blank, p. [xii]; half-title, p. [1]; blank, p. [2]; text, pp. [3]–145 (with printers' slug at foot of p. 145); blank, pp. [146–148]; end paper.

ILLUSTRATIONS: None.

BINDING: Blue twilled cloth sides, vegetable vellum shelfback, with vertical gilt rule where cloth and vellum join. Blue paper label on spine lettered in gilt: OLD- | FASHIONED | ROSES | [*rule*] | RILEY  Double gilt rules are stamped at top and bottom of spine, with two single gilt rules at equal intervals between. Just above the double rule at foot of the spine is stamped: LONGMANS & Cº  Front and back covers un-lettered.

PUBLICATION DATE: October 5, 1888, according to the publishers' records.

NOTES: The American edition, produced at the same time and place as the English edition, is identical save for the following differences:

The publishers' imprint reads: INDIANAPOLIS | BOWEN-MERRILL CO., PUBLISHERS | 1889

The line *All rights reserved* does not appear on the title-page.

The verso of the title-page reads: *Copyright 1889* | *By* | *James Whitcomb Riley*

There is no publishers' name at foot of spine.

Of the 1,000 copies of the first edition, Longmans sent 715 copies to America, presumably those with the Bowen-Merrill imprint. The English edition was published at 5s., the American at $1.75.*

In 1891 the English publishers reissued the book in an edition of 2,750 copies, with *Second Edition* stated on the title-page. Later printings were similarly identified, the last appearing in 1912; the book was allowed to go out of print in 1928.

The proem from which the book took its name was issued separately in 1914, with illustrations by Howard Chandler Christy (see p. 200).

Why Mr. Riley's poems won the recognition of so prominent a British publishing firm thus early in his career is explained in a notice of the book that appeared in the *Chicago Herald*, October 20, 1888: "When Charles Longman was in this country last spring he was very much taken with J. Whitcomb Riley's poems and arranged with the author to publish a volume of them specially prepared for the London public. This selection, called 'Old-Fashioned Roses,' has just been issued in England."

CONTENTS: Of the poems in this volume the following 9 make their first appearance in book form:

The Days Gone By   *Indianapolis Journal*, September 9, 1882

An Old Sweetheart of Mine†   *Indianapolis Journal*, March 12, 1877; *The Elocutionist's Annual*, No. 16 (1888)

A Fruit-Piece   *Indianapolis Journal*, September 16, 1882

The Little White Hearse   *Indianapolis Journal*, March 10, 1883

"Curly Locks"   *Indianapolis Journal*, August 2, 1885

The Ripest Peach   *Indianapolis Journal*, April 17, 1881

Puck   *Sun (New York)*, April 18, 1880

To the Cricket   *Indianapolis Journal*, July 21, 1881 (with title: Sonnet—To the Cricket)

The Serenade ("The midnight is not more bewildering")   *Cosmopolitan*, December, 1887

---

*Part of the American edition was destroyed in the Bowen-Merrill Company's big fire; see Riley's letter to W. H. Calkins, April 28, 1890, in *Letters of James Whitcomb Riley*, edited by William Lyon Phelps (1930), p. 100.

†See *Biographical Edition*, Vol. 1, notes, p. 405, for Riley's brief letter in rhyme on the identity of "the old sweetheart." It begins: "Dear Mister McGrew." See *An Old Sweetheart of Mine* (1902) for discussion of the poem's development.

# 1888

# Nye and Riley's Railway Guide

NYE AND RILEY'S | RAILWAY GUIDE | BY | EDGAR W. NYE | AND | JAMES WHITCOMB RILEY | [*rule*] | Illustrated by Baron DeGrimm E. Zimmerman | Walt. McDougall and others | [*rule*] | CHICAGO | THE DEARBORN PUBLISHING COMPANY | 88 AND 90 LA SALLE STREET | NEW YORK 1888 SAN FRANCISCO

COLLATION: [1–14]⁸, wire-stitched. The leaf measures 7⅜″ x 5¼″, all edges trimmed. Printed on white wove paper.

PAGINATION: End paper, red and white all-over design; blank, pp. [i–iii]; caricature of Bill Nye, p. [iv]; caricature of J. W. Riley (with tissue guard), p. [v]; blank, p. [vi]; title-page, p. [vii]; copyright notice in name of Bill Nye and James Whitcomb Riley, with date 1888, p. [viii]; preface, *Why it was done*, pp. [ix]–xiii (should be xi); blank, p. [xii]; table of contents, pp. [xiii]–xvi (should be xiv); text, pp. [1]–203; blank, p. [204]; advertisements, pp. [205–206]; blank, pp. [207–210]; end paper.

[Note: Pages x–xi mispaged xii–xiii; p. xiv mispaged xvi.]

ILLUSTRATIONS: The full-page caricatures of Nye and Riley are, as noted above, integral parts of the first signature. Text illustrations throughout the book.

BINDING: Issued simultaneously in both cloth and pictorial wrappers. *Mustard-colored twilled cloth:* Some of the text illustrations are stamped in black on the front cover, above, and at the left of, a design of a locomotive with headlight directed toward: NYE & RILEY'S | RAILWAY GUIDE   The date is stamped at the foot: 1888   Above the locomotive are two overlapping gilt medallions embossed with names and portraits of Bill Nye and James Whitcomb Riley. *Flemming, Eng.* appears on one of the black-stamped tracks. With the exception of the gilt-stamped medallions, all stamping is in black. The spine is stamped in gilt: [*double rule*] | NYE | AND | RILEY'S | RAILWAY | GUIDE | [*double rule*] Back cover blank.

*Mustard-colored pictorial wrappers:* The illustration on the front cover is a slightly reduced copy of that on the cloth-bound copies. It differs in detail and the publishers' imprint is added: Published by | The Dearborn Publishing Co. | Chicago. The spine is lettered vertically, running down: NYE & RILEY'S RAILWAY GUIDE. Back wrapper blank.

PUBLICATION DATE: November, 1888. A copyright deposit copy is stamped received November 30, 1888.

PUBLICATION PRICE: Cloth, $1.00; paper, 50c.

NOTES: The only examined wrappered copy is wire side-stitched; lacks the blank leaf in front, and the back wrapper follows the leaf of advertisements.

The first state is as collated. In the later state the signatures are as follows: Two unsigned leaves, [1–13]⁸, [14]⁴, one unsigned leaf. A copy in this state has end papers with tan and white all-over design, and lacks the tissue guard. Type wear throughout indicates its later status.

The first edition was exhausted in a week, according to a statement in the *St. Louis Post Dispatch*, December 16, 1888, which further stated that "another large edition is being issued."

The error in the table of contents, *Lines On Turning Over A Pass— Nye*, listed as on page 96, actually on page [97], remains uncorrected in all examined copies.

In the *Chicago Times*, August 3, 1889, there is a statement that "*Nye & Riley's Railway Guide*, illustrated, is published by F. T. Neely, New York and Chicago, in a 'double number' in 'Neely's Series.'" The article further states: "It has been read and enjoyed by thousands before, having been copyrighted a year or more ago."

The work reappeared under a variety of titles, some of which are:

*Poems by James Whitcomb Riley Yarns by Bill Nye*, Chicago & New York, F. T. Neely, 1891; cover title: *Poems and Yarns [by] James Whitcomb Riley, [and] Bill Nye*. Reissued, in wrappers, as Vol. II, No. 12, in "Neely's Series"; dated December, 1891,* on cover. Reissued, in wrappers, as Vol. I, No. 11 of "Neely's Popular Library," dated September, 1892*, on cover.

*Nye and Riley's Wit and Humor (Poems—Yarns)*, Chicago & New York, F. T. Neely, 1896; wrappers. The title-page states that this is No. 57 of "Neely's Popular Library," Jan. 15, 1896.* The book contains a biographical sketch of Nye and account of his death on February 22,

---

*These dates are all open to suspicion. In order to secure the lowest possible postal rates, Neely, like some other publishers of the period, used the device of issuing books as individual numbers in serials. Under the then-existing law, books so issued were accepted as second-class matter. In order to maintain the fiction of serial publication, the publishers dated the books at set intervals as required by postal regulations. Hence many of the printed dates are arbitrary and have only

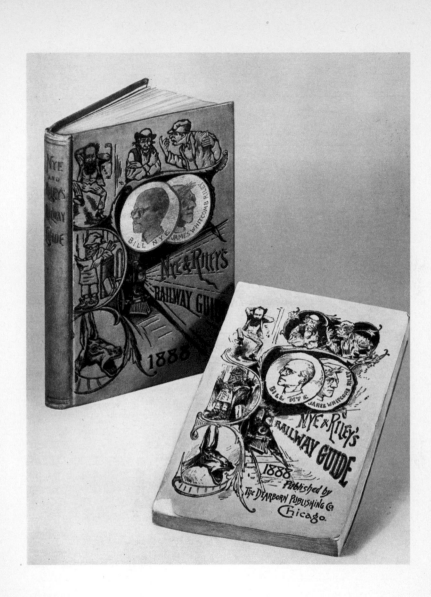

1896. This obituary includes Riley's sonnet beginning, "O William in thy blithe companionship," previously in *Armazindy* (1894).

*Nye and Riley's Wit and Humor* (*Poems and Yarns*), Chicago, Thompson & Thomas [1900]. This occurs in two known states with priority undetermined: with or without mention on the title-page of No. 57 of "Neely's Popular Library."

*Nye & Riley's Wit and Humor, Amusing Prose Sketches and Quaint Dialect Poems by Edgar Wilson Nye and James Whitcomb Riley*, Chicago, W. B. Conkey Co. [1902]. The copyright notice, dated 1902, is in the name of the Homewood Publishing Company.

*Nye and Riley's Wit and Humor* (*Poems and Yarns*), Chicago, Thompson & Thomas [1905]; cover title: *Poetry and Mirth by James Whitcomb Riley & Bill Nye*. A copy was deposited in the Copyright Office, November 24, 1904. Book title same as issue with 1900 copyright date. Later issued with imprint of Charles C. Thompson Co., Chicago.

*On the "Shoe-String" Limited with Nye and Riley*, Chicago, Thompson & Thomas [1905]. Noted in pictorial wrappers only. The title was entered for copyright January 21, 1905, and a copy was deposited February 23, 1905.

Since Riley and Nye did not collaborate on any other book, it is safe to assume that any joint compilation by them, under any title, remains essentially the same: *Nye and Riley's Railway Guide*.

CONTENTS: Prose by Nye, poetry by Riley; latter all first publications in a Riley book with the exception of one poem. These first appearances are:

Why it was done   (prose, by Nye and Riley)

Never Talk Back   *Indianapolis Journal*, April 5, 1884 (with title: "Cordaroy" Poetry | Never Talk Back)

The Gruesome Ballad of Mr. Squincher   *Indianapolis Journal*, January 11, 1880

A Fall-Crick View of the Earthquake   *Indianapolis Journal*, September 5, 1886

August ("O mellow month and merry month")   *Indianapolis Journal*, August 19, 1882

His First Womern   *Indianapolis Journal*, April 12, 1885 (title in *Biographical Edition:* My First Womern)

This Man Jones   *Kokomo Tribune*, August 2, 1879; also reprinted in broadside form (see p. 149)

---

slight relation to the actual time of publication. For example, *Nye and Riley's Wit and Humor* (*Poems–Yarns*) bears the statement on the title-page that it is No. 57 of "Neely's Popular Library, Jan. 15, 1896." This date is obviously false since the book contains an obituary of Nye, who died February 22, 1896.

The Boy-Friend  *Indianapolis Journal*, September 14, 1884

In the Afternoon  *Indianapolis Journal*, June 28, 1884

From Delphi to Camden  *Indianapolis Journal*, August 24, 1884

His Crazy-Bone  *Indianapolis Journal*, February 25, 1882

Craqueodoom  *Anderson Democrat*, June 1, 1877*

Mr. Silberberg  *Indianapolis Journal*, December 17, 1881 (with title: The Jew Father)

Spirits at Home  *Indianapolis Journal*, April 26, 1885

Lines on Hearing a Cow Bawl  *Saturday Herald* (*Indianapolis*), July 5, 1879

Me and Mary  *Indianapolis Journal*, March 29, 1884

That Night  *Indianapolis Journal*, August 5, 1882

A Black Hills Episode  *Indianapolis Journal*, August 1, 1880

The Rossville Lecture Course  *Indianapolis Journal*, March 28, 1886

A Character ("Swallowed up in gulfs of tho't")

The Man in the Moon  *Indianapolis Journal*, May 12, 1883

His Christmas Sled  *Indianapolis Journal*, December 25, 1884

Ezra House  *Saturday Herald* (*Indianapolis*), January 12, 1878

A Hint of Spring  *Indianapolis Journal*, February 23, 1881

A Treat Ode†  *Saturday Herald* (*Indianapolis*), August 2, 1879 (title in *Biographical Edition:* The Tree-Toad)

My Bachelor Chum  *Saturday Herald* (*Indianapolis*), July 12, 1879

"A Brave Refrain"  *Indianapolis Journal*, November 18, 1882

Good-bye er Howdy-Do  *Indianapolis Journal*, July 16, 1883

While Cigarettes to Ashes Turn  *Life*, May 3, 1883; *Life's Verses* (1885)

Says He§  *Indianapolis Journal*, January 18, 1885 (title in separate printing in *Biographical Edition:* Whatever the Weather May Be)

McFeeters' Fourth  *Indianapolis Journal*, July 5, 1883

In a Box  *Indianapolis Journal*, May 14, 1880

A Dose't of Blues  *Indianapolis Journal*, November 22, 1885 (title in *Biographical Edition:* A Dos't o' Blues)

Sutter's Claim  *Indianapolis Journal*, August 26, 1882

---

*Not seen except as a clipping with manuscript note of date.

†See *Biographical Edition*, Vol. 2, p. 491, for introduction to the poem, used by Riley in recitations.

Riley made the following statement in a letter of December 30 [1881], in *James Whitcomb Riley's Letter from Boston* . . . Privately Printed (1922): "You know the fool-dialect verses on the 'Tree toad'—well, they [Redpath Lyceum Bureau] have printed that along with the announcement card [for Riley's entertainment January 3, 1882, at Tremont Temple, Boston]."

§Incorporated later into prose sketch, "A Wild Irishman," in *Pipes o' Pan at Zekesbury* (1889).

# 1889
## (*Published 1888*)

# Pipes O' Pan at Zekesbury

Pipes O' Pan at Zekesbury | BY | JAMES WHITCOMB RILEY | INDIANAPOLIS | BOWEN-MERRILL CO., PUBLISHERS | 1889

COLLATION: One unsigned leaf, [1]–[4]⁸, 5–15⁸, 16⁴, one unsigned leaf. Leaf measures 7″ x 4⅛″, all edges trimmed, top edge gilt. Printed on white wove paper.

PAGINATION: End paper, same as book stock; fly leaf (its conjugate pasted down under the lining paper); fly title, p. [i]; list of books *By Same Author*, p. [ii]; title-page, p. [iii]; copyright notice with date 1888 and slug: *Carlon & Hollenbeck | Printers And Binders*, p. [iv]; dedication to John A. Riley, p. [v]; blank, p. [vi]; table of contents, pp. vii–viii; half-title, p. [ix]; blank, p. [x]; proem, p. [xi]; blank, p. [xii]; text, pp. 13–245; blank, pp. [246–248]; fly leaf (its conjugate pasted down under the lining paper); end paper.

ILLUSTRATIONS: None.

BINDING: Cloth, various colors, no priority. Front cover stamped in black with an illustration depicting a "Hoosier" Pan sitting on a rock, playing on his pipes, and lettered in black: Pipes o' Pan | AT | ZEKESBURY   A heavy rule is stamped immediately below the picture. Spine stamped in gilt: [*ornament*] | Pipes [*ornament*] | o' Pan | at | Zekesbury | [*ornament*] | JAMES | WHITCOMB | RILEY. Back cover blank.

Also issued in illuminated boards, extra gilt cloth shelfback. Neither the Pan illustration nor the title appears on the front cover. The spine, in addition to the ornamental gilt stamping, carries the same lettering as the cloth-bound copies.

PUBLICATION DATE: December 13, 1888,* according to advertisements of the Bowen-Merrill Company and Indianapolis booksellers, in the *Indianapolis Journal.*

---

*See *Letters of James Whitcomb Riley*, edited by William Lyon Phelps (1930), p. 86, for Riley's comments on this book, "with printers now," written to Bill Nye on October 3, 1888.

NOTES: The earliest copies are printed on wove paper; the printers' slug is present on the copyright page; the word *farmer* is present on p. 79, third stanza, first line.

Later the book appeared printed on laid paper; the printers' slug does not appear on the copyright page; the word *farmer* has dropped out on p. 79, third stanza, first line.

Still later the book appeared with flowered end papers and with an inserted portrait frontispiece.

The earliest bindings are those described above. There is a variety of later bindings, none of which have the Pan illustration on the front cover.

The publication price was $1.25.

CONTENTS: All but 5 poems, of the poems and prose sketches herein, are first appearances in a Riley book:

[Proem]   (Title in *Biographical Edition:* The Pipes of Pan)

At Zekesbury (prose; includes poems:   [The Song of Yesterday—"But yesterday"]; [The Happy Little Cripple—"I'm thist a little crippled boy"]; and 8-line poem, beginning: "F'r instunce, now, when *some* folks gits")   The poem, "The Song of Yesterday," had appeared separately in the *Indianapolis Journal*, August 1, 1880 (with title: Yesterday); the entire prose sketch first appeared in the *Current* (*Chicago*), April 24, 1886 (with title: A Waste of Genius at Zekesbury)

Down around the River

Kneeling with Herrick   *Indianapolis Journal*, April 4, 1886 (with title: A Prayer for Content with Simple Store); *Judge*, January 22, 1887 (with title: A Prayer for Content)

Romancin'   *Kokomo Tribune*, June 21, 1879*

Has She Forgotten   *Indianapolis Journal*, May 23, 1886

A' Old Played-Out Song   *Indianapolis Journal*, November 8, 1885 (with title: Lines on a' Old Played-Out Song)

The Lost Path   *Indianapolis Journal*, October 6, 1878

The Little Tiny Kickshaw   *Saturday Herald* (*Indianapolis*), May 31, 1879

His Mother   *Independent* (*New York*), December 6, 1888

Kissing the Rod   *Indianapolis Journal*, June 17, 1880

How It Happened   *Pittsburgh Bulletin*, prior to May 20, 1888† (reprinted in *Indianapolis Journal* this date)

---

*The proem in *Riley Farm-Rhymes* (1901), beginning: "The deadnin' and the thicket's jes' a b'ilin' full o' June," consists of stanzas 6, 7 and 8 of "Romancin'."
†Not seen.

Babyhood  *Saturday Herald* (*Indianapolis*), June 15, 1878

Mrs. Miller (prose; includes a 4-line poem beginning: "Ring in the wind his wedding chimes")  *Indianapolis Journal*, August 9, 1884

A Worn-Out Pencil  *Saturday Herald* (*Indianapolis*), July 26, 1879 (with title: To a Worn-Out Pencil)

The Stepmother  *Indianapolis Journal*, March 27, 1887

The Rain ("The rain! the rain! the rain!")  *World* (*New York*), October 23, 1887

The Legend Glorified  *Indianapolis Journal*, November 14, 1886

Want to Be Whur Mother Is (in table of contents: Whur Mother Is)  *Indianapolis Journal*, April 4, 1886; *Judge*, May 8, 1886

Old Man's Nursery Rhyme  *Indianapolis Journal*, December 19, 1886

Three Dead Friends  *Indianapolis Journal*, May 15, 1887

In Bohemia  *Illustrated Graphic News* (*Chicago*), October 9, 1886

In the Dark  *Indianapolis Journal*, March 16, 1877

Wet Weather Talk  *Indianapolis Journal*, July 28, 1883

Where Shall We Land  *Indianapolis News*, August 7, 1879

An Old Settler's Story (prose)  *Indianapolis Journal*, October 27* and November 3, 1878

Marthy Ellen  *Kokomo Tribune*, September 6, 1879; also reprinted in broadside form (see p. 149)

Moon-Drowned

Long afore He Knowed Who Santy-Claus Wuz  *Judge*, Christmas, 1887 (title in *Biographical Edition:* Who Santy Claus Wuz)

Dear Hands  *Indianapolis Journal*, November 4, 1882 (with title: The Touches of Her Hands

To My Good Master

When the Green Gits Back in the Trees  *World* (*New York*), May 13, 1888; *Judge*, June 30, 1888

At Broad Ripple  *Indianapolis Journal*, July 20, 1882

When Old Jack Died  *Indianapolis Journal*, August 7, 1887

Doc Sifers  *World* (*New York*), December 11, 1887; *Indiana Medical Journal*, July, 1888; *Transactions of the Indiana State Medical Society*, 1888

At Noon—and Midnight  *Indianapolis Journal*, April 19, 1885

A Wild Irishman† (prose; includes 3 poems: "Says He," "Chairley

---

*In the newspaper there is an introduction to the sketch, which is reprinted in the *Biographical Edition*, Vol. 6, p. 400.

†The "wild Irishman" is said to have been a real person whom Riley knew in his early sign-painting days: Frank J. Murphy, of South Bend, Indiana; see *South Bend Tribune*, October 5, 1912.

Burke['s in Town]" and "The Duck-Hunters of the Kankakee")
*Indianapolis Journal*, August 2, 1884. (The two poems first-named
do not appear in the *Journal*, but "Chairley Burke's in Town"
had been printed in the *Illustrated Graphic News* (*Chicago*) August
7, 1886, then in *Standard Comic Recitations*, #21, September,
1888*; "Says He" had been collected in *Nye and Riley's Railway
Guide*, 1888)

When My Dreams Come True    *Current* (*Chicago*), April 9, 1887

The Bat    *Indianapolis Journal*, August 12, 1882

The Way It Wuz    *Indianapolis Journal*, August 2, 1885

The Drum    *Sun* (*New York*), August 15, 1880

Tom Johnson's Quit    *Kokomo Tribune*, May 31, 1879

Lullaby ("The maple strews the embers of its leaves")    *Indianapolis Journal*, October 20, 1878; sheet music, 1879—composer:
Will H. Pontius (with title: Baby Bye; see p. 148)

In the South    *Indianapolis Journal*, April 11, 1886

The Old Home by the Mill    *Northwestern Miller*, Christmas, 1887;
*Indianapolis Journal*, January 8, 1888 (title in both: At the Old
Home by the Mill)

A Leave-Taking    *Indianapolis Sentinel*, February 1, 1885

Wait for the Morning    *Indianapolis Journal*, July 18, 1886

When June Is Here    *Indianapolis Journal*, April 19, 1885

The Gilded Roll (prose; includes 4 poems: A Backward Look;
Billy's Alphabetical Animal Show; [Her] Beautiful Hands; and
a poem without title beginning, "Here lies a young man")    *Indianapolis Journal*, July 26, 1884. (The poem, "Beautiful Hands,"
did not appear in the *Journal* but had been printed separately in
the *Indianapolis Sentinel*, February 20, 1876; later, in *His Pa's
Romance* [1903], it appeared separately with title: Her Beautiful
Hands)

---

*Not seen. "Chairley Burke" appeared later, in Vol. 4 of the *Homestead
Edition* (1898), as part of "A Wild Irishman"; also in Vol. 7 of the same edition
(1898), separately, with two added stanzas, as "Chairley Burke's in Town."

# Rhymes of Childhood

RHYMES OF | CHILDHOOD | BY | JAMES WHITCOMB RILEY | IN-
DIANAPOLIS | THE BOWEN-MERRILL CO | 1891

COLLATION: One unsigned leaf, [1–12]⁸, [13]⁴, one unsigned leaf.
Leaf measures 7¼″ x 4¾″, all edges trimmed, top edge gilt. Printed on
white laid paper.

PAGINATION: End paper, same as book stock; fly leaf (its conjugate
pasted down under the lining paper); fly title, p. [i]; list of books *By
The Same Author*, p. [ii]; frontispiece with tissue guard (inserted); title-
page, p. [iii]; copyright notice with date 1890, p. [iv]; dedication *To
The Little Nephew   Henry Edmund Eitel*\*, p. [v]; *Prefatory Note*, p. [vi];
table of contents, pp. [vii–x] (with acknowledgements at foot of p. [x]);
half-title, p. [xi]; blank, p. [xii]; proem, *The Rider Of The Knee*, p.
[xiii]; blank, p. [xiv]; text, p. [1]–186; fly leaf (its conjugate pasted down
under the lining paper); end paper.

ILLUSTRATIONS: Inserted frontispiece, on coated paper, with tissue,
from a photograph of Riley with his nephew on his lap.

BINDING: Twilled cloth, various colors. Front cover gilt-stamped:
RHYMES OF CHILDHOOD | [*decoration, a child's face showing through clouds
and surrounded by stars*] | JAMES WHITCOMB RILEY   Spine gilt-stamped:
RHYMES | OF | CHILDHOOD | [*rule*] | RILEY   Back cover blank.

PUBLICATION DATE: Announced for sale and reviewed in the *Indianapolis Journal* of December 14, 1890. The title was entered for copyright on December 19, 1890 and copies were deposited December 22,
1890.

PUBLICATION PRICE: $1.25.

NOTES: The book has been noted in two states:
   *State* 1: Page 64, line 12 of text, first word *Sometimes* (later
   *Sometime*)

---

\*The transposition in the nephew's name (it should read: *Edmund Henry Eitel*)
persisted through succeeding editions of the book.

Page 105, second stanza, second line, *sunshiney* (later *sunshiny*)

Page 137, last stanza, sixth line, *goin' to do* (later *comin' to*)

Page 152, last stanza, third line, *cataba* (later *catawba*)

State 2: Page 64, line 12 of text, first word *Sometime* (earlier *Sometimes*)

Page 105, second stanza, second line, *sunshiny* (earlier *sunshiney*)

Page 137, last stanza, sixth line, *comin' to* (earlier *goin' to do*)

Page 152, last stanza, third line, *catawba* (earlier *cataba*)

There are two states of the binding: as described above; and particolored cloth with all the lettering on the dark upper portion, and the design of the child's face present on the lower portion. So far no copies with sheets of the first state have been found in the parti-colored cloth binding.

In 1895 the book appeared in red cloth, extra gilt spine.

In 1898, as Vol. 5 of the *Homestead Edition, Rhymes of Childhood* is considerably altered: twenty of the poems of the first edition are omitted and seventeen others are included of which five are first book appearances (see p. 74).

CONTENTS: Of the 102 poems herein, 82 are first appearances in a Riley book:

The Rider of the Knee (proem)

The Raggedy Man   *Century Magazine*, December, 1890

The Little-Red-Apple Tree   *St. Nicholas Magazine*, October, 1890

A Boy's Mother   *Century Magazine*, December, 1890

The Pixy People   *Wide Awake*, August, 1884 (with title: The Little Pixy People); *Lothrop Annual* (1889?)*

Uncle Sidney

Pansies   *Indianapolis Journal*, July 12, 1881

Waitin' fer the Cat to Die   *Harper's New Monthly Magazine*, February, 1889

The Fishing Party   *Century Magazine*, December, 1890; *Indianapolis Journal*, December 2, 1890

Mother Goose   *Wide Awake*, June, 1881; *The Poet and the Children*, ed. by M. H. Lothrop (1882)

The Boy Lives on Our Farm   *Century Magazine*, December, 1890

The Robins' Other Name

To Hattie—on Her Birthday

---

*Not seen.

Mabel   *Indianapolis Journal*, April 8, 1881

Little Girly-Girl   *Indianapolis Journal*, March 2, 1881

The Runaway Boy   *Century Magazine*, December, 1890 (with title: The Runaway)

Time of Clearer Twitterings   *Indianapolis Journal*, October 19, 1884 (with title: October)

On the Sunny Side*   *Indianapolis Journal*, April 19, 1884

The All-Golden   *Indianapolis Journal*, March 17, 1883

Longfellow's Love for the Children

Winter Fancies   *Indianapolis Journal*, November 18, 1882 (with title: It's a Cold Day)

The Prayer Perfect   *Indianapolis Journal*, September 20, 1880 (with title: Amen)

A Mother-Song   *Indianapolis Journal*, July 18, 1880 (with title: Sleep, Little Brother!)

In the Night

The Funny Little Fellow   *Indianapolis Journal*, April 13, 1877 (with title: A Funny Fellow)

Uncle Sidney's Views   *Saturday Review (Indianapolis)*, October 30, 1880 (second stanza only, with title: The True Age of Wisdom); *Indianapolis Journal*, July 20, 1890; *Judge*, October 4, 1890

When Early March Seems Middle May   *Indianapolis Journal*, March 3, 1883 (with title: When Knotted Horse-Tails Are Untied); *Judge*, June 11, 1887 (with title: Signs of Coming of Spring)

The Nine Little Goblins   *Indianapolis Journal*, December 5, 1880 (with title: Nightmare)

The Little Coat   *Indianapolis Journal*, March 8, 1884

Our Hired Girl   *Century Magazine*, December, 1890

The Dream of the Little Princess

The Land of Used-to-Be   *Wide Awake*, August, 1881; *Saturday Review (Indianapolis)*, November 5, 1881; *Christmas Carols and Midsummer Songs* (1881)

When Our Baby Died   *Saturday Herald (Indianapolis)*, July 12, 1879

Christine Braibry (prose; including poem: Christine's Song)   *Indianapolis Journal*, November 4, 1882 (without title)

The Squirt-Gun Uncle Maked Me

The Youthful Press

---

*Part of "On the Sunny Side," beginning, "Where's a heart as mellow" appeared without title in a letter to school children of Port Fulton, published in the *Indianapolis News*, November 6, 1914.

That-Air Young-Un   *Northwestern Miller*, Christmas, 1888

Baby's Dying   *Indianapolis Journal*, July 16, 1881

The Boys   *Indianapolis Journal*, October 19, 1884

Max and Jim

The Circus-Day Parade   *Wide Awake*, August, 1882; *The Poet and the Children* (1882)

The Old Hay-Mow

John Tarkington Jameson

Dwainie—A Sprite Song (Incorporated later in Act I of *The Flying Islands of the Night*, first edition, p. 31)

Guineypigs

Busch and Tommy

Babe Herrick   *Indianapolis Journal*, April 4, 1886 (with title: To a Babe Sleeping, under caption: In the Manner of Herrick)

The Land of Thus-And-So   *Indianapolis Journal*, October 25, 1885; *The Elocutionist's Annual*, No. 17 (1889)

Grandfather Squeers   *Kokomo Tribune*, May 1, 15, 22, 29 and June 12, 1880 (in parts with titles, respectively: My Grandfather Squeers; His Grandpa; The Elderly Squeers; Squeers the Ancient; The Antique Squeers)

The Lugubrious Whing-Whang   *Indianapolis Journal*, June 30, 1881 (last 3 stanzas, without title, part of prose sketch: Science and Poetry); *The Humbler Poets* by Slason Thompson (1886; pub. 1885? see p. 169; 3 stanzas with title: The Mad, Mad Muse)

Lawyer and Child   *Indianapolis Journal*, November 29, 1879

The Funniest Thing in the World

Little Johnts's Chrismus   *Book Buyer*, December, 1888; *Indianapolis Journal*, December 16, 1888

The Boys' Candidate   *Indianapolis Journal*, August 31, 1890 (with title: The Boy's Friend)

The Bumble-Bee

He Called Her in   *Indianapolis Journal*, September 22, 1883

When the World Bu'sts Through   *Indianapolis Journal*, September 5, 1886

A Prospective Glimpse

The Old Tramp

The Pet Coon

A Nonsense Rhyme   *St. Nicholas*, November, 1880; *Indianapolis Journal*, October 31, 1880

Naughty Claude   *St. Nicholas*, January, 1889

The Old, Old Wish   *Indianapolis Journal*, July 14, 1880 (with title: The Old Wish)

"The Preacher's Boy"   *Indianapolis Journal*, June 2, 1883

An Impetuous Resolve

A Sudden Shower   *Indianapolis Journal*, July 14, 1883; *Judge*, September 1, 1883

The Hunter Boy   (No previous publication located save for 8 lines which appeared as part of "Just a Fiddler" in the *Indianapolis Journal*, April 18, 1880)

A Child's Home—Long Ago   *Indianapolis Sentinel*, August 4, 1878 (with title: At Oakland, August 3, 1878); *Twenty-Eighth Annual Report of the Indiana State Board of Agriculture* (1879) (with title: Old Settlers)

Billy Goodin'

A Passing Hail   *Home Magazine*, November, 1888; *Indianapolis Journal*, November 26, 1888 (title in both: Rest)

Prior to Miss Belle's Appearance   *Anderson Democrat*, May 11, 1877 (with title: Willie)*

Sprite Serenade   *Indianapolis Journal*, June 21, 1885 (with title: Song. This was later incorporated in Act II of *The Flying Islands of the Night*, first edition, p. 38)

Honey Dripping from the Comb   *Indianapolis Journal*, February 24, 1877 (with title: A Whisper)

In Swimming-Time   *Century Magazine*, September, 1883

She "Displains" It   *St. Nicholas*, February, 1888

The Way the Baby Slept   *Indianapolis Journal*, April 7, 1883 (with title: The Baby)

The Jolly Miller   *Northwestern Miller*, Christmas, 1886 (with title: The Restored Romaunt of "The Jolly Miller")

With the Current   *Indianapolis Journal*, July 21, 1883

A Sleeping Beauty   *Saturday Herald* (*Indianapolis*), June 28, 1879; *Life*, September 11, 1884 (title in both: Mirage)

At Aunty's House

The Whitheraways

Envoy ("Many pleasures of Youth have been buoyantly sung")   *Indianapolis Journal*, November 18, 1882 (with title, as in *Biographical Edition*: As I Sit in the Silence; begins: "All the pleasures of home have been numbered and sung")

NOTES: The book contains "Little Mahala Ashcraft" which had appeared in "*The Old Swimmin'-Hole*," *and 'Leven More Poems* (1883) as, "On the Death of Little Mahala Ashcraft." Another poem, "Cradle Song," had appeared in *Pipes o' Pan at Zekesbury* (1889), as "Lullaby."

---

*Not seen except as a clipping with manuscript note of date.

# Neghborly Poems

"THE OLD SWIMMIN'-HOLE" AND | 'LEVEN MORE POEMS | [*rule*] | NEGHBORLY POEMS | ON FRIENDSHIP | GRIEF AND | FARM-LIFE | BY | BENJ. F. JOHNSON, OF BOONE | [JAMES WHITCOMB RILEY.] | 1891 | THE BOWEN-MERRILL CO | INDIANAPOLIS, IND
    [Note: Brackets enclosing the author's name actually appear on the title-page.]

COLLATION: One unsigned leaf, [1]⁸, *1⁸, 2–5⁸, 6⁴, [7]², one unsigned leaf. Sigs. 3, 4, 5, 6 signed on pp. 33, 49, 65, 81 respectively (see pagination below). Leaf measures 7¼″ scant x 4¾″; all edges trimmed, top edge gilt. Printed on white laid paper.

PAGINATION: End paper, same as book stock; fly leaf (its conjugate pasted down under the end paper); fly title, p. [i]; list of books *By The Same Author*, p. [ii]; title-page, p. [iii]; dedication and copyright notice with date 1891, p. [iv]; *Preface And Sub-Preface*, pp. v–ix (dated at end July 1891); blank, p. [x]; table of contents, p. [xi]; blank, p. [xii]; half-title, p. [xiii]; blank, p. [xiv]; proem, p. [xv]; blank, p. [xvi]; illustration (inserted); text, pp. 1–90 (should be 92); fly leaf (its conjugate pasted down under the lining paper); end paper.
    [Note: Page 33 *et seqq.* mispaged 31 *et seqq.*]

ILLUSTRATIONS: Six illustrations on white coated paper, inserted opposite pp. 1, 16, 24, 33, 59, 86. The first three are by R. B. Gruelle, the fourth is unidentified, the last two are from photographs.

BINDING: Parti-colored cloth, various colors, darker color forming the upper third. The front cover is stamped in gilt: NEGHBORLY POEMS | By | Benj. F. Johnson, of Boone | (James Whitcomb Riley)   The author's name appears in parentheses as indicated. Spine gilt-stamped: NEGHBORLY | POEMS | [*wavy rule*] | RILEY   Back cover blank.

PUBLICATION DATE: The title was entered for copyright May 13, 1891. The *Indianapolis Journal*, in a brief review September 2, 1891, refers to an "advance copy" of the book.*  The Copyright Office received

---

*Presentation copies have been noted with inscriptions dated as early as September 18, 1891.

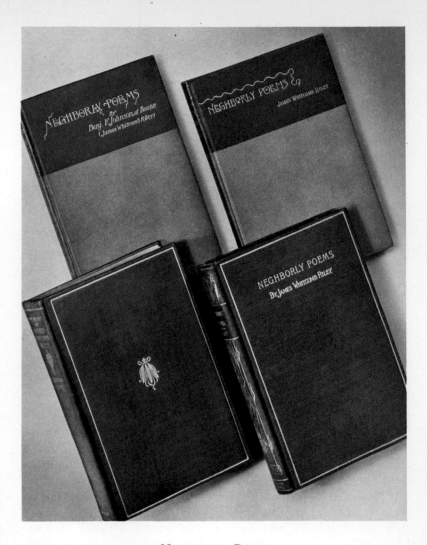

NEGHBORLY POEMS

*First edition in two states of binding,*
together with Homestead and Greenfield Edition bindings

copies October 5, 1891. The Bowen-Merrill Company's first local advertisement of the book, in the *Indianapolis Journal*, October 22, 1891, makes apparent that some delay attended actual publication. The advertisement reads in part: "We have at last succeeded in getting a sufficient quantity of this new book of Mr. Riley's from the bindery, and are now prepared to fill all orders promptly."

PUBLICATION PRICE: $1.25.

NOTES: The book appeared in two states.

> *State* 1: On p. [ii] there is no mention of *The Flying Islands of the Night* or *An Old Sweetheart of Mine*
> The copyright notice has the single copyright date, 1891
> On p. 23, second stanza, first line, the word *you* does not appear
> Page 61, last stanza, second line, "*Buckeyes*" (later in single quotation marks)
> Page 62, line 12, *bookeyes* (later *buckeyes*)
> Page 79, first stanza, fifth line *reco'nize* (later *recko'nize*)
> The illustrations appear as above described
>
> *State* 2: Page [ii] includes mention of *The Flying Islands of the Night* and *An Old Sweetheart of Mine*
> The copyright notice has two copyright dates: 1883 and 1891
> Page 23, second stanza, first line, *you* is added after *see*
> Page 61, last stanza, second line, '*Buckeyes*' (note single quotation marks)
> Page 62, line 12, *buckeyes* (earlier *bookeyes*)
> Page 79, first stanza, fifth line, *recko'nize* (earlier *reco'nize*)
> The illustration which appeared opposite p. 1 in the earlier state is here used as a frontispiece.

There are two states of the binding: as described above, and with the front cover gilt-stamped: NEGHBORLY POEMS | JAMES WHITCOMB RILEY   A wavy gilt rule is carried from the spine to the front cover, above and extending to the right of the title. Both states of binding appear with sheets of State 1 and with the author's inscriptions dated as early as September, 1891. It is significant that thus far no copy of the *Benj. F. Johnson* binding has been found with sheets in the later state.

The 1895 edition, bound in red cloth, extra gilt spine, reprints the text of the earlier edition but contains an added essay, "Dialect in Literature," pp. 95–112, previously in *The Forum*, December, 1892. In December of the same year, the publishers issued the book in a limited edition of 100 numbered and signed copies, bound in red silk cloth (see

p. 4). Vol. I of the *Homestead Edition* (1897) is entitled: *Neghborly Poems and Dialect Sketches*. It contains the same material as the earlier editions of the work, rearranged, and with numerous additions none of which are first appearances in a Riley book.

CONTENTS: Of the 36 poems, the following 20 are first appearances in a Riley book:

[Proem]   ("The delights of our childhood is soon passed away") (title in *Biographical Edition:* An Old Man's Memory)

Us Farmers in the Country . . .   (proem to second section of the book, uncaptioned at p. 31; title taken from table of contents)

Erasmus Wilson   See *Our Kind of a Man*, (p. 154)

My Ruthers   *Indianapolis Journal*, September 14, 1890; *Judge*, Oc-* tober 11, 1890

On a Dead Babe (in table of contents: To a Dead Babe)

"Coon-Dog Wess"

Lines to Perfesser John Clark Ridpath (in table of contents: Perfesser John Clark Ridpath)

"Mylo Jones's Wife"

On a Splendud Match   *Kokomo Tribune*, December 27, 1879 (with title: John Golliher's Third Womern)

Old John Clevenger on Buckeyes   See *A Buckeye Ballad*, (p. 152)

The Hoss   *Indianapolis Journal*, November 1, 1885; Vigo County Fair Premium List for 1890*

A Pen-Pictur' of a Certin Frivvolus Old Man

Thoughts on a Pore Joke†

A Mortul Prayer   *Sun* (*New York*), April 25, 1880 (with title: The Skeptic's Prayer)

The First Bluebird   *Indianapolis Journal*, April 19, 1891 (with title: The First Boone County Bluebird)

Evagene Baker

On Any Ordenary Man in a High State of Laughture and Delight

Town and Country   *Indianapolis Journal*, April 10, 1891 (with title: The Sooburbs)§

Lines fer Isaac Bradwell (in table of contents: Lines Writ fer Isaac Bradwell)

Decoration Day on the Place

---

*Not seen but referred to in the *Terre Haute* (*Indiana*) *Evening Gazette*, August 12, 1890.

†The first 8 lines of stanza 2 of this poem had appeared in *Pipes o' Pan at Zekesbury* (1889), without title, as part of the prose sketch, "At Zekesbury." The part begins: "F'r instunce, now, when *some* folks gits"

§See *New Suburban Train Service*, (p. 200).

# 1892
*(Published 1891)*

# The Flying Islands of the Night

THE FLYING ISLANDS | OF THE NIGHT | BY | JAMES WHITCOMB RILEY | "A thynge of wytchencref—an idle dreme." | INDIANAPOLIS | THE BOWEN-MERRILL CO. | 1892

COLLATION: [1–14]⁴ signed in 8: [1]–[7]. The leaf measures 7⅟₁₆″ x 5″, top edge gilt, other edges uncut. Printed on white laid paper.

PAGINATION: Lining paper, pp. [i–ii]; blank, pp. [iii–viii]; fly title, p. [ix]; list of books *By the Same Author*, p. [x]; title-page, p. [xi]; copyright notice with date 1891, p. [xii]; dedication to Madison Cawein, p. [xiii]; blank, p. [xiv]; proem, p. [xv]; blank, p. [xvi]; text, pp. [1]–88; blank, pp. [89–96] (pp. [95–96] used as lining paper).

ILLUSTRATIONS: None.

BINDING: White flexible boards, embossed with winged heads, clouds and stars. Front cover lettered in silver or gilt (no known priority, if any): THE FLYING ISLANDS | OF THE | [*wavy rule*] NIGHT | James Whitcomb Riley   Spine and back cover unlettered.

PUBLICATION DATE: The title was entered for copyright October 15, 1891. A copy was deposited for copyright November 12, 1891. The book was advertised for sale by the Bowen-Merrill Company in the *Indianapolis Journal*, December 10, 1891, as "now ready."

PUBLICATION PRICE: $1.25.

NOTES: The sheets exist in two states. In the first state the signatures are signed as above indicated, with the signature marks printed in the customary place, below the last line of text. In the second state there appears a supplementary set of signature marks, [1]–12, which are printed close to the inner margins.

The earliest state of the binding is as described. The parti-colored cloth binding, similar to that of *Neghborly Poems* (1891), appeared later.

Apparently the book had a slow sale, for as late as 1895 the publishers were still issuing copies made up of the 1892 sheets. Some of these later issues contain inserted advertisements dated 1895.

37

It has been frequently stated that this book was first offered for sale at the Indianapolis Flower Mission Fair, November, 1891. The evidence does not support this claim. According to contemporary newspaper accounts* of the fair the souvenirs sold at the Riley booth consisted of the *Golden Rod* (see p. 173) and a Riley blotter (see p. 154).

The first known change in date of title-page occurred in 1895, when the book appeared so dated and bound in the familiar red cloth, extra gilt spine.

In 1898 the book appeared as Vol. 6 of the *Homestead Edition*, with added songs and speeches in the fantasy itself, and with an added section: *Spirk And Wunk Rhymes | Rounds And Catches*, consisting of 28 poems, 24 of which are first appearances in a Riley book (see p. 76).

It was reissued (ᶜ1900) with this added material. Heretofore copies with the additions had been sold only as part of the *Homestead Edition*.

In 1913 the extended version of 1898 was published in large 8vo format, with colored illustrations by Franklin Booth, and with the text printed within brown decorative borders.

CONTENTS: The following is a record of the original appearances of the text of *The Flying Islands of the Night*.

Its earliest version was published in the *Saturday Herald* (*Indianapolis*), August 24, 1878.†

In the *Indianapolis Journal*, February 4, 1879, were published two songs: "Of the Whole World Mine" (incorporated in the first edition in "Songs of the Seven Faces," p. 2); and "Song" (beginning: "I follow you forever on," incorporated in the first edition in the "Chorus of Swarming Faces," p. 4).

The *Saturday Herald* (*Indianapolis*), June 28, 1879, contained a poem, "Night," which was not incorporated into "The Flying Islands of the Night" until the *Homestead Edition* (1898) appeared.

The same newspaper on July 5, 1879, published a poem, "Glimpse," which also was not incorporated into "The Flying Islands of the Night" until the *Homestead Edition* (1898).

The *Saturday Herald* (*Indianapolis*), September 6, 1879, published the poem, "Delilah," which is incorporated in Act III of the first edition, p. 85.

The *Indianapolis Journal*, March 24, 1883, contained a poem entitled, "Sweet Bells Jangled," which appears in Act III of the first edition, p. 77, as "Wraith-Song of Spraivoll."

---

*Indianapolis Journal* and *Indianapolis Sentinel*, November 4, 1891.

†An anonymous criticism of the poem, written by Riley himself according to *The Youth of James Whitcomb Riley* by Marcus Dickey (1919), p. 37, appears in the *Saturday Herald* (*Indianapolis*), September 14, 1878.

The *Indianapolis Journal*, August 18, 1883, printed a poem, "A Mere Outline," which appears in the first edition as part of Amphine's song at the beginning of Act II, p. 34.

The *Indianapolis Journal*, December 28, 1884, contained a poem entitled, "What Shall We Pray For" which is incorporated in the first edition as Jucklet's prayer to Aeo at end of Act II, p. 73.

Two parts which made first book appearance in *Rhymes of Childhood*, are discussed elsewhere. See pp. 32, 33.

This composition of Riley's aroused almost as much publicity as did his famous poem, "Leonainie." When it first appeared in the *Saturday Herald* (*Indianapolis*), August 24, 1878, under the heading "Respectfully Declined Papers of the Buzz Club," Number IV, it evoked an editorial of praise from the *Indianapolis News*, but an ironical note by Enos B. Reed in the *People* (*Indianapolis*), which brought about a so-called "War of Poets." This "war" went on for months, with Riley's admirers rallying to his defense in the *Saturday Herald*, and Reed leading a vituperative attack in the *People*. It led to Riley's writing an uncomplimentary poem to Enos B. Reed, entitled, "To the Bard," which Reed answered in poetical form: "The 'Bard' Responds to the Son of 'Wunkland.' "

The *Pittsburgh Commercial Gazette*, December 18, 1891, thus summarized the general attitude toward the fantasy: "You can hardly realize that it emanated from the same brain that gave birth to 'The Raggedy Man,' 'When the Frost Is on the Punkin,' and 'Goodbye Jim.' . . . This work will not be as satisfactory to the general readers as his others, although some admire it most of all."

During the summer of 1891, Riley visited England and it was rumored that he had written "an operatic libretto" which he hoped Sir Arthur Sullivan might set to music. The rumor seems to have originated with his traveling companion, Myron Reed, who made a statement that was quoted in an interview published in the Denver (Colorado) newspapers, *News* and *Times*, September 18, 1891. Eugene Field, in the *Chicago News*, said that he did not believe the rumor. Riley issued a statement published in the *Critic*, September 26, 1891, which we quote in part: "What may have given rise to this report is my taking with me a poetic drama which, for a long time, I have been elaborating. . . . This performance . . . will, as originally intended, first appear as a literary venture—a book—a drama in verse."

And so *The Flying Islands of the Night* did appear, just a few weeks later, and remained the author's "strong weakness" as he called it in a letter to Thomas Bailey Aldrich, October 27, 1896.*

---

*\*Letters of James Whitcomb Riley*, edited by William Lyon Phelps (1930), p. 208. For further comments by the author see pp. 149, 153, 157, 159.

# 1893
## *(Published 1892)*

# Green Fields and Running Brooks

GREEN FIELDS AND | RUNNING BROOKS | BY | JAMES WHITCOMB RILEY | INDIANAPOLIS | THE BOWEN-MERRILL COMPANY | 1893

COLLATION: One unsigned leaf, [1–14]⁸, one unsigned leaf. Leaf measures 7 3/16″ x 4¾″, all edges trimmed, top edge gilt. Printed on white laid paper.

PAGINATION: End paper, same as book stock; fly leaf (its conjugate pasted down under the lining paper); fly title, p. 1; list of books *By The Same Author*, p. [2]; title-page, p. [3]; copyright notice with date 1892, p. 4; dedication, *To My Sisters Elva And Mary*, p. 5; blank, p. [6]; table of contents, pp. 7–10; half-title, p. 11; blank, p. [12]; proem, p. 13; blank, p. [14]; text, pp. 15–224; fly leaf (its conjugate pasted down under the lining paper); end paper.

ILLUSTRATIONS: None.

BINDING: Parti-colored cloth, various colors, the darker color forming the upper third. The front cover is stamped in gilt: GREEN FIELDS | AND RUNNING BROOKS. [*ornamented*] | JAMES WHITCOMB RILEY  Spine gilt-stamped: GREEN | FIELDS | AND | RUNNING | BROOKS | [*rule*] | RILEY A wavy gilt rule is carried from the spine to the front cover, above and extended to the right of: GREEN FIELDS

PUBLICATION DATE: The title was entered for copyright November 21, 1892. The book was advertised for sale by the publishers in the *Indianapolis Journal*, December 10, 1892, but copies were apparently not available since the Indianapolis booksellers, Cathcart & Cleland, announced on December 11th, in the same newspaper, that the book would be published "this week," and stated that they would take advance orders. The earliest review located is in the *Indianapolis News*, December 17, 1892. A copyright deposit copy is stamped as received December 17, 1892.

PUBLICATION PRICE: $1.25.

NOTES: There are three distinct states of the book.

State 1: Page 10, next to last line, no accent mark over second
*e* in *Blessed*
Page 16, first line, . . . *miles on miles*
Page 33, second stanza, first line, no comma after *w'y*
Page 43, second stanza, first line, no comma after *away*
Page 48, first stanza, first line, capital *T* in *The*
Page 94, last stanza, sixth line, *my* (later *may*)
State 2: Same as State 1 except for change on p. 16, line 1,
which reads: . . . *mile on mile*
State 3: Page 10, next to last line has accent mark over second
*e* in *Blésséd* [*sic*]
Page 16 as in State 2
Page 33, second stanza, first line has comma after *w'y*,
Page 43, second stanza, first line has comma after *away*,
Page 48, first stanza, first line, small *t* in *the*
Page 94, last stanza, sixth line, *may* (earlier *my*)
In 1895 the book appeared in red cloth, extra gilt spine.

In 1897, as Vol. 7 of the *Homestead Edition*, it appeared with the
original contents minus 13 poems (which were included in other volumes of the *Homestead Edition*) and with 2 poems added, neither of
which are first appearances in a Riley book.

CONTENTS: All of the poems are first appearances in a Riley book:
[Proem]   ("Ho! green fields and running brooks!") (title in *Bio-
graphical Edition:* Green Fields and Running Brooks)
The Artemus of Michigan   *Morning News* (*Chicago*), March 30, 1886
As My Uncle Used to Say   *Indianapolis Journal*, August 28, 1892
At Utter Loaf   *Indianapolis Journal*, June 13, 1880 (with title: June)
August ("A day of torpor in the sullen heat")   *Indianapolis Jour-
nal*, August 14, 1877
Autumn ("As a harvester, at dusk")   *Indianapolis Journal*, Septem-
ber 15, 1883 (with title: A Dream of Autumn)
Bedouin   *Indianapolis Journal*, April 24, 1881
Being His Mother   *Lippincott's Monthly Magazine*, June, 1892
Blind ("You think it is a sorry thing")   *Indianapolis Journal*, Sep-
tember 12, 1880
The Blossoms on the Trees   *Indianapolis Journal*, May 10, 1884
By Any Other Name   *Indianapolis Journal*, March 2, 1890 (with
title: A Rose by Any Other Name)
By Her White Bed
The Chant of the Cross-Bearing Child   *Indianapolis Journal*, April
24, 1887

A Country Pathway   *Indianapolis Journal*, September 22, 1877

A Cup of Tea   *Indianapolis Journal*, December 12, 1880

The Curse of the Wandering Foot   *Indianapolis Journal*, August 7, 1892*

The Cyclone   *Indianapolis Journal*, March 13, 1887

Dan Paine   *Saturday Herald* (*Indianapolis*), September 14, 1878 (with title: To My Friend, Dan Paine)

Dawn, Noon and Dewfall

A Discouraging Model   *Indianapolis Journal*, September 10, 1880

A Ditty of No Tone   *Indianapolis Journal*, April 30, 1881 (with title: Summertime)

Donn Piatt of Mac-o-chee (table of contents: Don Piatt of Mac-o-chee)   *Indianapolis Journal*, August 16, 1884

Dot Leedle Boy   *People* (*Indianapolis*), January 1, 1876 (with title: Karl Schronz's Christmas Story); Broadside [n. p., n. d.], probably before 1880 (with title: Dot Leedle Poy of Mine) (see p. 151); *Bulletin of Pharmacy*, Parke, Davis & Company, July, 1891

A Dream of Autumn ("Mellow hazes, lowly trailing")   *Saturday Herald* (*Indianapolis*), August 9, 1879

Elizabeth ("Elizabeth! Elizabeth!")   *Indianapolis Journal*, May 1, 1891 (with title: Elizabeth Meredith Steele)

Envoy ("Just as of old! The world rolls on and on")   *Indianapolis Journal*, September 19, 1880 (title in *Journal* and in *Biographical Edition:* Just As of Old)

Farmer Whipple—Bachelor   *Greenfield News*, February 28, 1874†; *Saturday Herald* (*Indianapolis*), November 16, 1878

A Full Harvest   *Kokomo Tribune*, July 12, 1879

A Glimpse of Pan   *Indianapolis Journal*, May 12, 1883

Go, Winter!

Her Beautiful Eyes   *Indianapolis Journal*, April 4, 1886; *Judge*, August 23, 1890

The Hereafter   *Indianapolis Journal*, December 24, 1881 (with title: Our Fortunes)

His Mother's Way

His Vigil   *Ladies' Home Journal*, January, 1891

Home at Night   *Indianapolis Journal*, June 26, 1880; *Life*, July 12, 1883 (with title: Kate)

The Home-Going   *Indianapolis Journal*, March 27, 1881 (with title: Der Heimgang); *Poems* (published by Indianapolis Flower

---

*With the prose introduction by Riley which is quoted also in the *Biographical Edition* (1913), Vol. 4, p. 528.

†Not seen except as a clipping with manuscript note of date.

Mission, 1890; with title: Home; see p. 171); (title in *Biographical Edition:* We Must Get Home)

The Hoodoo *Indianapolis Journal,* September 10, 1891 (with title: Benj. F. Johnson on Skates)

The Hoosier Folk-Child

How John Quit the Farm

The Iron Horse *Indianapolis Journal,* July 13, 1878; *Locomotive Firemen's Monthly Magazine,* September, 1879

Iry and Billy and Jo *Indianapolis News,* July 5, 1890

Jack, the Giant-Killer *Indianapolis Journal,* August 27, 1880 (with title: A Bad Boy's Version of "Jack the Giant-Killer")

Jap Miller *Indianapolis Journal,* August 4, 1889; *Judge,* October 5, 1889*

John Alden and Percilly *Judge,* Christmas, 1888 (with title: John and Percilly)

John Brown

John McKeen *Indianapolis Journal,* August 31, 1884

Judith *Indianapolis Journal,* October 31, 1886

June at Woodruff *Indianapolis Journal,* June 8, 1890

Just to Be Good *Indianapolis Journal,* August 8, 1881 (with title: Enough)

Last Night—And This *Indianapolis Journal,* February 27, 1881

Let Us Forget *Indianapolis Journal,* October 17, 1880

The Little Fat Doctor *Indianapolis Journal,* April 12, 1884

Longfellow† ("The winds have talked with him confidingly")

A Lounger *Indianapolis Journal,* August 13, 1881

A Monument for the Soldiers *Indianapolis Journal,* June 12, 1884

Mr. What's-His-Name *Indianapolis Journal,* August 20, 1881

My Friend *Indianapolis Journal,* April 12, 1884

Nessmuk *Indianapolis Journal,* August 21, 1887 (with title: A Character)

North and South *Indianapolis Journal,* September 2, 1882

The Old Retired Sea Captain *Indianapolis Journal,* September 12, 1886

Old Winters on the Farm *Indianapolis Journal,* September 13, 1891

The Old Year and the New *Indianapolis Journal,* January 1, 1881

On the Banks o' Deer Crick *Indianapolis Journal,* August 16, 1885

---

*Jap Miller used the poem on numerous undated cards he had printed; possibly some preceded the book appearance.

†For Riley's tribute in prose to Longfellow, beginning: "The happiest forms of poetic expression are cast in simplest phraseology and seeming artlessness," see *Biographical Edition,* Vol. 4, p. 526.

Out of Nazareth   *Indianapolis Journal*, July 12, 1885
The Passing of a Heart   *Kokomo Tribune*, May 15, 1880 (with title:
    Just with Your Hands)
The Plaint Human   *Indianapolis Journal*, January 17, 1886
The Quarrel*   *Saturday Herald* (*Indianapolis*), December 19, 1885
    (with title: A Last Meeting, beginning: "As brown as dusk of
    death is brown")
The Quiet Lodger   *Indianapolis Journal*, January 28, 1882
Reach Your Hand to Me   *Indianapolis Journal*, March 20, 1881
Right Here at Home   *Indianapolis Journal*, February 7, 1892
The Rival ("I so loved once, when Death came by I hid")   *Kokomo
    Tribune*, June 19, 1880 (with title: The Rivals)
The Rivals; or the Showman's Ruse   *Indianapolis Journal*, Septem-
    ber 14, 1884
Robert Burns Wilson   *Critic*, November 24, 1888 (with title: To
    Robert Burns Wilson)
The Rose   *Cincinnati Commercial*, December 3, 1877 (with title:
    My Rose)
September Dark   *Indianapolis Journal*, September 28, 1884 (with
    title: December Dark)
The Shoemaker   *Indianapolis Journal*, October 18, 1880
The Singer   *Kokomo Tribune*, December 27, 1879
Sister Jones's Confession   *Indianapolis Journal*, March 10, 1880
Sleep ("Orphaned, I cry to thee")   *Indianapolis Journal*, March 21,
    1880
Some Scattering Remarks of Bub's
A Song of Long Ago   *Indianapolis Journal*, February 17, 1883
A Southern Singer   *Indianapolis Journal*, May 11, 1890
Suspense   *Indianapolis Journal*, October 31, 1880
Thanksgiving ("Let us be thankful—not alone because")   *Indi-
    anapolis Journal*, November 25, 1880
Their Sweet Sorrow
Them Flowers†   *Locomotive Firemen's Magazine*, November, 1887
To an Importunate Ghost   *Indianapolis Journal*, April 12, 1885
To Hear Her Sing   *Indianapolis Journal*, September 21, 1884
Tom Van Arden   *Saturday Herald* (*Indianapolis*), July 6, 1878
To the Serenader   *Indianapolis Journal*, December 13, 1880 (with
    title: The Serenade)

---

*Riley used frequently as a recitation a poem written by Miss Anna H. Poe,
"The Lily-Bud," but listed on his programs as "The Quarrel." It is quite different
from Riley's own poem, "The Quarrel," listed above.
†See p. 188 for mention of a later appearance of stanza 3 of "Them Flowers."

Tugg Martin

The Twins ("One's the pictur' of his Pa,") *Indianapolis Journal*, January 26, 1881

The Wandering Jew *Indianapolis Journal*, May 28, 1880

The Watches of the Night [*Tribute to Mrs. William J. Kinsley, of Shenandoah, Iowa*, pub. 1890?] (see p. 153); *Indianapolis Journal*, April 5, 1891 (stanza 4 only); *Independent*, November 26, 1891 (entire poem)

A Water-Color *Indianapolis Journal*, July 30, 1880 (with title: A Bit of Nature)

We to Sigh Instead of Sing *Indianapolis Journal*, June 2, 1883

What Chris'mas Fetched the Wigginses (See *A Christmas Story. What Chris'mas Fetched the Wigginses*, p. 156)

When Age Comes On *Indianapolis Journal*, July 29, 1882

Where-Away *Indianapolis Journal*, October 14, 1882

While the Musician Played *Indianapolis Journal*, February 6, 1881

The Wife-Blessèd [*sic*] *Belford's Magazine*, August, 1888; *Indianapolis Journal*, August 19, 1888 (title in both: The Wife)

A Wraith of Summertime *Indianapolis Journal*, August 22, 1880

# 1893

# Poems Here at Home

POEMS HERE | AT HOME | BY | JAMES WHITCOMB RILEY | [*floret*] |
PICTURES BY E. W. KEMBLE | [*publishers' emblem*] | NEW YORK |
THE CENTURY CO. | 1893

COLLATION: One unsigned leaf, [1]–24⁴. Leaf measures 6⅞″ x 4⅜″,
top edge gilt, other edges untrimmed. Printed on white coated paper.

PAGINATION: End paper, same as book stock; fly leaf (its conjugate
pasted down under the lining paper); fly title, p. [1]; list of *Other Books
by James Whitcomb Riley*, p. [2]; blank, p. [3]; frontispiece, p. [4]; title-
page, p. [5]; copyright notices with final date 1893, and imprint of De
Vinne Press, p. [6]; dedication *To My Father*, p. [7]; blank, p. [8]; proem,
pp. 7–9 (should be 9–11); blank, p. [12]; table of contents, pp. 11–14
(should be 13–16); text, pp. 15–187 (should be 17–189); blank, p. [190];
end paper.

[Note: The conjugate of pp. 183–184 (*sic*) is pasted down under
the lining paper.]

ILLUSTRATIONS: Frontispiece and numerous text illustrations all
integral parts of the book.

BINDING: Green cloth or vellum. Front cover gilt-stamped: POEMS |
HERE | [*floret*] | AT | [*floret*] | HOME [*preceding 4 lines within single rule
box*] | JAMES | WHITCOMB | RILEY   All of the foregoing appears within
an ornamental gilt border. Spine gilt-stamped: [*ornament*] | [*rule*] |
POEMS | HERE | AT | HOME | [*floret*] | RILEY | [*floret*] | THE | CENTURY |
CO. | [*rule*] | [*ornament*]   Back cover gilt-stamped, identical with the
front cover.

PUBLICATION DATE: The title was entered for copyright August 30,
1893. A copy of the book was received by the Copyright Office September 15, 1893. It was advertised by the Bowen-Merrill Company in the
*Indianapolis Journal*, October 7, 1893, as "ready October 10." The earliest located presentation inscriptions are dated October 10, 1893*. There
were "two large editions before issue," according to the Century Com-

---

*With the exception of one copy in which the author absent-mindedly wrote
the date *October 10, 1892* (!)

POEMS HERE AT HOME

*Green cloth, back cover blind-stamped;*
*green cloth, back cover gilt; vellum*

pany's advertisement in the Christmas Number of the *Publishers' Weekly*, 1893.

The Bowen-Merrill Company advertised the book without mention of the Century Company as publishers. British reviews, as early as November 3, 1893, do not mention the American publishers, but refer instead to Longmans, Green and Co., London, and give the price as 6s. Since no copies of the book have been found bearing Longmans' imprint, it may be assumed that the book was simply distributed by them, just as the Bowen-Merrill Company advertised and sold copies in the Middle West.

PUBLICATION PRICE: Cloth, $1.50; vellum, $2.50.

NOTES: The sheets exist in two states.

> State 1: In the advertisements at p. [2], *Neighborly* (later *Neghborly*)
>
> Page 50, first stanza, line 5, *girls* (later *gyrls*)
>
> State 2: In the advertisements at p. [2], *Neghborly* (earlier *Neighborly*)
>
> Page 50, first stanza, line 5, *gyrls* (earlier *girls*)

The cloth binding occurs in two states: with back cover gilt-stamped, or blind-stamped. Although the copyright deposit copy is in the latter state, it is significant that the known reprints do not have the stamping in gilt on the back cover.

On November 4, 1893, the Bowen-Merrill Company advertised, in the *Indianapolis News*, a "Special Photogravure Edition" of the book. On November 10th they advertised further: ". . . *Poems Here at Home* issued by Bowen-Merrill in a special Photogravure edition. No other edition contains the author's new Photogravure portrait and autograph also personally written by Mr. Riley. This edition necessarily is limited." This edition consisted of nothing more than ordinary copies of the book in which Bowen-Merrill had inserted, between the copyright page and the dedication, a photogravure portrait of the author. The portrait measures 3¹³⁄₁₆″ x 2⁹⁄₁₆″ and is set within a 4¹⁵⁄₁₆″ x 3⅜″ panel. The first state of the portrait carries an 1893 copyright notice in the name of the Bowen-Merrill Company*; later printings of the portrait lack the copyright notice. The text occurs in both states, with, or without, the typographical changes noted, at p. [2] and p. 50.

The Bobbs-Merrill Company later issued the book with a cancel title-page bearing their imprint.

---

*The Eitel copy contains a portrait measuring the full area of the panel and lacks the copyright notice. It was inscribed by Riley, October 10, 1893, and is apparently proof before letters.

A *Birthday Dinner Edition*, so stated on the front cover, was issued October 7, 1915, bound in gray boards with white cloth shelfback. A list of the committees, speakers, etc., follows the dedication page. The book contains a facsimile of the manuscript of stanzas III and IV of Riley's poem, "America—1901" ("O thou America—Messiah of Nations!"). This edition was boxed, and mounted on the box appears the poem beginning, "Season halest of the year" which is stanza III of "Time of Clearer Twitterings." Both box and binding carry the recipient's name.

CONTENTS: Of the 61 poems herein, 52 make their first appearance in a Riley book:

Proem   *Century Magazine*, November, 1892 (title in *Century* and in *Biographical Edition:* The Poems Here at Home)

The Absence of Little Wesley   *Century Magazine*, May, 1888

The Used-to-Be   *Indianapolis Journal*, June 3, 1880; *Judge*, April 26, 1890

At "The Literary"   *Century Magazine*, February, 1888; *Indianapolis Journal*, January 29, 1888

One Afternoon   *Indianapolis Journal*, June 23, 1883

Down to the Capital*   *Century Magazine*, March, 1889

The Poet of the Future   *Century Magazine*, January, 1889

The Old Man and Jim†   *Century Magazine*, January, 1888; *The Elocutionist's Annual No. 16* (1888); *Gems from an Old Drummer's Grip* (1889)

Thoughts on the Late War   *Century Magazine*, January, 1890; *Indianapolis Journal*, January 5, 1890 (with title: Thoughts of the Late War)

The Old Band   *Century Magazine*, February, 1890; *Indianapolis Journal*, February 9, 1890

"Last Christmas Was a Year Ago"   *Century Magazine*, December, 1888; *Indianapolis Journal*, December 9, 1888; *Ideal Series: Select Readings and Recitations for Christmas, No. 4* (1891)

The All-Kind Mother   *Century Magazine*, February, 1889; *Indianapolis Journal*, February 10, 1889

Goin' to the Fair   *Golden-Rod* (Indianapolis Flower Mission Magazine, November 3, 1891)

Gladness   *Century Magazine*, July, 1888

---

*See *Biographical Edition*, Vol. 4, p. 488, for introduction to the poem, used by Riley in recitations.

†See *Biographical Edition*, Vol. 3, p. 561, for introduction to the poem, used by Riley in recitations.

Fessler's Bees   *Indianapolis Journal*, May 31, 1885

A Life Term   *Indianapolis Journal*, June 30, 1883

"The Little Man in the Tin-Shop"   *Century Magazine*, April, 1890

From a Balloon   *Indianapolis Journal*, September 12, 1881

"Tradin' Joe"   *Saturday Herald* (*Indianapolis*), July 6, 1878*

Uncle William's Picture   *Century Magazine*, January, 1891; *Western Association Writers, Sayings and Doings of the Sixth General Meeting, 1891* (1892) (with title: Uncle William's Photo)

Squire Hawkins's Story   *Saturday Herald* (*Indianapolis*), February 9, 1878

Dead Selves   *Indianapolis Journal*, May 22, 1877

Song of the Bullet   *Indianapolis Journal*, December 13, 1890

Dead, My Lords   *Indianapolis Journal*, February 26, 1888

Home Again ("I'm bin a-visitun 'bout a week")   *Century Magazine*, December, 1892

A Sea-Song from the Shore   *Indianapolis Journal* and *Indianapolis Sentinel*, December 28, 1890 (in advertisement for The When)

The Spoiled Child   *Century Magazine*, December, 1892

The Kind Old Man   *Indianapolis Journal*, May 24, 1884

The Doodle-Bugs's Charm   *Century Magazine*, December, 1892

Little Cousin Jasper   *Century Magazine*, December, 1892; *Standard Recitations No. 38* (1893)

Give Me the Baby   *Indianapolis Journal*, October 13, 1883

The Bee-Bag   *Century Magazine*, December, 1892

Little Marjorie   *Indianapolis Journal*, March 13, 1892

The Truly Marvelous   *Century Magazine*, December, 1892

'Mongst the Hills o' Somerset   *Century Magazine*, November, 1888

Old John Henry   *Indianapolis Journal*, April 17, 1892†

My First Spectacles   *Indianapolis Journal*, November 8, 1880

Scotty   *Current* (*Chicago*), April 19, 1884; *Sun* (*New York*), April 27, 1884

My White Bread   *Indianapolis Journal*, September 10, 1881 (without title)

Back from Town   *Century Magazine*, February, 1891

A Man by the Name of Bolus   *World* (*New York*), April 8, 1888

---

*See *Biographical Edition*, Vol. 1, p. 401, for introduction to the poem, used by Riley in recitations and for reference to an earlier newspaper appearance.

†"Old John Henry" appears in *Dick's Recitations and Readings No. 18* (1893). According to records in Washington, the title of this compilation was entered for copyright August 31, 1893, just one day later than the title of *Poems Here at Home*. Copies were deposited October 3, 1893, after *Poems Here at Home* had been received in the Copyright Office.

Old Chums   *Critic*, January 7, 1893

What a Dead Man Said   *Indianapolis Journal*, December 18, 1880

Cuored o' Skeerin'   *Indianapolis Journal*, September 12, 1891

Your Violin   *Indianapolis Journal*, May 20, 1882

To a Skull   *Indianapolis Journal*, July 7, 1880

A Vision of Summer   *Indianapolis Journal*, April 21, 1883

Bereaved   *Century Magazine*, November, 1890; *Indianapolis Journal*, November 2, 1890

A Song of the Cruise   *Indianapolis Journal*, July 22, 1882

The Dead Wife ("Always I see her in a saintly guise")   *Indianapolis Journal*, July 30, 1881

Someday   *Indianapolis Journal*, January 20, 1881

Close the Book   *Indianapolis Journal*, March 6, 1881

For Riley's own comments on *Poems Here at Home*, see his letter to William Carey, June 29, 1893, published in *Letters of James Whitcomb Riley* edited by William Lyon Phelps (1930), p. 188. Rudyard Kipling's comments on it are quoted on p. 333 of the same collection.

# 1894

# Armazindy

ARMAZINDY | BY | JAMES WHITCOMB RILEY | [*floret*] | INDI-
ANAPOLIS | THE BOWEN-MERRILL CO. | 1894

COLLATION: 1–11⁸, [12]⁴. Leaf measures 7¼″ x 4¾″, all edges
trimmed, top edge gilt. Printed on white laid paper with horizontal wire
marks.

PAGINATION: End paper, same as book stock; fly title, p. i; list of
books *By The Same Author*, p. ii; frontispiece with tissue guard (inserted);
title-page, p. [iii]; copyright notice with date 1894, p. iv; dedication to
Henry Eitel, p. v; blank, p. [vi]; table of contents, pp. vii–viii; blank,
pp. [ix–x]; text, pp. 1–169 (should be 171; blank leaf following p. 76 is
not figured in the printed pagination); blank, p. [172]; end paper.

[Note: The conjugate of pp. 165–166 (*sic*) is pasted down under
the lining paper. Some copies have inserted advertisements. For further
comment see discussion of State 1, p. 52.]

ILLUSTRATIONS: Frontispiece with tissue guard, inserted: a sepia
photogravure of a woman with a fishing pole crossing a water-gap*.

BINDING: Parti-colored cloth, darker color forming upper third.
The front cover is stamped in gilt: ARMAZINDY | JAMES WHITCOMB RILEY
The spine is gilt-stamped: ARMAZINDY | [*ornament resembling a question
mark in reverse*] | RILEY   The wavy rule above the lettering on the spine
is carried to the front cover above, and extends to the right of, the title.

PUBLICATION DATE: The title was entered for copyright October 1,
1894 and a copy of the regular edition was deposited in the Copyright
Office on October 8, 1894; the Holiday Edition was deposited November 16, 1894.

PUBLICATION PRICE: Regular edition, $1.25; Holiday Edition, $2.00.

NOTES: Reviews of advance copies† appeared in the Indianapolis

---

*According to an article in the *Nicholasville Democrat*, November 30, 1894, this
illustration is from a photograph of Miss Susie Little, taken while she was crossing
a water gap on Long Run Creek, near Nicholasville, Ky.

†These were issued in plain wrappers, stamped on front cover and title page:
*For editorial use*. The leaves are trimmed, top edge ungilded; no illustrations; otherwise same as State 1.

newspapers October 6, 1894. The publishers announced in the *Indianapolis Journal*, October 7, 1894, that the book would be offered to the public "this week," and that "two editions are being prepared—one in uniform style with Mr. Riley's other volumes, . . . the other handsomely illustrated and with ornamental cover as a holiday edition." A presentation copy of the regular edition has been noted with inscription dated October 8, 1894, the date of copyright deposit. There was, however, some delay in publication. On October 27, 1894, in the *Indianapolis News*, the publishers announced the book as "ready for delivery today"; both editions are described in the advertisement. It may be that preparation of the Holiday Edition delayed publication, for presentation copies of it are usually dated "October, 1894," and the earliest so far seen that reads more definitely is one dated October 27, 1894.

The book occurs in the following states:

*State* 1: Page ii: numbered; Longmans, Green & Co. mentioned
Table of contents, pp. vii–viii
Blank leaf that follows p. 76 unnumbered
Page 110 has 26 lines (later 27)*
Copies occur with or without advertisements inserted at back: 4 signatures in 4. When they are present the last leaf of the final signature of the book proper is a free blank, not pasted down under the lining paper. Priority, if any, undetermined.

*State* 2: Typographically same as State 1 but p. 110 has the added line, fourth from the top, reading: *But found myself as suddenly beset.* This state has so far been found only in copies of the Holiday Edition (see description of Holiday Edition below).

*State* 3: Page ii: numeral omitted; list of books by Riley changed in form and Longmans, Green & Co. not mentioned
Table of contents, pp. vii–x; reset and arranged in alphabetical order
Blank page following p. 76 numbered 76½
Page 110 has 27 lines as in State 2
The first signature is in 2, followed by 11 in 8, and the 12th in 4. Printed on same paper as the Holiday Edition but with all edges trimmed.

---

*The author usually wrote the missing line in presentation copies, in its proper place. Since the space between lines in the book is negligible, only a minute and precise script such as his could be squeezed therein.

*State* 4: Same as State 3 but printed on paper similar to State 1 except heavier. The signatures consist of 12 in 8, with last leaf of final signature pasted down under the lining paper. In one examined copy the last leaf of the final signature is used as the lining paper

The bindings occur in the following states:

Parti-colored cloth, as described in the collation.

Holiday Edition binding: red buckram gilt-stamped, or green buckram with silver stamping. Front cover stamped: ARMAZINDY | JAMES WHITCOMB RILEY Spine stamped: ARMAZINDY | [*ornament, head of grain*] | RILEY | BOWEN-MERRILL At top and bottom of spine is stamped a band which extends to the front cover and borders the top, fore and bottom edges. Back cover blank. All stamping either gilt or silver, as described.

A variant, probably trial, binding of the Holiday Edition has the spine stamped: ARMAZINDY | HOOSIER | AIRS | AND | OTHERS | [*rule*] | RILEY | BOWEN-MERRILL It occurs in both colors: red with gilt, green with silver.

The sheets of all examined copies of the Holiday Edition fall into typographical States 2 or 3. Thus far no copy has been seen with sheets in State 1. This edition is printed on heavy deckle-edged paper with vertical wire marks. It contains a portrait frontispiece and 5 inserted photogravure plates: opposite p. 1 (illustration used as frontispiece in State 1), p. 37, p. 52, p. 77, p. 134.

Later states of the book appear in the parti-colored cloth binding. A copy in State 3 has the ornament on the spine which follows the title turned so as to resemble a question mark in its proper position.

A limited edition of 100 numbered and signed copies bound in red silk cloth, published at $5.00, was issued in December, 1894. It contains the portrait and illustrations as in the Holiday Edition.

The book was reissued in 1895 in red cloth, extra gilt spine.

In 1898, as Vol. 9 of the *Homestead Edition*, the book appeared with two poems omitted (included in other volumes) and with one added, which is not a first appearance in a Riley book.

CONTENTS: All of the poems and the prose sketch herein are first appearances in a Riley book:

Armazindy*  *Indianapolis Journal*, September 5, 1893

The Old Trundle-Bed†  *Life*, June 14, 1883

Natural Perversities  *Indianapolis Sentinel*, March 26, 1876 (with title: Lusus Naturae)

The Old School-Chum  *Indianapolis Journal*, December 6, 1880 (with title: Tears)

Writin' Back to the Home-Folks

The Blind Girl  *Indianapolis Journal*, November 1, 1884

We Defer Things  *Indianapolis Journal*, February 9, 1885 (without title)

The Muskingum Valley  *Life*, March 8, 1883

For This Christmas§

A Poor Man's Wealth  *Indianapolis Journal*, August 4, 1883

The Little Red Ribbon  *Indianapolis Journal*, May 12, 1883

"How Did You Rest, Last Night?"  *Atlanta Constitution*, April 16, 1893

A Good-Bye  *Indianapolis Journal*, June 24, 1882 (with title: Some Other Evening)

When Maimie Married  *Life*, April 12, 1883; *Life's Verses* (1885)

"This Dear Child-Hearted Woman That Is Dead"‖

To a Poet-Critic

An Old-Timer  *Indianapolis Journal*, May 16, 1880

The Silent Victors  *New Castle Mercury*, June 1, 1876 (without title; part only); *Anderson Democrat*, June 1, 1877 (with title: Decoration Poem)¶; *Indianapolis Journal*, May 31, 1878 (without title)

Up and Down Old Brandywine  *Cosmopolitan*, May, 1894

---

*There is in the Rare Book Collection in the Library of Congress a large sheet, scant 24″ x full 15″, headed: Armazindy . . . "*A Borned Soldier and Hero.*" . . . followed by text of the poem in three columns. This bears the Copyright Office stamp dated August 30, 1893. It is printed on news pulp. Comparing it with the full-page spread of the first newspaper appearance, in the *Indianapolis Journal*, September 5, 1893, there seems no doubt that the same type was used for both. Two words were changed to italics in the newspaper publication, and a great many illustrations, by Will Vawter, were added throughout the text, extending it to five columns.

†Not listed in table of contents, States 1 and 2.

§"For This Christmas" appears in the *Indianapolis Star*, September 10, 1943, under the title, "God Bless You, Merry Gentlemen!"

‖Under the title "Transfigured" stanzas 3 and 4 of the poem "This Dear Child-Hearted Woman That Is Dead" appeared in *The Youth of James Whitcomb Riley* by Marcus Dickey (1919), p. 72.

¶Not seen except as a clipping with manuscript identification.

Three Singing Friends  *Indianapolis Journal*, November 19, 1893 (part III only, with title: To a Western Singer—James Newton Matthews); *Indianapolis Journal*, December 3, 1893 (part I only, with title: Master and First Song-Friend—Lee O. Harris); *Indianapolis Journal*, December 10, 1893 (part II only, with title: The Clearer Hail—Benjamin S. Parker)

A Noon Lull  *Indianapolis Journal*, February 21, 1892 (in advertisement for The When)

A Windy Day  *Indianapolis Journal*, June 3, 1882

My Henry  *Kokomo Tribune*, July 10, 1880; *Kokomo Tribune* advertising circular (see p. 168)

The Song I Never Sing  *Indianapolis Journal*, November 10, 1878

To Edgar Wilson Nye

Little David

Out of the Hitherwhere  *Indianapolis Journal*, December 22, 1883

Rabbit in the Cross-Ties  *Indianapolis Journal* and *Indianapolis Sentinel*, December 27, 1891 (in advertisement for The When)

Serenade—To Nora  *Life*, March 8, 1883; *Life's Verses* (1885)

He and I  *Indianapolis Journal*, September 10, 1881 (without title)

What Redress  *Indianapolis Journal*, September 29, 1880 (with title: Redress)

Dreamer, Say  *Saturday Herald* (*Indianapolis*), May 11, 1878 (without title); *Indianapolis Journal*, August 8, 1886 (with title: Alkazar)

When Lide Married *Him*

My Bride That Is to Be  *Indianapolis Journal*, October 13, 1878

"Ringworm Frank"

An Empty Glove*  *Indianapolis Journal*, July 19, 1881

Our Own  *Indianapolis Journal*, August 13, 1880

The Frog  *Anderson Democrat*, 1877†; *Saturday Herald* (*Indianapolis*), July 6, 1878; *Life*, January 18, 1883

"Twiggs and Tudens" (prose)  *Saturday Herald* (*Indianapolis*), September 28, 1878; *Golden-Rod* (Indianapolis Flower Mission Magazine, November 3, 1891; with title: Tale of a Manuscript)

An Idyl of the King§  *Saturday Herald* (*Indianapolis*), September 28, 1878

---

*The *Hancock Democrat*, August 11, 1881, contains part of this poem, beginning: "White fruited cocoa shown against the shell"; without title.

†"The Frog" appeared in the *Anderson Democrat* during 1877, as evidenced by its inclusion in *Riley's First Poems* (1901).

§Part of "An Idyl of the King," beginning "Oh, bright is gleaming morn on mountain height" appeared in the *Sun* (*New York*), May 30, 1880, with title: "Song | Imitated from Tennyson's Idyls of the King."

Dolores  *Indianapolis Journal*, August 26, 1882

When I Do Mock  *Indianapolis Journal*, August 26, 1882 (with title: Sonnet)

My Mary  *Indianapolis Journal*, June 16, 1883

Eros  *Indianapolis Journal*, January 21, 1882

Orlie Wilde  *Indianapolis Journal*, April 19, 1877*

Leonainie  *Kokomo Dispatch*, August 2, 1877; sheet music (1879; see p. 147)

To a Jilted Swain  *Indianapolis Journal*, April 4, 1886

The Voices  *Indianapolis Journal*, July 9, 1880

A Barefoot Boy  *Indianapolis Journal*, May 12, 1883 (with title: Sonnet unto a Barefoot Boy)

The Youthful Patriot

Ponchus Pilut

A Twintorette  *Indianapolis Journal*, September 17, 1881 (with title: A Rondel)

Slumber-Song  *Indianapolis Journal*, June 4, 1880

The Circus Parade  *Indianapolis Journal*, May 9, 1880

Folks at Lonesomeville  *Indianapolis Journal*, December 23, 1890 (in advertisement for The When)

The Three Jolly Hunters  *Indianapolis Journal*, December 16, 1890 (in advertisement for The When)

The Little Dog-Woggy  *Indianapolis Journal*, April 5, 1891 (in advertisement for The When; with title: The Doggy That Walked Round the World)

Charms: I—For Corns and Things; II—To Remove Freckles—Scotch Ones†  *Indianapolis Journal*, December 27, 1890 (in advertisement for The When; two poems, with titles: "This Will Knock a Corn Silly"; and "To Take Off Freckles—Scotch Ones")

A Few of the Bird-Family  *Indianapolis Journal*, May 3, 1891 (in advertisement for The When)

Through Sleepy-Land  *Indianapolis Journal*, December 19, 1890 (in advertisement for The When)

The Trestle and the Buck-Saw  *Indianapolis Journal* and *Indianapolis Sentinel*, March 22, 1891 (in advertisement for The When)

The King of Oo-Rinktum-Jing  *Indianapolis Journal*, December 29, 1890 (in advertisement for The When)

---

*Riley's reply to criticism of this poem, in the form of a letter, appears in the *Indianapolis Journal*, April 21, 1877; captioned "Card from Mr. J. W. Riley."

†The table of contents lists "To Remove Freckles" as a separate poem, but its only appearance here and elsewhere in Riley books is as part II of "Charms."

The Toy Penny-Dog  *Indianapolis Journal*, March 22, 1891 (in advertisement for The When; with title: The Little Toy Penny-Dog)

Jargon-Jingle

The Great Explorer  *Indianapolis Journal*, December 20, 1890 (in advertisement for The When; with title: Stanley)

The Schoolboy's Favorite  *Modern Art*, October 1, 1894

Albumania—*caption title for 6 short poems:* Friendship; Life; Life's Happiest Hours; Marion-County Man Homesick Abroad; Birdy! Birdy!; and quatrain, without title, beginning: "When o'er this page in happy years to come." (No previous publication located save for 2 of the poems which appeared in the *Indianapolis Journal*, February 22, 1891, in advertisement for The When, under title, "Choice Verses for Autograph Albums": [Birdy! Birdy!], and the quatrain beginning, "When on [o'er] this page, in happy years to come")

The Little Mock-Man

Summer-Time and Winter-Time  *Indianapolis Journal*, October 18, 1891 (in advertisement for The When)

Home-Made Riddles  *Indianapolis Journal*, January 4, 1891 (in advertisement for The When; with title: Some Custom-Made Riddles)

The Lovely Child  *Indianapolis Journal* and *Indianapolis Sentinel*, December 13, 1891 (in advertisement for The When; with title: A Child's Choice)

The Yellow-Bird  *Indianapolis Journal*, December 6, 1891 (in advertisement for The When)

Envoy ("When but a little boy, it seemed")  *Indianapolis Journal*, April 19, 1891 (in advertisement for The When; with title: The Two Dreams) (Title in *Biographical Edition:* Sad Perversity)

The author is said to have read the poem "Armazindy" at a G. A. R. assembly in Indianapolis shortly after its publication in the newspaper. It brought him a rebuke* from Prof. Charles H. Wood, head of the public school in New Harmony, Indiana, who thought that Riley was poking fun at the town in the lines about Jule Reddinhouse:

> "*She'd* ben to school at *New Harmony*, i gum!—
> Fool before, but that hepped *some*—
> 'Stablished-like more confidence
> 'at she *never* had no sense."

---

*See *New Harmony Times*, September 22, 1893.

Miss Louise Husband, Librarian of The Workingmen's Institute, New Harmony, tells us that the other members of the community understood and felt that Riley meant to compliment the town because of its early history and school system. The letter which Prof. Wood wrote to Riley was, however, sufficient to make him change the name of the town where Jule got her education from "New Harmony" to a fictitious "New Thessaly." In all examined editions of the book, "New Thessaly" appears, and not "New Harmony."

# 1895

# The Days Gone By

THE DAYS GONE BY | AND OTHER POEMS | BY | JAMES WHITCOMB RILEY | [*publishers' emblem*] | CHICAGO: | E. A. WEEKS & COMPANY | 521–531 WABASH AVENUE

COLLATION: [*]⁴, [1–5]⁸, 6–[12]⁸, 13⁸, 14⁴. Leaf measures 6¾" x 4¼", top edge gilt, other edges untrimmed. Printed on white laid paper.

PAGINATION: End paper, same as book stock; frontispiece (inserted); title-page, p. [i]; copyright notice in the name of E. A. Weeks & Company with date 1895 and printers' imprint, p. [ii]; table of contents, pp. iii–v; blank, p. [vi]; divisional half-title, p. [vii]; blank, p. [viii]; text, pp. [1]–214; blank, pp. [215–216]; end paper.

ILLUSTRATIONS: Frontispiece, and 3 full-page plates inserted opposite pp. 57, 107 and 113. All plates on coated paper.

BINDING: Dark blue cloth. Front cover gilt-stamped with small ornaments and lettered in gilt within gilt festoons that form a shield-shaped design: THE | DAYS GONE BY | AND | [*dot*] OTHER POEMS [*dot*] | [*dot*] | JAMES WHITCOMB RILEY. Spine gilt-stamped: [*fillet*] | [*2 ornaments*] | THE | DAYS | GONE BY | AND | OTHER POEMS | [*ornament*] | [*fillet*] | [*wreath, within which is lettered;*] JAMES | WHITCOMB | RILEY. | [*at foot of spine:*] E. A. WEEKS | & COMPANY. | [*fillet*] Back cover blank.

PUBLICATION DATE: Copies were deposited in the Copyright Office on December 5, 1895. The title was entered for copyright December 9, 1895.

PUBLICATION PRICE: $1.00(?)

NOTES: This pirated edition of Riley's poems was suppressed by law, together with *A Tinkle of Bells*, issued the same year. Riley and his publishers, the Bowen-Merrill Company, brought suit against E. A. Weeks & Company and George W. Ogilvie for infringement of copyright. They further claimed that mutilated and improper versions of his works had damaged Riley's reputation. Judgment was in the author's favor on every point. The court ordered confiscation of all books, sheets and plates and issued a permanent injunction against the Chicago pub-

59

lishers preventing further publication of Riley's works. The copyright was renewed in April, 1930, but with Mary Riley Payne, the author's sister, as claimant.

The errors and "improprieties" were noted by the author in a copy* which he corrected for his authorized publishers. His pencil was busy with corrections on almost every page.

CONTENTS: The book contains the following poems and sketches written by others than Riley: "To James Whitcomb Riley" by Frank Preston Smart; "James Whitcomb Riley" by Robert J. Burdette; and "An Answer to Riley's 'Deer Crick' " [by William W. Pfrimmer]; and the concluding sketch, "A Wholesale Poet." "O, Pinching-Bug!" signed "Poet of the Waste-Basket," is not Riley's; its only connection lies in the subtitle which is a quotation from him†. The first part of "When We Three Meet," with subtitle "R. C. M.," is by J. N. Matthews; Riley's reply, headed "M. C. R.," follows it. The poem, "Only Wanted a Chance," had previously appeared as "The Tree-Toad," and "Song" had appeared as "Sprite Serenade."

Of the other poems and prose sketches herein, all reprinted from the *Indianapolis Journal*, the following are first appearances in a Riley book:

> The Baby (3 parts, of which 2 here make first appearances in a Riley book§) *Indianapolis Journal*, April 7, 1883; *Ideal Series, Select Readings and Recitations, No. 9* (1891) (later title of the 2 parts: The Way the Baby Came; The Way the Baby Woke)
>
> Becalmed  *Indianapolis Journal*, May 10, 1885
>
> A Local Politician from Away Back  *Indianapolis Journal*, January 30, 1887
>
> Dan O'Sullivan  *Indianapolis Journal*, January 22, 1888
>
> The Mute Singer  *Indianapolis Journal*, February 6, 1887
>
> Song ("O I would I had a lover")  *Indianapolis Journal*, April 26, 1885
>
> Uninterpreted  *Indianapolis Journal*, July 12, 1884
>
> Unless  *Indianapolis Journal*, February 24, 1883
>
> The Iron Pup‖  *Indianapolis Journal*, December 2, 1882
>
> Two Sonnets to the June-Bug  *Indianapolis Journal*, June 16, 1883
>
> The Way That Billy Could Ride  *Indianapolis Journal*, September 13, 1885 (title in *Biographical Edition:* Billy Could Ride)

---

*In the private library of Mr. Lee Burns, Indianapolis.
†"Circumstances alters cases"—from poem, "Down on Wriggle Crick"
§For third part, see: "The Way the Baby Slept," p. 33.
‖The only appearance in a Riley book.

The Willow  *Indianapolis Journal*, May 3, 1885 (later incorporated, without title, in "The Old Home-Folks")

The Christ  *Indianapolis Journal*, September 14, 1884

When We Three Meet  *Indianapolis Journal*, October 11, 1885 (with title: M. C. R.)

Dave Field  *Indianapolis Journal*, September 27, 1885

Written in John Boyle O'Reilly's "In Bohemia"  *Indianapolis Journal*, December 12, 1886; *Life of John Boyle O'Reilly* by J. J. Roche (1891) (title in *Biographical Edition:* On a Fly-Leaf)

Grant  *Indianapolis Journal*, August 9, 1885 (the last stanza had appeared in the *Indianapolis Journal*, July 26, 1885, as the first stanza of "The Dead Leader")

An Impromptu on Roller Skates  *Indianapolis Journal*, March 29, 1884

The Law of the Perverse  *Indianapolis Journal*, June 28, 1885

The Best Is Good Enough for Me  *Indianapolis Journal*, September 8, 1883

A Trancient [*sic*] Dental Monody*  *Indianapolis Journal*, June 23, 1883 (with title: A Transient Dental Monody)

The Assassin ("Fling him amongst the cobbles of the street")  *Indianapolis Journal*, June 23, 1883

Mrs. Robert J. Burdette* (prose)  *Indianapolis Journal*, May 31, 1884

---

*The only appearance in a Riley book.

# 1895

# A Tinkle of Bells

A TINKLE OF BELLS | AND OTHER POEMS | BY | JAMES WHITCOMB RILEY | [*publishers' emblem*] | CHICAGO: | E. A. WEEKS & COMPANY | 521–531 WABASH AVENUE

SIGNATURES: [*]⁴, [1]–[11]⁸, 12–[13]⁸, [14]⁴. Leaf measures 6¾″ x 4¼″, top edge gilt, other edges untrimmed. Printed on white laid paper.

PAGINATION: End paper, same as book stock; blank, pp. [i–ii]; frontispiece (inserted); title-page, p. [iii]; copyright notice in the name of E. A. Weeks & Company with date 1895 and printers' imprint, p. [iv]; table of contents, pp. iii–v (should be v–vii); blank, p. [viii]; text, pp. 1–210; blank, pp. [211–216]; end paper

ILLUSTRATIONS: Frontispiece, and 3 full-page plates inserted opposite pp. 99, 136 and 192. All plates on coated paper.

BINDING: Dark blue cloth. Front cover gilt-stamped with small ornaments and lettered in gilt within gilt festoons that form a shield-shaped design: A | TINKLE OF BELLS | AND | [*dot*] OTHER POEMS [*dot*] | [*dot*] | JAMES WHITCOMB RILEY. Spine stamped in gilt: [*fillet*] | [*2 ornaments*] | A | TINKLE | OF | BELLS | AND | OTHER POEMS | [*ornament*] | [*fillet*] | [*wreath, within which is lettered:*] JAMES | WHITCOMB | RILEY. | [*at foot of spine:*] E. A. WEEKS | & COMPANY. | [*fillet*]  Back cover blank.

PUBLICATION DATE: The title was entered for copyright December 21, 1895; copies were deposited in the Copyright Office December 23, 1895.

PUBLICATION PRICE: $1.00(?)

NOTES: This is a pirated edition of Riley's poems, uniform with *The Days Gone By*, and suppressed by law with the latter book (see p. 59). The copyright was renewed in April, 1930, but with Mary Riley Payne as claimant.

CONTENTS: Of the poems and prose sketches herein, all reprinted from the *Indianapolis Journal*, the following 21 are first appearances in a Riley book.

The poem, "A Summer Day," had previously appeared as "A Summer's Day." The poem, "God Moves in a Mysterious Way" had previously been published as "A Hymb of Faith." "As I Sit in the Silence" had appeared as "Envoy."

A Tinkle of Bells  *Indianapolis Journal*, January 12, 1884
In Days to Come  *Indianapolis Journal*, March 20, 1887
An Ideal*  *Indianapolis Journal*, September 14, 1884
Noon  *Indianapolis Journal*, August 24, 1884 (title in *Biographical Edition:* A Noon Interval)
"Jack in the Box"  *Indianapolis Journal*, June 2, 1883
Our Old Friend Neverfail  *Indianapolis Journal*, January 22, 1888
Back from a Two Years' Sentence  *Indianapolis Journal*, August 28, 1887
Luther A. Todd  *Indianapolis Journal*, August 7, 1887
Pap's Old Sayin'  *Indianapolis Journal*, May 3, 1885
All Alone*  *Indianapolis Journal*, November 25, 1882
At Madame Manicure's  *Indianapolis Journal*, August 24, 1884
Lincoln  *Indianapolis Journal*, October 26, 1884
The Dead Wife* ("I looked from the window. The smoke goes straight") *Indianapolis Journal*, March 22, 1885; broadside, undated, with "Alone" by Robert J. Burdette (see p. 172)
In State  *Indianapolis Journal*, May 17, 1884
Nonsense Jingles  *Indianapolis Journal*, April 12, 1884 (title in *Biographical Edition:* The Strange Young Man)
The Amiable Old Sister*  *Indianapolis Journal*, February 21, 1886
At Ninety in the Shade  *Indianapolis Journal*, July 7, 1883
To a Benedict Friend*  *Indianapolis Journal*, June 16, 1883
Written in Bunner's "Airs from Arcady"  *Indianapolis Journal* April 5, 1884
Josh Billings  *Indianapolis Journal*, October 18, 1885
Kismet ("Our fortunes! O we need not waste")*  *Indianapolis Journal*, September 21, 1884

---

*Only appearance of the poem in a Riley book.

# A Child-World

A CHILD-WORLD | BY | JAMES WHITCOMB RILEY | [*floret*] | INDI-
ANAPOLIS AND KANSAS CITY | THE BOWEN-MERRILL COMPANY |
1897

COLLATION: [1–28]⁴ signed in 8: [1]–[14]. The publishers' advertisements are an integral part of the book. Leaf measures 7″ full x 4¾″,
all edges trimmed, top edge gilt. Printed on white laid paper, with horizontal wire marks.

PAGINATION: End paper, same as book stock; blank, pp. [i–ii]; fly
title, p. [iii]; list of *Mr. Riley's Books*, p. [iv]; frontispiece with guard
(inserted); title-page, p. [v]; copyright notice with date 1896, p. [vi];
dedication to Mr. and Mrs. Charles L. Holstein, p. [vii]; blank, p. [viii];
proem, p. [ix]; blank, p. [x]; table of contents, pp. [xi–xiii]; blank, p.
[xiv]; half-title, p. [xv]; blank, p. [xvi]; text, pp. 17–209; blank, p. [210];
title-page for publishers' catalogue, p. [211]; advertisements, pp. [212–
224]; end paper.

ILLUSTRATIONS: Sepia photogravure frontispiece, by Will Vawter,
with guard, inserted. Facsimile of sheet music, "Mountain Maid's Invitation" (not by Riley), inserted opposite p. 126.

BINDING: Smooth red cloth. Front cover stamped in gilt within
single rule border: A CHILD-WORLD | BY JAMES WHITCOMB RILEY  Spine
extra gilt-stamped with decorative design of vine-like scrolls, single rule
at top, lettered within single rules: A | CHILD- | WORLD | [*rule*] | RILEY
and, at foot of spine, between single rules: BOWEN-MERRILL  Back cover
blank. This binding is uniform with that of eight other volumes of
Riley's works, but it is the first of the Riley books to have it as a first
edition binding.

PUBLICATION DATE: A copyright deposit copy is dated received
October 12, 1896. A publishers' advertisement in the *Indianapolis Jour-
nal*, October 10, 1896, and a review of the book in the same newspaper,
October 11, 1896, announce the book as due to appear on October 12th.

The *Indianapolis Journal* of September 29, 1896 contains an article which states: "Mr. Riley's new book, entitled *A Child-World* is to be issued simultaneously here by the Bowen-Merrill Company and in London by Longmans, Green & Co. sometime in October. There is no doubt about its success. Having been privileged to see some of the advance sheets, ... I predict for it a greater popularity than any of his books have hitherto attained." Although publication date in America was the 12th, an earlier date, October 9th, had been agreed upon by the Indianapolis and London publishers. In a letter dated July 3, 1939, Longmans, Green & Company state that their edition was published October 9, 1896. There exist a number of presentation copies of the Bowen-Merrill Company edition with an inserted leaf bearing the author's inscription dated October 9, 1896*. This is accounted for by the fact that Riley had left Indianapolis on October 8th to give a reading in Colorado on the 13th, and some time before the books were ready, in expectation of their issuance on the 9th, he had prepared these leaves for insertion.

PUBLICATION PRICE: $1.25.

NOTES: There are several states of the American edition
  *State* 1: Title-page with single imprint, as described
    Proem at p. [ix]
    Table of contents headed I, II and III; lists proem as at p. 15
    Half-title at p. [xv]
    Advertisement at p. [224], of Nye's *A Guest at the Ludlow*, has *The Bowen-Merrill Co., Indianapolis* present
    Printed on laid paper with horizontal wire marks; all edges trimmed
  *State* 2: Title-page has added imprint: *London | Longmans, Green & Co.*
    Proem at p. [xi]
    Table of contents reset: headings I, II, III, omitted; proem listed without reference to page; titles distributed differently on second and third pages
    Half-title at p. [ix]
    Advertisement at p. [224] lacks imprint: *The Bowen-Merrill Co., Indianapolis*
    Printed on laid paper with vertical wire marks; fore edge and bottom edge untrimmed.

---

*The *Biographical Edition*, Vol. 4, Notes, p. 551, contains the author's poetical inscription in a copy of the book presented to his brother, October 7, 1896. It begins: "In this book of simple rhyme"

Later states have the signatures gathered in 8 and the publishers' catalogue in back, still dated 1897, varies. The advertisement for *A Guest at the Ludlow* is elaborated and does not appear on the last page of the catalogue. Copies have been noted with and without the imprint, Braunworth, Munn & Barber, on the copyright page. The Bowen-Merrill imprint on the spine is in larger type than in the earlier states and lacks the hyphen.

### FIRST ENGLISH EDITION

A CHILD-WORLD | BY | JAMES WHITCOMB RILEY | [*floret*] | LONGMANS, GREEN, AND CO. | LONDON AND BOMBAY | 1896 | All rights reserved

COLLATION: [A]–I⁸, K⁴. Leaf measures 6¼" x 3¾", top edge gilt, other edges untrimmed. Printed on white laid paper watermarked *K P T & Co.*

PAGINATION: End paper, off-white laid; blank, pp. [i–ii]; fly title, p. [iii]; list of books *By The Same Author*, p. [iv]; title page, p. [v]; copyright notice with date 1896, p. [vi]; dedication to Mr. and Mrs. Charles L. Holstein, p. [vii]; blank, p. [viii]; proem, p. [ix]; blank, p. [x]; table of contents, pp. [xi]–xiii; blank, p. [xiv]; half-title, p. [xv]; blank, p. [xvi]; text, pp. [1]–135 (with printers' slug at foot of p. 135); blank, p. [136]; end paper.

ILLUSTRATIONS: None.

BINDING: Blue pebbled cloth, vegetable vellum shelfback, vertical gilt rule where cloth and vellum join. Light blue paper label on spine gilt-stamped: A | CHILD- | WORLD | [*rule*] | RILEY   Double gilt rules are stamped at top and bottom of spine, with two single gilt rules at equal intervals between. Front and back covers unlettered. The book is uniform in binding with *Old-Fashioned Roses* (1888).

NOTES: This issue was evidently set up in England from advance sheets of the American edition*. Longmans, Green and Company's records show that the first printing consisted of 1,250 copies, 1,000 of which were sent to America. The English edition was published at 5 shillings. A later printing, with date 1897 on the title-page, is on paper watermarked *I D & Co* and has the Vawter frontispiece.

On December 3, 1896, the Bowen-Merrill Company advertised the book in the *Indianapolis Journal*, "in five different styles for the holidays."

---

*For discussion of date of appearance see p. 65.

One of the five was a limited edition of 100 numbered and signed copies in red silk· cloth, with limitation notice and author's signature on the title page, as in the case of *Neghborly Poems* (see "*The Old Swimmin'-Hole*," p. 4). The regular edition in red cloth, extra gilt spine, and the English edition account for two more of the "styles." Calf and half calf bindings constituted the remaining two, but we have not located these.

By June of 1897 the book was in its thirtieth thousand, according to a notice in the *Bookman* of that date.

In 1898 it was incorporated in the *Homestead Edition* as Vol. 10, with contents same as earlier editions.

CONTENTS: All of the poems herein are first appearances in a Riley book:

[Proem]  ("The Child-World—long and long since lost to view")

The Child-World

The Old Home Folks   Includes: "The Willow," previously in *The Days Gone By* (1895); "While the Heart Beats Young," *Ladies' Home Journal*, August, 1896; otherwise no previous appearance. Also includes "Almon Keefer," "Noey Bixler" and " 'A Noted Traveler' " all three of which are listed separately in the table of contents although here and in other Riley books they are part of "The Old Home Folks." Also includes "Nocturnal Ranger" and "The Child-Heart" which are indexed in the *Biographical* and the *Homestead Editions* but which make no separate appearance.

A Prospective Visit

At Noey's House (includes "That Little Dog")   *Danbury* (*Conn.*) *News*, April 8, 1874 (part only: That Little Dog, with title: That Little Dorg)

The Loehrs and the Hammonds   (No previous publication located save for the part beginning, "In the warm, health-giving weather," which appeared in the *Ladies' Home Journal*, December, 1895, with title, "At the Gate.")

The Hired Man and Floretty

The Evening Company

Maymie's Story of Red Riding Hood   *Saturday Herald* (*Indianapolis*), June 15, 1878 (in prose form, with title: A Child's Version of Little Red Riding Hood)

Limitations of Genius

Mr. Hammond's Parable   *Hearth and Home*, April 10, 1875 (with title: A Destiny); *Indianapolis Sentinel*, April 13, 1875 (with title: The Farmer Dreamer)

Floretty's Musical Contribution

Bud's Fairy-Tale   *Indianapolis Journal*, December 3, 1879 (in prose
   form, with title: Trillpipe's Boy)
A Delicious Interruption
Noey's Night-Piece
Cousin Rufus' Story
Bewildering Emotions
The Bear Story (table of contents: Alex Tells a Bear Story)
The Pathos of Applause
Told by "The Noted Traveler"
Heat Lightning
Uncle Mart's Poem
"Little Jack Janitor"

For Riley's comment on *A Child-World*, written to Mrs. Edgar Wilson Nye, May 6, 1896, see *Letters of James Whitcomb Riley* (1930), p. 207;
see also pp. 208–209.

# 1897

# Rubáiyát of Doc Sifers

[*orange rule*] | RUBÁIYÁT OF DOC SIFERS | BY JAMES WHITCOMB RILEY | [*orange rule*] | ILLUSTRATED | BY | C. M. RELYEA | [*publishers' emblem, black and orange*] | PUBLISHED BY THE CENTURY CO. | NEW YORK  M DCCC XC VII | [*orange rule*]

COLLATION: [\*]⁸, 1–7⁸. Leaf measures 7½″ x 5″, all edges trimmed, top edge gilt. Printed on white coated paper.

PAGINATION: End paper, white laid; blank, pp. [i–iv]; fly title, p. [v]; list of *Other Books by James Whitcomb Riley*, p. [vi]; blank, p. [vii]; frontispiece, p. [viii]; title-page, p. [ix]; copyright notices dated 1897, and imprint of the De Vinne Press, p. [x]; dedication to Dr. Franklin W. Hays, p. [xi]; blank, p. [xii]; proem, pp. ix–x (should be xiii–xiv); half-title, p. [xv]; vignette, p. [xvi]; text, pp. 1–111; blank, p. [112]; end paper. [Note: Each page of the text has the page number at the head between single orange rules with an orange rule below the text.]

ILLUSTRATIONS: Frontispiece and 26 full-page illustrations are integral parts of the book and are figured in the pagination. In addition there are numerous text illustrations.

BINDING: Sage green cloth. At the top of the front cover is a silhouette of the doctor in his horse and buggy, stamped in colors, within a single rule gilt box. Below this, within a single rule gilt box, is gilt stamped: RUBAIYAT OF DOC SIFERS | BY JAMES WHITCOMB RILEY | PUBLISHED BY THE CENTURY CO. The whole of the foregoing is enclosed within a single rule gilt box. The spine is gilt-stamped: RUBÁIYÁT | OF | DOC | SIFERS | BY | JAMES | WHITCOMB | RILEY | THE | CENTURY | CO. Back cover bears publishers' emblem stamped in gilt.

PUBLICATION DATE: Copies were deposited in the Copyright Office November 2, 1897. The book was advertised by the publishers in the *Indianapolis Journal* of December 4, 1897 as "now ready."

The book was reviewed in the *British Medical Journal*, March 26, 1898 and referred to as published by Longmans, Green & Company; similarly referred to in the *Indian Medical Gazette* of November, 1898. Since no copies of the book have been found bearing a Longmans,

Green & Company imprint, it may be assumed that the book was simply distributed by them.

PUBLICATION PRICE: $1.50.

NOTES: A limited edition of 100 numbered and signed copies, bound in red silk, was offered for sale on December 16, 1897. In these copies a portrait and limitation page precede the fly title.

CONTENTS: The poem of 105 quatrains of which the book is composed, had appeared in the *Century Magazine* of November and December, 1897, with the same title, "Rubáiyát of Doc Sifers." Riley had previously written a much shorter poem, entitled "Doc Sifers," which appeared in the *World* (*New York*), December 11, 1887, and was recited by the author at a banquet given by the Marion County Medical Society on June 5, 1888 (see p. 169). For the story of this banquet and the growth of the poem into the "Rubáiyát," see the *Indianapolis News*, September 9, 1907.

*The Homestead Edition*, Vol. 11, published 1902, combines *Home-Folks* (1900) with the *Rubáiyát of Doc Sifers*.

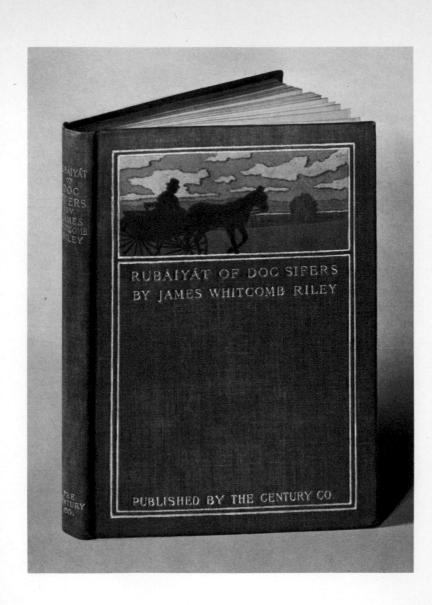

# 1898

## THE HOMESTEAD EDITION, VOL. III*
# Afterwhiles

THE POEMS AND PROSE | [2 *florets*] SKETCHES OF [2 *florets*] | JAMES WHITCOMB RILEY | AFTERWHILES [*in red, with 4 florets in red making a decorative design of the word*] | CHARLES SCRIBNER'S | SONS [*floret*] NEW YORK [*floret*] 1898

[Note: All the preceding appears within a red single rule box.]

COLLATION: [1]⁶, [2–13]⁸. Leaf measures 7⅜″ x 5″, top edge gilt, other edges untrimmed. Printed on white laid paper watermarked with Riley's monogram.

PAGINATION: End paper, same as book stock; blank, pp. [i–ii]; fly title: The Works Of James | Whitcomb Riley [2 *florets*] | Vol. III, p. [iii]; blank, p. [iv]; frontispiece with printed tissue guard (inserted); title-page, p. [v]; copyright notice with final date 1898 and acknowledgement, p. [vi]; dedication, p. [vii]; blank, p. [viii]; table of contents, pp. vii–x (should be ix–xii); half-title, p. [1]; blank, p. [2]; proem, pp. 3–5; blank, p. [6]; text, pp. 7–187; insignia of De Vinne Press, p. [188]; blank, pp. [189–190]; end paper.

[Note: The conjugate of pp. 177–178 is pasted down under the lining paper.]

ILLUSTRATIONS: Frontispiece: sepia photogravure, by C. M. Relyea, with tissue guard printed in sepia, inserted.

BINDING: Brown satin-finished cloth. The front cover bears a design of 3 ears of corn gilt-stamped in the center, and a gilt single rule

---

*This is the first volume of the *Homestead Edition* to contain first edition material.

Riley suggested, in a letter to Arthur H. Scribner, June 26, 1897, that he would like to get "that good-omen-ish word Home" in the name of the edition, and he suggested three possibilities: Homestead, Old-Home, Home-Folks Edition. In a postscript to a letter addressed to Arthur H. Scribner, October 12, 1897, Riley expressed his appreciation of this edition of his works. The letter appears in *Letters of James Whitcomb Riley*, edited by William Lyon Phelps (1930), p. 220. The postscript was quoted in part in a leaflet issued by Scribner's, 1902, advertising the *Homestead Edition*.

border. The spine is gilt-stamped: [*rule*] | THE WORKS | OF | JAMES | WHITCOMB | RILEY | ·[*ear of corn*] | AFTERWHILES | SCRIBNERS | [*rule*] Back cover has a blind-stamped single rule border.

PUBLICATION DATE: Published January 22, 1898, according to the publishers' records. Deposited for copyright January 24, 1898.

PUBLICATION PRICE: Sold by subscription: 10-volume set (1898), cloth, $15.00; half Levant morocco, $30.00. 14-volume set (1902), cloth, $21.00; half Levant morocco, $42.00; Japan paper edition, $80.00.

NOTES: This also appeared in a limited edition of 204 numbered copies on Japan paper, bound with vellum shelfback and corners, wood veneer sides. Spine has raised bands and a wood veneer paper label printed in blue. The verso of the fly title carries the limitation notice, and the frontispiece has the illustration on tissue, mounted.

CONTENTS: 3 of the poems in this volume are here first collected: Indiana  *Indiana's Gift to the Battleship Indiana* (*ca.* 1896; see p. 176) To Santa Claus  *Arena*, December, 1897 (with title: Santa Claus) Where the Children Used to Play  *Once a Year* (Indianapolis Flower Mission Magazine, 1897); *Indianapolis Journal*, November 14, 1897 (title in both: An Old-Home Song)

# 1898

## *THE HOMESTEAD EDITION, VOL. IV*
## Pipes O' Pan at Zekesbury

THE POEMS AND PROSE | [*2 florets*] SKETCHES OF [*2 florets*] | JAMES WHITCOMB RILEY | PIPES O' PAN [*2 florets; all in red*] | AT ZEKES-BURY [*in red*] | CHARLES SCRIBNER'S | SONS [*floret*] NEW YORK [*floret*] 1898
[Note: All the preceding appears within a red single rule box.]

COLLATION: [1]⁴, [2–14]⁸. Leaf measures 7⅜" x 5", top edge gilt, other edges untrimmed. Printed on white laid paper watermarked with Riley's monogram.

PAGINATION: End paper, same as book stock; fly title: *The Works Of James* | *Whitcomb Riley* [*2 florets*] | *Vol. IV*, p. [i]; blank, p. [ii]; frontis-piece with printed tissue guard (inserted); title-page, p. [iii]; copyright notice with final date 1898 and acknowledgement, p. [iv]; dedication, p. [v]; blank, p. [vi]; table of contents, pp. vii–ix; blank, p. [x]; half-title, p. [1]; proem, p. [2]; text, pp. 3–204; insignia of De Vinne Press, p. [205]; blank, p. [206]; end paper.

ILLUSTRATIONS: Frontispiece: sepia photogravure, by B. West Clinedinst, with tissue guard printed in sepia, inserted.

BINDING: Uniform with the *Homestead Edition*, Vol. III. For de-scription see p. 71.

PUBLICATION DATE: The title was entered for copyright February 5, 1898; copies were deposited in the Copyright Office February 10, 1898. Published February 12, 1898, according to the publishers' records.

NOTES: Also issued in a limited edition of 204 numbered copies on Japan paper. For further description see p. 72.

CONTENTS: Of all the poems and prose in this volume, only one prose sketch is a first appearance in a Riley book:
The Champion Checker-Player of Ameriky *Indianapolis Journal*,
September 5, 1880

1898

## THE HOMESTEAD EDITION, VOL. V

# Rhymes of Childhood

THE POEMS AND PROSE | [*2 florets*] SKETCHES OF [*2 florets*] | JAMES WHITCOMB RILEY | RHYMES OF [*floret; all in red*] | CHILDHOOD [*in red*] | CHARLES SCRIBNER'S | SONS [*floret*] NEW YORK [*floret*] 1898 [Note: All the preceding appears within a red single rule box.]

SIGNATURES: [1]⁴, [2–15]⁸. Leaf measures 7⅜″ x 5″, top edge gilt, other edges untrimmed. Printed on white laid paper watermarked with Riley's monogram.

PAGINATION: End paper, same as book stock; fly title: *The Works Of James* | *Whitcomb Riley* [*2 florets*] | *Vol. V*, p. [i]; blank, p. [ii]; frontispiece with printed tissue guard (inserted); title-page, p. [iii]; copyright notice with final date 1898 and acknowledgement, p. [iv]; dedication, p. [v]; blank, p. [vi]; *Prefatory Note*, p. [vii]; blank, p. [viii]; table of contents, pp. ix–xii; half-title, p. [1]; proem, p. [2]; text, pp. 3–216; insignia of De Vinne Press, p. [217]; blank, pp. [218–220]; end paper.

ILLUSTRATIONS: Frontispiece: sepia photogravure, by Alice Barber Stephens, with tissue guard printed in sepia, inserted.

BINDING: Uniform with the *Homestead Edition*, Vol. III. For description see p. 71.

PUBLICATION DATE: Published March 21, 1898, according to the publishers' records. Deposited in the Copyright Office March 23, 1898.

NOTES: Also issued in a limited edition of 204 numbered copies on Japan paper. For further description see p. 72.

CONTENTS: Of the poems in this volume, 5 here make their first appearance in a Riley collection:
Christmas Afterthought
The Christmas Long Ago   *Interior*, December 13, 1894
Exceeding All
Little Mandy's Christmas-Tree   *Interior*, December 10, 1896
Song—For November   *A November Leaf* (Indianapolis Flower
   Mission Magazine, 1896; see p. 176)

# 1898

## THE HOMESTEAD EDITION, VOL. VI

# The Flying Islands of the Night

THE POEMS AND PROSE | [*2 florets*] SKETCHES OF [*2 florets*] | JAMES WHITCOMB RILEY | THE FLYING ISLANDS [*in red*] | OF THE NIGHT [*3 florets; all in red*] | CHARLES SCRIBNER'S | SONS [*floret*] NEW YORK [*floret*] 1898
[Note: All the preceding appears within a red single rule box.]

COLLATION: [1]⁴, [2–12]⁸, [13]², [14]⁴. Leaf measures 7⅜" x 5", top edge gilt, other edges untrimmed. Printed on white laid paper watermarked with Riley's monogram.

PAGINATION: End paper, same as book stock; fly title: *The Works Of James* | *Whitcomb Riley* [*2 florets*] | *Vol. VI.*, p. [i]; blank, p. [ii]; frontispiece with printed tissue guard (inserted); title-page, p. [iii]; copyright notice with final date 1898 and acknowledgement, p. [iv]; dedication, p. [v]; blank, p. [vi]; table of contents, pp. vii–viii; half-title, p. [1]; quotation: "*A thynge of wytchencreft—an idle dreme,*" p. [2]; proem, p. [3]; *Dramatis Personae*, p. [4]; text, pp. 5–187; insignia of De Vinne Press, p. [188]; end paper.

ILLUSTRATIONS: Frontispiece: sepia photogravure, by Adrien Marcel, with tissue guard printed in sepia, inserted.

BINDING: Uniform with the *Homestead Edition*, Vol. III. For description see p. 71.

PUBLICATION DATE: Copies were deposited in the Copyright Office April 30, 1898; publication date same, according to the publishers' records.

NOTES: Also issued in a limited edition of 204 numbered copies on Japan paper. For further description see p. 72.
In a letter to Scribners, dated April 4, 1898, Riley asked for a half dozen unbound copies of this volume. These are, apparently, the copies specially bound in light blue cloth with paper label on the front cover reading: [*space for recipient's name*] Personal copy of | The Flying Islands of the Night | From the author [*space for author's signature*] Inside the

75

front cover is pasted a printed note which states: "This volume is one of six copies, which are—by especial permission of the publishers to the author—thus detached from The Homestead Edition to be had only in the complete set, comprising ten volumes." The six were given to Madison Cawein, Young E. Allison*, Rupert Hughes, Dr. James Newton Matthews, Eugene F. Ware and F. G. Darlington.*

CONTENTS: The volume contains additions to "The Flying Islands of the Night": p. 15 [The Lovely Husband†]; pp. 59–60; pp. 73–76; "Song—Fold me away in your arms, O night," p. 76. It also contains 24 poems first collected:

After Death   *Indianapolis Journal*, January 23, 1880

Death   *Indianapolis Journal*, November 1, 1879

"Dream" ("Because her eyes were far too deep")   *Indianapolis Journal*, February 16, 1878

[A Dream of Inspiration] ("To loll back, in a misty hammock, swung"—proem to "Spirk and Wunk Rhymes")   *Indianapolis Journal*, June 27, 1880 (title in *Biographical Edition*: A Dream of Inspiration)

Ere I Went Mad   *Indianapolis Journal*, May 18, 1880 (with title: Yrsule)

Eternity   *Saturday Herald* (*Indianapolis*), July 19, 1879

For You   *Indianapolis Journal*, November 7, 1880

Laughter   *Indianapolis Journal*, April 3, 1880

The Light of Love   *Indianapolis Journal*, June 20, 1880 (with title: Song)

Out of the Dark and the Dearth   *Dawn* (Indianapolis High School No. 1, October 26, 1893, with title: After the Dark the Dawn)

An Out-Worn Sappho   *Indianapolis Journal*, November 21, 1880 (with title: Tired)

The Quest   *Indianapolis Journal*, April 12, 1885

The Rain   *Saturday Herald* (*Indianapolis*), July 12, 1879 (title in *Biographical Edition:* The Laughter of the Rain)

The Romaunt of King Mordameer   *Indianapolis Journal*, October 27, 1878 (with title: The Romaunt of King Valdemere)

Song of Parting   *Indianapolis Journal*, May 23, 1880; *Say Farewell & Let Me Go* (sheet music, 1891; see p. 155)

Songs Tuneless   *Indianapolis Journal*, March 7, 1880

---

*The Allison and Darlington copies are in the possession of the respective families; other four copies unlocated.

†This also appears separately, with music, on pp. 116–119.

The Speeding of the King's Spite   *Danbury (Conn.) News*, July 18,
   1874 (with title: An Oriental Idyl)
Three Several Birds*
To the Wine-God Merlus   *Indianapolis Journal*, November 8, 1879
   (with title: To Gambrinus)
A Variation   *Indianapolis Journal*, July 4, 1880
We Are Not Always Glad When We Smile   *Indianapolis Journal*,
   December 14, 1877
The Werewife   *Indianapolis Journal*, January 6, 1880 (with title:
   My Ghoul)
The Witch of Erkmurden   *Saturday Herald (Indianapolis)*, August
   2, 1879
A Wrangdillion   *Anderson Democrat*, July, 1877?†

---

*Part III of "Three Several Birds" made separate appearances later: as "Book-
man's Catch" in *Book Lovers' Verse* compiled by Howard S. Ruddy (1899); as the
dedicatory poem in *Riley Songs of Friendship* (1915); revised by Riley, beginning,
"Your roses are the phrase and word," in the *William Winter Testimonial* (1916).

†Not seen except in *Indianapolis Journal* appearance, July 14, 1877, where it is
ascribed to the *Anderson Democrat* and appears with a prose introduction captioned,
"Strange Experiences of a Poet—How Fool Rhymes Are Born." This introduction was published later in *Riley's First Poems* (1901) and in the *Biographical Edition*, Vol. 1, p. 422.

# The Golden Year

THE GOLDEN YEAR | From the Verse and Prose | OF | JAMES WHITCOMB RILEY | COMPILED BY | CLARA E. LAUGHLIN | [*5-line quotation from Tennyson*] | [*floret*] | LONGMANS, GREEN, AND CO. | 39 PATERNOSTER ROW, LONDON | NEW YORK AND BOMBAY | 1898 | All rights reserved

COLLATION: [A]⁶, B-I⁸, K-M⁸, N². Leaf measures 6⅛″ x 3¾″, top edge gilt, other edges untrimmed. The book is printed on white laid paper watermarked *I D & Co*

PAGINATION: End paper, white laid; blank leaf, pp. [i–ii]; fly title, p. [iii]; list of *Works by James Whitcomb Riley*, p. [iv]; frontispiece with tissue guard printed in red (inserted); title-page, p. [v]; blank, p. [vi]; proem, p. [vii]; blank, p. [viii]; *Compiler's Note*, pp. [ix]–viii (should be ix–x); table of contents, p. [xi]; blank, p. [xii]; text, pp. [1]–176; *L'Envoy*, p. [177]; printer's slug, p. [178]; blank, pp. [179–180]; end paper.

ILLUSTRATIONS: Sepia frontispiece with tissue guard printed in red, inserted.

BINDING: Blue pebbled cloth, vegetable vellum shelfback, vertical gilt rule where cloth and vellum join. Light blue paper label on spine gilt-stamped: THE | GOLDEN | YEAR | [*rule*] | RILEY Double gilt rules are stamped at the top and bottom of the spine, with two single gilt rules at equal intervals between. Front and back covers unlettered. Uniform in binding with *Old-Fashioned Roses* (1888).

PUBLICATION DATE: October 3, 1898, according to the publishers' records. Reviewed in the *Indianapolis Journal*, October 31, 1898.

PUBLICATION PRICE: 5 shillings; $1.75.

NOTES: Longmans, Green & Company's records show that first printing consisted of 2,250 copies, 2,000 of which were sent to America. No copy has been located with Bowen-Merrill Company's imprint, but the book was so issued according to the *Biographical Edition*, Vol. 6, p. 423. According to a review in the *Indianapolis Journal*, October 31,

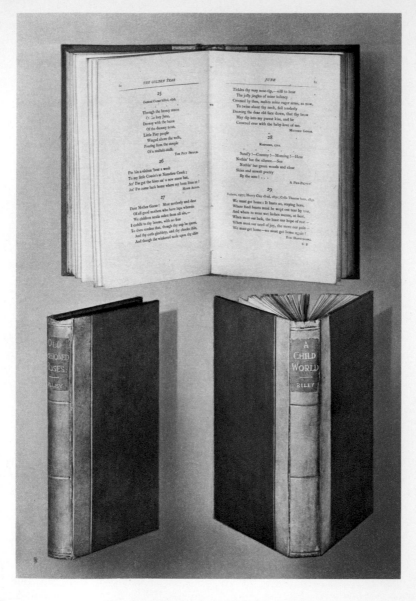

*The three Riley books published in London
by Longmans, Green & Co.*

1898, *The Golden Year* was published in London and "handled in this country by the Bowen-Merrill Company." The earliest located copy with an American imprint is a *Fourth Impression* with Bobbs-Merrill, 1907, imprint.*

CONTENTS: Selections from Riley, for each day of the year, of which only the proem (beginning, "THE YEAR goes on and on and on!—) and "L'Envoy" are first appearances in a Riley book. The latter poem appeared later in the *Biographical Edition* under the title, "Snow in the Air."

---

*In the collection of the Bobbs-Merrill Company.

# 1899

# Riley Love-Lyrics

RILEY | LOVE-LYRICS [*in red*] | JAMES WHITCOMB RILEY | WITH | LIFE PICTURES [*in red*] | BY | WILLIAM B. DYER | INDIANAPOLIS, INDIANA, U. S. A. | THE BOWEN-MERRILL COMPANY

COLLATION: [1–24]⁴. Leaf measures 7¾″ x 5⁵⁄₁₆″, all edges trimmed. Printed on white coated paper.

PAGINATION: End paper, cream-white coated; blank, pp. [i–iv]; fly title, second line in red, p. [v]; list of *Other Books by James Whitcomb Riley*, caption in red and all within red single rule box, p. [vi]; blank, p. [vii]; frontispiece (with tissue guard), p. [viii]; title-page, p. [ix]; copyright notice with final date 1899 and imprint of Braunworth, Munn & Barber*, p. [x]; dedication, p. [xi]; blank, p. [xii]; proem, p. [xiii]; blank, p. [xiv]; table of contents (with the word *Contents* lettered in red), pp. xv–xvi; list of illustrations (with the word *Illustrations* lettered in red), pp. xvii–xx; half-title; p. [xxi]; blank, p. [xxii]; text, pp. 23–190; vignette, p. [191]; blank, p. [192]; end paper.

ILLUSTRATIONS: Frontispiece with tissue guard; this and all other illustrations are integral parts of the book. The list of illustrations is highly inaccurate but the errors are common to all copies up to the 1905 reissue.

BINDING: Sage green, satin-finished cloth. Front cover bears design of a woman's head outlined in black on a gilt-stamped heart, surrounded by white-stamped flowers, below which is gilt-stamped: RILEY | LOVE-LYRICS | [*ornament*]   All within a gilt-stamped single rule border. Spine gilt-stamped: [*double rule*] | RILEY | LOVE- | LYRICS | WITH | PICTURES | BY DYER | [*lighted torch*] | BOWEN-MERRILL | [*double rule*].

PUBLICATION DATE: Deposited in the Copyright Office October 19, 1899. Advertised in the *Chicago Times-Herald*, October 31, 1899 as "to be published at once," but the earliest review located is in the *Indianapolis Press*, December 13, 1899.

---

*Copyright deposit copy No. 2 (only one located) does not have the imprint. It is the only copy so far examined in which the imprint does not appear.

PUBLICATION PRICE: $1.25.

NOTES: The book occurs in two states:

> *State 1:* Table of contents, p. xvi, lists *Passing Of A Heart, The*
> as at p. 71 (should be p. 44)
> Signatures in 4
>
> *State 2:* Table of contents, p. xvi, lists *Passing Of A Heart, The*
> as at p. 44 (not p. 71)
> Signatures in 8

The above change was made before February 13, 1900; a copy with this date inscribed on a preliminary leaf is in State 2

Copies with the Bobbs-Merrill imprint in place of Bowen-Merrill (*ca.* 1902) have a few minor corrections; recopyrighted in 1905, with some changes in illustrations; new edition in limp leather advertised December 19, 1907; recopyrighted 1921, with new format and illustrations by Will Vawter.

CONTENTS: 45 poems, of which only one is first collected:
The Sermon of the Rose   *Atlantic Monthly*, September, 1898; *Indianapolis Journal*, September 11, 1898

The poem, "Why I Loved Her," listed here in table of contents (with tailpiece called for in list of illustrations) does not appear in the book, nor is there any record that Riley ever wrote a poem with this title. Mention of it is dropped in later states.

The dedication consists of a 4-line poem beginning: "To the Elect of Love,—or side-by-side."

"The Touches of Her Hands" had previously appeared under title, "Dear Hands"; "A Very Youthful Affair" had previously appeared as "Home Again." The proem consists of the last two stanzas of "In the South," which had made previous appearances. "Her Waiting Face" had been incorporated, without title, in Act I of *The Flying Islands of the Night* (1892). "Blooms of May" is part of a longer poem, "The Song of Yesterday," which had made previous appearances. "Her Face and Brow" had been published in the *Indianapolis Journal*, August 18, 1883, with title, "A Mere Outline," then incorporated in the book, *The Flying Islands of the Night* (1892), Act II.

# 1900

# Home-Folks

HOME-FOLKS | JAMES WHITCOMB RILEY | [*floret*] | INDIANAPOLIS | THE BOWEN-MERRILL COMPANY | PUBLISHERS

COLLATION: [*]⁸, [1–2]⁸, 3–11⁸. The lining papers are integral parts of the first and last signatures, respectively. The leaf measures 7″ x 4¾″, all edges trimmed, top edge gilt. Printed on white laid paper.

PAGINATION: Lining paper, pp. [i–ii]; blank, pp. [iii–iv]; fly title, p. [v]; blank, pp. [vi–vii]; list of *Books by James Whitcomb Riley*, p. [viii]; frontispiece with guard (inserted); title-page, p. [ix]; copyright notice with date 1900 and imprint of Braunworth, Munn & Barber, p. [x]; dedication to Myron W. Reed and quotation from Joel Chandler Harris, p. [xi]; blank, p. [xii]; table of contents, pp. [xiii–xv]; blank, p. [xvi]; half-title, p. [xvii]; blank, p. [xviii]; proem, p. [xix]; blank, p. [xx]; text, pp. 1–166; blank, pp. [167–172] (pp. [171–172] used as lining paper).

ILLUSTRATIONS: Frontispiece with guard, inserted.

BINDING: Smooth red cloth*. Front cover stamped in gilt within single rule border: HOME-FOLKS | BY JAMES WHITCOMB RILEY  Spine extra gilt-stamped with decorative design of vine-like scrolls, single rule at top, lettered within single rules: HOME-FOLKS | [*ornament*] | RILEY and, at foot of spine, between single rules: BOWEN MERRILL  Back cover blank. Binding uniform with *A Child-World* (1897).

PUBLICATION DATE: Title entered for copyright September 15, 1900. Reviewed in the *Indianapolis News*, October 6, 1900. Deposited in the Copyright Office November 14, 1900.

PUBLICATION PRICE: $1.00.

NOTES: The book has been noted in three states:
> *State 1:* Page 59, part of the heading repeated: YOUR HEIGHT IS OURS | TO RICHARD HENRY STODDARD, AT THE STOD-DARD | BANQUET BY THE AUTHORS' CLUB, | NEW YORK, MARCH 25, 1897 | AT THE STODDARD BANQUET BY THE AUTHORS' | CLUB, NEW YORK, MARCH 25, 1897

---

*Copies in green cloth with fore edge and bottom edge untrimmed are part of the *Greenfield Edition*, (10 volumes of Riley's works), published December, 1900.

*State 2:* Page 59 on a stub, with heading corrected: YOUR HEIGHT IS OURS | TO RICHARD HENRY STODDARD, AT THE STODDARD | BANQUET BY THE AUTHORS' CLUB, NEW YORK, MARCH 25, 1897

*State 3:* Page 59 an integral part of the signature but reading as in State 2

Both of the copyright deposit copies in Washington are in State 2.

CONTENTS: Of the 68 poems herein, 63 are first appearances in a Riley book:

Proem ("You Home-Folks:—Aid your grateful guest")

As Created   *Indianapolis Journal*, January 14, 1881 (with title: The Human Heart)

At Crown Hill*

At His Wintry Tent

At Sea   *Indianapolis Journal*, August 29, 1880

A Ballad— | With a Serious Conclusion   *Saturday Mirror (Indianapolis)*, May 11, 1872

The Ballade of the Coming Rain

The Bed   *Century Magazine*, October, 1900

Cassander   *Ladies' Home Journal*, June, 1896

Christmas along the Wires   *Chicago Tribune*, supplement, December 19, 1897 (with title: Christmas Times along the Wires)

The Edge of the Wind

Emerson   *Indianapolis Journal*, April 29, 1882

The Enduring   *Scribner's Magazine*, July, 1899

Equity—?

Eugene Field   *The Writings in Prose and Verse of Eugene Field*, Vol. 4 (1898)

A Feel in the Chris'mas-Air   *Ideal Series No. 10* (1892); *Cosmopolitan*, December, 1894; *Freeman (Indianapolis)*, December 22, 1894

The Green Grass of Old Ireland   *Century Magazine*, August, 1895 (with title: The Green Grass av Owld Ireland)

Henry W. Grady   *New York Tribune*, December 24, 1889; *Joel Chandler Harris' Life of Henry W. Grady* (1890)

The Hired Man's Faith in Children

His Love of Home

"Home Ag'in"†   *Century Magazine*, August, 1894

---

*The first stanza only appeared later in the *Indianapolis Journal*, May 26, 1901, with title, "At Home."

†The autograph manuscript of "Elviry," offered in auction catalogue No. 325 of the Parke-Bernet Galleries, Inc., is the poem, " 'Home Ag'in.' "

Home-Folks   *Indianapolis Journal*, October 28, 1900

The Home-Voyage*   *Indianapolis Journal*, February 6, 1900;
*Interior*, March 1, 1900

Hymn Exultant   *Indianapolis Journal*, April 18, 1897

An Idiot   *Indianapolis Journal*, January 9, 1880

In the Evening   *Lippincott's Monthly Magazine*, January, 1890;
*Indianapolis Journal*, January 12, 1890

Let Something Good Be Said   *Sun* (*New York*), June 20, 1880
(with title: Something Good); *Ideal Series: Selected Readings and
Recitations, No. 13* (1894)

The Loving Cup

Mister Hop-Toad   *St. Nicholas*, November, 1897

Moonshiner's Serenade

The Mother Sainted   *Kokomo Tribune*, March 19, 1881 (with title:
Kate Kennedy Philips)

Mr. Foley's Christmas   *Ideal Series: Select Readings and Recitations,
No. 12* (1895); *Interior*, December 9, 1897

My Dancin'-Days Is Over   *Century Magazine*, November, 1895
(with title: His Dancin' Days)

The Name of Old Glory†   *Atlantic Monthly*, December, 1898;
*Indianapolis News*, December 10, 1898

The Naturalist   *Ohio State Journal*, April 23, 1899 (with title: To
Oliver Davie—The Naturalist); *The Hesperian Tree, An Annual of
the Ohio Valley* (1900) (with title: To a Naturalist)

The Noblest Service   *Indianapolis Journal*, December 31, 1899
(with title: Dr. Wickliffe Smith)

The Old Guitar   *Indianapolis Sentinel*, January 9, 1876

"O Life! O Beyond!"   *Arena*, June, 1897

On a Youthful Portrait of Stevenson   *Scribner's Magazine*, Decem-
ber, 1897 (with title: On a Youthful Portrait of Robert Louis
Stevenson); *Chicago Tribune*, December 19, 1897 (with title: New
Portrait of Stevenson)

One with a Song   *Indianapolis Journal*, June 25, 1898 (with title:
Frank L. Stanton)

The Onward Trail   *Indianapolis Journal*, January 31, 1899

---

*The poem was published in leaflet form, undated, entitled "The Home
Voyage: A Tribute to Major General H. W. Lawton, U. S. A.," with imprint,
Huntington, Pa. Whether this was printed before or after the book has not been
determined.

†The speech by Riley introducing this poem at ceremonies honoring Rear-
Admiral Henry Clay Taylor, is printed in *Indianapolis Journal*, February 24, 1903,
and in *Biographical Edition*, Vol. 5, p. 446.

Oscar C. McCulloch   *Indianapolis Journal*, December 12, 1891; *In Memoriam: Oscar C. McCulloch, Sepulture, December 12, 1891* (leaflet, see p. 173)

Our Boyhood Haunts

Our Queer Old World   *McClure's Magazine*, August, 1897

A Peace-Hymn of the Republic*   *Indianapolis Journal*, September 13, 1895; *A Peace Hymn* (broadside), September, 1895 (see p. 157)

Red Riding Hood   *Saturday Herald* (*Indianapolis*), June 26, 1875

The Rhymes of Ironquill   *Fort Scott* (*Kansas*) *Daily Tribune*, April 25, 1893

Say Something to Me   *Indianapolis Journal*, August 5, 1877

A Short'nin' Bread Song—Pieced Out

The Silent Singer   *Indianapolis Journal*, May 1, 1895

The Smitten Purist

A Song of the Road†   *Lippincott's Monthly Magazine*, July, 1899; sheet music (1900; see p. 158)

"Them Old Cheery Words"   *Century Magazine*, December, 1896

To Robert Louis Stevenson   *World* (*New York*), December 11, 1887 (with title: Robert Louis Stevenson)

To the Judge   *Saturday Herald* (*Indianapolis*), May 30, 1885

To "Uncle Remus"

The Traveling Man   *Saturday Review* (*Indianapolis*), February 12, 1881

Uncle Sidney's Logic

The Unheard§   *Ideal Series: Selected Readings and Recitations*, No. 8 (1891)

What the Wind Said   *Kokomo Dispatch*, October 4, 1877

Whittier—at Newburyport   *Indianapolis News*, September 7, 1892

A Wholly Unscholastic Opinion

Your Height Is Ours‖   *Critic*, April 3, 1897 (without title)

NOTE: "On a Fly-Leaf" had previously appeared with the title, "Written in John Boyle O'Reilly's 'In Bohemia.'"

---

*See *Biographical Edition*, Vol. 4, p. 545, for introduction used by Riley when reciting the poem.

†Riley wrote to Miss Constance Maud, of London, on October 12, 1899, and gave her permission to set to music his poem, "A Song of the Road." If her composition was published we have not been able to see or find a record of it.

§"The Unheard" also appeared in *The Impromptu*, annual magazine of the Indianapolis Flower Mission, 1894, under title, "The Master-Song."

‖The publication of the poem in *The Book Buyer*, April, 1897, was probably a few days later than *The Critic*.

# 1902

# The Book of Joyous Children

THE BOOK | OF JOYOUS CHILDREN | JAMES | WHITCOMB | RILEY | Illustrated by | J. W. VAWTER | NEW YORK, | CHARLES SCRIBNER'S SONS | 1902
[Note: All the preceding on background of woodland scene with children and a dog; all enclosed by a single rule box.]

COLLATION: [1]⁶, [2–8]⁸, [9]⁶. Leaf measures 7½" x 5", top edge gilt, other edges untrimmed. Printed on white wove paper.

PAGINATION: End paper, same as book stock; fly title, p. [i]; blank, p. [ii]; frontispiece with guard* (inserted); title-page, p. [iii]; copyright notice with statement: *Published October, 1902* and imprint of De Vinne Press, p. [iv]; dedication to Joel Chandler Harris, p. [v]; proem, p. [vi]; table of contents, pp. ix–xi (should be vii–ix); blank, p. [x]; list of full-page illustrations, pp. xiii–xiv (should be xi–xii); half-title, p. [1]; blank, p. [2]; text, pp. 3–175; tailpiece, p. 176; blank, pp. [177–178]; end paper.

ILLUSTRATIONS: Frontispiece, with guard*, and 27 other full-page halftones on coated paper inserted but figured in the pagination. Numerous text illustrations throughout.

BINDING: Green, blue or red cloth. Front cover stamped in gilt: THE BOOK | OF JOYOUS CHILDREN | JAMES | WHITCOMB | RILEY  The lettering appears above and at right of a gilt-stamped woodland scene with children playing under a tree. Spine gilt-stamped: [*rule*] | [*ornament: clover blossom*] | [*rule*] | THE BOOK | [*ornament*] OF [*ornament*] | JOYOUS | CHILDREN | [*ornament*] | RILEY | [*rule*] | [*child holding doll, with birds above and clover blossoms below*] | [*fillet*] | SCRIBNERS | [*fillet*]  Back cover stamped in gilt in the lower left corner with a boy and girl bowing.

PUBLICATION DATE: Title entered for copyright October 8, 1902; copies deposited in the Copyright Office October 9, 1902; advertised in Indianapolis newspapers October 11, 1902, as "now ready."

PUBLICATION PRICE: $1.20.

---

*Not present in all copies.

NOTES: Reviews of the book in newspapers throughout the country, October, 1902, if they mention the binding at all, describe it as green and gold; a copyright deposit copy is also in the green binding. Scribners, on the other hand, in an undated but surely contemporary advertising leaflet describe it as bound in blue. The red binding was probably issued at the same time as the others; no textual differences have been noted between copies in the various colors.

The *Homestead Edition*, Vol. 12, 1902, is a reissue of the book with 9 poems added (see p. 95).

The *Author's Edition* (so stated on title-page), 1903, bound in green limp leather with *Author's Edition* stamped on front cover has contents same as Vol. 12 of the *Homestead Edition*. It was announced in the *Indianapolis Journal*, September 13, 1903, as "just issued." This announcement mentions inclusion of several poems not found in the original edition of the book and states further that "the new volume is not on sale, but the additional poems will, of course, be included in the next volume added to the uniform edition of the poet's works." The statement indicates that the *Author's Edition* preceded the *Homestead Edition*, but the records prove otherwise.

The Bobbs-Merrill Company, some time later, reissued the book from the plates of the *Homestead Edition*, undated but for the 1902 copyright date.

CONTENTS: All of the poems in this volume are first appearances in a Riley book:

[Proem] beginning "You who to the rounded prime" (title in *Biographical Edition:* To Joel Chandler Harris)

The Book of Joyous Children

An Impromptu Fairy-Tale

Dream-March   *St. Nicholas*, December, 1895 (with title: Dream March of the Children)

Elmer Brown

No Boy Knows

When We First Played "Show"

A Diverted Tragedy   *Century Magazine*, January, 1902

The Rambo-Tree

Find the Favorite

The Boy Patriot

Extremes

Intellectual Limitations

A Masque of the Seasons

Thomas the Pretender   *Century Magazine*, January, 1902

Little Dick and the Clock
Fool-Youngens    *Century Magazine*, January, 1902
The Katydids
Billy and His Drum    *Century Magazine*, January, 1902
The Noble Old Elm
The Penalty of Genius    *Century Magazine*, February, 1900
Evensong
The Twins | "Igo and Ago"
The Little Lady
"Company Manners"
In Fervent Praise of Picnics    *Century Magazine*, February, 1900
The Good, Old-Fashioned People
The Best Times
"Hik-Tee-Dik!"
A Christmas Memory    *Life*, Christmas number, 1895; *Notable Single Poems* (1895); *Taken from Life* (1897)
"Old Bob White"
A Session with Uncle Sidney
    I One of His Animal Stories
    II Uncle Brightens Up—(includes verses without title, printed elsewhere as: A Pet of Uncle Sidney's; In the Kindergarten of Noble Song. "A Pet of Uncle Sidney's" had appeared in *Century Magazine*, February, 1900, and in *Indianapolis Press*, February 3, 1900; "In the Kindergarten of Noble Song" had appeared in *Century Magazine*, January, 1902)
    III Sings a "Winky-Tooden" Song—
    IV And Makes Nursery Rhymes
      1 The Diners in the Kitchen
      2 The Imperious Angler
      3 The Gathering of the Clans
      4 "It"
      5 The Daring Prince
A Dubious "Old Kriss"    *Ladies' Home Journal*, December, 1896
A Song of Singing
The Jaybird
A Bear Family
Some Songs after Master Singers
    I Song ("With a hey! and a hi! and a hey-ho rhyme")
    II To the Child Julia
    III The Dolly's Mother
    IV Wind of the Sea

V Subtlety

VI Born to the Purple

Old Man Whiskery-Whee-Kum-Wheeze   *Century Magazine*, February, 1900; *Indianapolis Press*, February 3, 1900

Little-Girl-Two-Little-Girls   *Century Magazine*, February, 1900; *Indianapolis Press*, February 3, 1900, (title in both: The Little Girl That Was Two Little Girls)

A Gustatory Achievement   *Century Magazine*, January, 1902 (with title: A Gustatory Memory)

Climatic Sorcery

A Parent Reprimanded   *Century Magazine*, February, 1900; *Indianapolis Press*, February 3, 1900

The Treasure of the Wise Man

For Riley's enthusiastic announcement of plans for the book, in a letter to Joel Chandler Harris, May 5, 1902, see *Letters of James Whitcomb Riley*, edited by William Lyon Phelps (1930), p. 258.

# 1902

# An Old Sweetheart of Mine

An Old | Sweetheart of Mine | James Whitcomb Riley | Draw-ings by | Howard Chandler Christy | Decorations by | Virginia Keep | The Bowen-Merrill Company | Publishers   Indianapolis
[Note: All but the imprint appears within a rose-red floral wreath.]

COLLATION: [1–6]⁸. Leaf measures 8⅜" x 6¼", all edges trimmed. Printed on white coated paper.

PAGINATION: End paper, floral design printed in rose-red on white, lettered in black with title, author's name, *With Studies From Life*, illus-trator's name; blank, p. [i]; vignettes, pp. [ii–iv]; fly title, p. [v]; vi-gnettes, pp. [vi–vii]; frontispiece, p. [viii]; title-page, p. [ix]; copyright notice with final date 1902 and imprint of Braunworth & Co., p. [x]; half-title, p. [xi]; blank, p. [xii]; dedication to George C. Hitt, p. [xiii]; blank, p. [xiv]; list of illustrations, pp. [xv–xvii]; blank, p. [xviii]; proem, p. [xix]; blank, p. [xx]; text, pp. [21–90]; illustration, p. [91]; blank, p. [92]; vignettes, pp. [93–95]; blank, p. [96]; end paper.

ILLUSTRATIONS: The frontispiece and other illustrations in black and white and rose-red are integral parts of the book. The vignettes are in rose-red and each page of letterpress has floral decorations in rose-red. The illustrations are by Howard Chandler Christy, the decora-tions, including the end papers, by Virginia Keep.

BINDING: Dark red, vertically ribbed cloth. Front cover* gilt-stamped: AN OLD SWEETHEART | OF MINE | [*oval colored halftone inlaid within a white-stamped border which is itself within a white and orange heart-shaped garland*] | JAMES | WHITCOMB | RILEY | ILLUSTRATED BY | HOWARD CHANDLER CHRISTY   The spine is gilt-stamped: AN OLD | SWEET- | HEART | OF | MINE | [*floral ornament, white and orange*] | JAMES | WHIT-COMB | RILEY | [*floral ornament, white and orange*] | BOWEN | MERRILL Back cover blank.

Also issued in light green cloth with floral decorations on front covet and spine stamped in pale green and orange. Thus far no copy in the green binding has been seen with text in State 1.

---

*Designed by G. Alden Pierson; see *Indianapolis Journal*, Nov. 27, 1902.

PUBLICATION DATE: Deposited for copyright November 28, 1902. Advertised by the publishers in the *Indianapolis Journal*, December 4, 1902.

PUBLICATION PRICE: $2.50.

NOTES: The book occurs in two states, the most noticeable differences as follows:

*State 1:* Signatures in 8

End papers lettered in black

Eleventh stanza (beginning: 'Tis a fragrant retrospection—) line 1, next to last word not in italics (later *fragrant* in italics)

Eighteenth stanza (beginning: When all the air, to toss and quaff,) line 3: ...shout... (later: ...song...)

Twentieth stanza (beginning: And from "Recess" romp in again) line 3, last word *reader* (later "*lesson*")

Twenty-fifth stanza (beginning: Again I make her presents,) line 4, no parentheses (later added)

Twenty-seventh stanza: (beginning: I give my *treasures* to her—all,—) line 4, no italics (later *mine* and *hers* appear in italics)

Thirty-second stanza (beginning: Where the vines were ever fruited,) line 1, comma at end (later omitted); line 4, period at end (later 4 dots)

Thirty-fourth stanza (beginning: And we should be so happy) line 4, exclamation point at end (later a period)

Last stanza, line 3, no italics (later *living* in italics)

*State 2:* Signatures in 4

End papers lettered in rose-red

Eleventh stanza, line 1, *fragrant* (earlier not in italics)

Eighteenth stanza, line 3: ...song... (earlier: ...shout...)

Twentieth stanza, line 3, last word: "lesson" (earlier: reader)

Twenty-fifth stanza, line 4 in parentheses (earlier no parentheses)

Twenty-seventh stanza, line 4, *mine* and *hers* (earlier these words not in italics)

Thirty-second stanza, line 1, no punctuation at end (earlier a comma); line 4, 4 dots at end (earlier a period)

Thirty-fourth stanza, line 4, period at end (earlier an exclamation point)

Last stanza, line 3, *living* (earlier not in italics)

In January, 1903, the Bowen-Merrill Company became the Bobbs-Merrill Company. *An Old Sweetheart of Mine* continued to be issued with copyright in the name of the Bowen-Merrill Company but with the Bobbs-Merrill imprint on the title-page and binding. One copy has been noted with Bobbs-Merrill on the title-page but with Bowen-Merrill on the spine. The Bobbs-Merrill edition is slightly shorter; the decorations on the front cover and spine of the dark red binding are pink and orange instead of white and orange.

Of the quarto edition of 1903, in tan boards, boxed, 400 copies were issued with an inserted leaf bearing the following statement: "Each of the first four hundred copies of this edition is autographed by the author and numbered, and this book is No.    [signed] James Whitcomb Riley."

Copies in blue-green cloth binding, similar in format and decoration to the first edition, have been noted with a printed slip inserted in the front which states: "This special copy of *An Old Sweetheart of Mine* is presented to [*space for recipient's name*] with the compliments of the author The Bobbs-Merrill Company and Braunworth & Co. Christmas, 1903." The back cover is gilt-stamped: CHRISTMAS GREETINGS | ... OF ... | THE AUTHOR | THE BOBBS-MERRILL COMPANY | BRAUNWORTH & CO.

Later issues include the following:

Green cloth with large rectangular colored inlay by Christy on front cover; spine lettered in white; plain end papers.

Plain green cloth lettered in dark green.

Green cloth with oval colored halftone inlaid on front cover but differing from the earlier one, the garland that encloses it is blind-stamped, the lettering is in white with name of illustrator omitted from front cover; plain end papers; many of the preliminary pages are omitted and the text is printed on the verso of the illustrations.

In 1916 the book appeared in altogether different format and without the Christy illustrations, with a portrait frontispiece; bound in pale blue cloth, and red leather.

CONTENTS: An extended version of the single poem, "An Old Sweetheart of Mine," which had first appeared in the *Indianapolis Journal*, March 12, 1877, and had been collected in numerous Riley books before 1902. Before 1902 the poem had fewer stanzas; here it has a proem, six new 4-line stanzas at the beginning, and four new 4-line stanzas at the end. In his public readings Riley had been using this longer version which is here first published.

Printings subsequent to 1902 contain no added material.

# 1902

*THE HOMESTEAD EDITION, VOL. XI*

# Rubáiyát of Doc Sifers
# and Home-Folks

THE POEMS AND PROSE | [*2 florets*] SKETCHES OF [*2 florets*] | JAMES WHITCOMB RILEY | RUBÁIYÁT OF DOC [*in red*] | SIFERS [*2 florets*] AND [*all in red*] | HOME-FOLKS [*3 florets; all in red*] | CHARLES SCRIBNER'S | SONS [*floret*] NEW YORK [*floret*] 1902
[Note: All the preceding appears within a red single rule box.]

SIGNATURES: [1]⁴, [2–16]⁸. Leaf measures 7⅜" x 5", top edge gilt, other edges untrimmed. Printed on white laid paper watermarked with Riley's monogram.

PAGINATION: End paper, same as book stock; fly title: *The Works Of James* | *Whitcomb Riley* [*2 florets*] | *Vol. XI*, p. [i]; blank, p. [ii]; frontispiece with printed tissue guard (inserted); title-page, p. [iii]; copyright notice with date 1902 and acknowledgements, p. [iv]; table of contents, pp. v–viii; half-title, p. [1]; dedication, p. [2]; proem, p. [3]; blank, p. [4]; text, pp. 5–237; insignia of De Vinne Press, p. [238]; blank, pp. [239–240]; end paper.

ILLUSTRATIONS: Frontispiece: sepia photogravure [by C. M. Relyea], with tissue guard printed in sepia, inserted.

BINDING: Uniform with the *Homestead Edition*, Vol. III. For description see p. 71.

PUBLICATION DATE: Copies deposited in the Copyright Office, December 4, 1902.

NOTES: Also issued in a limited edition of 204 numbered copies on Japan paper. For further description see p. 72.

CONTENTS: Of the poems herein the following are first appearances in a Riley book:

An Old Friend  *Saturday Herald* (*Indianapolis*), July 19, 1879

The Paths of Peace  *Indianapolis News*, February 15, 1901; *Independent* (*New York*), February 21, 1901 (title in both: Maurice Thompson)

The Tribute of His Home  *Cincinnati Enquirer*, March 15, 1901 (with title: Harrison's Home Tribute)

Old Hec's Idolatry (the first 44 lines are new; the rest of the poem had previous book publication as "An Idyl of the King")

Note: The poem entitled "Sing" which appears on p. 158 is stanza 2 of "A Song of Singing" which had made previous appearances.

*THE HOMESTEAD EDITION, VOL. XII*

# The Book of Joyous Children

THE POEMS AND PROSE | [*2 florets*] SKETCHES OF [*2 florets*] | JAMES WHITCOMB RILEY | THE BOOK OF [*2 florets; all in red*] | JOYOUS CHILDREN [*in red*] | CHARLES SCRIBNER'S | SONS [*floret*] NEW YORK [*floret*] 1902

[Note: All the preceding appears within a red single rule box.]

COLLATION: [1]⁴, [2–11]⁸. Leaf measures 7⅜″ x 5″, top edge gilt, other edges untrimmed. Printed on white laid paper watermarked with Riley's monogram.

PAGINATION: End paper, same as book stock; fly title: *The Works Of James* | *Whitcomb Riley* [*2 florets*] | *Vol. XII*, p. [i]; blank, p. [ii]; frontispiece with printed tissue guard (inserted); title-page, p. [iii]; copyright notice with date 1902, p. [iv]; dedication, p. [v]; proem, p. [vi]; table of contents, pp. vii–x; half-title, p. [1]; blank, p. [2]; text, pp. 3–154; insignia of De Vinne Press, p. [155]; blank, pp. [156–158]; end paper.

ILLUSTRATIONS: Frontispiece: violet-black photogravure [by Will Vawter], with tissue guard printed in sepia, inserted.

BINDING: Uniform with the *Homestead Edition*, Vol. III. For description see p. 71.

PUBLICATION DATE: Copies deposited in the Copyright Office December 4, 1902.

NOTES: Also issued in a limited edition of 204 numbered copies on Japan paper. For further description see p. 72.

CONTENTS: 9 of the poems herein make their first appearance in a Riley book:

Fire at Night
"Go Read Your Book!"
The Lisper
Old Granny Dusk
A Session with Uncle Sidney
 (part IV, with title, "And

Another of Our Betsy," here
 makes first appearance)
Some Christmas Youngsters
Twilight Stories
When Uncle Doc Was Young
The Young Old Man

# 1903

# His Pa's Romance

His Pa's Romance | James Whitcomb Riley | With Illustrations by | Will Vawter and a Portrait by | John Cecil Clay | Indianapolis | The Bobbs-Merrill Company | Publishers

COLLATION: [1–12]⁸. Leaf measures 7⅟₁₆″ x 4¾″, all edges trimmed, top edge gilt. Printed on white laid paper.

PAGINATION: Lining paper, pp. [i–ii]; blank, pp. [iii–vii]; list of *Books by James Whitcomb Riley*, p. [viii]; frontispiece with tissue guard (inserted); title-page, p. [ix]; copyright notice with date 1903 and imprint of Braunworth & Co., p. [x]; half-title, p. [xi]; blank, p. [xii]; dedication to Edgar Wilson Nye (with last 6 lines of poem, "Edgar Wilson Nye"*), p. [xiii]; blank, p. [xiv]; table of contents, pp. [xv–xvi]; divisional half-title, p. [xvii]; blank, p. [xviii]; text, pp. 1–168; blank, pp. [169–174] (pp. 173–174 used as lining paper).

ILLUSTRATIONS: Frontispiece: a tinted portrait of Riley by John Cecil Clay, with tissue guard, inserted. Also 3 full-page plates, inserted opposite p. 6, p. 52 and p. 120. Numerous text illustrations.

BINDING: Red cloth†. Front cover stamped in gilt within single rule border§: HIS PA'S ROMANCE | BY JAMES WHITCOMB RILEY Spine extra gilt-stamped with decorative design of vine-like scrolls, single rule at top, lettered within single rules: HIS PA'S | ROMANCE | [*ornament*] | RILEY and, at foot of spine, between single rules: BOBBS-MERRILL Back cover blank. Uniform with *A Child-World* (1897) and *Home-Folks* (1900).

PUBLICATION DATE: Copies were deposited for copyright November 23, 1903. A review in the *Indianapolis News* of November 26, 1903, states that the book is "issued today." Both the Bobbs-Merrill Company and the author filed applications for copyright, the former on November 21, 1903, the latter December 7, 1903, but only Riley's application was completed.

PUBLICATION PRICE: $1.00.

---

*The entire poem appears in the book on p. 132.
†Noted in both smooth and comparatively rough-finished cloths.
§One copy examined has border blind-stamped.

NOTES: Of the errors in the book, lamented by the author\*, the only glaring one is on p. 105, line 6: *Of the froth of our streets as we gallop away.* Correction was not made (*steeds* for *streets*) until the book appeared in the *Greenfield Edition* in 1905. The latter contains in the back "a complete index to the works of James Whitcomb Riley."

Copies of the first edition, inscribed by the author with a stanza from "Art and Poetry: Some of Wess's Views," were given by the author in January, 1904, to each of the newspaper artists represented in an exhibit in the Claypool Hotel (Indianapolis), and to the promoter of the exhibit, Malcolm Gunn. Inserted in each book was a typewritten copy of the entire poem. No copy has been located, but the story is told in the *Indianapolis News*, January 27, 1904†; two stanzas of the poem appear in the *Biographical Edition*, Vol. 5 (1913).

CONTENTS: 12 of the poems herein are first appearances in a Riley book:

Almost Beyond Endurance   *Ladies' Home Journal*, March, 1903
Billy Miller's Circus-Show   *Interior*, Chicago, August 10, 1899
Edgar Wilson Nye ("The saddest silence falls when Laughter lays")   *Indianapolis Journal*, February 23, 1896
His Pa's Romance   *Ladies' Home Journal*, January, 1903
His Room   *Indianapolis Journal*, January 12, 1879 (with title: My Room)
Lockerbie Fair   *A Souvenir of Lockerbie Fair* (June, 1903); *Indianapolis Journal*, June 25, 1903 (2 stanzas only, without title); *Indianapolis News*, June 27, 1903 (complete.)
Song—The Old Man of the Sea   *Collier's*, September 26, 1903 (title in table of contents and in *Biographical Edition:* The Old Man of the Sea)
Prose or Verse?   *The Bow-Legged Ghost and Other Stories*, by Leon Mead (1899) (Proem)
A Simple Recipe   *Collier's*, February 28, 1903
Songs of a Life-Time   *Songs of a Life-Time*, by Sarah T. Bolton (1892)
Toil   *Indianapolis Journal*, December 15, 1878
The Toy-Balloon   *Ladies' Home Journal*, March, 1903

The poem, "Our Betsy," had made previous appearance in the *Homestead Edition*, Vol. 12 (1902), as part of "A Session with Uncle Sidney," captioned "And Another of Our Betsy."

---

\*See his letter to Wilbur D. Nesbit, January 8, 1904, in *Letters of James Whitcomb Riley*, edited by William Lyon Phelps (1930), p. 285.
†The poem, "Art and Poetry: Some of Wess's Views," is printed here in its entirety.

# 1904

# Out to Old Aunt Mary's

Out to | Old Aunt Mary's | By | James Whitcomb Riley | [*floret*] | Drawings by | Howard Chandler Christy | Decorations by | Margaret Armstrong | [*floret*] | The Bobbs-Merrill Company | Indianapolis
[Note: The foregoing appears on a field of pale buff enclosed by a buff decorative border of grape-vine design.]

COLLATION: [1–12]⁴. Leaf measures 8¾″ x 6⁵⁄₁₆″, all edges trimmed. Printed on ivory-finished plate paper.

PAGINATION: Pictorial end paper, green printed on cream-colored wove paper, bearing title, author's name, *With Studies From Nature*, illustrator's name; blank, pp. [i–ii]; fly title, p. [iii]; blank, pp. [iv–v]; frontispiece, p. [vi]; title-page, p. [vii]; copyright notice with final date 1904, and imprint of Braunworth & Co., p. [viii]; dedication to Robert J. Burdette, p. [ix]; blank, p. [x]; proem, p. [xi]; blank, p. [xii]; half-title, p. [xiii]; blank, p. [xiv]; illustration, with quotation, p. [xv]; text, pp. [16–92]; illustration, p. [93]; blank, pp. [94–96]; end paper.

ILLUSTRATIONS: The frontispiece, a vignette in dark sepia, is an integral part of the book. The fly title, dedication, proem and half-title are printed within decorative buff borders. Each page of text appears on a buff field within buff floral border; each small illustration with quotation is similarly decorated. In addition there are 20 full-page illustrations in dark sepia and buff; all illustrations are integral parts of the book. The illustrations are by Howard Chandler Christy, the decorations, including end papers, by Margaret Armstrong.

BINDING: Sage green, levant-grained cloth. Front cover stamped in gilt: OUT TO | OLD AUNT MARY'S | [*oval halftone in color inlaid within a white-stamped border which is itself within a heart-shaped, white-stamped garland*] | JAMES | WHITCOMB | RILEY | ILLUSTRATED BY HOWARD CHANDLER CHRISTY The spine is lettered in gilt: OUT | TO | OLD | AUNT | MARY'S | [*floral ornament, white-stamped*] | JAMES | WHITCOMB | RILEY | [*floral ornament, white-stamped*] | BOBBS | MERRILL Back cover blank.

PUBLICATION DATE: Deposited in the Copyright Office December 2, 1904. Advertised in the *Indianapolis News* December 5, 1904.

PUBLICATION PRICE: $2.00.

NOTES: The text was printed in different sizes of type, a defect that the publishers corrected. This resulted in two states of the book, the most noticeable differences being:

> *State* 1: Proem: the over-all depth of text is 1⅜" (later a scant 1½")
> Second stanza (beginning: *"Me and you"—And the morning fair,*), line 3: . . . *cherry* . . . (later . . . *cherrv* . . .)
> Seventh stanza (beginning: *And the woodland echoes with yells of mirth*), line 2 ends with two dots (later with four dots)
>
> *State* 2: Proem: the over-all depth of text is a scant 1½" (earlier 1⅜")
> Second stanza, line 3, . . . *cherrv* . . . (earlier . . . *cherry* . . .)
> Seventh stanza, line 2 ends with 4 dots (earlier with 2 dots)

Issued in a decorated box. Later bindings include leather, and cloth with large colored rectangular illustration inlaid on front cover. The sheets of the latter measure 9½" x 7"; still later copies measure 8⅝" x 6⅛".

A copy of the poem, sent in sheet form for copyright purposes, received in Washington January 29, 1903, has been preserved in the Library of Congress.

A facsimile of the manuscript of the poem appeared in a pamphlet, published December, 1912. It can be distinguished from the facsimile edition of October 7, 1913, by the gilt rectangular border on all but last page; the later printing (presented to the school children of Indianapolis by Mr. Riley in appreciation of their poetry shower and exercises on his birthday) has green borders in place of gilt, and other differences.*

CONTENTS: The single poem, "Out to Old Aunt Mary's." This was first collected in *Afterwhiles* (1888) under the title, "Old Aunt Mary's," and consisted of 6 stanzas only. In this separate publication it is extended to 20 stanzas. Here, too, it appears with a proem, previously unpublished, beginning: "You who have journeyed the wide world through—"

---

*The 1913 facsimile contains a 4-line, untitled greeting which was later collected in the *Biographical Edition*, Vol. 5, under the title, "To the Children."

# 1904

# A Defective Santa Claus

A Defective Santa Claus [*in red*] | JAMES WHITCOMB RILEY | With Pictures by | C. M. RELYEA | and | WILL VAWTER | INDIANAPOLIS | THE BOBBS-MERRILL COMPANY | PUBLISHERS

COLLATION: [1–12]⁴. Leaf measures 7¾″ x 5¼″, all edges trimmed. Printed on white coated paper.

PAGINATION: End paper, white wove; blank, p. [i]; vignettes in red, pp. [ii–iv]; fly title, p. [v]; illustration in red, p. [vi]; blank, p. [vii]; frontispiece (with tissue guard), p. [viii]; title-page, p. [ix]; copyright notice with date 1904, *December*, and imprint of Braunworth & Co., p. [x]; dedication to Hewitt Hanson Howland, with 4-line poem beginning, *Little Boy! Halloo!—halloo!*\*, p. [xi]; vignette in red, p. [xii]; half-title, p. [xiii]; illustration, p. [xiv]; text, pp. 1–[78]; vignettes in red, pp. [79–81]; blank, p. [82]; end paper.

ILLUSTRATIONS: Frontispiece, with tissue guard, and 19 full-page illustrations integral parts of the book, unnumbered but figured in the pagination. Numerous text illustrations throughout and vignettes in red as noted above.

BINDING: Sage green, satin-finished cloth with design of holly leaves and berries stamped in light green and red on the front cover and spine. Front cover bears a gilt-stamped wreath within which is gilt-stamped: A | Defective | Santa Claus | James Whitcomb | Riley   The spine is gilt-stamped: A | DEFECTIVE | SANTA | CLAUS | JAMES | WHIT-COMB | RILEY | BOBBS | MERRILL   Back cover blank.

PUBLICATION DATE: Deposited for copyright December 7, 1904. Reviewed in the *Indianapolis Star*, December 9, 1904 and advertised by the publishers December 10, 1904.

PUBLICATION PRICE: $1.00.

CONTENTS: The single poem, "A Defective Santa Claus," had appeared previously in *Collier's*, December 3, 1904.

---

\*This same poem had been inscribed by Riley in a copy of *The Book of Joyous Children* (1902) which he gave to Madison Cawein, August 5, 1903; see *The Story of a Poet: Madison Cawein*, by Otto A. Rothert (1921).

## 1905

# Riley Songs O' Cheer

RILEY | SONGS O' CHEER [*in red*] | JAMES WHITCOMB RILEY | WITH PICTURES BY | WILL VAWTER | INDIANAPOLIS | THE BOBBS-MERRILL COMPANY | PUBLISHERS

COLLATION: [1–12]⁸. Leaf measures 7¾″ scant x 5³⁄₁₆″, all edges trimmed. Printed on white coated paper.

PAGINATION: End paper, white wove; blank, pp. [i–iv]; list of *Books by James Whitcomb Riley* (caption and single rule box in red), p. [v]; proem, p. [vi]; frontispiece with tissue guard (inserted); title-page, p. [vii]; copyright notice with final date 1905, and imprint of Charles Francis Press, p. [viii]; dedication to Bliss Carman, with poem*, pp. [ix–x]; table of contents, pp. [xi–xii]; list of illustrations, pp. [xiii–xvi]; half-title, p. [xvii]; blank, p. [xviii]; text, pp. 19–195; tailpiece, p. [196]; blank, pp. [197–202]; end paper.

ILLUSTRATIONS: Colored frontispiece with tissue guard, inserted and not included in the pagination. The five other colored plates, inserted opposite p. [42], p. [72], p. [116], p. [128] and p. [184], are unnumbered but included in the pagination. All other full-page illustrations are integral parts of the book. Halftones and line drawings are profuse as head and tailpieces.

BINDING: Dark green, vertically ribbed cloth, with design of a young man, waist-length, stamped in cream-white, outlined in black on a circular gilt background. A branch of green leaves, outlined in black, starts at the upper right corner of the front cover and traverses the circle. Below it is gilt-stamped: RILEY | SONGS O' CHEER  All the preceding appears within a rectangular single rule border, blind-stamped. The spine is gilt-stamped: [*double rule*] | RILEY | SONGS | O' CHEER | WITH | PICTURES | BY VAWTER | [*bird on branch of a fruit-tree: bird and fruit gilt-stamped, branch and leaves outlined in black*] | BOBBS-MERRILL | [*double rule*]  Back cover blank.

PUBLICATION DATE: Deposited for copyright October 23, 1905.

---

*This poem appeared in later books with title, "Bliss Carman."

Earliest located advertisement by the publishers appeared in the *Indianapolis News* of November 27, 1905.

PUBLICATION PRICE: $1.25.

NOTES: The binding occurs in three states: as described above, with figure cream-white and border blind-stamped; or, with figure snow-white and border gilt-stamped; or with figure snow-white and border blind-stamped. The deposit copies and copies with earliest presentation inscriptions are in the first-described state. Copies in the third-described state have all the plates in black and white, all integral parts of the book.

A bright red binding occurs on copies offered as a premium, about 1907, together with *Riley Love-Lyrics* (1899), *Riley Child Rhymes* (1899) and *Riley Farm-Rhymes* (1901) with subscriptions to the *Home Magazine*, published by the Bobbs-Merrill Company.

CONTENTS: Several of the poems herein had previously appeared under different titles: "The Rapture of the Year" as "Song—for November"; "There Is Ever a Song Somewhere" as "A Song"; "There Was a Cherry-Tree" as part of "The Child-World," without title; "Whatever the Weather May Be" as "Says He."

The following 4 poems are first appearances in a Riley book:

Songs o' Cheer [proem]    *Reader Magazine*, November, 1905* (title in *Biographical Edition:* A Song o' Cheer)

To Bliss Carman [dedication]†

A Christmas Carol§    *Reader Magazine* [front cover of], Christmas, 1904 (second stanza only, with title: A Carol) (title in *Biographical Edition:* Child's Christmas Carol)

Her Smile of Cheer and Voice of Song    *Indianapolis News*, April 3, 1905 (without title)

---

*The book is recorded as copyrighted October 23rd; whether the magazine appeared before or after this date is not known.

†"To Bliss Carman" appeared in the *Homestead Edition*, Vol. 14 (1913) as "Bliss Carman."

§Riley used this poem on his Christmas greeting (broadside) of 1912. His Christmas greetings of 1914 and 1915 contained the second stanza only, beginning, "O brother mine of birth divine" (without title).

# While the Heart Beats Young

[*illustration, tinted*] | While the Heart Beats Young | By | James Whitcomb Riley | With Pictures By | Ethel Franklin Betts | [*illustration, tinted*] | Indianapolis | The Bobbs-Merrill Company | Publishers
[Note: All the preceding appears within a decorative tinted border of floral design.]

COLLATION: [1–10]⁴. Leaf measures 9¼″ x 6⅞″, all edges trimmed. Printed on white plate paper.

PAGINATION: End paper, tinted halftone illustration printed on white; illustrations, tinted, pp. [i–ii]; fly title, p. [iii]; blank, p. [iv]; frontispiece, colored (inserted); title-page, p. [v]; copyright notice with final date 1906, p. [vi]; dedication, p. [vii]; blank, p. [viii]; proem, pp. [ix–x]; table of contents, pp. [xi–xii]; list of full-page pictures, pp. [xiii–xiv]; half-title, p. [xv]; blank, p. [xvi]; text, pp. 17–110; end paper.

ILLUSTRATIONS: Colored frontispiece, inserted. Also 15 full-page colored plates inserted, unnumbered but figured in the pagination. Tinted illustrations are used as head and tailpieces, on preliminary pages and throughout the text.

BINDING: Sage green twilled* or light blue-green, silk-finished cloth. A colored illustration, 8¹¹⁄₁₆″ x 5¾″, is inlaid on the front cover. It depicts a boy and girl seated in a field of white flowers; above them is printed in gilt: WHILE the HEART BEATS YOUNG | JAMES WHITCOMB RILEY   The lettering and illustration each appear within a panel formed by a gray border. Spine stamped in gilt: WHILE | the | HEART | BEATS | YOUNG | [*floret*] | JAMES | WHITCOMB | RILEY | ILLUSTRATED | BY | ETHEL | FRANKLIN | BETTS | BOBBS | MERRILL   Back cover blank.

PUBLICATION DATE: Deposited for copyright October 8, 1906. The book was reviewed in the *Indianapolis News*, November 3, 1906.

PUBLICATION PRICE: $2.50.

---

*A copyright deposit copy is bound in sage green twilled cloth.

NOTES: The text occurs in two states:

State 1: Has errors in the table of contents. Only two poems, "At Aunty's House" and "The Bear Story," can be found at the pages indicated; all of the other poems, with two exceptions, are listed two pages short of actual appearance. For example, "Almost Beyond Endurance," listed as at p. 38, appears at p. 40. The two exceptions are "The Boys' Candidate," listed as at p. 66, actually at p. 69; "Little Johnts's Chris'mus," listed as at p. 106, actually at p. 96.

State 2: Has table of contents corrected.

A freak copy in the Eitel collection* has the following features: no fly title; has title-page printed from type (the regular title-page is from hand-drawn lettering); lacks copyright notice on verso of the title-page; has table of contents in State 2; has only some of the pages numbered; has plain end papers and is printed on different paper. Two of the plates differ from all other copies examined: the one that accompanies "The Lisper," and the one accompanying "Our Hired Girl." The illustration inlaid on the front cover shows a boy and girl—the girl holding a doll—with background of a hedge of tall flowers.

CONTENTS: Only two of the poems herein are first appearances in a Riley book:

Her Lonesomeness  *Youth's Companion*, February 26, 1903

What Little Saul Got for Christmas  *Cosmopolitan*, December, 1904; *Indianapolis News*, December 6, 1904

---

*At the Indianapolis Public Library.

# 1907

# Morning

MORNING | JAMES WHITCOMB RILEY | INDIANAPOLIS | THE
BOBBS-MERRILL COMPANY | PUBLISHERS

COLLATION: [1–11]⁸. Leaf measures 7″ x 4¾″; all edges trimmed,
top edge gilt. Printed on white laid paper.*

PAGINATION: End paper, white wove; blank, p. [i]; list of *Books by
James Whitcomb Riley*, p. [ii]; frontispiece, with tissue guard printed in
red† (inserted); title-page, p. [iii]; copyright notice with date 1907,
*October*, p. [iv]; half-title, p. [v]; blank, p. [vi]; dedication to Meredith
Nicholson, p. [vii]; blank, p. [viii]; table of contents, pp. [ix–xi]; blank,
p. [xii]; half-title, p. [xiii]; blank, p. [xiv]; text, pp. 1–162; end paper.

ILLUSTRATIONS: Inserted frontispiece portrait of the author, in sepia, by John Singer Sargent, with tissue guard printed in red†. The
three advance copies (see below) were not provided with a frontispiece.

BINDING: Smooth red cloth. Front cover stamped in gilt within
single rule border: MORNING | BY JAMES WHITCOMB RILEY   Spine extra
gilt-stamped with decorative design of vine-like scrolls, single rule at
top, lettered within single rules: MORNING | [*ornament*] | RILEY   and, at
foot of spine, between single rules: BOBBS-MERRILL   Back cover blank.
Uniform with *A Child-World* (1897).

Also issued in green vertically ribbed, and, green twilled cloths. The
front cover is gilt-stamped: MORNING | BY JAMES WHITCOMB RILEY
within a blind-stamped box having a trefoil at each inner corner. Spine
gilt-stamped: MORNING | [*ornament*] | RILEY | BOBBS | MERRILL   Back
cover blank.

Note: The two copyright deposit copies and an advance copy in
the Frank G. Darlington collection are bound in the smooth red cloth.
The green cloth binding described above apparently followed shortly
thereafter and was in the nature of a trial binding, soon discarded in
favor of the red cloth with extra gilt spine, similar to the advance copies.

---

*Copies occur printed on laid paper, wove paper and mixed laid and wove
papers. Study of the advance copies and early inscribed copies indicates beyond
doubt that use of laid paper preceded use of wove paper.

†Also occurs unprinted. Earliest examined copies have tissue printed.

PUBLICATION DATE: Deposited for copyright August 12, 1907. Reviewed in the *Indianapolis News*, October 5, 1907.

PUBLICATION PRICE: $1.25.

NOTES: The book occurs in two states:
> *State 1:* Page [ii], title of first book listed: *Neghborly Poems*
> *State 2:* Page [ii], title of first book listed: *Neighborly Poems*

The copyright deposit copy, received August 12th, has the spelling *Neghborly*. The first reprints in the *Greenfield Edition* (1908) have the spelling as in State 2 but when the advertisements in the *Greenfield Edition* were revised, the correct(!) *Neghborly* spelling was used.

CONTENTS: Two of the poems herein had appeared previously in Riley books; all of the others are here first collected:

America   *Chicago Evening Post*, November 30, 1901 (with title: America, Sept. 14, 1901); *Indianapolis News*, May 10, 1902 (with music and with title: The Messiah of Nations); *The Messiah of Nations*, sheet music (1902) (see p. 162); *Official Souvenir Indiana Soldiers and Sailors Monument* (1902) (with title: The Messiah of Nations)

An Autumnal Tonic   *Indianapolis Journal*, October 22, 1883

The Children of the Childless   *Collier's*, April 2, 1904; *The Children of the Childless*, broadside (1904) (see p. 164)

Christine   *Indianapolis Journal*, August 31, 1890 (with title: Wilhelmina)

A Christmas Glee   *Reader Magazine*, December, 1905 (with music by Riley); *Indianapolis News*, November 29, 1905 (with music); *A Christmas Glee*, leaflet (see p. 164)

The Country Editor   *Indianapolis Journal*, July 21, 1882 (with title: The Editor)

The Doctor*   *Indianapolis Star*, April 29, 1907

An Empty Nest   *Indianapolis Journal*, February 7, 1877

Even As a Child   *Boston Daily Globe* (McKinley Memorial Edition), September 19, 1901; *The Shield*, Phi Kappa Psi, October, 1901

General Lew Wallace†   *Collier's*, March 4, 1905

A Golden Wedding   *Hancock Democrat*, Dec. 25, 1884 (untitled)

---

*The *Transactions of the Indiana State Medical Association* (1907), contains the poem in an obituary of Dr. Wm. B. Fletcher by Dr. Roscoe H. Ritter. It is not known whether this was published before or after August 12, 1907.

†Later Riley added four new stanzas and the longer version is printed in *Proceedings in Statuary Hall . . . upon the Unveiling, Reception and Acceptance . . . of the Statue of General Lew Wallace* (1910). It appears also in the *Biographical Edition*, Vol. 5, p. 476.

*Green cloth and red cloth bindings; the latter
a uniform binding for numerous Riley books*

A Good Man  *Indianapolis Journal*, January 18, 1901

The Great God Pan  *Indianapolis Journal*, May 12, 1883 (part of "A Glimpse of Pan")

Henry Irving  *Collier's*, October 28, 1905

His Heart of Constant Youth  *Indianapolis Journal*, January 25, 1901; *Major Charles L. Holstein*, (pamphlet; see p. 179)

His Last Picture  *Saturday Herald* (*Indianapolis*), July 3, 1880 (with title: In Memoriam | John W. Love)

A Hoosier Calendar

The Hoosier in Exile  *Indianapolis Journal*, December 18, 1901

A Humble Singer  *Topeka State Journal*, September 15, 1899 (with title: On Reading Eugene Ware's "Old Kansas Veteran")

Laughing Song  *Saturday Herald* (*Indianapolis*), August 2, 1879 (with title: Song)

Life at the Lake  *Indianapolis Journal*, August 10, 1890; *Judge*, September 13, 1890 (title in both: Maxinkuckee)

Lincoln—the Boy  *Collier's*, February 10, 1906

The Little Woman  *Indianapolis Journal*, April 27, 1877 (with title: My Little Woman)

Longfellow | 1807—February 27—1907  *Collier's*, March 2, 1907; *Indianapolis Star*, March 3, 1907

The Loveliness

Morning ("Breath of Morning—breath of May")

My Foe

Nicholas Oberting

The Old Days  *Collier's*, December 5, 1903

On Reading Dr. Henry van Dyke's Volume of Poems—Music (Title in table of contents: On Reading Dr. van Dyke's Poems—Music) *Reader Magazine*, March, 1905; [Program of] *Indiana State Teachers Association*, 1906 (see p. 181).

Our Little Girl  *Hancock Democrat*, December 7, 1876\*, with title: Minnie

Ours  *Louisville Courier-Journal*, December 9, 1906

"Out of Reach"?†

A Parting Guest

The Quest of the Fathers  *Detroit Free Press*, December 21, 1901

The Rainy Morning  *Indianapolis Journal*, November 24, 1877

The Rest

---

\*Not seen.

†See *Indianapolis News*, August 3, 1916, for an account of the poem's origin and version beginning, "They?—'Out of Reach'—our loyal dead?"

The Rose-Lady*
Sis Rapalye  *Collier's*, April 15, 1905
The Soldier  *Indianapolis News*, May 15, 1902; *The Soldier*, 1902
    (pamphlet, see p. 161); *Critic*, June, 1902
Some Imitations  *Reader Magazine*, October, 1905 (parts I–III only,
    with title: Imitations of Three Southern Singers)
A Spring Song and a Later
To Edmund Clarence Stedman  *New York Times*, December 22, 1900
The Voice of Peace  *Reader Magazine*, July, 1905
We Must Believe
What Title?
You May Not Remember
"Blue-Monday" at the Shoe Shop
Bub Says
Goldie Goodwin
Grampa's Choice
Her Poet-Brother
The Hired Man's Dog-Story†
Hoosier Spring-Poetry  *Century Magazine*, June, 1904
I' Got to Face Mother To-Day!  *Reader Magazine*, September, 1905
It's *Got* to Be  *Success*, December, 1903
A Little Lame Boy's Views
Lizabuth-Ann on Bakin'-Day
"Mother"§
Name Us No Names No More
Perversity
The Poor Student
Rabbit  *Reader Magazine*, May, 1906
The Raggedy Man on Children
Symptoms
Thinkin' Back  *Reader Magazine*, April, 1905; *Thinkin' Back* (remi-
    niscences of John Wanamaker, Philadelphia; see p. 180)
The Thoughts of Youth
Uncle Sidney's Rhymes
A Very Tall Boy  *Indianapolis Journal*, December 12, 1890 (in ad-
    vertisement for The When, with title: The Very Tall Boy)

---

*A clipping dated "Greenfield, Ind., August, 1879," entitled "Roses [For the
*Saturday Evening Call*]" is probably from the Peoria, Illinois, *Call, ca.* August, 1879.
  †This appeared in *Uncle Remus's Magazine*, October, 1907, before the book
appeared on the market, but after copyright deposit.
  §This appeared in *Century Magazine*, October, 1907, before the book appeared
on the market, but after copyright deposit.

# 1907

# The Raggedy Man

The Raggedy Man | By | James Whitcomb Riley | [*illustration, black and red*] | With illustrations by | Ethel Franklin Betts | [*decorative design*] | Indianapolis [*ornament, red*] | The Bobbs Merrill Company | Publishers

[Note: The foregoing appears within a black single rule box. The title-page is from a hand-drawn design. No attempt has been made to indicate the illustrator's use of mixed upper and lower case letters.]

COLLATION: [1–6]⁴. Leaf measures 11⅞″ x 10½″, all edges trimmed. Printed on white plate paper.

PAGINATION: End paper, white wove; fly title, p. [i]; blank, pp. [ii–iii]; frontispiece, p. [iv]; title-page, p. [v]; copyright notice with date 1907, p. [vi]; dedication to Lesley and Elizabeth [and other children; in verse], p. [vii]; decoration, p. [viii]; half-title, p. [ix]; decoration, p. [x]; text, pp. [1–35]; tailpiece, p. [36]; blank, pp. [37–38]; end paper.

ILLUSTRATIONS: Frontispiece and 7 full-page illustrations, colored, all integral parts of the book. The printed pages which precede the text have ornaments and illustrations printed in black and red; each page of text bears an illustrated headpiece, tailpiece and decorative border printed in these same colors.

BINDING: Colored pictorial boards, with: THE RAGGEDY MAN | BY JAMES WHITCOMB RILEY printed in black. Dark green cloth shelf-back. Both covers identical. Issued in pictorial colored dust wrapper.

PUBLICATION DATE: A copy was deposited in the Copyright Office on October 12, 1907 and another on October 18, 1907. The earliest advertisement of it so far noted is one that appeared in the *Indianapolis News*, December 16, 1907.

PUBLICATION PRICE: $1.50.

NOTES: The book has been noted in three states:
 *State* 1: Pictorial boards, both covers identical
   Fly title, p. [i]
   Final leaf blank

*State* 2: Green cloth with large pictorial inlay on front cover, back cover blank
First leaf blank; fly title, p. [iii]
Final leaf: recto text, verso tailpiece
*State* 3: Same as State 2 but for binding which is plain light-green cloth, with title and author's name stamped in blue on the front cover.

CONTENTS: The dedicatory poem, beginning: "To Lesley and Elizabeth," (preceded by: *Dedication | Most Lovingly And Loyally Signed Over*) had no previous appearance. The poem, "The Raggedy Man," is extended to eight stanzas. In *Rhymes of Childhood* (1891) and other previous appearances it consisted of 4 stanzas only. Other poems herein are reprinted from earlier Riley books.

# The Boys of the Old Glee Club

[*headpiece*] | THE BOYS OF | THE OLD | GLEE CLVB [*sic*] | BY JAMES WHITCOMB RILEY [*on scroll-like panel*] | [*decoration*] | INDIANAP-OLIS | THE BOBBS-MERRILL COMPANY | [*dot*] PVBLISHERS [*sic*] [*dot*] [Note: The publishers' imprint appears on a scroll-like panel.]

COLLATION: [1–7]⁴, [8]². Leaf measures 9″ x 5⅝″, all edges trimmed. Printed on white wove paper.

PAGINATION: End paper, yellow-green printed on white, with title, and names of author, illustrator and decorator on decorative panels; blank, pp. [i–ii]; fly title, p. [iii]; blank, p. [iv]; frontispiece with tissue guard (inserted); title-page, p. [v]; copyright notice with date 1907, *November*, p. [vi]; dedication to Newton Booth Tarkington, p. [vii]; blank, p. [viii]; divisional half-title, names of illustrator and designer, p. [ix]; blank, p. [x]; list of illustrations, p. [xi]; blank, p. [xii]; list of illustrations continued, p. [xiii]; blank, p. [xiv]; half-title, p. [xv]; blank, p. [xvi]; text, pp. [17–55]; blank, pp. [56–60]; end paper.

[Note: With the exception of the title-page, which has the copyright notice on verso, all the leaves are printed on one side only.]

ILLUSTRATIONS: Colored frontispiece with tissue guard and 12 other full-page colored plates on coated paper, inserted. Illustrations by Will Vawter; decorations on preliminary pages and on each page of text by Franklin Booth.

BINDING: Light yellow-green, vertically-ribbed cloth, with design stamped in dark green on front cover, white flowers, gilt title on ivory scroll: THE BOYS OF | THE OLD | GLEE CLVB [*sic*]  The author's name is gilt-stamped below the green design: JAMES WHITCOMB RILEY  Spine gilt-stamped: THE | BOYS | OF | THE | OLD | GLEE | CLVB [*sic*] | JAMES | WHIT- | COMB | RILEY | BOBBS | MERRILL

PUBLICATION DATE: Deposited for copyright November 27, 1907; advertised in the *Indianapolis News*, December 7, 1907.

PUBLICATION PRICE: $1.50.

NOTES: The binding occurs in three states: (A), as described above; (B), same except that the cloth is blue-green instead of yellow-green;

(C), yellow-green cloth with title on front cover stamped on a panel of cover color instead of ivory and with the flowers in dark green instead of white. The copyright deposit copies are in the first described state, as is the copy presented by the author to the dedicatee, Booth Tarkington, called the "very first copy" in the inscription which is dated November 30, 1907. Other presentation copies, inscribed early in December of the same year, are likewise in this state.

The copyright deposit copies have plain end papers, same as the book stock. Copies in the late *C* binding have been noted with either decorated or plain end papers.

CONTENTS: The Boys of the Old Glee Club   *Reader*, November, 1907

# 1908

# The Orphant Annie Book

THE ORPHANT ANNIE BOOK | By James Whitcomb Riley | Illustrated by | Ethel Franklin Betts | [*decorative design in orange and green*] | [*illustration in orange and green*] | Indianapolis | [*ornament, orange and green*] The Bobbs-Merrill Company [*ornament, orange and green*] | Publishers

[Note: The foregoing appears within a decorative green border; except as noted, wholly printed in green. The title-page is from a hand-drawn design. No attempt has been made to indicate the illustrator's use of mixed upper and lower case letters.]

COLLATION: [1–6]⁴. Leaf measures 11⅜″ x 10¼″, all edges trimmed. Text printed in green on white plate paper.

PAGINATION: End paper, white wove; blank, pp. [i–ii]; fly title, p. [iii]; blank, pp. [iv–v]; frontispiece, p. [vi]; title-page, p. [vii]; copyright notice with final date 1908, p. [viii]; dedication *To all the little children . . .*, p. [ix]; decoration, p. [x]; proem, p. [xi]; decoration, p. [xii]; text, pp. [1–35]; decoration, p. [36]; end paper.

ILLUSTRATIONS: Frontispiece and 7 full-page illustrations, orange and green, all integral parts of the book. The printed pages which precede the text have ornaments and illustrations printed in orange and green; each page of text bears an illustrated headpiece, tailpiece and decorative border printed in the same colors.

BINDING: Colored pictorial boards with: THE ORPHANT ANNIE BOOK | BY JAMES WHITCOMB RILEY printed in green. Green cloth shelf-back. Back and front covers identical. The dust wrapper is a repetition of the covers except for a minor difference in color.

PUBLICATION DATE: Deposited for copyright September 14, 1908.

PUBLICATION PRICE: $1.50.

NOTES: The book was reissued in the following forms:
*Little Orphan Annie* (1908) [*i.e.* 1910]. Contents same but arranged differently.

*Little Orphan Annie* (cover title: *Ef You Don't Watch Out*) (1908)
[*i.e.* 1911]. Reissue of part of *The Orphant Annie Book* (1908)
*The Boy Lives on Our Farm* (1908) [*i.e.* 1911]. Reissue of part of
*The Orphant Annie Book* (1908)

CONTENTS: The only poem herein that had not appeared previously
in a Riley book is the proem which begins: "Little Orphant Annie she
knows riddles, rhymes and things!"

# 1908

## THE HOMESTEAD EDITION, VOL. XIII

# His Pa's Romance

THE POEMS AND PROSE | [2 *florets*] SKETCHES OF [2 *florets*] | JAMES WHITCOMB RILEY | HIS PA'S ROMANCE [*in red*] | CHARLES SCRIBNER'S | SONS [*floret*] NEW YORK [*floret*] 1908
[Note: All the preceding appears within a red single rule box.]

COLLATION: [1–9]⁸, [10]⁴. Leaf measures 7⅜″ x 5″, top edge gilt, other edges untrimmed. Printed on white laid paper watermarked with Riley's monogram.

PAGINATION: End paper, same as book stock; fly title: *The Works Of James | Whitcomb Riley* [2 *florets*] | *Vol. XIII*, p. [i]; blank, p. [ii]; frontispiece with printed tissue guard (inserted); title-page, p. [iii]; copyright notice with date 1908 and acknowledgement, p. [iv]; dedication, p. [v]; blank, p. [vi]; table of contents, pp. vii–viii; half-title, p. [1]; blank, p. [2]; text, pp. 3–140; insignia of Scribner Press, p. [141]; blank, pp. [142–144]; end paper.

ILLUSTRATIONS: Frontispiece: sepia photogravure [by Will Vawter], with tissue guard printed in sepia, inserted.

BINDING: Uniform with the *Homestead Edition*, Vol. III. For description see p. 71.

PUBLICATION DATE: Copies deposited in the Copyright Office November 20, 1908.

NOTES: Also issued in a limited edition of 204 numbered copies on Japan paper. For further description see p. 72.

CONTENTS: The following 13 poems here make first appearance in a Riley book:
Christmas Season
Envoy    *Indianapolis Journal*, February 16, 1881 (with title: The New Friend. Title in *Biographical Edition:* Be Our Fortunes as They May)

"Friday Afternoon"   *Indianapolis Sentinel*, January 30, 1876; *History of Hancock County, Indiana* (1882)

He Cometh in Sweet Sense   *Indianapolis Journal*, August 22, 1886

I Smoke My Pipe   *Sunday Herald* (*Indianapolis*), January 24, 1875

Kathleen Mavourneen   *Indianapolis Journal*, April 16, 1892; leaflet announcing Riley's appearance in Cleveland, October 25 [1898] (without title; see p. 177)

Larry Noolan's New Year   *Indianapolis Journal*, January 1, 1891 (in advertisement for The When)

Lisping in Numbers

A Lost Love   *Kokomo Tribune*, October 2, 1880; *Judge*, April 19, 1890 (with title: Lost)

An Order for a Song   *Indianapolis Journal*, January 18, 1880

Song Discordant

With a Child-Book

Ylladmar   *Indianapolis Journal*, March 16, 1878

# 1908

# Riley Songs of Summer

RILEY | SONGS OF SUMMER [*in red*] | JAMES WHITCOMB RILEY | WITH PICTURES BY | WILL VAWTER | INDIANAPOLIS | THE BOBBS-MERRILL COMPANY | PUBLISHERS

COLLATION: [1–12]⁸. Leaf measures 7⅜″ x 5¼″, all edges trimmed. Printed on white coated paper.

PAGINATION: End paper, white wove; blank, pp. [i–iv]; fly title, p. [v]; blank, p. [vi]; list of *Books by James Whitcomb Riley*, heading and border rule in red, p. [vii]; blank, pp. [viii–ix]; frontispiece, p. [x]; title-page, p. [xi]; copyright notice with final date 1908 and imprint of Charles Francis Press, p. [xii]; dedication to Lee O. Harris, p. [xiii]; proem, p. [xiv]; table of contents, pp. [xv–xvi]; half-title, p. [xvii]; blank, p. [xviii]; text, pp. 19–[190]; blank, pp. [191–192]; end paper.

ILLUSTRATIONS: The full-page illustrations, including the frontispiece, are integral parts of the book. They are unnumbered but figured in the pagination. Numerous headpieces and tailpieces.

BINDING: Dark green, vertically ribbed cloth. The front cover bears a design of a young man in profile, waist-length, outlined in black against a circular gilt-stamped background. A branch of a tree with a bird perched on it is outlined in black in the upper left corner and on part of the gilt field; below is gilt-stamped: RILEY | SONGS OF SUMMER All the preceding appears within a blind-stamped single rule border. The spine is stamped in gilt: [*double gilt rule*] | RILEY | SONGS | OF | SUMMER | WITH | PICTURES | BY VAWTER | [*sheaves of wheat and birds*] | BOBBS-MERRILL | [*double gilt rule*] Back cover blank.

PUBLICATION DATE: Deposited for copyright September 14, 1908. Advertised by the publishers and reviewed in the *Indianapolis News*, December 5, 1908.

PUBLICATION PRICE: $1.00*.

---

*Listed by the publishers at $1.00 in the earliest located advertisement, December 5, 1908. *The Publishers' Weekly*, December 12, 1908, gives price as $1.25, leather $2.00. No leather-bound copy has been located, nor is there any other record found of the book's appearance in leather.

CONTENTS: Of all the poems herein, only the proem makes a first appearance in a Riley book:

The Summer-Time  *Kokomo Tribune*, May 22, 1880; broadside (see p. 150)

NOTE: The poem, "To Loll Back in a Misty Hammock" had appeared without title in the *Homestead Edition*, Vol. 6 (1898). In the *Biographical Edition* the same poem is entitled, "A Dream of Inspiration."

"Pomona" had previously appeared as Part I of "Some Imitations." In the *Reader Magazine*, October, 1905, this same part was entitled, "Melpomene," not "Pomona."

# 1911

# The Lockerbie Book

The Lockerbie Book | Containing Poems Not in Dialect | By | James Whitcomb Riley | Collected and Arranged by | Hewitt Hanson Howland | INDIANAPOLIS | THE BOBBS-MERRILL COMPANY | PUBLISHERS

COLLATION: [1–20]¹⁶, [21]⁸. Leaf measures 6½″ x 4⅜″, all edges gilt. Printed on India paper.

PAGINATION: End paper, white wove; fly title, p. [i]; blank, p. [ii]; title-page, p. [iii]; copyright notice with date 1911, p. [iv]*; dedication to Judge E. B. Martindale, p. [v]; blank, p. [vi]; *Introduction* signed H. H. H., pp. [vii–viii]; half-title, p. [ix]; blank, p. [x]; text, pp. 1–611; blank, p. [612]; divisional title-page, p. [613]; blank, p. [614]; divisional half-title, p. [615]; blank, p. [616]; indexes, pp. 617–646; end paper.

ILLUSTRATIONS: None.

BINDING: Blue cloth. Front cover gilt-stamped within decorative gilt border: The Lockerbie Book | of | Riley Verse    Spine gilt-stamped: [*ornamental rule*] | The | Lockerbie | Book | [*rule*] | Riley | Bobbs | Merrill | [*ornamental rule*]    On the back cover the ornamental border is blind-stamped.

Also issued in limp black morocco with rounded corners; single rule border blind-stamped on both covers; front cover lettered in gilt: The Lockerbie Book | of Riley Verse    Spine has a single rule blind-stamped at top and bottom and the following stamped in gilt: The | Lockerbie | Book | [*rule*] | Riley    The end papers are black coated on white and a fly leaf is present both front and back.

Both bindings were available on October 7, 1911.

PUBLICATION DATE: Deposited for copyright October 4, 1911. According to the publishers' statement in the Copyright Office, publication date was September 15, 1911, but copies were not received in Washington until October 4th and the earliest advertisement located appears in the *Indianapolis News*, October 7th.

---

*Later the copyright page has imprint of Braunworth & Co. added.

PUBLICATION PRICE: Cloth, $1.75; limp morocco, $2.50.

NOTES: The book occurs in two states:
  State 1: Pages 617–630, titles indexed by page
  State 2: Pages 617–630, titles indexed by number
The copies in State 1, so far seen, have been found in the private libraries of persons associated in some way with the publishers; two of these measure ¾″ across sheets. The deposit copy in the Library of Congress, in State 1, and other copies noted, measure ⅜″ as in later printings. Copies with early presentation inscriptions, so far examined, have text in State 2. Several of the author's friends were given copies in a trial binding of dark red leather, with red coated end papers, but with text in State 2.

CONTENTS: Of the 411 poems in this collection, only one makes first appearance in a Riley book:
To Benj. S. Parker   *Indianapolis Star*, March 15, 1911

NOTE: See *The Hoosier Book* (1916) for the companion volume to *The Lockerbie Book*.

# 1913

# The Riley Baby Book

THE | RILEY BABY BOOK | Autograph Verses | Reproduced in Facsimile | By JAMES WHITCOMB RILEY | Illustrated by | WILLIAM COTTON | INDIANAPOLIS | THE BOBBS-MERRILL COMPANY | PUBLISHERS

[Note: All the preceding printed in sepia within a sepia single rule box.]

COLLATION: The book is composed of 19 unnumbered leaves of cream-colored flexible boards hinged on linen. The leaf measures 8⅜″ x 6⅜″ full, all edges trimmed.

PAGINATION: End paper, cream-colored rough paper; fly title, p. [i]; blank, pp. [ii–iii]; frontispiece, p. [iv]; title-page, p. [v]; copyright notice with date 1913, and imprint of Charles Francis Press, p. [vi]; facsimile inscription: *Very truly your friend | —James Whitcomb Riley*, p. [vii]; text, pp. [8–36]; illustration, p. [37]; blank, p. [38]; end paper.

[Note: All printed in sepia.]

ILLUSTRATIONS: Frontispiece: an oval colored halftone mounted above a quatrain by Riley. Also 15 full-page illustrations in sepia on recto of each leaf from pp. [9–37], inclusive.

BINDING: Red vertically-ribbed cloth. Front cover stamped in gilt within an ornamental gilt design: JAMES | WHITCOMB | RILEY | BABY | BOOK   all within a blind-stamped double rule border. Spine and back cover blank.

PUBLICATION DATE: October 11, 1913. Deposited for copyright October 15, 1913.

PUBLICATION PRICE: $1.50.

NOTES: The inspiration for *The Riley Baby Book* was a book entitled: *My Little Friends: A Choice Collection of Children's Portraits Accompanied by Appropriate Poems*, by E. Heinrichs, published Boston [1891]. The author sent a copy to Riley in April, 1892. Apparently the pictures appealed to Riley for he wrote his own interpretation, in ink, below or on each photograph*. The text of *The Riley Baby Book* (1913) is a selection from these inscribed verses, reproduced in facsimile and accompanied by William Cotton's illustrations.

*The Riley Baby Book* was reissued, 1914, as *Baby Ballads*, bound in gray wrappers tied with blue ribbon, with the colored halftone, used as a frontispiece in the original edition, mounted on the front cover.

CONTENTS: All the poems, untitled, are first appearances in a Riley book, with the exception of the poem beginning, "GIUNTS is *biggest* mens they air"; this had been collected in *Poems Here at Home* (1893) under the title, "The Truly Marvelous."

[FIRST LINE:]

IF one of the little Cherubim (below frontispiece)
IS it "Good-night" or "Good-morning," Dear?—
*Don't* disturve me, Mommy!—Say,
LOOK so very
LITTLE Injun boys, like me,
THIS is ist a *'tend-like boat*, an'
'SPECT you think I'm "a tough old jay"
WHAT you think I care fer STILE,
I'M a Papoosie, an' Muvver's a Squaw,—
I'M a very *serious* baby—
I'M ist a little too skeer'd to know
*GIVEN*-NAME is 'MANCIPATION,
MA says—Couldn't mucher prize
DINAH she aint pleased at all
HERE'S a Water-Kelpie's daughter—

---

*This copy is in the Edmund Henry Eitel Collection loaned to the Indianapolis Public Library. Another copy of the Heinrichs book was similarly annotated by Riley, for the parents of Benjamin Harrison McKee, the baby to whom Heinrichs dedicated his book. The *Indianapolis Star*, May 26, 1940, contains a story of this copy with facsimile of the frontispiece bearing Riley's inscribed verses beginning "Grandpa's name ain't much comparison"

# 1913

# Biographical Edition

THE COMPLETE WORKS | OF | JAMES WHITCOMB RILEY | IN WHICH
THE POEMS, INCLUDING A NUMBER HERETOFORE UNPUBLISHED, |
ARE ARRANGED IN THE ORDER IN WHICH THEY WERE WRIT-
TEN, | TOGETHER WITH PHOTOGRAPHS, BIBLIOGRAPHIC NOTES |
AND A LIFE SKETCH OF THE AUTHOR | COLLECTED AND EDITED
BY | EDMUND HENRY EITEL | BIOGRAPHICAL EDITION | VOLUME
ONE [TWO, THREE, FOUR, FIVE, SIX] | INDIANAPOLIS | THE
BOBBS-MERRILL COMPANY | PUBLISHERS

## VOL. I

COLLATION: [1–29]⁸. Leaf measures 7½" x 5⅛", top edge gilt, other
edges untrimmed. Printed on white wove paper.

PAGINATION*: Fly title, p. [i]; blank, p. [ii]; frontispiece with tissue
guard (inserted); title-page, p. [iii]; copyright notice with final date 1913
and imprint of Braunworth & Co., p. [iv]; dedication *To My Father And
Mother*, p. [v]; blank, p. [vi]; *Acknowledgement*, p. [vii]; blank, p. [viii];
table of contents, pp. [ix–xii]; half-title, p. [xiii]; blank, p. [xiv]; text,
pp. 1–363; blank, p. [364]; divisional half-title, p. [365]; blank, p. [366];
*James Whitcomb Riley—A Sketch* [by Edmund Henry Eitel], pp. 367–387;
blank, p. [388]; divisional half-title, p. [389]; blank, p. [390]; illustration
(inserted); *Notes*, pp. 391–449; blank, p. [450].

ILLUSTRATIONS: Frontispiece: sepia portrait of Riley, by Sargent,
with tissue guard, inserted. Also inserted are the following plates: opposite pp. 30, 66, 100, 168, 198, 258, 300, 350, [390]; between pp. 138 and
139 (5 plates on 3 leaves) and between pp. 234 and 235 (2 plates on 1
leaf).

---

*The set was issued in 5 different bindings. The inserted preliminary and ter-
minal leaves vary with the bindings and are disregarded in the collation. Some
copies contain leaf in front of Vol. I which reads: "THIS SET is one of the First
Thousand Printed Impressions of the BIOGRAPHICAL EDITION of the COMPLETE
WORKS of JAMES WHITCOMB RILEY which have been reserved by the Publishers at
the request of the Author for his friends and neighbors."

BINDING: Issued in 5 different bindings: green cloth, red cloth, ¾ morocco, ¾ calf, full morocco*. Lettered on the spine: [4 *ornaments*] THE | COMPLETE | WORKS OF | JAMES [2 *ornaments*] | WHITCOMB | RILEY [3 *ornaments*] | I [II, III, IV, V, VI] | BIOGRAPHICAL | EDITION [3 *ornaments*] |BOBBS [*ornament*] | MERRILL    Tooling varies with the type of binding. The thin paper edition in limp leather appeared in 1915. Sets in a ¾ red imitation leather with gray cloth sides are probably later.

PUBLICATION DATE: November 26, 1913, according to publishers' statement in the Copyright Office; advertised by the Indianapolis stores and reviewed in the *Indianapolis News* November 29, 1913. Deposited for copyright December 5, 1913.

PUBLICATION PRICE: Cloth, $12.00; ¾ morocco or ¾ calf, $18.00; full morocco, $24.00.

CONTENTS: The following poems had not previously appeared in Riley books:

At Last   *Danbury (Conn.) News*, February 25, 1874 (repeated February 28, 1874)

An Autumnal Extravaganza   *Saturday Herald (Indianapolis)*, November 3, 1877

Bryant   *Indianapolis Journal*, June 14, 1878

Dead in Sight of Fame   *Hancock Democrat*, September 7, 1876 (with title: Dunbar)

Dead Leaves | Dawn, Dusk, Night†   *New Castle Mercury*, November 16, 1876 (with title: Three Sonnets to Autumn)

A Dream ("I dreamed I was a spider")   *Saturday Herald (Indianapolis)*, May 11, 1878

A Dream of Long Ago   *Indianapolis Journal*, June 1, 1877

A Dream Unfinished   *Hancock Democrat*, August 1, 1878 (without title; included in prose sketch: Memorial | Nellie M. Cooley)

Father William   *Saturday Herald (Indianapolis)*, September 22, 1877

Job Work   *People (Indianapolis)*, July 19, 1874

John Walsh   (Funeral announcement, see p. 167*n*)

"Johnson's Boy"   *Hancock Democrat*, February 10, 1876

A Letter to a Friend   *Saturday Herald (Indianapolis)*, April 18, 1885 (without title; preceded by 6 uncollected stanzas beginning, "Dear Friend, You want a letter")

Liberty   *Indianapolis Journal*, July 5, 1878 (part only, with title:

---

*According to contemporary advertisements (see the *Indianapolis News* of November 29, 1913); also see *Biographical Edition*, Vol. 6, p. 443.

†The third of these sonnets appeared later in the *Homestead Edition*, Vol. 15 (1914), under the title "Night."

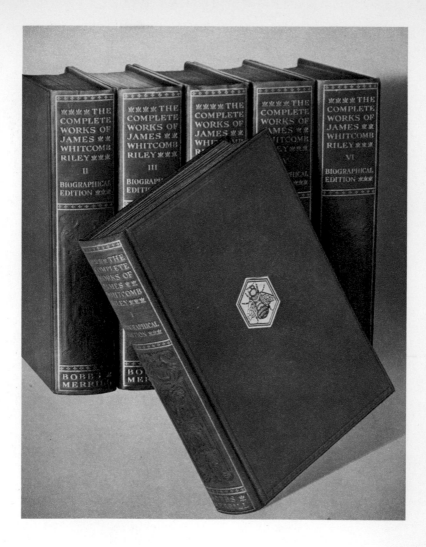

Independence Bell); *New Castle Mercury*, July 6, 1878 (part only, with title: Bire [Bird] Song)

Lines for an Album

Luther Benson *Kokomo Tribune*, January 5, 1878

Man's Devotion *Saturday Mirror (Indianapolis)*, March 30, 1872

The Merman *Saturday Herald (Indianapolis)*, November 17, 1877

Morton *Indianapolis Journal*, November 2, 1877

My Jolly Friend's Secret *Danbury (Conn.) News*, May 23, 1874

A New Year's Plaint *Indianapolis Journal*, January 1, 1878

The Old Times Were the Best *High School Budget (Greenfield)*, June, 1899

An Old Year's Address

Only a Dream

Over the Eyes of Gladness *Hancock Democrat*, November 23, 1876 (without title)

Philiper Flash*

Plain Sermons†

Private Theatricals *Danbury (Conn.) News*, August 15, 1874

The Same Old Story *Greenfield Commercial*, September, 1870§

Song of the New Year *Indianapolis Journal*, January 10, 1877

A Summer Afternoon *Danbury (Conn.) News*, July 11, 1874

A Summer Sunrise *Indianapolis Journal*, December 21, 1877

T. C. Philips *Kokomo Tribune*, July 20, 1878

To a Boy Whistling

To Annie

What Smith Knew about Farming

When Evening Shadows Fall *Indianapolis Journal*, January 12, 1890 (without title)

In addition to the above, there are printed in the notes to this volume a letter to C. B. Foote, November 22, 1886; a letter to Benj. S. Parker, November 6, 1876‖ and letters to John A. Riley of February 9,

---

*See *Biographical Edition* Vol. 1, p. 392, for reference to an early newspaper appearance.

†See *Biographical Edition* Vol. 1, p. 401, for reference to an early newspaper appearance.

§Not seen except as a clipping with partial identification.

‖The date of this letter is later given by Mr. Eitel as November 4, 1876 (in *Harper's Magazine*, February, 1918, p. 326); in *Letters of James Whitcomb Riley* edited by William Lyon Phelps (1930), p. 12, the date appears as December 5, 1876. The latter date is undoubtedly correct. Henry Wadsworth Longfellow Dana states in a letter of October 13, 1943: "In my grandfather's manuscript list of letters written, I find under the date of November 30, 1876, the name 'J. W. Riley.' There is no such name under November 3."

April 6, May 7 and May 14, 1872. Other letters in this and succeeding volumes are printed in part only, hence not listed. Riley's reply in verse to an inquiry concerning "An Old Sweetheart of Mine," beginning, "Dear Mister McGrew" is printed on p. 405 of this volume.

## VOL. II

COLLATION: [1–36]⁸.

PAGINATION: Blank, pp. [i–iv]; fly title, p. [v]; blank, p. [vi]; frontispiece with tissue guard (inserted); title-page, p. [vii]; copyright notice with final date 1913 and imprint of Braunworth & Co., p. [viii]; table of contents, pp. [ix–xvi]; half-title, p. [xvii]; blank, p. [xviii]; text, pp. 1–471; blank, p. [472]; divisional half-title, p. [473]; blank, p. [474]; *Notes*, pp. 475–552; blank, pp. [553–558].

ILLUSTRATIONS: Frontispiece: sepia photographic view of "the old swimmin'-hole" with tissue guard, inserted. Also inserted are the following plates: opposite pp. 72, 206, 354, 446; between pp. 140 and 141 (4 plates on 2 leaves), between pp. 266 and 267 (2 plates on 2 leaves) and between pp. 416 and 417 (3 plates on 2 leaves).

CONTENTS: The following had not appeared previously in a Riley book:

After the Frost   *Indianapolis Journal*, October 22, 1881
Another Ride from Ghent to Aix   *Indianapolis Journal*, April 16, 1881
Apart   *Indianapolis Journal*, December 8, 1878
An Assassin ("Cat-like he creeps along where ways are dim")   *Indianapolis Journal*, November 23, 1881 (with title: The Assassin)
At Bay   *Saturday Herald (Indianapolis)*, July 26, 1879
At Dusk   *Indianapolis Journal*, April 10, 1881
A Ballad from April   *Indianapolis Journal*, January 23, 1881
The Ballad of Smiles and Tears   *Kokomo Tribune*, August 2, 1879
Because   *Indianapolis Journal*, Juy 9, 1881
Best of All   *Indianapolis Journal*, December 3, 1881
Bin A-Fishin'   *Indianapolis Journal*, April 22, 1882
Brudder Sims*
A Case in Pint   *Indianapolis Journal*, August 16, 1880
Charles H. Philips   *Indianapolis Journal*, November 7, 1881 (with title: C. H. P.)
The Conqueror   *Indianapolis Journal*, January 21, 1880

---

*For reference to an early newspaper appearance see *Biographical Edition* (1913), Vol. 2, p. 522.

A Custom-Made Valentine (facsimile of manuscript.)

The Dead Joke and the Funny Man   *Indianapolis Journal*, March 19, 1880

Deformed   *Indianapolis Journal*, February 4, 1881

The Empty Song   *Saturday Herald* (*Indianapolis*), June 21, 1879

An End   *Indianapolis Journal*, August 6, 1880

Faith   *Indianapolis Journal*, February 15, 1881

False and True   *Indianapolis Journal*, January 22, 1881

Friend of a Wayward Hour   *Saturday Herald* (*Indianapolis*), July 12, 1879 (with title: To H. S. T.)

From Below   *Indianapolis Journal*, April 5, 1880

The Ginoine Ar-Tickle   *Kokomo Tribune*, November 8, 1879

Glamour   *Indianapolis Journal*, April 11, 1880

Good-By, Old Year   *Indianapolis Journal*, January 3, 1881

The Guide   *Indianapolis Journal*, August 26, 1882

Guinevere   *Indianapolis Journal*, January 4, 1880

Her Choice   *Indianapolis Journal*, August 9, 1880

Her Valentine   *Saturday Herald* (*Indianapolis*), August 30, 1879

Hope   *Saturday Herald* (*Indianapolis*), September 27, 1879

The Hour before the Dawn

In the Corridor   *Indianapolis Journal*, October 29, 1880

In the Heart of June   *Indianapolis Journal*, June 25, 1881

An Invocation   *Indianapolis Journal*, April 4, 1880

Last Words   *Saturday Herald* (*Indianapolis*), July 26, 1879

Lelloine   *Saturday Herald* (*Indianapolis*), August 9, 1879*

Lines | On Receiving a Present from an Unknown Friend   *Saturday Herald* (*Indianapolis*), July 5, 1879

Lines to an Onsettled Young Man   *Indianapolis Journal*, November 24, 1879

The Little Dead Man   *Saturday Herald* (*Indianapolis*), June 7, 1879

The Little Old Poem That Nobody Reads   *Saturday Herald* (*Indianapolis*), June 28, 1879

The Lost Thrill   *Indianapolis Journal*, March 20, 1881

Louella Wainie   *Indianapolis Journal*, November 1, 1880

Love's As Broad As Long   *Indianapolis Journal*, July 11, 1880

The Mad Lover   *Indianapolis Journal*, January 25, 1880

Michael Flynn and the Baby   *Indianapolis Journal*, December 15, 1879

---

*For reference to an earlier newspaper appearance see *The Youth of James Whitcomb Riley* by Marcus Dickey (1919), p. 228. A clipping bearing this poem has been examined; it is identified in manuscript as from the *Greenfield News*.

Monsieur Le Secretaire   *Indianapolis Journal*, September 21, 1890 (without title)

My Boy   *Indianapolis Journal*, July 2, 1881

My Laddie wi' the Bashfu' Grace   *Indianapolis Journal*, May 2, 1880

My Night

My Old Friend   *Sun (New York)*, June 13, 1880

O Her Beauty   *Indianapolis Journal*, May 20, 1880

The Old-Fashioned Bible   *Indianapolis Journal*, July 26, 1881

The Old Hand-Organ   *Indianapolis Journal*, June 23, 1880

Ole Bull   *Indianapolis Journal*, August 19, 1880

One Angel   *Indianapolis Journal*, March 24, 1880

A Phantom   *Indianapolis Journal*, September 26, 1880

The Piper's Son   *Indianapolis Journal*, July 1, 1880

Plantation Hymn   *Indianapolis Journal*, November 29, 1879

Requiescat   *Indianapolis Journal*, August 28, 1880

A Rose in October   *Saturday Herald (Indianapolis)*, June 21, 1879

Shadow and Shine   *Indianapolis Journal*, June 10, 1882

Since My Mother Died   *Saturday Herald (Indianapolis)*, August 16, 1879

Soldiers Here To-Day   *Indianapolis Journal*, May 24, 1882 (without title)

Somep'n Common-Like   *Sun (New York)*, August 29, 1880

A Song for Christmas   *Indianapolis Journal*, December 25, 1880; *Reader Magazine*, December, 1906

Stanzas for a New Song   *Indianapolis Journal*, November 24, 1879

Sun and Rain   *Indianapolis Journal*, May 28, 1881

A Test   *Indianapolis Journal*, December 19, 1880

The Text   *Indianapolis Journal*, November 15, 1880

Thanksgiving Day at Hunchley's   *Indianapolis Journal*, December 1, 1878

There Is a Need   *Indianapolis Journal*, July 5, 1880

To Leonainie   *Kokomo Tribune*, February 1, 1879 (with title: Leonainie)*

The Touch of Loving Hands   *Indianapolis Journal*, December 5, 1880

A Tress of Hair   *Indianapolis Journal*, May 9, 1880

Uncle Dan'l in Town over Sunday   *Indianapolis Journal*, April 22, 1882

Uncomforted   *Indianapolis Journal*, August 23, 1881

---

*Not the "Leonainie" poem of the famous Poe hoax (see p. 147) but one written later in memory of Leonainie Titus.

Unknown Friends   *Indianapolis Journal*, July 31, 1880
Unspoken   *Indianapolis Journal*, November 24, 1878
The Vision of Rabbi Ben Isaac   *Indianapolis Journal*, August 29, 1878
Wait   *Saturday Herald (Indianapolis)*, August 9, 1879
What They Said   *Indianapolis Journal*, October 22, 1881
When It Rains   *Indianapolis Journal*, November 19, 1881
Why   *Indianapolis Journal*, December 5, 1880
William Brown   *Indianapolis Journal*, November 28, 1880
With Her Face

In addition to the above, the following are printed in the notes to this volume:

P. 543, The Circus Season (prose), including poem beginning, "Season of myths and monster circuses"; previously in *Indianapolis Journal*, May 14, 1881

P. 549, an 8-line poem which had appeared earlier in advertisements for the Apollo Player Piano in the Indianapolis—and probably other—newspapers (see *Indianapolis News*, October 10, 1908, where it is entitled: "Lines Penned on an Apollo | To Melville Clark—With Another Order")

P. 549, The Old Fiddler (prose), previously in the *Indianapolis Journal*, August 20, 1881

## VOL. III

COLLATION: [1–36]⁸.

PAGINATION: Fly title, p. [i]; blank, p. [ii]; frontispiece with tissue guard (inserted); title-page, p. [iii]; copyright notice with final date 1913 and imprint of Braunworth & Co., p. [iv]; table of contents, pp. [v–xi]; blank, p. [xii]; half-title, p. [xiii]; blank, p. [xiv]; text, pp. 1–497; blank, p. [498]; divisional half-title, p. [499]; blank, p. [500]; *Notes*, pp. 501–568; blank, pp. [569–570].

ILLUSTRATIONS: Frontispiece: sepia portrait of Riley, by Steele, with tissue guard, inserted. Also inserted are the following plates: opposite pp. 176, 358, 426; between pp. 72 and 73 (3 plates on 2 leaves), between pp. 250 and 251 (3 plates on 2 leaves), between pp. 266 and 267 (2 plates on 1 leaf), between pp. 290 and 291 (2 plates on 1 leaf), between pp. 480 and 481 (1 plate on a folded sheet).

CONTENTS: The following had not appeared previously in a Riley book:

As We Read Burns   *Saturday Herald (Indianapolis)*, April 18, 1885
Autographic

The Earthquake    *Indianapolis Journal,* September 5, 1886 (caption: The Earthquake; title: Charleston)
Her Light Guitar    *Life,* March 15, 1883
Lewis D. Hayes    *Indianapolis Journal,* December 30, 1886
Lord Bacon    *Indianapolis Journal,* April 12, 1885
To James Newton Matthews    *Saturday Herald (Indianapolis),* November 21, 1885 (with title: Par Nobile Fratrum)
Which Ane    *Indianapolis Journal,* January 31, 1886

In the notes to this volume, on p. 540, appears the second (and last) stanza of "The Dead Leader." The first stanza was used as the last stanza of "Grant" (see *The Days Gone By* [1895], p. 61 of this bibliography). "The Dead Leader" had appeared in the *Indianapolis Journal,* July 26, 1885.

## VOL. IV

COLLATION: [1–36]⁸.

PAGINATION: Fly title, p. [i]; blank, p. [ii]; frontispiece with tissue guard (inserted); title-page, p. [iii]; copyright notice with final date 1913 and imprint of Braunworth & Co., p. [iv]; table of contents, pp. [v–xi]; blank, p. [xii]; half-title, p. [xiii]; blank, p. [xiv]; text, pp. 1–483; blank, p. [484]; divisional half-title, p. [485]; blank, p. [486]; *Notes,* pp. 487–560; blank, pp. [561–562].

ILLUSTRATIONS: Frontispiece in sepia: Vawter illustration from *A Child-World,* with tissue guard, inserted. Also inserted are the following plates: opposite pp. 110, 206, 312, 454, 482; between pp. 354 and 355 (2 plates on 1 leaf), between pp. 412 and 413 (2 plates on 1 leaf).

CONTENTS: The following had not appeared previously in a Riley book:
Christmas Greeting    *World (New York),* December 25, 1890
God's Mercy
The Gudewife    *Lippincott's Monthly Magazine,* January, 1892
John Boyle O'Reilly    *Indianapolis Journal,* August 17, 1890
Little Maid-o'-Dreams    *Ladies' Home Journal,* February, 1896
Meredith Nicholson    *Indianapolis Journal,* September 7, 1890
Mrs. Benjamin Harrison    *Indianapolis News,* October 25, 1892; *Mrs. Benjamin Harrison,* by Harriet McIntire Foster (1908) (title in both: Mrs. Harrison)
Rosamond C. Bailey    *Indianapolis News,* October 1, 1892
Tennyson    *Indianapolis News,* October 6, 1892; *Critic,* October 15, 1892
To Almon Keefer    *Hancock Democrat,* December 24, 1895(?)

To Elizabeth  *Mrs. Charles E. Coffin* (1893?) (with title: Elizabeth; see p. 175)

To Rudyard Kipling

To—"The J. W. R. Literary Club"  *Dawn* (Indianapolis High School No. 1), May 6, 1893

In addition to the above, the following are printed in the notes:

P. 498, Science and Poetry (prose), previously in *Indianapolis Journal*, June 30, 1881

P. 502, Just a Fiddler, previously in *Indianapolis Journal*, April 18, 1880

P. 514, The Common Patriot (prose), previously in *Chicago Times*, October 9, 1891

P. 518, Trillpipe on Puns (prose), previously in *Indianapolis Journal*, September 15, 1881

P. 536, letter in rhyme, without title, addressed to Benjamin S. Parker, which had appeared in the *Indianapolis Journal*, February 20, 1883 (with title: An Open Letter | To Ben S. Parker)

P. 542, From Pad to Verse, previously in blotting pad, Indianapolis Flower Mission Souvenir (1895) (see p. 157)

P. 545, poem without title, beginning: "Dear singing friend, your genial rhyme" written for Mrs. D. M. Jordan *ca.* 1885. It had appeared in the *Indianapolis Journal*, February 9, 1885. The same poem, in broadside form, was used by Riley as a card of appreciation of poems written in honor of his birthday, October 7, 1913.

P. 547, prose tribute, without title, to Edgar Wilson Nye, beginning: "Especially favored, as for years I have been, with close personal acquaintance"

## VOL. V

COLLATION: [1–32]⁸.

PAGINATION: Fly title, p. [i]; blank, p. [ii]; frontispiece with tissue guard (inserted); title-page, p. [iii]; copyright notice with final date 1913, and imprint of Braunworth & Co., p. [iv]; table of contents, pp. [v–xii]; half-title, p. [xiii]; blank, p. [xiv]; text, pp. 1–437; blank, p. [438]; divisional half-title, p. [439]; blank, p. [440]; *Notes*, pp. 441–493; blank, pp. [494–498].

ILLUSTRATIONS: Frontispiece: sepia portrait of Riley, from a crayon sketch by John Cecil Clay, with tissue guard, inserted. Also inserted are the following plates: opposite pp. 72, 148, 210, 280, 360, 424.

CONTENTS: The following had not appeared previously in a Riley book:

Abe Martin  *Indianapolis News*, May 12, 1906 (with title: To Kin Hubbard—The Father of His Countryman, Abe Martin); *Abe Martin of Brown County, Indiana*, by Kin Hubbard (1906) (with title: To Kin Hubbard)

America's Thanksgiving  *World* (*New York*) (*supplement*), November 25, 1900

Art and Poetry  *Indianapolis News*, January 27, 1904; *Reader Magazine*, March, 1904 (without title)

Benjamin Harrison  No previous appearance located save as part of "The Tribute of His Home" in *Indianapolis News*, October 27, 1908; and same in: *The Addresses . . . on . . . the Unveiling . . . of the Statue of Benjamin Harrison* (1909)

Claude Matthews  *Indianapolis Journal*, August 30, 1898

The Highest Good  Annual [of] *Shortridge High School*, 1912 (without title, addressed: To the Shortridge High School Seniors, 1912)

John Clark Ridpath  *Indianapolis Press*, January 21, 1901 (without title)

Lee O. Harris | Christmas Day—1909  *Indianapolis Star*, December 27, 1909

"Mona Machree"

A Motto  *Indianapolis Press*, December 9, 1894 (with facsimile); *James Whitcomb Riley in Prose and Picture* (1903), in facsimile, without title

My Conscience  *Century Magazine*, July, 1913

New Year's Nursery Jingle

O. Henry  *Rolling Stones*, by O. Henry (1912)

Old Indiany

To a Poet on His Marriage

To Frank L. Stanton  *Atlanta Constitution*, August 5, 1901

To Lesley  *Indianapolis Journal*, February 19, 1899

To My Sister

To the Boy with a Country

To the Mother  *Indianapolis Journal*, December 29, 1901

To the Quiet Observer  *The Quiet Observer*, May 3, 1900; *Pittsburgh Gazette*, March 16, 1904

William McKinley  *Indianapolis News*, September 30, 1907

William Pinkney Fishback  *Indianapolis Journal*, January 17, 1901

In addition to the above, the following are printed in the notes to this volume:

P. 474, A Manhattan Christmas Voice

P. 483, two poems, without title, written for Dr. Joseph Eastman. One begins: "Take the best man ever wuz"; the other begins: "First laureate of humanity,"

## VOL. VI

COLLATION: [1–37]⁸, [38]².

PAGINATION: Blank, pp. [i–ii]; fly title, p. [iii]; blank, p. [iv]; frontispiece with tissue guard (inserted); title-page, p. [v]; copyright notice with final date 1913, and imprint of Braunworth & Co., p. [vi]; table of contents, p. [vii]; blank, p. [viii]; half-title, p. [ix]; blank, p. [x]; text, pp. 1–396; divisional half-title, p. [397]; blank, p. [398]; *Notes*, pp. 399–408; divisional half-title, p. [409]; blank, p. [410]; table of contents for bibliography, p. [411]; blank, p. [412]; bibliography, pp. 413–467; blank, p. [468]; divisional half-title, p. [469]; blank, p. [470]; indexes, pp. 471–586.

ILLUSTRATIONS: Frontispiece: sepia portrait of Riley from a photograph, with tissue guard, inserted. Also inserted are the following plates: opposite pp. 80, 154, 230, 310.

CONTENTS: The following not previously in a Riley book:
A Caller from Boone (prose)
Dreams (prose)   *Kokomo Tribune*, May 24, 1879
Ez (prose)   *Indianapolis Journal*, May 23, 1880
The Judkins Papers (prose)   Previous partial appearances as follows:
  Father and Son—In: *Indianapolis Journal*, September 10, 1881
    (with title: Mr. Trillpipe at Home)
  Judkins' Boy on the Mud-Turtle—In: *Life*, March 29, 1883
  On Frogs—In: *Anderson Democrat*, July 20, 1877* (with title:
    Trillpipe's Boy on Frogs); *Life*, April 5, 1883 (with title:
    Judkins' Boy on Frogs)
  On Piruts—In: *Life*, April 19, 1883 (with title: Judkins' Boy)
  On Hackmens—In: *Life*, May 17, 1883 (with title: Judkins' Boy)
  On Dudes—In: *Life*, May 31, 1883 (with title: Judkins' Boy)
  On Red Hair—In: *Life*, June 7, 1883 (with title: Judkins' Boy)
  The Cross-Eyed Girl—In: *Indianapolis Journal*, August 22, 1881
  Homesickness—In: *Indianapolis Journal*, August 27, 1881
The Object Lesson (prose)
The Old Soldier's Story (prose)   *Ninety-Second Anniversary Celebration of the New England Society in the City of New York*, December 22, 1897 (without title)

---

*Not seen except as a clipping with manuscript identification.

# Riley Songs of Friendship

RILEY | SONGS OF FRIENDSHIP | JAMES WHITCOMB RILEY | WITH PICTURES BY | WILL VAWTER | INDIANAPOLIS | THE BOBBS-MERRILL COMPANY | PUBLISHERS

COLLATION: [1–12]⁸. Leaf measures 7½″ x 5⅛″, all edges trimmed. Printed on white plate paper.

PAGINATION: End paper, white wove; blank, pp. [i–ii]; fly title, p. [iii]; blank, pp. [iv–v]; frontispiece, p. [vi]; title-page, p. [vii]; copyright notice with final date 1915, and imprint of Braunworth & Co., p. [viii]; dedication *To Young E. Allison—Bookman*, p. [ix]; blank, p. [x]; proem, p. [xi]; blank, p. [xii]; table of contents, pp. xv–xvi (should be xiii–xiv); list of illustrations, pp. xvii–xix (should be xv–xvii); blank, p. [xviii]; half-title, p. [xix]; blank, p. [xx]; text, pp. [23]–[190] (should be 21–188); blank leaf; one page of advertisements; one blank page; end paper.

ILLUSTRATIONS: The frontispiece and all other full-page illustrations are integral parts of the book, unnumbered but figured in the pagination. Headpieces and tailpieces appear throughout.

BINDING: Green vertically-ribbed cloth. Front cover bears design of two boys and a tree stamped in black and gilt. Below the design is stamped in gilt: RILEY | SONGS OF FRIENDSHIP all within a blind-stamped border rule. Spine gilt-stamped: [*double rule*] | RILEY | SONGS | OF | FRIEND- | SHIP | [*design of a fireplace in black and gilt*] | BOBBS-MERRILL | [*double rule*] Back cover blank.

PUBLICATION DATE: Published August 27, 1915, according to the publishers' statement in the Copyright Office. Deposited for copyright August 30, 1915. A presentation copy, from the author to the dedicatee, bears an inscription dated September 17, 1915. The book was advertised in the *Publishers' Weekly*, September 25, 1915; earliest local advertisement is in the *Indianapolis News*, October 5, 1915.

PUBLICATION PRICE: $1.25.*

---

*The book was advertised in the *Indianapolis News*, December 16, 1915, as available in cloth, $1.25; leather, $2.00. The latter is unlocated.

NOTES: The book was recopyrighted in 1921 with some changes but with no added first edition material.

CONTENTS: Only 5 of the poems are here first collected:
A Hobo Voluntary*
Uncle Sidney to Marcellus
A Song by Uncle Sidney
The Poet's Love for the Children†
James B. Maynard   *Indianapolis Sentinel*, September 14, 1902
What "Old Santa" Overheard   *Collier's*, December 12, 1914

The dedicatory poem, "To Young E. Allison—Bookman," had appeared previously as part of "Three Several Birds." The proem had appeared under the title, "Unknown Friends."

---

*According to Bliss Carman in the *Indianapolis Star*, November 11, 1914, Riley had set music (the chant of the old stagecoach drivers) to "The Hobo Voluntary" and had sold it to one of the "leading magazines" where it would appear within the next few months. So far the magazine appearance has not been located.

†The first stanza of this poem had appeared in the *Biographical Edition*, Vol. 3, p. 503, in notes to "Longfellow's Love for the Children."

# 1915

# The Old Soldier's Story

THE | OLD SOLDIER'S STORY | Poems and Prose Sketches | JAMES WHITCOMB RILEY | [*open book*] | INDIANAPOLIS | THE BOBBS-MERRILL COMPANY | PUBLISHERS

COLLATION: [1–13]⁸, [14]⁴. Leaf measures 7″ full x 4¾″, all edges trimmed, top edge gilt. Printed on white wove paper.

PAGINATION: End paper, white wove; fly title, p. [i]; blank, p. [ii]; title-page, p. [iii]; copyright notice with final date 1915 and imprint of Braunworth & Co., p. [iv]; dedication to George Thompson, p. [v]; blank, p. [vi]; table of contents, pp. [vii–ix]; blank, p. [x]; half-title, p. [xi]; blank, p. [xii]; text, pp. 1–[202]; blank, pp. [203–204]; end paper.

ILLUSTRATIONS: None.*

BINDING: Red cloth†. Front cover stamped in gilt within a blind-stamped single rule border: THE OLD SOLDIER'S STORY | BY JAMES WHITCOMB RILEY   Spine extra gilt-stamped with decorative design of vine-like scrolls, single rule at top, lettered within single rules: THE OLD | SOLDIER'S | STORY | [*ornament*] | RILEY   and, at foot of spine, between single rules: BOBBS-MERRILL   Back cover blank. Binding uniform with *A Child-World* (1897).

Also noted with spine unstamped but for the following, in gilt: THE OLD | SOLDIER'S | STORY | [*ornament*] | RILEY | BOBBS | MERRILL

PUBLICATION DATE: October 23, 1915, according to the publishers' statement in the Copyright Office. Deposited for copyright October 27, 1915. Advertised in the *Indianapolis News*, December 16, 1915.

PUBLICATION PRICE: $1.25.†

---

*The advertisement in the *Indianapolis News*, December 16, 1915, mentions a frontispiece, but thus far no examined copy has this feature.

†The publishers advertised the book in the *Indianapolis News*, December 16, 1915 as in red cloth, $1.25; limp leather, $1.50. No limp leather copy has been located.

NOTES: The book contains numerous type imperfections. The same imperfections are common to all copies examined, including the copyright deposit copy.

CONTENTS: Only one poem herein is a first appearance in a Riley book:

George A. Carr*    *Indianapolis Star*, July 22, 1914

---

*This poem, printed on a slip of paper, 5½″ x 3½″, is mounted on an inserted leaf in Vol. 6 of Mr. Edmund Henry Eitel's copy of the *Elizabeth Marine Riley Edition* (q.v.). It bears a note, "Hitherto unpublished in book form." It is not present in the other sets of this edition so far examined.

# 1916

## The Hoosier Book

The Hoosier Book | Containing Poems in Dialect | By | James Whitcomb Riley | Collected and Arranged by | Hewitt Hanson Howland | INDIANAPOLIS | THE BOBBS-MERRILL COMPANY | PUBLISHERS

COLLATION: [1–19]¹⁶. Leaf measures 6⅛″ x 4⅜″, all edges gilt. Printed on India paper.

PAGINATION: End paper, white wove; fly title, p. [i]; blank, p. [ii]; title-page, p. [iii]; copyright notice with final date 1916, and imprint of Braunworth & Co., p. [iv]; dedication *To Johnty*, p. [v]; blank, p. [vi]; introduction, pp. [vii–viii] (signed *H.H.H.*); half-title, p. [ix]; blank, p. [x]; text, pp. 1–572; divisional title-page, p. [573]; blank, p. [574]; divisional half-title, p. [575]; blank, p. [576]; indexes, pp. 577–598; end paper.

ILLUSTRATIONS: None.

BINDING: Blue cloth. Front cover gilt-stamped within gilt ornamental border: The Hoosier Book | of | Riley Verse   Spine gilt-stamped: [*ornamental rule*] | The | Hoosier | Book | [*rule*] | Riley | Bobbs | Merrill | [*ornamental rule*]   Back cover has ornamental border blind-stamped.

Also issued in limp black morocco with rounded corners; single rule border blind-stamped on both covers; front cover lettered in gilt: The Hoosier Book | of Riley Verse   The spine has a single rule blind-stamped at top and bottom and the following gilt-stamped: The | Hoosier | Book | [*rule*] | Riley   The end papers are black coated on white and a fly leaf is present both front and back.

Both bindings were available at time of publication.

PUBLICATION DATE: Advertised in the *Publishers' Weekly*, September 23, 1916. Published October 25, 1916, according to the publishers' statement in the Copyright Office. Deposited for copyright October 28, 1916.

PUBLICATION PRICE: Cloth, $2.00; limp morocco, $3.00.

NOTES: Uniform with *The Lockerbie Book* (1911).

A later state of the cloth-bound book has the ornamental border on the front cover blind-stamped; edges ungilded; statement added to copyright page: *Printed in the United States of America.*

CONTENTS: Contains only one poem not previously in a Riley book:

A Happy Dream*    *Indianapolis News,* July 25, 1916

---

*This poem is said to be the last one written by Riley. According to the story (see *Indianapolis News,* July 25, 1916) a little girl, Cornelia Allison, had sent him a poem on June 26, 1916. It delighted him, and as soon as he had read it he sat down and wrote one for her, using her title.

# 1916

# Memorial Edition

Memorial Edition | [*rule*] | James Whitcomb Riley's | Complete Works | Including Poems and Prose Sketches, many of which have | not heretofore been published; an authentic Biog- | raphy, an elaborate Index and numerous | Illustrations in color from Paintings | by Howard Chandler Christy | and Ethel Franklin Betts | In Ten Volumes [*in orange*] | Publishers | The Bobbs-Merrill Company | Indianapolis    New York | 1916
[Note: The foregoing appears within a tinted floral border.]

This collection of Riley's works* is the same as the *Biographical Edition* (1913), except that the sketch of Riley's life (by Edmund Henry Eitel), at the end of Vol. I, is altered slightly and includes more data, chiefly relating to the close of the poet's life; ten poems have been added, of which seven make first appearances in a Riley book. These previously uncollected poems appear in Volumes V, VII and IX.

## VOL. V

COLLATION: [1–18]⁸. Leaf measures 8⅜" x 5¾", all edges gilt. Printed on white wove paper.

PAGINATION: End paper, white moiré-finished paper; fly leaf; frontispiece with tissue guard (inserted); title-page (inserted; copyright notice with final date 1916, on verso); table of contents, pp. [i–iv]; text, pp. 1141–1422; blank, pp. [1423–1424]; fly leaf; end paper.

ILLUSTRATIONS: Colored frontispiece by Howard Chandler Christy, reprinted from a plate used in an earlier Riley book, with tissue guard, inserted. The inserted title-page, decorated with a tinted floral border, is of plate paper. Other illustrations, by Christy and Ethel Franklin Betts, all reprints, are inserted opposite pp. 1164, 1170, 1186, 1286, 1364, 1416.

---

*Reissued in 1917 by Harper & Brothers (under a contract dated August 1, 1917), with the title: *Memorial Edition: The Complete Works of James Whitcomb Riley in Ten Volumes. . .* A Collier edition appeared in 1931. Some sheets of the Harper edition were used by Colliers, with the Collier imprint on the binding.

BINDING: Full maroon morocco; single rule border blind-stamped on front and back covers which are otherwise unstamped. Spine lettered in gilt: JAMES | WHITCOMB | RILEY'S | COMPLETE | WORKS | VOLUME V [VII, IX] | MEMORIAL | EDITION   There is also an arrangement of sunflowers and horizontal rules blind-stamped on the spine.

Also issued in cloth; and, half morocco.*

PUBLICATION DATE: December 6, 1916, according to the publishers' statement in the Copyright Office. Deposited for copyright December 9, 1916.

PUBLICATION PRICE*: Cloth, $19.50; half morocco, $27.50; morocco, $35.00.

CONTENTS: Volume V contains one poem which makes a first appearance in a Riley book:
Youth and Age   *Collier's*, April 22, 1916; *Indianapolis News*, April 17, 1916 (with statement: "Reprinted from *Collier's Weekly*")

## VOL. VII

COLLATION: [1–16]⁸, [17]⁶.

PAGINATION: End paper (same as Vol. V); fly leaf; frontispiece with tissue guard (inserted); title-page (inserted; copyright notice with final date 1916, on verso); table of contents, pp. [i–iii]; blank, p. [iv]; text, pp. 1705–1965; blank, pp. [1966–1968]; fly leaf; end paper.

ILLUSTRATIONS: Colored frontispiece, by Ethel Franklin Betts, reprinted from a plate used in an earlier Riley book, with tissue guard, inserted. Other illustrations, by Betts and Howard Chandler Christy, all reprints, are inserted opposite pp. 1724, 1760, 1864, 1954.

CONTENTS: Volume VII contains one poem which makes a first appearance in a Riley book:
St. Lirriper   *Phoenix*, May, 1915†

## VOL. IX

COLLATION: [1–17]⁸, [18]⁴.

PAGINATION: End paper (same as Vol. V); fly leaf; frontispiece with tissue guard (inserted); title-page (inserted; copyright notice with final

---

*According to the *United States Catalog Supplement, Books Published 1912–1917*.
†Not seen, but it had appeared herein according to a footnote in the *Phoenix* of September, 1916.

date 1916 on verso); table of contents, pp. [i–ii]; text, pp. 2239–2516; fly leaf; end paper.

ILLUSTRATIONS: Colored frontispiece, by Ethel Franklin Betts, reprinted from plate used in an earlier Riley book, with tissue guard, inserted. Other illustrations, by Howard Chandler Christy and Will Vawter, all reprints, are inserted opposite pp. 2254, 2348, 2364, 2486.

CONTENTS: Volume IX contains 5 poems not previously collected:
Something   *Collier's*, December 25, 1915
A Christmas-Time Jingle   *Indianapolis Journal*, December 14, 1890
    (in advertisement for The When, with title: The Babes in the
    When)
When Baby Played   *Collier's*, November 27, 1915
When Baby Slept   *Collier's*, April 3, 1915
When Baby Woke   *Collier's*, April 3, 1915

## 1922

# Love Letters of the Bachelor Poet

LOVE LETTERS [*in red*] | OF | THE BACHELOR POET | JAMES WHITCOMB RILEY | TO | MISS ELIZABETH KAHLE | NOW FIRST PRINTED FROM THE ORIGINALS | WITH NUMEROUS FACSIMILES | [*Bibliophile Society's insignia, in green*] | PRIVATELY PRINTED, EXCLUSIVELY FOR | MEMBERS OF | THE BIBLIOPHILE SOCIETY [*in red*] | BOSTON—MCMXXII

COLLATION: 4 unsigned leaves, [1–20]⁴, 4 unsigned leaves. Leaf measures 8¾" x 6½", top edge gilt, other edges untrimmed. Printed on white Strathmore and Alexandra papers, both used within the same book.

PAGINATION: 4 blank leaves, the first being the lining paper; fly title, p. [i]; blank, p. [ii]; engraved colophon (inserted); frontispiece, with tissue guard printed in red (inserted); title-page, p. [iii]; copyright notice with date 1922, p. [iv]; *Foreword* signed *H. H. H.*, pp. 9–18 (should be v–xiv); half-title, p. [xv]; blank, p. [xvi]; text, pp. 19–161 (should be 17–159); blank page; 4 blank leaves, the last being the terminal lining paper.

ILLUSTRATIONS: Plates inserted as follows: engraved colophon on ivory-finished paper, following the fly title; frontispiece: two pictures of Riley and facsimile of a manuscript, with tissue guard printed in red; facsimiles and portraits (the plate opposite p. 154 and the portraits have tissue guards) opposite pp.* 46, 64, 84, 104, 154; between pp. 16 and 17 (4 plates on 2 leaves† with 3 tissue guards), between pp. 20 and 21 (12 plates on 6 leaves), between pp. 72 and 73 (6 leaves), between pp. 102 and 103 (6 plates on 3 leaves), between pp. 106 and 107 (4 leaves), between pp. 142 and 143 (2 leaves).

BINDING: Light tan boards with pumpkin-colored pebbled cloth shelfback. Spine stamped in gilt: LOVE | LETTERS | OF | JAMES | WHITCOMB | RILEY | [*Bibliophile Society's insignia*] | THE | BIBLIOPHILE | SOCIETY Both covers blank.

---

*References according to the printed pagination.
†Facsimile of the "New Year's Greeting of the Carriers of the Indianapolis Daily Journal. 1881."

PUBLICATION DATE: September 20, 1922, according to the statement of The Bibliophile Society in the Copyright Office. Deposited for copyright October 10, 1922.

NOTES: The colophon states that only 475 copies were printed, for members of The Bibliophile Society. Each copy was issued in a light tan board slip case with cloth top and bottom and with paper label on back.

CONTENTS: The letters herein had not been published previously. The foreword concludes with the following paragraph:

"In a sworn statement which accompanies the letters, their former owner declares that they have been in her possession ever since she received them; that none of them have ever been published, and that not more than ten persons—mostly her family and close friends—have ever read the originals. The Bibliophile Society was indeed fortunate in acquiring possession of this treasure-trove, which was accomplished through the kind mediation of one of our members, Mr. John Needels Chester, of Pittsburgh, who procured them for us direct from their owner."

The poem on p. 27, "Mine: An Extravaganza," is a combination of two poems: the first 39 lines had appeared in the *Indianapolis Journal*, February 4, 1879, as part of the poem, "Of the Whole World, Mine," and these lines were later altered and incorporated in *The Flying Islands of the Night* (1892); "Of the Whole World, Mine" appears in the *Biographical Edition*, Vol. 1 (1913), *Notes*, p. 441. The last 4 stanzas of "Mine: An Extravaganza" had appeared in the *Indianapolis Journal*, February 16, 1878, with the title "Dream," collected in the *Homestead Edition*, Vol. 6 (1898).

Spirit messages, allegedly from Riley, received by Mrs. Brunn (*née* Elizabeth Kahle) through a medium, appear on pp. 154–160. These include a poem, "After Death," pp. 154–155, together with a facsimile of the slate upon which the poem was written. The editor, on p. 160, makes the following statement regarding the messages: "As to what, if any, part Riley's spirit took in dictating these lines, or any of the preceding verses, is a question upon which the opinions of readers may differ; but certainly all must agree that he could hardly have written such mediocre verse while in his mortal state."

# 1930

# Letters of James Whitcomb Riley

LETTERS | of | James Whitcomb Riley | [*red rule*] | Edited by William Lyon Phelps | [*red bee*] | Illustrated | [*red rule*] | THE BOBBS-MERRILL COMPANY | Publishers [*dot*] Indianapolis
[Note: All of the foregoing enclosed by a red single rule box.]

COLLATION: [1–23]⁸, [24]⁴. Leaf measures 9⅜" x 6¼", top edge trimmed, other edges untrimmed. Printed on cream-colored laid paper.

PAGINATION: End paper, same as book stock; fly title, p. [i]; blank, p. [ii]; frontispiece (inserted); title-page, p. [iii]; copyright notice with final date 1930, with statements: *First Edition* and *Printed in the United States of America*, also imprint of Braunworth & Co., p. [iv]; *Acknowledgement*, p. [v]; blank, p. [vi]; tables of contents, pp. [vii–xvi]; list of illustrations, p. [xvii]; blank, p. [xviii]; half-title, p. [xix]; blank, p. [xx]; foreword, pp. 1–9 (signed *William Lyon Phelps* and dated *7 April 1930*); text, pp. 10–322; *Afterword*, pp. 323–326 (signed *W. L. P.*); divisional half-title, p. [327]; blank, p. [328]; appendix, pp. 329–335; blank, p. [336]; divisional half-title, p. [337]; blank, p. [338]; index, pp. 339–349; blank, pp. [350–356]; end paper.

ILLUSTRATIONS: Frontispiece, halftone from the portrait of Riley by John Singer Sargent, inserted. Also inserted are the following plates: opposite pp. 74, 120, 166, 212, 318; between pp. 28 and 29 (2 plates on 1 leaf), between pp. 256 and 257 (2 plates on 1 leaf), and between pp. 292 and 293 (2 plates on 1 leaf).

BINDING: Dark red twilled, silk-finished cloth. Border rule blind-stamped on front cover, which is otherwise unstamped. Spine gilt-stamped: Letters | of | JAMES | WHITCOMB | RILEY | Edited | by | WILLIAM | LYON | PHELPS | BOBBS | MERRILL  Back cover blank.

PUBLICATION DATE: November 3, 1930, according to publishers' statement in the Copyright Office. A review in the *Indianapolis Sunday Star*, November 9, 1930, states that the letters "will be issued in book form tomorrow." Deposited for copyright November 17, 1930.

PUBLICATION PRICE: $5.00.

NOTES: The letters, pp. 10–322, cover the period from 1876 to 1915.

Most of them here make first appearances in print; a few had previously appeared in the Marcus Dickey books, in Bliss Carman's *James Whitcomb Riley: An Essay* (1918), and other books (see *Contributions*, pp. 183, 188).

The contents are grouped under nine chapter headings, with subtitles and with notes identifying persons, books and poems mentioned in the letters. The appendix contains letters to Riley from Mark Twain, Rudyard Kipling and others; also a letter from W. D. Howells to Meredith Nicholson and one from George Ade to D. L. Chambers, about Riley. In addition to the notes, William Lyon Phelps contributed the foreword and afterword.

The following uncollected poems are included in the letters:

Honest Old Sam Hungerford    p. 123

Thanksgiving    p. 222    *Omaha World-Herald*, November 21, 1897; *Robert J. Burdette: His Message*, ed. by Clara B. Burdette (1922), p. 174

[Without title, beginning:]

"Being a Jimpsy-jumpsy boy"    p. 301    *Harper's Monthly Magazine*, December, 1917

"Fame, says I, go 'way from *me*"    p. 192

"It is the lecture agent"    p. 62

"Miss Medairy Dory-Ann"    p. 255    *Harper's Monthly Magazine*, December, 1917

"Our teacher Miss King"    p. 255

"Rain! Rain! Rain!"    p. 10

"Sister, sister, come and see"    p. 297    *Harper's Monthly Magazine*, December, 1917

"The Devil's feelings e'en were spared"    p. 285

"The first book far too bad to go"    p. 285

"The women came running"    p. 59

"When Dory Ann she gave a tea"    p. 281    *Harper's Monthly Magazine*, December, 1917

"When Shakespeare's voice was heard of old"    p. 135    *New York Morning Journal*, May 1, 1892

"With joy too great for pen to state"    p. 281    *Harper's Monthly Magazine*, December, 1917

"You may break—you may shatter the little"    p. 92    *Pastels of Men*, by Eugene V. Debs (1919); *Debs: His Authorized Life and Letters*, by David Karsner (1919)

Note: The poem beginning: "Peace kindo' sorto' suits my diet," included in the letter to Samuel L. Clemens, at p. 54, is the last stanza of "Thoughts on the Late War," first collected in *Poems Here at Home* (1893).

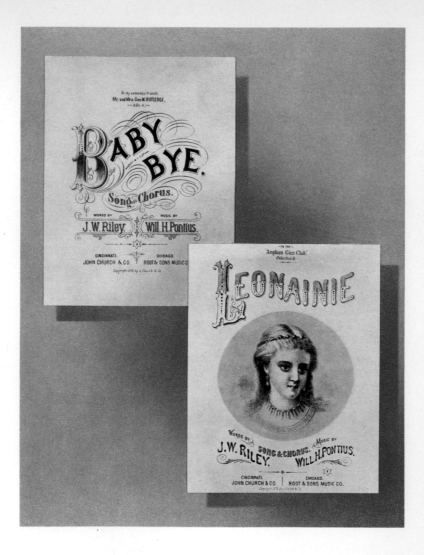

# Ephemeral Publications

## 1879
## Leonainie

TO THE | "Amphion Glee Club," | Columbus, O. | LEONAINIE | [*girl's head*] | SONG & CHORUS. | WORDS BY | J. W. RILEY. | MUSIC BY | WILL. H. PONTIUS. | 4 | CINCINNATI. | JOHN CHURCH & CO. | CHICAGO. | ROOT & SONS MUSIC CO. | Copyright, 1879 by J. Church & Co.

[Note: The alignment of the above wording on the front cover is not indicated exactly. For the alignment and the decorations see illustration opposite p. 146]

COLLATION: Sheet music. A single sheet folded to make 4 pages, with a leaf loosely inserted. Leaf measures 14″ x 10¾″, all edges trimmed.

PAGINATION: Front cover, p. [1]; blank, p. [2]; words and music, pp. 3–5 (pp. 3–4 on the inserted leaf); blank, p. [6].

[Note: The plate number, 2842–4, appears at foot of pp. 4 and 5.]

PUBLICATION DATE: Deposited in the Copyright Office March 14, 1879.

PUBLICATION PRICE: 40c.

NOTES: The poem, "Leonainie," had appeared in the *Kokomo Dispatch*, August 2, 1877, signed E. A. P., in the famous "Poe hoax"* which led to a furor of criticism and world-wide publication of the poem in periodicals. It was first collected in *Armazindy* (1894).

---

*Many accounts of the hoax have been published. Riley's own story of it is told in some of his letters. His letter of July 23, 1877, to J. Oscar Henderson, proposing the hoax, appears in *The Youth of James Whitcomb Riley* by Marcus Dickey (1919),

# 1879

# Baby Bye

To my esteemed friends, | Mr. and Mrs. Geo. W. RUTLEDGE, | Ada, O. | BABY | BYE. | Song AND Chorus. | WORDS BY | J. W. RILEY. | MUSIC BY | WILL. H. PONTIUS. | 3 | CINCINNATI. | JOHN CHURCH & CO. | CHICAGO. | ROOT & SONS MUSIC CO. | Copyright 1879 by J. Church & Co.

[Note: The alignment of the above wording on the front cover is not indicated exactly. For the alignment and the decorations see illustration opposite p. 146]

COLLATION: Sheet music. A single sheet folded to make 4 pages, with a leaf loosely inserted. Leaf measures 14″ x 10⅝″, all edges trimmed.

PAGINATION: Front cover, p. [1]; blank, p. [2]; words and music, pp. 3–5 (pp. 3–4 on the inserted leaf); blank, p. [6].

[Note: The plate number, 3230–4, appears at foot of pp. 4 and 5.]

PUBLICATION DATE: Deposited in the Copyright Office July 2, 1879.

PUBLICATION PRICE: 30c.

---

p. 372, and in *Letters of James Whitcomb Riley* edited by William Lyon Phelps (1930), p. 14. His letter of October 25, 1877, to John M. Anderson, appears in the *Cincinnati Commercial*, November 5, 1877, and in *Letters of James Whitcomb Riley* edited by William Lyon Phelps, p. 16. Another letter, March 15, 1879, to Miss Elizabeth Kahle, appears in *Love Letters of the Bachelor Poet* (1922), p. 38; one to Charles B. Foote, November 22, 1886, is in the *Biographical Edition* (1913), Vol. 1, p. 431 (also, in full with introductory phrase, in *Letters of James Whitcomb Riley* edited by William Lyon Phelps, p. 63). In the latter book appears also, at p. 144, a letter to John Patterson, October 24, 1891, and, at p. 163, one to Miss Helen Carter. All of these deal with "Leonainie" in the words of the author. He also discussed it in interviews reported in *McClure's Magazine*, February, 1894, p. 226; *Cincinnati Commercial Gazette*, December 9, 1894; *Indianapolis News*, September 20, 1902; *Indianapolis Star*, July 20, 1903; *Indianapolis Sentinel*, April 13, 1904.

Riley wrote two parodies of "Leonainie," one with the same title, beginning, " 'Leonainie'—Riley named her," published anonymously in the *Saturday Herald* (*Indianapolis*), September 1, 1877. The other, entitled "Leoloony," appeared anonymously in the *Kokomo Tribune* on the same day. Contemporary correspondence identifies Riley as the author of both. Other parodies of the poem are not his.

Paul G. Henderson, son of J. O. Henderson, is preparing for publication a detailed and documented story of the hoax.

*Printed a few slips like this to send to exchanges. Good scheme, eh?*

### THIS MAN JONES.

This man Jones was what you'd call
A feller as hed no sand at all;
Kindo' consumpted, and undersize,
And sailor-complected, with big sad eyes,
And a kind-of-a sort-of-a hang-dog style,
And a sneakin' sort-of-a half-way smile
That kindo' give him away to us
As a preacher, maybe, or somepin' wuss.

Didn't take with the gang—well, no—
But still we managed to use him, though—
Coddin' the gilley along the route,
And drivin' the stakes that he pulled out;—
For I was one of the bosses then,
And of course stood in with the canvasmen—
And the way we put up jobs, you know,
On this man Jones jes' beat the show!

Used to rattle him scandalous,
And keep the feller a-dodgin' us,
And a-shyin' round jes' skeered to death,
And afeerd to whimper above his breath;
Give him a cussin', and then a kick,
And then a kind-of-a back-hand lick—
Jes' for the fun of seein' him climb
Around with a head on half the time.

But what was the curioust thing to me,
Was along o' the party—let me see,—
Who was our "Lion Queen" last year?—
Mamzelle Zanty or De La Pierre—
Well, no matter!—a stunnin' mash,
With a red-ripe lip, and a long eye-lash,
And a figure sich as the angels owns—
And one too many for this man Jones.

He'd always wake in the afternoon
As the band waltzed in on the lion tune,
And thar, from the time that she'd go in,
Till she'd back out of the cage agin,
He'd stand shaky and limber-kneed—
'specially when she come to "feed
The beasts raw meat with her naked hand"—
And all that business, you understand.

And it was resky in that den—
For I think she juggled three cubs then,
And a big "green" lion as used to smash
Collar bones for old Frank Nash:
And I reckon now she haint forgot
The afternoon old "Nero" sot
His paws on HER!—but as for me,
Its a sort-of-a mixed-up mystery:—

Kindo' remember an awful roar,
And see her back for the bolted door—
See the cage rock—heerd her call
"God have mercy!"—and that was all—
For thar haint no livin' man can tell
What it's like when a thousand yell
In female tones, and a thousand more
Howl in bass till their throats is sore!

But the keeper said as dragged her out,
They heerd some feller laugh and shout:—
"Save her! Quick! I've got the cuss!"
....And yit she waked and smiled on us—
And we daren't flinch, for the doctor said,
Seein' as this man Jones was dead,
Better to jes' not let her know
Nothin' o' that for a week or so.

—John C. Walker, in the Kokomo TRIBUNE.

*Exchange slip, for distribution to newspapers.*
*Note use of pseudonym*

NOTES: This poem, beginning, "The maple strews the embers of its leaves," had first appeared in the *Indianapolis Journal*, October 20, 1878, under the title, "Lullaby." It was first collected in *Pipes o' Pan at Zekesbury* (1889) under the same title, "Lullaby." In *Rhymes of Childhood* (1891) the poem appeared as "Cradle Song."

It was set to music by Fritz Krull, published Indianapolis, Wulschner-Stewart Co., 1907, as "Lullaby." Under the title "Cradle Song" it was included in *Ten Songs of Childhood*, by Archie A. Mumma: Dayton, Archie A. Mumma & Co., 1913.*

# 1879 (?)

# This Man Jones

THIS MAN JONES.
[n.p., n.d., Kokomo, Ind., 1879?]

A single sheet of white paper, 10¹¹⁄₁₆" x 5⅛", all edges trimmed, verso blank. Contains the poem, "This Man Jones," signed: *John C. Walker, in the Kokomo Tribune*. On the only copy so far seen is a penciled note in what appears to be Riley's early handwriting: "Printed a few slips like this to send to Exchanges. Good scheme, eh?"

This poem appeared in the *Kokomo Tribune*, August 2, 1879; first collected in *Nye & Riley's Railway Guide* (1888).

# 1879 (?)

# Marthy Ellen

MARTHY ELLEN.
[n.p., n. d., Kokomo, Ind., 1879?]

A single sheet of white paper, 8⅞" x 4⅛", all edges trimmed, verso blank. Contains the poem, "Marthy Ellen," signed: *John C. Walker, in Kokomo Tribune*. Probably issued for newspaper exchanges (see "This Man Jones" above).

The poem appeared in the *Kokomo Tribune*, September 6, 1879; first collected in *Pipes o' Pan at Zekesbury* (1889).

---

*For record of an 1896 musical setting see *Biographical Edition*, Vol. 6, p. 461.

# 1880

# New Year's Address

1880. | New Year's Address | FOR | The Carriers | OF THE | Indianapolis Daily Journal. | BAKER & RANDOLPH, PRINTERS, INDIANAPOLIS.

[Note: The foregoing is printed with decorations on the first page; the imprint appears at foot.]

COLLATION: Leaflet, 4 pages. Leaf measures 6⅞" x 5⅜", all edges trimmed. Printed on white paper.

PAGINATION: Title-page, p. [1]; text, pp. [2–3]; blank, p. [4].

ILLUSTRATIONS: Decorations on title-page, at top of p. [2] and at foot of p. [3].

BINDING: Leaflet, 4 pages, without covers.

PUBLICATION DATE: January 1, 1880.*

CONTENTS: A single poem beginning: *O, singer, in these later times;* unsigned, uncollected.

# 1880 (?)

# The Summer-Time

THE SUMMER-TIME.
[n.p., n.d., Kokomo, Ind., 1880?]

A single sheet of white paper, 5⅞" x 3⅞", all edges trimmed, verso blank. Contains the poem, "The Summer-Time," signed: *John C. Walker in the Kokomo Tribune.* Probably issued for newspaper exchanges (see "This Man Jones," p. 149).

This poem appeared in the *Kokomo Tribune,* May 22, 1880; first collected in *Riley Songs of Summer* (1908).

---

*Distributed by the newsboys to their customers who, in conformance with a custom which still persists in some localities, paid whatever sum they felt inclined to give as reward for the year's service.

1880.

New Year's Address

FOR

The Carriers

OF THE

Indianapolis Daily Journal.

BAKER & RANDOLPH, PRINTERS, INDIANAPOLIS.

# [*ca.* 1880]

# "Dot Leedle Poy of Mine"

"DOT LEEDLE POY OF MINE"

A single sheet of white paper, 9¹³⁄₁₆″ x 4⅛″, all edges trimmed, verso blank. Contains the poem, "Dot Leedle Poy of Mine," signed J. W. *Riley.*

Under the title, "Karl Schronz's Christmas Story," signed with Riley's pseudonym, *Jay Whit,* the same poem appeared in the *People* (*Indianapolis*), January 1, 1876. In 1892 it was first collected, in *Green Fields and Running Brooks* (1893), under the title, "Dot Leedle Boy." Both punctuation and spelling underwent considerable revision between the time of newspaper and book appearance, and this undated broadside seems to represent an intermediate state. About 1880 Riley dropped the *J. W. Riley* form and signed himself successively *James W. Riley* and *James Whitcomb Riley.*

# 1881

# New Year's Greeting

NEW YEAR'S GREETING | OF THE | Carriers | OF THE | Indianapolis Daily Journal. | 1881

[The foregoing is printed with decorations on the first page. Below it, with further decorations, appear the first two and a half stanzas of a poem, beginning: *It was the night, ere New Year's night,*]

COLLATION: Leaflet, 4 pages.*

PAGINATION: Title and text, p. [1]; text, pp. [2–4].

ILLUSTRATIONS: Decorations on all four pages.

BINDING: Leaflet, 4 pages, without covers.

---

*The description is from a facsimile in the *Love Letters of the Bachelor Poet* (1922); original unlocated.

PUBLICATION DATE: January 1, 1881.

NOTES: The poem is unsigned and uncollected save in the form of a photographic facsimile in the *Love Letters of the Bachelor Poet* (1922), *q.v.* In the brief account of it that appears on pp. 16–17 of the latter book, it is conjectured that "a very limited number of the leaflets were issued, and owing to the fact that the poem was unsigned, and the further fact that newspaper 'carriers' are not usually gifted with the collector's instinct, it is doubtful if many copies were long preserved." Certainly the leaflet is rare, but probably thousands were printed in order that the carriers might present them to their customers on New Year's day.

# 1890

# A Buckeye Ballad

A BUCKEYE BALLAD | BY | JAMES WHITCOMB RILEY THE HOOSIER POET | COMPLIMENTS OF PASSENGER DEPARTMENT BUCKEYE ROUTE | TALE OF A MILLION

[Printed in brown on front wrapper. With the exception of the last line, all the lettering appears on a printed ribbon; no attempt has been made to indicate the exact position of the wording. All the preceding is from a hand-drawn plate and is decorated with a spray of buckeyes (the illustrator's name below it) and with dots sprinkled throughout the lettering. A train is indicated on a distant landscape.]

SIGNATURES: 10 unnumbered leaves printed on recto only. On each printed page a portion of the poem appears in black, surrounded by illustrations and a portion of the text of "Tale of a Million" in maroon. Leaf measures 6″ full x 9″, all edges trimmed. Printed on white coated paper.

BINDING: Issued in wrappers same as the book stock, trimmed to size of leaf; the front, printed in brown, serves as the title-page. Back cover blank. Inside the front cover, printed in maroon, is the copyright notice with date 1890, the statement *Illustrated By W. H. Mullay* and imprint of the *Ohio State Journal*. Inside the back cover is the imprint, in white on black, of the Columbus, Hocking Valley and Toledo Railway. Through the inner margin of the pamphlet passes a brown ribbon fastened to a buckeye which is stamped *Buckeye Route*.

PUBLICATION DATE: December, 1890. Distributed as a Christmas souvenir by the Passenger Department of the Buckeye Route.

CONTENTS: Single poem, "A Buckeye Ballad," not previously published. The marginal prose sketch, "Tale of a Million," is not by Riley.

"A Buckeye Ballad" was reprinted in the *Cincinnati Commercial*, January 7, 1891, under the title, "Buckeyes." It was later collected in Riley books with twenty lines added at the beginning, under the title, "Old John Clevenger on Buckeyes."

# 1890 (?)

# The Watches of the Night

A poem, without title, beginning: *One guides us through the watches of the night.* Below the poem it is stated: this "is a part of an unpublished poem by her* old friend, James Whitcomb Riley, and was placed by him, as his offering, near her casket." [n.p., n.d.]

Printed on a single sheet of white calendered paper, 3⅛″ x 5″, verso blank, all edges trimmed.

This has been identified as a tribute to Mrs. William J. Kinsley of Shenandoah, Iowa, who died on December 25, 1890. It apparently was printed at the same time as the sheet containing the Riley poem, "The Dead Wife," with Burdette's poem, "Alone" (see p. 172).

The poem appeared under the title, "The Watches of the Night," in the *Indianapolis Journal*, April 5, 1891. With three new stanzas preceding it, it was published in *The Independent*, November 26, 1891, and was collected in *Green Fields and Running Brooks* (1893).

---

*Referring to Mrs. William J. Kinsley.

# 1891

# Our Kind of a Man (Erasmus Wilson)

OUR KIND OF A MAN. | [FROM JAMES WHITCOMB RILEY'S response to | the toast: "Our Kind of a Man," delivered on | the occasion of the annual dinner of The Pitts- | burg Press Club, January 29, 1891. The poem | is dedicated to his long-time personal friend, | Erasmus Wilson, (Quiet Observer) on the edi- | torials (*sic*) taff of The Pittsburg *Commercial Gazette*.]

COLLATION: Leaflet, 4 pages. Leaf measures 6″ x 3¾″, all edges trimmed. Printed on white paper (two types noted).

PAGINATION: Text, pp. [1–4]. The speech follows the heading above quoted and includes the poem beginning: *'Ras Wilson, I respect you, 'cause.*

BINDING: Leaflet, 4 pages, without covers.

PUBLICATION DATE: *ca.* January 29, 1891.

CONTENTS: Only part of the speech which Riley gave on the occasion is here printed; for its entirety see the *Pittsburgh Commercial Gazette*, January 30, 1891. The poem, first collected in *Neghborly Poems* (1891) under the title "Erasmus Wilson," is not the same as the poem entitled "Our Kind of a Man," beginning: *The kind of a man for you and me*, first collected in *Afterwhiles* (1888). The latter refers to Myron W. Reed.

# 1891

# Blotting Pad

A blotting pad, 5⅛″ x 8⅛″. Sold at the Riley Booth, Indianapolis Flower Mission Fair, opening November 3, 1891. In the *Indianapolis Journal*, November 4, 1891, this is described as having "an original verse on the fly-leaf and his [Riley's] name on the last leaf, written as if blotted on." The only copy located lacks the "fly leaf" and consists only of two pieces of blotting paper, white above blue, tied with cream-colored, satin-back ribbon. The white piece has, in facsimile of Riley's autograph, the following in reverse: *Ever thine,* | *James Whitcomb Riley.* The effect is as if the "inscription" had been picked up by the blotting paper.

The *Indianapolis Sentinel*, November 4, 1891, describes the blotter in less detail but mentions that the inscription is in facsimile, and prints the poem, beginning: *He took his pen in hand, and then* The poem is otherwise unpublished.

# 1891

# Say Farewell and Let Me Go

Dedicated by Permission to | Miss Lillian Russell. | Say Farewell & let me go. | BALLAD. | WORDS BY | James Whitcomb Riley, | MUSIC BY | BELLE DANOLDS. | CINCINNATI: | PUBLISHED BY THE JOHN CHURCH CO. 74 WEST FOURTH ST. | 4 [*at left of the numeral appears:*] Chicago, | ROOT & SONS MUSIC CO. | 200 Wabash Avenue. [*at right of the numeral appears:*] New York, | THE JOHN CHURCH CO. | 13 East 16th St.

[Note: The foregoing is printed on a decorated cover, in blue on a tan field, within a decorative blue border. *PEARSON, N. Y.* appears at lower left.]

COLLATION: Sheet music. A single sheet folded to make 4 pages, with a leaf loosely inserted. Leaf measures 14" x 10⅝", all edges trimmed.

PAGINATION: Front cover, p. [1]; words and music, pp. 2–5 (pp. 3–4 on the inserted leaf); blank, p. [6].

[Note: The plate number, 7939-4-T appears on pp. 2, 3, 4 and 5.]

PUBLICATION DATE: Deposited for copyright December 17, 1891.

PUBLICATION PRICE: 40c

NOTES: Previously published in the *Indianapolis Journal*, May 23, 1880, under the title, "Song of Parting," and under this title it was first collected in the *Homestead Edition*, Vol. 6, 1898.

## 1891
### (*Published 1892*)

# What Chris'mas Fetched the Wigginses

A CHRISTMAS STORY. | [*wavy rule*] | [*circular ornament*] | WHAT | CHRIS'MAS | FETCHED | THE | WIGGINSES | [*circular ornament*] | BY JAMES WHITCOMB RILEY. | ILLUSTRATED BY | E. W. KEMBLE. | [*circular ornament*] | LOUISVILLE: | PRESS OF COURIER-JOURNAL JOB PRINTING CO. | 1891.

COLLATION: A single signature of 8 leaves. Leaf measures 9⅝" x 6¹¹⁄₁₆", all edges trimmed. Printed on white wove paper.

PAGINATION: Title-page, p. [i]; copyright notice with date 1891, p. [ii]; text, pp. [1–14].

ILLUSTRATIONS: All the illustrations, by E. W. Kemble, are integral parts of the pamphlet.

BINDING: Pictorial cream-colored wrappers, trimmed to size of leaf, printed in black, brown and gilt with a design that extends to the back cover. On the front cover are several vignettes, the date 1892, a reproduction in miniature of top half of the front page of the *Louisville Times* of November 23, 1891, and engravers' imprint: *Courier-Journal Eng—* | *Louisville—* Inner covers blank. Wire saddle-stitched.

PUBLICATION DATE: January 1, 1892.

NOTES: This pamphlet was planned in March, 1890, as a joint enterprise between Riley and his friend, Young E. Allison, of Louisville, Kentucky, but it finally appeared as the carriers' address of the *Louisville Times*, January 1, 1892.*

CONTENTS: The single poem, "What Chris'mas Fetched the Wigginses," which had no previous appearance in print.

---

*Distributed by the newsboys to their customers who, in conformance with a custom which still persists in some localities, paid whatever sum they felt inclined to give as reward for the year's service.

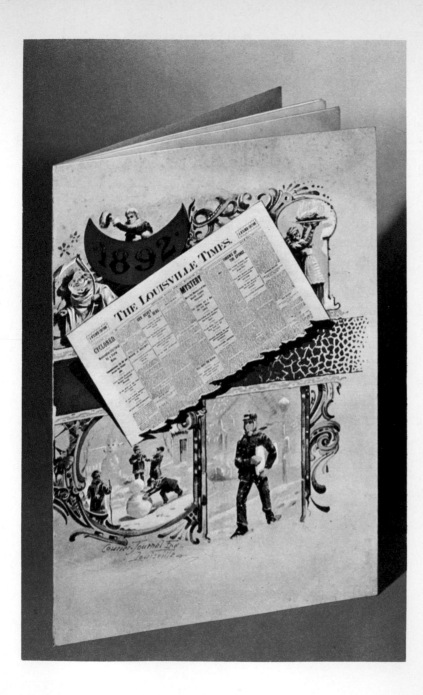

# 1895

## A Peace Hymn

The following Peace Hymn was read at the National | Encampment of the Grand Army of the Republic, held at | Louisville, Ky., Sept., 1895, by its author, James Whitcomb | Riley. | Air.—John Brown's Body. | (12th Mass.—Webster-Regiment War Song) | [double rule] | A PEACE HYMN [text of poem follows, within a triple rule box]

A sheet of white paper, 9⅝" x 5¾", edges trimmed, verso blank. The poem, "A Peace Hymn," appeared in the *Indianapolis Journal*, September 13, 1895; collected in *Home-Folks* (1900) as "A Peace-Hymn of the Republic."

# 1895 (?)

## Blotting Pad

A blotting pad, 7⅛" x 10". Consists of two sheets of white blotting paper, on top of which are two sheets of white wove paper, the whole tied with light green ribbon. The top sheet (of the only copy examined) is inscribed by Riley: *Forgers do their plotting bad | When they use a BLOTTING-PAD. | —James Whitcomb Riley.* Printed on the under sheet of paper is the poem, "From Pad to Verse," which appears in the *Biographical Edition*, Vol. 4, *Notes*, p. 542 (and which includes, as the sixth couplet, the two lines used as inscription).

Judging by contemporary correspondence, Riley wrote the poem and autographed the blotters for a charity fair in October, 1895. Search of the Indianapolis newspapers between October 1 and December 31, 1895 reveals no mention of the blotters or account of a fair at which they might have been distributed.

The poem, "From Pad to Verse," is composed of twelve couplets. From evidence in the correspondence, Riley used other couplets besides the sixth for his inscriptions.

1900 (?)

# The Home Voyage

The Home Voyage. | [*triple rule*] | A Tribute to | Major General
H. W. Lawton, U.S.A. | [*American flag, colored*] | By James
Whitcomb Riley. [n.d.]

COLLATION: Leaflet, 4 pages. Leaf measures 9⅜″ x 4¹³⁄₁₆″, all
edges trimmed. Printed on white Strathmore Deckle-Edge paper.

PAGINATION: Title-page, p. [1]; statement: *Reprinted by J. C. Blair
Company, Manufacturing Stationers, Huntingdon, Pa., U.S.A.*, p. [2]; text,
p. [3]; blank, p. [4].

PUBLICATION DATE: After February 6, 1900.

CONTENTS: The single poem, "The Home Voyage," which appeared first in the *Indianapolis Journal*, February 6, 1900. It was first
collected in *Home-Folks* (deposited for copyright November 14, 1900).
The reprint notice on the second page may refer either to the newspaper
or the book. Issued in a blue mailing envelope.

1900

# A Song of the Road

SINGER'S REPERTOIRE. | I Cannot Help Loving Thee. A. L.
Brown .30 | [*followed by list of ten other songs, then:*] A Song
of the Road. Kate Vannah .30 | Philadelphia. | Theodore
Presser. | 1708 Chestnut Str.

[Note: The foregoing is printed on a decorated cover; decorations
printed in pale yellow and dark blue-green.]

COLLATION: Sheet music. A single sheet folded to make 4 pages,
with a leaf loosely inserted. Leaf measures 13¾″ x 10¹⁵⁄₁₆″, all edges
trimmed.

PAGINATION: Front cover, p. [1]; blank, p. [2]; words and music, pp. 3–5 (pp. 3–4 on the inserted leaf); publishers' advertisements, p. [6].

[Note: Page 3 bears information not on the front cover: the dedication, *To Mrs. Wm. Rogers Chapman;* catalogue number, 2899; the name of James Whitcomb Riley and acknowledgement: *With permission of the author, and of the Lippincots* [sic]; the copyright notice with date, 1900. The plate number, 2899–3, appears at foot of pp. 4 and 5.]

PUBLICATION DATE: The title was registered for copyright March 15, 1900 and copies were deposited in the Copyright Office April 3, 1900.

PUBLICATION PRICE: 30c.

NOTES: The poem, "A Song of the Road," was published in *Lippincott's Monthly Magazine*, July, 1899. It was first collected in *Home-Folks* (1900), published some months after the appearance of this musical setting by Kate Vannah.

Another musical setting, by Edward Baxter Felton, with the title, "O, I Will Walk with You, My Lad," was published in Cincinnati by John Church Company in 1900; this, however, was not deposited for copyright until September 29, 1900. In 1913 another musical setting, by Jean Bohannan, with title, "A Song of the Road," was published in Boston by the B. F. Wood Music Company.

# 1901

# Riley's First Poems

RILEY'S FIRST POEMS. | COLLECTED AND PUBLISHED BY | DORY BIDDLE, | ANDERSON,—INDIANA, | CHRISTMAS, 1901.

SIGNATURES: [1]², one unsigned leaf, [2–5]⁴, [6]². Wire side-stitched. Leaf measures 6¾" full x 9", all edges trimmed. Printed on white coated paper.

PAGINATION: Blank, pp. [i–ii]; title-page, p. [iii]; blank, p. [iv]; foreword, p. [v]; blank, p. [vi]; text, pp. [1]–17 (should be 33); blank, p. [34]; blank leaf.

[Note: The text is printed on recto only of 17 leaves.]

ILLUSTRATIONS: Reproductions of the woodcuts by Samuel Richards which had accompanied the poems in their original newspaper appearance.

BINDING: Gray wrappers, trimmed to leaf size. Front cover has a line-cut portrait of Riley on a blue-green rectangular background, with title printed below: Riley's [ornament] | [ornament] First Poems. A decorative panel in red and green appears at the left, and a red single rule border encloses the whole. Back cover blank.

PUBLICATION DATE: Issued by Dory Biddle, an Anderson newspaperman, as a Christmas souvenir, December 16, 1901. Publication was reported in the *Indianapolis News*, December 17, 1901.

NOTES: This is a selection from Riley's early writings in the *Anderson (Indiana) Democrat*. It has especial significance in view of the fact that no file of the 1877 issues of the newspaper can be located. In 1913 these issues were found* in the County Recorder's office, Madison County Court House; they have disappeared since that time.

Lon Taylor, of Anderson, interviewed on June 21, 1943, recalls printing this pamphlet and states that only 200 copies were issued. At the time, 1901, Dory Biddle was an owner of the *Anderson Daily Bulletin* (successor to the *Anderson Democrat*), and Mr. Taylor worked in the printing room.

CONTENTS: Contains 13 poems that make first appearance in a Riley book. These have not been checked in their original Anderson newspaper publication for reason stated above, but the entire issue of August 17, 1877 has been examined, also clippings from some of the other issues. Two of the poems here make their only appearance in a Riley book: "Police Poetry" and "Now We Can Sleep, Mother."

Maud Muller   *Anderson Democrat*, 1877; *Cincinnati Commercial*, December 26, 1877 (title in *Biographical Edition:* That Other Maud Muller)

Police Poetry   *Anderson Democrat*, 1877

When Mother Combed My Hair   *Indianapolis Sentinel*, February 6, 1876; *Anderson Democrat*, August 17, 1877

George Mullen's Confession   *Anderson Democrat*, 1877

Scraps   *New Castle Mercury*, June 8, 1876; *Anderson Democrat*, 1877

Now We Can Sleep, Mother   *Anderson Democrat*, 1877

Wash Lowry's Reminiscence   *Anderson Democrat*, 1877; *Saturday Herald (Indianapolis)*, August 16, 1879 (with title: One View of It); *Puck on Wheels, No. IV*, Summer, 1883 (with title: Rural Advice to a Poet)

Harlie   *Anderson Democrat*, July 20, 1877†

---

*See account in the *Indianapolis Star*, September 14, 1913, p. 17, c. 3.
†Not seen except as a clipping with manuscript identification.

"Tired Out"   *Anderson Democrat*, 1877; *Indianapolis Journal*, December 17, 1879

A Test of Love   *Anderson Democrat*, 1877

A Poet's Wooing   *Danbury (Conn.) News*, August 8, 1874; *Anderson Democrat*, 1877

The Ancient Printerman   *Greenfield News, ca.* 1875*; *Anderson Democrat*, June 22, 1877*

A Man of Many Parts   *Anderson Democrat*, May 4, 1877*

Note: Of the other 9 poems, 6 are not first book appearances; one, "A Sog of Subber," is not by Riley but by Lee O. Harris, and two others are, so far as we know, not Riley's: the untitled poem beginning "If you should see a fellow man with trouble's flag unfurled" and another, beginning "This world at best is but a hash of pleasure and of pain."

# 1902

# The Soldier

THE SOLDIER | MONUMENT DEDICATION, INDIANAPOLIS | MAY FIFTEENTH, NINETEEN HUNDRED AND TWO | A POEM | BY | JAMES WHITCOMB RILEY | INDIANAPOLIS | THE BOWEN-MERRILL COMPANY | PUBLISHERS

COLLATION: 4 leaves. Leaf measures 9¼″ x 6⅞″, all edges trimmed. Printed on white laid paper.

PAGINATION: Title-page, p. [1]; copyright notice, with date 1902, p. [2]; text, pp. [3, 5, 7] (versos blank).

ILLUSTRATIONS: None.

BINDING: Gray wrappers, trimmed to size of leaf. On the front cover is printed in blue-black: THE SOLDIER   Back cover and inner covers blank. Sewn with blue silk floss.

PUBLICATION DATE: Title entered for copyright April 25, 1902; copies deposited May 8, 1902. Issued for the monument dedication, May 15, 1902.

---

*Not seen except as a clipping with manuscript identification.

CONTENTS: The single poem, "The Soldier." Published the same day, May 15, 1902, in the *Indianapolis Journal's* gray-wrapped souvenir entitled: *Official Souvenir Indiana Soldiers and Sailors Monument;* and, in the *Indianapolis News'* gray-wrapped souvenir entitled: *The Indianapolis News Souvenir Dedication Ceremonies and History Indiana Soldiers' and Sailors' Monument.* In the *Journal's* souvenir, the poem appears in facsimile of the manuscript. Both contain much matter in addition to "The Soldier," and were not deposited for copyright. The *Indianapolis News* of May 15, 1902 also contains the poem.

# 1902

# The Messiah of [the] Nations

THE MESSIAH OF THE NATIONS | A HYMN | BY | JAMES WHITCOMB RILEY | WITH MUSIC | BY | JOHN PHILIP SOUSA | WRITTEN AND COMPOSED ESPECIALLY FOR | THE DEDICATION OF | THE SOLDIERS' AND SAILORS' MONUMENT | AT INDIANAPOLIS | MAY FIFTEENTH NINETEEN HUNDRED TWO | PRESENTED WITH THE COMPLIMENTS OF | THE BOWEN-MERRILL COMPANY
[Note: The foregoing is printed in black on the front cover, over an engraving, in maroon, of the monument; the following appears in the lower left of the design: *Indpls. Eng. Elec. Co.*]

COLLATION: A single sheet folded to make 4 pages, pasted within cream-colored wrappers. The leaf measures 10⅞" x 6⅝", all edges trimmed. Front cover, p. [1]; blank, p. [2]; words and music, pp. 3–6; back cover, blank. [The heading at the top of p. 3 is *The Messiah of Nations* (not *The Messiah of the Nations* as on cover). The copyright notice, in the name of The John Church Company, dated MCMII, and the plate number, 14200–2*, appear at the foot of p. 3.]

PUBLICATION DATE: Deposited in the Copyright Office May 9, 1902.

CONTENTS: The single poem, "The Messiah of Nations." It had appeared without music in the *Chicago Evening Post*, November 30,

---

*The copyright deposit copy so marked.

1901, under the title, "America, Sept. 14, 1901." It was first collected in *Morning* (1907), under the title, "America" (see p. 106).

NOTES: A later musical setting, with title "America," appeared in *The Ward-Stephens Musical Settings of Selected Poems by James Whitcomb Riley* (1915).

# 1903
# Lockerbie Fair

A Souvenir of | Lockerbie Fair
[Printed on front cover to the right of a floral design in black and yellow.]

COLLATION: A single sheet of white coated paper, French fold. Leaf measures 9⅛" x 6"; fore edge and bottom edge trimmed.

PAGINATION: Picture of Riley, p. [1]; text, pp. [2–3]; picture of Lockerbie Street, p. [4].

ILLUSTRATIONS: Pictures on first and last pages; floral ornaments on the two pages of text.

BINDING: Red wrappers, measuring 9⅜" x 6¼". The front wrapper, printed in black and yellow, serves as the title-page. The back cover has imprint of The Hollenbeck Press, Monument Place, Indianapolis. Inner covers blank. Sewn with red silk floss.

PUBLICATION DATE: June, 1903.

PUBLICATION PRICE: With autograph signature, $1.00; without autograph, 50c.

NOTES: The pamphlet was issued by the Indianapolis Flower Mission for the fair held on Lockerbie Street during the last week in June, 1903. Some copies have Riley's name in autograph at end of text; others have it printed in italics; both were issued at the same time.

CONTENTS: The single poem, "Lockerbie Fair." No prior appearance.

# 1904

# The Children of the Childless

The Children Of The Childless | By James Whitcomb Riley

A broadside, measuring 22″ x 14½″, white calendered paper, containing the poem, "The Children of the Childless," printed within an illustrated border by Charles A. Winter. At the foot is the statement: *Copyright 1904 by Collier's Weekly.*

The poem had appeared in *Collier's*, April 2, 1904, p. 18, with the Winter decorations. The broadside is printed from the same plate.

# 1905

# A Christmas Glee

A CHRISTMAS | GLEE

[The foregoing is printed in green on a pictorial green and orange panel on the first page. Below is printed in green: FROM FEIGNED ELIZABETHAN COMEDY | Words and Music by James Whitcomb Riley followed by text: 2 stanzas and chorus.]

COLLATION: Leaflet, 4 pages. Leaf measures 10⅜″ x 7¾″, all edges trimmed. Printed on cream-colored coated paper.

PAGINATION: Title and text (in green), p. [1]; words and music (in green), pp. [2–3]; decoration (in green and orange), p. [4].

ILLUSTRATIONS: Pictorial panel on first page and decoration on last page, by John Cecil Clay; in green and orange.

NOTES: Issued as an insert in the Christmas number of *The Reader*, December, 1905. Reviewed and reprinted, with the music, in the *Indianapolis News*, November 29, 1905. No records regarding the leaflet described above have been found; it would seem to be a separate issue for private distribution.

The poem was first collected in *Morning* (1907), but here and in the *Biographical* and *Homestead* editions it appears without the music.

# 1913

# [Card of Appreciation]

Issued by Riley in appreciation of a poetry shower honoring his birthday, October 7, 1913. Measures 3¼″ x 5¾″. Contains poem beginning, "Dear singing friend, your genial rhyme" followed by his signature, in facsimile; with portrait.

The poem was originally written for Mrs. Dulcina Mason Jordan of Richmond, Indiana, and probably appeared first in a Richmond newspaper, shortly before its publication in the *Indianapolis Journal*, February 9, 1885; first collected in the *Biographical Edition* (1913), Vol. 4, *Notes*, p. 545.

# 1922

# James Whitcomb Riley's Letter from Boston

JAMES WHITCOMB RILEY'S | Letter from Boston | Written when he first felt that he was gaining | Recognition | [*illustration, tinted*] | Privately Printed | For a few Friends by W. K. Bixby | Saint Louis | 1922

COLLATION: 10 unnumbered leaves; sewn. Leaf measures 8½″ x 5½″, all edges untrimmed. Printed on white laid paper.

PAGINATION: Lining paper, pp. [i–ii]; blank, pp. [iii–iv]; fly title, p. [v]; blank, p. [vi]; title-page, p. [vii]; blank, p. [viii]; facsimile of the letter, pp. [1–4]; printed transcript, pp. [5–8]; colophon, p. [9]; blank, p. [10]; lining paper, pp. [11–12].

ILLUSTRATIONS: View of the doorway of the Longfellow house at Cambridge, engraved on wood by Rudolph Ruzicka, tinted, on title-page.

BINDING: Green paper folded loosely over flexible boards. Front cover printed as follows, within decorative box: A Letter of | James Whitcomb Riley   Spine and back cover blank.

PUBLICATION DATE: Printed September, 1922, according to the colophon. Not copyrighted.

NOTES: Five hundred copies were printed by D. B. Updike, The Merrymount Press, Boston.

The name of the addressee is not stated. The letter was written in 1881, but dated merely *Dec. 30*\*. It begins: "Didn't mail first letter last night when written—thought I'd have other matters to communicate— and I have." The "other matters" concern his experiences in Boston, and his visit to Longfellow at Cambridge.

# 1930

# The Bold Rory McMoore

THE BOLD RORY MCMOORE | A Hitherto Unpublished Poem by | James Whitcomb Riley | With an Introduction by the Late | Will F. Meek | of Greenfield, Indiana | Indianapolis | 1930

COLLATION: A single signature of 6 leaves. Leaf measures 6¾″ x 4⅜″, all edges trimmed.

PAGINATION: Blank, pp. [i–ii]; title-page, p. [iii]; copyright notice with date 1930, in name of Mrs. William F. Meek, p. [iv]; text, pp. [1–6]; blank, pp. [7–8].

ILLUSTRATIONS: None.

BINDING: Wrappers of gray cloud paper on white, measuring 7″ x 4¾″. The front cover repeats the first 3 lines of the text of the title-page. Back cover blank. Wire saddle-stitched.

PUBLICATION DATE: Deposited for copyright September 6, 1930.

NOTES: The Riley poem, entitled "Bold Rory McMoore," consists of a previously unpublished poem of 28 lines. The introduction and ex- planation of the poem's origin make up the bulk of the pamphlet's text.

---

\*Written over a period of two days, December 30 and 31.

# Contributions

~~~~~~~~~~~~~~~~~~~~~~~~~~~~~~~~~~~~~~~~~~~~~~~~

A CHECK LIST of books, pamphlets, leaflets, etc., by authors other than Riley, which contain material by him. The list includes only those works which contain first edition matter. Unless otherwise described, the items are cloth-bound books.

Among omissions are books containing Riley letters printed in part only, and those containing extremely brief contributions. Catalogues of book auction sales and bookdealers' lists have also been omitted although they frequently quote letters and inscriptions otherwise unpublished.

## 1879*

TWENTY-EIGHTH ANNUAL REPORT OF THE INDIANA STATE BOARD OF AGRICULTURE, Vol. XX, 1878, including the Proceedings of the Annual Meeting of 1879. Indianapolis, Indianapolis Journal Co., 1879

Contains at p. 400, poem, "Old Settlers" (later entitled, "A Child's Home—Long Ago"), written for an Old Settlers' Meeting, August 3, 1878; read by Riley at the first convention of the Pioneer Association of Indiana, October 2, 1878.

An extract from the above-named report, pp. [375]–423, was issued separately with the title: *The First Convention of the Pioneer Association of Indiana, Inaugurated at the State Fair of 1878;* bound in wrappers.

---

*For reference to a funeral announcement containing the poem, "John Walsh," dated February 23, 1877, see the *Biographical Edition*, Vol. 1, p. 419.

# 1880 (?)

THE KOKOMO TRIBUNE [advertising circular]. Kokomo, Ind., T. C. Philip's Sons [n.d.]

A single sheet, 5½" x 9½", folded in three.
Contains poem, "My Henry," written for the *Kokomo Tribune* and published therein on July 10, 1880, signed *John C. Walker*.

# 1881

CHRISTMAS CAROLS AND MIDSUMMER SONGS. By American Poets. Boston, D. Lothrop & Company, Franklin Street [1881]

Contains poem, "The Land of Used-to-Be," p. 47.

# 1882

HISTORY OF HANCOCK COUNTY, INDIANA. By J. H. Binford. Greenfield, Ind., King & Binford, 1882

Contains poem, "Friday Afternoon," p. 493, similar in form to its earliest known printing, in the *Indianapolis Daily Sentinel*, January 30, 1876. Printed with the poem in this book is a portrait of Riley and his signature in facsimile (an interesting example of his early handwriting).

THE POET AND THE CHILDREN. Edited by Matthew Henry Lothrop. Boston, D. Lothrop & Company, Franklin Street [1882]

Contains three poems by Riley of which the following two are first known appearances in a book: "Mother Goose," p. 136; "The Circus-Day Parade," p. 243.

# 1885

THE ELOCUTIONIST'S ANNUAL, No. 13. Compiled by Mrs. J. W. Shoemaker. Philadelphia, National School of Elocution and Oratory, 1885

Cloth; wrappers. Contains poem, "Out to Old Aunt Mary's," p. 38.

LIFE'S VERSES. New York, Mitchell & Miller [1885]

Boards, cloth shelfback. Contains five poems by Riley, all of which make first known book appearance here: "All She Could Do," uncollected; "Says He Would Smile," uncollected; "Serenade to Nora"; "When Maimie Married"; "While Cigarettes to Ashes Turn"; pp. 26, 12, 66, 75 and 87.

# 1886

THE HUMBLER POETS. A Collection of Newspaper and Periodical Verse . . . by Slason Thompson. Chicago, Jansen, McClurg & Co., 1886

Of the five poems by Riley in this collection, the following two are first known book appearances: "Like His Mother Used to Make," p. 227; "The Mad, Mad Muse" (last 3 stanzas of the poem entitled, "The Lugubrious Whing-Whang"), p. 445.

The book was deposited for copyright January 4, 1886 but the title had been entered for copyright on November 17, 1885. If publication preceded *The Boss Girl* (December 19, 1885), another poem of the five is a first book appearance: "The Orchard Lands of Long Ago," p. 191.

# 1888

THE HARRISON LOG CABIN SONG BOOK OF 1840. REVISED FOR THE CAMPAIGN OF 1888. Edited by O. C. Hooper. Columbus, O., A. H. Smythe, 1888

Wrappers. Contains poem, "Set Him There K-Sock," p. 63; uncollected. This poem, beginning: *And they's still another idy 'at I ort to here append*, is said to have been written and recited by Riley on the occasion of a banquet for Benjamin Harrison in the fall of 1888. It was appended to his poem, "When the Frost is on the Punkin."

Another issue, probably later, called the *Music Edition*, contains the poem, unsigned, at p. 43.

TRANSACTIONS OF THE INDIANA STATE MEDICAL SOCIETY, 1888. Thirty-Ninth Annual Session Held in Indianapolis, June 5th and 6th, 1888. Indianapolis, Baker & Randolph, 1888.

Contains "Doc Sifers," p. 169, as recited by Riley at the banquet given by the Marion County Medical Society to the Indiana State

Medical Society, June 5, 1888. The report of the banquet is here reprinted from the *Indiana Medical Journal*, July, 1888. According to the prefatory note, the "Transactions" were ready for issue September 1.

STANDARD COMIC RECITATIONS No. 21, September, 1888

Wrappers. Contains the poem, "Chairley Burke's in Town." Reported but not seen.

THE ELOCUTIONIST'S ANNUAL, No. 16. Compiled by Mrs. J. W. Shoemaker. Philadelphia, National School of Elocution and Oratory, 1888

Copyrighted October 1, 1888. Contains two poems that make first known book appearance: "An Old Sweetheart of Mine," p. 56; "The Old Man and Jim," p. 117. The other Riley poem herein, "The Elf-Child" ("Little Orphant Annie") had appeared in *The Boss Girl* (1886). The copy examined is cloth bound; probably issued also in wrappers.

[Program for banquet tendered James Whitcomb Riley, by the Western Association of Writers and other friends, October 18, 1888]

Wrappers. Contains a poem of 11 lines beginning: *Gadzooks! My dainty lady typewriter* following the toast, "Our Guest." This poem appeared later in *Letters of James Whitcomb Riley*, edited by William Lyon Phelps (1930), p. 87.

[Advertising matter, leaflets and broadsides, issued by Major James B. Pond, New York, for the Nye and Riley entertainments, season 1888–1889]

Containing "The Autobiography of Bill Nye, written by himself, through James Whitcomb Riley." This, and *not* "The Autobiography of James Whitcomb Riley" (actually written by Bill Nye), is a Riley contribution. For the story of the origin of the "autobiographies" see *Eccentricities of Genius*, by Pond (1900), pp. 241–246.

Riley's publishers, the Bowen-Merrill Company, used "The Autobiography of James Whitcomb Riley" on circulars issued in the early '90's.

# 1889

THE ELOCUTIONIST'S ANNUAL, No. 17. Compiled by Mrs. J. W. Shoemaker. Philadelphia, The Penn Publishing Co., 1889

Cloth; wrappers. Contains, "The Land of Thus and So," p. 94.

The book was copyrighted October 15, 1889. It was republished in 1890 under the title, *Shoemaker's Best Selections for Readings and Recitations, No. 17*, with the same Riley poem included.

LOTHROP ANNUAL. Boston, D. Lothrop Company, Washington Street opposite Bromfield [1889]

Contains the poem, "The Little Pixey People," (later entitled: "The Pixy People"), p. 160. Reported but not seen.

# 1890

JOEL CHANDLER HARRIS' LIFE OF HENRY W. GRADY INCLUDING HIS WRITINGS AND SPEECHES. New York, Cassell Publishing Co. [1890]

Contains the poem, "Henry W. Grady," p. 317. First edition has 628 pp., second edition, 645 pp.

SOUVENIR OF THE UNVEILING OF THE HENDRICKS MONUMENT, July 1st, 1890. [Indianapolis], Published by the Hendricks Club [July 10, 1890]

Leather. Contains "Hendricks," beginning: *Pride of thy Westland, and Loved of the Nation!*, p. 16. The poem had appeared in the *Indianapolis Sentinel* of July 2, 1890; otherwise unpublished.

POEMS. Indianapolis [Indianapolis Flower Mission], 1890

Issued in wrappers embossed in imitation of morocco, sold at the society's fair, November, 1890. Only 300 copies, according to the *Indianapolis Journal*, November 18, 1890. Riley's poem, "Home," is followed by poems of five other Indiana authors. It appeared later, in *Green Fields and Running Brooks* (1893) with title, "The Home-Going"; in *Morning* (1907) and later Riley books with title, "We Must Get Home."

## 1890 (?)

[A sheet, 6⅜″ x 3⅜″, n.p., n.d., 1890?]

Bears Riley's poem, "The Dead Wife," which begins: *I look from the window. The smoke goes straight.* Below it is printed Robert J. Burdette's poem, "Alone," and the following statement by W. J. Kinsley: "The above touching and singularly appropriate verses were clipped by Mrs. Kinsley's* own hands, and were found by me, among other clippings, 'since she went home.' "

This poem, "The Dead Wife," differs from the poem of the same title first collected in *Poems Here at Home* (1893); this one appears in *A Tinkle of Bells* (1895).

## 1891

LIFE OF JOHN BOYLE O'REILLY. By James Jeffrey Roche. Chicago, J. S. Hyland & Co. [1891]

Contains poem, p. 300, "Written in John Boyle O'Reilly's 'In Bohemia' " (in Riley books under this title, also under the title, "On a Fly-Leaf").

PROCEEDINGS OF THE NATIONAL CONFERENCE OF CHARITIES AND CORRECTION AT THE EIGHTEENTH ANNUAL SESSION, Held in Indianapolis, Ind., May 13–20, 1891. Edited by Isabel C. Barrows. Boston, Geo. H. Ellis, 1891

Contains, at p. 304, "A Character Study: an Incident of the Insane Asylum," beginning: *The story is true in every particular.* Riley's speech of introduction to this story of "Dutch Frank," a Greenfield shoemaker, is printed apparently in full, but the story itself, as he related it in broken German, is merely outlined. So far as known, this has no other appearance in print.

[Program of] BENEFIT PERFORMANCE FOR THE FAMILY OF THE LATE LEONARD DANE WASHBURNE. Thursday afternoon, Oct. 29, 1891. Chicago, The Columbia [Theatre, 1891]

---

*Mrs. William J. Kinsley, of Shenandoah, Iowa, who died December 25, 1890 (see p. 153).

Leaflet. Contains a poem, "The Reporter," which begins: *The Reporter! Honor to.* It appears also in the *Chicago Herald*, October 30, 1891; no known appearance elsewhere.

GOLDEN ROD: The Magazine of the Indianapolis Flower Mission. [Indianapolis, Indianapolis Flower Mission, November 3, 1891]

Wrappers. Contains the poem, "Going to the Fair" (later entitled, "Goin' to the Fair"), and a prose sketch, "Tale of a Manuscript" (later entitled, "Twiggs and Tudens"). This souvenir of the society's annual fair, sold at the Riley Booth, is not a magazine but a brochure.

IDEAL SERIES. SELECT READINGS AND RECITATIONS FOR CHRISTMAS. No. 4. Indianapolis, Bowen-Merrill Co. [1891]

Wrappers. Deposited for copyright November 12, 1891. Contains the first known printing in book form of the poem, "Last Christmas Was a Year Ago," p. 73. The other Riley poem in this compilation is not a first book appearance.

IDEAL SERIES. SELECT READINGS AND RECITATIONS. No. 8. Indianapolis, Bowen-Merrill Co. [1891]

Wrappers. Deposited for copyright December 3, 1891. Contains "The Unheard," p. 4.

IDEAL SERIES. SELECT READINGS AND RECITATIONS FOR YOUNG PEOPLE. No. 9. Indianapolis, Bowen-Merrill Co. [1891]

Wrappers. Deposited for copyright December 3, 1891. Contains "The Baby," p. 19. This is the first appearance in a book of the first two stanzas, later published as "The Way the Baby Came" and "The Way the Baby Woke." The third stanza had previously appeared under the title, "The Way the Baby Slept." The other Riley poem herein, "Curv'ture of the Spine," p. 31, had previously appeared as "The Happy Little Cripple."

IN MEMORIAM. Oscar C. McCulloch, Pastor Plymouth Church, Indianpolis (*sic*), (Sepulture, Dec. 12, 1891) [Indianapolis, 1891?]

Probably a leaflet; the only copy seen is a single sheet, 8¾" x 5¾", torn as if on a fold. Contains the poem, "Oscar C. McCulloch," from the *Indianapolis Sentinel**; with a poem by Chadwick on the verso of the page.

# 1892

JOSEPHINE [memorial volume to Josephine Bemis-Fuller Gill who died at Indianapolis, December 31, 1891] [n.p., n.d., Indianapolis, 1892?]

Contains "Josephine," a 4-line poem beginning: *Thrice blest are we by such fair lives as hers;* uncollected.

WESTERN ASSOCIATION WRITERS. Sayings and Doings of the Sixth General Meeting held at Eagle Lake, Warsaw, Ind., July 6 to 10, 1891. Cincinnati, Jones Brothers Publishing Co. [1892]

Binder's title: In-Gathering of Sketches, Essays, Poems by Western Writers. Contains Riley's poem, "Uncle William's Photo" (later entitled, "Uncle William's Picture"), p. 254.

FROM THE BOOKS OF LAURENCE HUTTON. New York, Harper & Bros., 1892

Contains a poem, "Lines on a Error," which Riley had inscribed in a copy of *Afterwhiles* after he had inadvertently written his name in the back instead of in the front of the book; uncollected. Also in: *Rochester (New York) Herald*, August 13, 1892, but the title of *From the Books of Laurence Hutton* had been registered on May 29, 1892, and copies were deposited in the Copyright Office on July 25, 1892.

SONGS OF A LIFE-TIME. By Sarah T. Bolton. Edited by John Clark Ridpath. Indianapolis, Bowen-Merrill Co., 1892

Contains a proem by Riley entitled, "Songs of a Life-Time."

IDEAL SERIES. SELECT READINGS AND RECITATIONS FOR ALL THE YEAR ROUND. No. 10. Indianapolis, Bowen-Merrill Co. [1892]

Wrappers. Deposited for copyright February 2, 1893. Contains poem, "A Feel in the Chris'mas-Air," p. 45.

---

*Although source of publication is stated on the page to be the *Indianapolis Sentinel,* a careful search of this newspaper around the time of McCulloch's death, fails to find the Riley poem therein. It did appear in the *Indianapolis Journal* of December 12, 1891.

# 1893

STANDARD RECITATIONS No. 38. Compiled by Frances P. Sullivan. New York, M. J. Ivers & Co. [1893]

Wrappers. Deposited for copyright May 5, 1893. Contains poem, "Little Cousin Jasper," p. 8.

MRS. CHARLES E. COFFIN [memorial volume]. [n.p., n.d., Indianapolis, 1893?]

Mrs. Coffin died on July 8, 1893; this book was probably published the same year, or early the next. Contains poem, p. 10, "Elizabeth" (later entitled, "To Elizabeth"), which begins: *O noble, true and pure and lovable*. This is not to be confused with Riley's other poem, "Elizabeth," a tribute to Elizabeth Meredith Steele.

# 1894

IDEAL SERIES. SELECT READINGS AND RECITATIONS FOR CHRISTMAS. No. 12. Indianapolis, Bowen-Merrill Co. [1894]

Wrappers. Deposited for copyright January 10, 1895. Contains poem, "Mr. Foley's Christmas," p. 11.

IDEAL SERIES. SELECT READINGS AND RECITATIONS. No. 13. Indianapolis, Bowen-Merrill Co. [1894]

Wrappers. Deposited for copyright January 10, 1895. Contains poem, "Let Something Good Be Said," p. 4.

# 1895

NOTABLE SINGLE POEMS. Buffalo, The Peter Paul Book Company [1895]

White boards. Running title reads: "The Magazine of Poetry and Literary Review, Vol. 8, No. 1, Single Poems Number, American Authors." Contains poem, "A Christmas Memory," reprinted from *Life*, December, 1895. The same poem appeared later in *Taken from Life*, published by Doubleday & McClure Co., New York, 1897.

# 1896

A NOVEMBER LEAF. [Indianapolis, Indianapolis Flower Mission], 1896

Wrappers. Sold at the society's fair in November, 1896. Contains poem, "Song for November," written for this brochure.

INDIANA'S GIFT TO THE BATTLESHIP INDIANA. Indianapolis [n.d., 1896?]

The second title of the book reads: "Story of the Subscription; Account of the Presentation, Description of the Silver Service, List of Books and Names of the Subscribers." The service and the library were presented on September 21, 1896. Contains the poem, "Indiana," dated September, 1896. A copy of the book has been noted with presentation inscription dated January 1, 1897.

# 1897

THE AUTHORS CLUB. Annual Report for 1896. Annual Meeting Held Thursday, January 14th, 1897.
[New York, The Authors Club, 1897?]

Includes, under the caption, *Obituaries*, "Edgar Wilson Nye," a prose tribute by Riley, with the statement: *Adopted April 28, 1896.* It begins: *The personality of Edgar Wilson Nye was as distinctly lovable as his genius was unique.* Uncollected. Thus far no complete copy of the report has been located.

[Program of an unidentified young men's club of Detroit, Michigan, meeting held March 5, 1897; imprint of Winn & Hammond on second page; cover title: *Old Fashioned Roses*]

Wrappers. Contains facsimile of a letter from Riley to H. S. Pingree, dated Feb. 4, 1897, beginning: *Your good request in behalf of your young men's Club is just in my hands.* The letter has no known appearance elsewhere.

"NO MEAN CITY"    A Response by Benjamin Harrison at a Dinner Given by the Commercial Club, Indianapolis, April 21, 1897. . . . [Indianapolis, Commercial Club, 1897]

A pamphlet, with self-cover. Contains Riley's speech in response to the toast, "Our Guest," p. 14, including a 4-line poem which begins: *Moving up from high to higher*. The speech appears also in the *Indianapolis Journal*, April 22, 1897. Part of it is printed in *The Maturity of James Whitcomb Riley*, by Marcus Dickey (1922), p. 363.

ONCE A YEAR. [Indianapolis, Indianapolis Flower Mission], 1897

Wrappers. Sold at the society's fair, November 9–13, 1897. Contains poem, "An Old-Home Song" (later entitled, "Where the Children Used to Play").

NINETY-SECOND ANNIVERSARY CELEBRATION OF THE NEW ENGLAND SOCIETY IN THE CITY OF NEW YORK . . . December 22, 1897. [New York, 1897]

Wrappers. Includes Riley's speech at the banquet, pp. 63–67; uncollected. Also contains the first known printing in book form of his prose sketch, "The Old Soldier's Story." Samuel L. Clemens, in *How to Tell a Story and Other Essays, by Mark Twain* (1897), under the heading, "The Wounded Soldier," relates the anecdote and describes Riley's manner of telling it.

The poem, "The Old Man and Jim," also recited by Riley on the occasion and here printed, is not a first book appearance.

# 1898

[Announcement of Riley's appearance for a reading* in Cleveland, Ohio, October 25, 1898, at the First M. E. Church]

Leaflet, 4 pages. Contains a poem without title which later appeared in Riley books as "Kathleen Mavourneen."

THE WRITINGS IN PROSE AND VERSE OF EUGENE FIELD [Sabine Edition], Vol. 4: Poems of Childhood. New York, Charles Scribner's Sons, 1898

Riley's poem, "Eugene Field," in facsimile of the manuscript, is used as the introduction.

---

*Riley gave recitations in many cities over a long period of years, and his appearance was heralded by quantities of ephemeral matter: posters, broadsides, leaflets and pamphlets. These frequently contain quotations from his poetry but, except in this one case, they are not first printings.

# 1899

DINNER AND TOASTS IN HONOR OF SENATOR ALBERT J. BEVER-
IDGE BY MR. AND MRS. CHARLES E. COFFIN, Friday Evening,
January 13, 1899. [Indianapolis, 1899]

Wrappers. Contains at p. 68, Riley's toast to Senator Beveridge,
beginning: *All the speeches I have listened to to-night;* uncollected.

LIFE OF OLIVER P. MORTON. By William Dudley Foulke. Indianapolis & Kansas City, Bowen-Merrill, 1899

Contains the poem, "Morton," Vol. 2, p. 534 (3 stanzas).

THE BOW-LEGGED GHOST AND OTHER STORIES. By Leon Mead.
Akron, Ohio [etc.], Werner [1899].

Contains a proem, p. v, which appeared later in Riley books under
the title, "Prose or Verse?"

# 1900

THE HESPERIAN TREE. An Annual of the Ohio Valley. Cincinnati, George C. Shaw [1900]

Contains "To a Naturalist" (later entitled, "The Naturalist"), p. 53;
a poetical tribute to Oliver Davie.

[Prospectus of] "THE QUIET OBSERVER," Erasmus Wilson, Editor. [n.p., n.d.]

Single sheet, 5¾" x 11¾", folded in 4 panels. Contains a letter
from Riley which begins: *Of course I don't know if your Pennsylvania country knows the old sugar camp to which my homely rhyme alludes,* and concludes: *All hail and Godspeed to your venture.* Uncollected.

This prospectus was issued *ca.* March, 1900. The Riley letter
herein reappeared in the first issue of the magazine, *The Quiet Observer,*
May 3, 1900 (see p. 305 of this bibliography for note regarding the
magazine's date of publication).

# 1901

MAJOR CHARLES L. HOLSTEIN, January 26, 1843—January 22, 1901 [Indianapolis, The Hollenbeck Press, n.d., 1901?]

Wrappers. Contains poem in tribute to Major Holstein: "His Heart of Constant Youth."

# 1902

EARLY RECOLLECTIONS OF JAMES WHITCOMB RILEY. By Major Ridgeway (pseudonym of William Ross Hartpence). Harrison, Ohio, 1902

Wrappers. Contains the following uncollected material:
*Letter to William Ross Hartpence*   p. [1]
*Limerick*, beginning: "There is an 'old war-horse' named Sanders," p. 55
*Advertising jingles*, originally published in the *Greenfield News, ca.* 1874–75: one with title, "He Was Right," the others without titles, beginning as follows:
"Fine! FINE!! SUPERFINE!!!" (advertising his own signs) p. 60
"Hootsy-tootsy, I declare!" p. 37
"Me and my little old man fell out;" p. 32
"O, tell me no more" p. 35
"O, where—tell me where" p. 37
"Of all the stores, the cheapest one" p. 36
" 'Old Santa Claus is coming!' " p. 35
"Sweet is the sound, when oft at evening's close," p. 37
"The deepest ice that ever froze," p. 36
"There are Bracelets rare," p. 34
"Those elegant designs" p. 32
"Though gently scan" p. 36
"Willow ware, rich and rare,—" p. 32
" 'Write me a rhyme of the present time;' " p. 37
"You'll find true happiness just begun," p. 33
The book also contains a poem originally published anonymously in the *Greenfield News*, attributed to Riley by Mr. Hartpence, entitled, "Apple Time."

# 1903

JAMES WHITCOMB RILEY IN PROSE AND PICTURE. By John A. Howland. Chicago, Handy & Higgins, 1903

Boards. Contains a poem in facsimile of the manuscript, which begins: "The *Brightest* Star's the *modestest*" (in the *Biographical Edition* later with the title, "A Motto").

# 1904

BIOGRAPHY OF MARY HARTWELL CATHERWOOD. By M. L. Wilson. Newark, O., American Tribune Printery, 1904

Contains a 6-line tribute to Mrs. Catherwood, p. [85], beginning: *Mrs. Catherwood was a dear friend of mine;* uncollected.

# 1905

THINKIN' BACK. [By John Wanamaker]. [Philadelphia, n.d., 1905?]

A single sheet, 14" x 5½" issued *ca.* April, 1905. Below the title appears the following: "A new poem by my old friend, James Whitcomb Riley, laid on the writer's desk this morning. It seems to have been written especially for our Anniversary." Riley's poem, "Thinkin' Back," follows, in format similar to its appearance in the *Reader Magazine* of April, 1905. On the verso of the sheet are John Wanamaker's reminiscences of his business experience in Philadelphia.

# 1906

IN HONOR OF JAMES WHITCOMB RILEY. Indianapolis, Bobbs-Merrill Co. [1906]

Gray wrappers over boards. An account of the meeting of the Indiana State Teachers' Association held in Indianapolis, December 28, 1905. Contains Riley's speech in response to the addresses, p. 48, beginning: *In a very humble life you have made a most distinctive and memorable day.* The speech is apparently unpublished elsewhere. The poems which Riley recited on the occasion, printed herein, are not first book appearances.

A special edition was issued at, or near, the same time as the regular edition. It differs in many respects; among other differences it has a title-page reading simply: IN HONOR | OF | JAMES WHITCOMB RILEY; bears the following on the verso of the page of acknowledgements: THIS BOOK IS NUMBER [*number stamped in*] OF A | SPECIAL EDITION. IT IS PRE-SENTED TO | [*space for recipient's name*] | WITH THE COMPLIMENTS OF D. C. HEATH | AND COMPANY BY E. R. SMITH* This issue, of which there were at least 1,000 printed, does not contain the sketch of Riley's life that appears at pp. [61]–89 of the regular edition, but ends with p. 60. The front wrapper has the title printed in red (regular edition in black) and the spine is blank (regular edition has title on spine).

Although the copyright page bears the statement, *Published, April,* the book did not appear until May 16, 1906, according to a review in the *Indianapolis News* of this date, but copyright deposit copies (regular edition) were received on May 7, 1906. A copy of the Special Edition, presented to Young E. Allison, is inscribed with the date May 10, 1906.

ABE MARTIN OF BROWN COUNTY, INDIANA. By Kin Hubbard. [Indianapolis], Levey Bros., 1906

Contains "To Kin Hubbard" (later entitled, "Abe Martin"). The same Riley poem appeared in several succeeding "almanacks" by Kin (Frank McKinney) Hubbard.

AN ACCOUNT OF THE PROCEEDINGS ON THE OCCASION OF THE SECOND ANNUAL BANQUET OF THE INDIANA SOCIETY OF CHI-CAGO, December 11, 1906. [n.p., n.d., Chicago, 1906?]

Wrappers. Contains, at p. 33, Riley's speech which begins: *I am more than privileged to be with you here to-night;* uncollected. The two poems herein printed are not first book appearances.

[Program of] INDIANA STATE TEACHERS ASSOCIATION. Meeting in honor of Dr. Henry van Dyke. Tomlinson Hall, December 28, 1906, Indianapolis. [Indianapolis, 1906]

Pamphlet? Leaflet? Only an excerpt from it has been located. Contains the poem, "On Reading Dr. Henry van Dyke's Latest Volume of Poems—Music."

---

*Immediately below this notice some copies have an inscription in Riley's autograph: *With greetings,—James Whitcomb Riley*

## 1907

HARVEST OF THOUGHTS. By Aaron Belford Thompson. Indianapolis, Published . . . By The Author, 1907

Contains an introduction by Riley, in facsimile of the manuscript, beginning: *It is gratifying to find so much of real poetic worth in these first published verses of Aaron Belford Thompson.*

## 1908

MRS. BENJAMIN HARRISON. By Harriet McIntire Foster. [n.p., Daughters of the American Revolution], 1908

Wrappers. Contains poem, "Mrs. Harrison, Washington, October 25, 1892" (later entitled, "Mrs. Benjamin Harrison").

SOUVENIR OF 32ND NATIONAL SAENGERFEST, Indianapolis, June 17–20, 1908. [n.p., n.d., Indianapolis, 1908?]

Wrappers. Contains a dedicatory poem of 6 lines, without title, beginning: *Forever old, forever young;* uncollected.

## 1909

THE ADDRESSES BY CHARLES WARREN FAIRBANKS, JOHN W. NOBLE, JOHN L. GRIFFITHS AND THE POEM BY JAMES WHITCOMB RILEY ON THE OCCASION OF THE UNVEILING AT INDIANAPOLIS, INDIANA, OCTOBER 27, 1908 OF THE STATUE OF BENJAMIN HARRISON. [Indianapolis, The Hollenbeck Press, 1909]

Wrappers. Contains "The Tribute of His Home," p. 19, consisting of three sonnets of which the first appears under the title, "The Tribute of His Home," in the *Biographical Edition*, and the other two under the title, "Benjamin Harrison."

## 1910

THE CLIFF-DWELLERS' YEAR BOOK. Chicago, 1910

Wrappers. Contains a letter to the Cliff-Dwellers, p. 51, congratulating the club on its housewarming in January, 1906, beginning: *It is with great delight that I just hear of your prospective housewarming;* uncollected.

# 1911

INDIANAPOLIS PUBLIC SCHOOLS. SOME SUGGESTIONS FOR THE OBSERVANCE OF RILEY DAY, OCTOBER 6 [7]. Prepared by a Committee of Supervising Principals. [Indianapolis, 1911]

Wrappers. Contains Riley's letter "To the School Children of Indianapolis," dated October 6, 1911, beginning: *You are conspirators— every one of you.* This letter was published in the *Indianapolis Star* and the *Indianapolis News* of October 6, 1911. Later it appeared in *The Maturity of James Whitcomb Riley* by Marcus Dickey (1922), p. 398, and in *The Letters of James Whitcomb Riley* edited by William Lyon Phelps (1930), p. 315.

# 1912

MCMXII: THE ANNUAL PUBLISHED BY SHORTRIDGE HIGH SCHOOL. [Indianapolis, Shortridge High School, 1912]

Wrappers. Contains a poem by Riley addressed to the Shortridge High School Seniors, 1912; later collected under the title, "The Highest Good." The annual is dedicated to Riley.

ROLLING STONES. By O. Henry (William Sydney Porter). Garden City, N. Y., Doubleday, Page & Co., 1912

Contains poem, "O. Henry," p. v.

THE HOOSIER ALMANACK AND FAMILY MAGAZINE. [Chicago], Indiana Society of Chicago, 1912.

Wrappers. A souvenir of the society's eighth annual dinner, December, 1912. Contains a greeting by Riley, p. 27, and a 4-line poem, "In an Album," p. 53, which begins: *What verse shall I write;* uncollected.

MARK TWAIN: A BIOGRAPHY. THE PERSONAL AND LITERARY LIFE OF SAMUEL LANGHORNE CLEMENS. By Albert Bigelow Paine. New York & London, Harper, 1912. 3 vols.

Contains a letter [written in 1897], beginning: *For a solid week— night sessions—I have been glorying in your last book;* Vol. 2, p. 1055. Uncollected. First edition of Vol. 2 has *I-M* at foot of copyright page.

# 1915

LITTLE VERSES AND BIG NAMES. New York, George H. Doran Co., 1915

Contains poem, "Why?" at p. 5, beginning: *Onc't little Wesley Offut watch;* uncollected.

SUGGESTIONS AND MATERIALS [for] RILEY DAY PROGRAMS. By Charles A. Greathouse. Indianapolis [1915]

Wrappers. Riley's letter to Governor Ralston, dated September 9, 1915, appears at p. 4; his letter to school children, October 7, 1912 (in *Indianapolis Star*, October 7, 1912), at p. 12. Three of his letters to children, printed herein, are first book appearances: to Elizabeth Page, August 30, 1912, at p. 12, beginning: *You have sent me a mighty good letter;* to James L. Murray, February 5, 1896, p. 13, beginning: *No-sir-ee! I couldn't write verses when I was nine years old like you;* to Mabel Wessels, April 10, 1897, p. 12, beginning: *One time a little girl*

THE WARD-STEPHENS MUSICAL SETTINGS OF SELECTED POEMS BY JAMES WHITCOMB RILEY. New York, Chappell & Co., Ltd., 1915

Wrappers. Contains a letter to Ward Stephens, dated October 11, 1915, beginning: *For the loving touch with which you set my verse to music*

# 1916

THE WILLIAM WINTER TESTIMONIAL, Century Theatre, March 14, 1916. [New York], 1916

Wrappers. Contains a letter from Riley, in tribute to William Winter, dated February 22, 1916, beginning: *On this merry occasion;* uncollected. The poem herein is adapted from "Three Several Birds," which had made previous appearance.

AN INVITATION TO YOU AND YOUR FOLKS FROM JIM AND SOME MORE OF THE HOME FOLKS. Compiled by George Ade for the Indiana Historical Commission. Indianapolis [1916]

Wrappers. Contains a letter, p. 4, beginning: *If it were given me to be infinitely persuasive;* uncollected. The poem included herein, "The Hoosier in Exile," is not a first book appearance.

REMINISCENCES OF JAMES WHITCOMB RILEY. By Clara E. Laughlin. New York & Chicago, Fleming H. Revell Co. [1916]

Boards, cloth shelfback. Contains numerous uncollected letters to Miss Laughlin, some of which include limericks and brief poems, also uncollected. These uncollected poems are: "Yatesesque," p. 53; and the following, without titles, beginning:

"A notable lady of letters was she,"   p. 110
"And so, in the face o' the sun by day,"   p. 47
"In jousts of old, with couchant quill,"   p. 108
"Kate Shane, the coquette iv all Dayton."   p. 67

The poem at p. 32, beginning: "He was a sawyer—blind from birth," may or may not be Riley's (see p. 234).

# 1917

A JAMES WHITCOMB RILEY AND A DOUGLASS SHERLEY VALENTINE. [n.p.], 1917

A single sheet, 10⅛" x 21", folded in 3 panels. Issued in a decorated envelope. The center panel contains a poem by Riley, "Upon Valentine-Designs by D.S.," dated February, 1896, in facsimile of manuscript. It begins: *Deft master of the most grotesque;* uncollected.

SONGS OF THE HEART AND SOUL. By Joseph Roland Piatt. Boston, Sherman, French & Co., 1917

Contains, at p. 107, "To Joseph Roland Piatt—The Poemer," written Christmas, 1901, in response to a poem from Piatt to Riley. The poem made its first known appearance in the *Cleveland World*, January 12, 1902, under the title: "James Whitcomb Riley to Joseph Roland Piatt"; uncollected.

# 1918

THE LIFE OF JOEL CHANDLER HARRIS. By Robert Lemuel Wiggins. Nashville, Tenn., Publishing House, M. E. Church, 1918

Contains, at p. 5, a letter to Joel Chandler Harris, dated December 30, 1905, beginning: *Your book of "New Stories of the Old Plantation" is here;* uncollected.

THE LIFE AND LETTERS OF JOEL CHANDLER HARRIS. By Julia Collier Harris. Boston & New York, Houghton Mifflin Co., 1918

Contains at p. 439, a letter dated March 5, 1901, beginning: *Wooooh! Ole man Winter round here yit;* also, at p. 498, a letter in rhyme beginning: *"Leventeen Hundred-an-full-er-flees."* | *Hit's mighty good news er new-Ol' Uncle Remus Rhymes,* Both letters, to Joel Chandler Harris, are uncollected.

JAMES WHITCOMB RILEY: An Essay by Bliss Carman. New York [1918]

Boards; morocco shelfback. Limited edition of 250 signed copies, printed for George D. Smith. Contains numerous previously unpublished letters to Bliss Carman written from August 30, 1898 to October 12, 1915. Most of the letters appear in both type and facsimile. Contains also a facsimile of an inscription by Riley in a book given to Bliss Carman, beginning: *Yet himself a child at play;* uncollected. The poem, "Bliss Carman," had appeared previously as "To Bliss Carman."

The sheets were reissued, Metuchen, N. J., 1925, with cancel title-page.

# 1919

THE YOUTH OF JAMES WHITCOMB RILEY. By Marcus Dickey. Indianapolis, Bobbs-Merrill [1919]

Also a limited signed edition of 500 large-paper copies, in boards with cloth shelfback. In addition to numerous letters, herein first published, this book contains the following uncollected works:

    The Anderson Democrat Is a Good Little Paper (prose) p. 351*
    A Fragment   p. 68
    Happy Bells!   p. 368*
    Invocation   p. 338
    Joe Biggsby's Proposal   p. 165
    The Last Waltz   p. 168
    Lines in a Letter Enclosing a Picture   p. 296
    The Poet's Realm   p. 217
    A Session of "The Singing Pilgrims" (prose)   p. 209
    A Tune   p. 158
Also, without titles:
    "Afterwhile—the poet-man"   p. 332  *Harper's Magazine*, May,

---

*Mr. Dickey here discusses an earlier newspaper appearance.

1918 (included in letter to Mrs. R. E. Jones, November 9, 1887)

"Carpets coarse and carpets fine" p. 228*

"Greenfield barbers cut my hair" p. 196

"I washed my face and combed my hair" p. 196

"If you ever live to see" p. 196

"In making my salam [*sic*] to the Anderson public" (prose), p. 334*

"My dear young friend, regaled with love" p. 287

"Neglected genius—truth be said" p. 241

"O he was a poet weird and sad"† p. 238

"Oh, Muse! Inspire our 'Faber No. 2' " p. 167

"Rain, rain, go away" p. 138

"Saddles and harness! O musical words" p. 140

"Sing for the Oak Tree" p. 140

"The farmer works his hired hand" p. 228

"The hands are as busy" p. 257

"There all day long the bullfrog cheeps" p. 139

"There were harrows" p. 257

"They who turn the whizzing wheel of labor should be blessed" p. 257

"We would advise you all to see" p. 112

"Where art thou, Love, still lost to me" p. 249

"Wherever blooms of health are blown" p. 130

Also, *Anderson Democrat* jingles (advertisements and locals),§ beginning:

"A hundred hearts beat happily; and when" p. 343

"And hence the Muse was prone to balk" p. 346

"And now the jolly Muse, with rosy lip" p. 347

"And when she still insisted" p. 346

"Come to the sanctum board to-night" p. 337

"Dear ever indulgent and generous Muse" p. 342

"Gilded bands and polished steel" p. 342

"Here on the balcony, a sign" p. 340

"Just across the street" p. 345

---

*Evidently printed in the *Anderson Democrat* in April, 1877; not seen except in proof sheet form.

†There is some similarity between this poem and another by Riley, uncollected, entitled, "The Stars Won't Wane and the Moon Won't Wax," published in *Life*, August 16, 1883.

§Some of these jingles have been noted in the form of unidentified newspaper clippings.

"Liquors that so strangely lubricate"   p. 347
"Make way for Liberty!" (he said)   p. 342
"Strop his razor till it gleams"   p. 344
"The praise of the Grocery men"   p. 346
"Twitter me something low and sweet"   p. 345
" 'What boots it?' Shakespeare asks"   p. 344
"When the heart like a plummet resounds in the dumps"   p.
347
"Where the goods are all new"   p. 344
"Who but he | Could read a watch's pedigree?"   p. 343

PASTELS OF MEN. By Eugene V. Debs. New York, Pearson's
(25c) Library, 1919

Wrappers. Contains, at p. 19, a letter* from Riley to Debs, beginning: *Do you think I've entirely forgotten all I owe you?* The letter contains a 4-line poem beginning: *You may break—you may shatter the little*
The same letter appears in David Karsner's *Debs: His Authorized Life
and Letters from Woodstock Prison to Atlanta,* published New York, Boni &
Liveright (1919); p. 211. The poems that appear at p. 212 are: stanza 3
of "Them Flowers," and part of stanza 3 of "Regardin' Terry Hut,"
both previously collected.

## 1920

THE LIFE OF MRS. ROBERT LOUIS STEVENSON. By Nellie Van de
Grift Sanchez. New York, Charles Scribner's Sons, 1920

Contains at p. 264, a letter to Mrs. Stevenson, dated Christmas,
1900, beginning: *Since your brief visit here last winter I've been remembering
you and your kindness every day* (later in *Letters of James Whitcomb Riley,*
edited by William Lyon Phelps [1930], p. 246).

## 1921

THE STORY OF A POET: MADISON CAWEIN. By Otto A. Rothert.
Louisville, Ky., John P. Morton & Company, Inc., 1921

Filson Club Publications, No. 30. Contains two letters to Cawein
which are first book appearances: one dated October 23, 1891 (at p.
333), beginning: *What's come of ye 'at you don't never let a fellow hear*

---

*Later in *Letters of James Whitcomb Riley,* edited by William Lyon Phelps (1930),
p. 92.

*nothin' of ye anymore?* The other, dated January 11, 1904, (at p. 336), begins: *Thank you—thank you! for the patient query reminding me of not having sent you a copy of the last book.*

# 1922

THE MATURITY OF JAMES WHITCOMB RILEY. By Marcus Dickey. Indianapolis, Bobbs-Merrill [1922]

Blue cloth, gilt stamped. Also a limited signed edition of 500 large-paper copies in boards with cloth shelfback. Later bound in olive-drab cloth, black-stamped. In addition to numerous letters, herein first published, the book contains uncollected poems: ["Crow's Nest"], beginning: *A little, dingy, dusty room*, p. 105; "The Autumn Leaves Is Falling," p. 253; also a number of uncollected poems without titles:

"And there was something in his tone" p. 45
"At La Ker-bie, nor mirth nor wit" p. 298
"I asked my tailor for a suit" p. 119
"I once thought myself quite a poet" p. 135
"Jes' my ortograph, you say" p. 196
"The burdened heart is lighter" p. 263
"What poverty like this! to laugh and sing" p. 111
"Your letter was almost as dear to me" p. 111

ROBERT J. BURDETTE: HIS MESSAGE. Edited from his writings by his wife, Clara B. Burdette. Pasadena, California, The Clara Vista Press, Published by the John C. Winston Company [1922]

Contains numerous letters to Burdette in the chapter entitled, "Friendship with Riley," pp. 163–186. One, written in 1881, contains an uncollected limerick, without title, beginning: *A carpenter up in Du Chien*. At p. 167 appears a poem entitled, "Little Jack Wiseman," also uncollected. The letter at p. 174 contains a poem entitled "Thanksgiving," previously in the *Omaha World-Herald*, November 21, 1897.

# 1924 (?)

[Advertisement of the Frederic ("Fritz") Krull program of Riley songs] [Indianapolis, n.d., 1924?]

Leaflet, 4 pages. Contains a letter to Fritz Krull dated January 9, 1904, in facsimile, beginning: *Thank you heartily for your good query;* uncollected.

# 1928

MARCHING ALONG. By John Philip Sousa. Boston, Hale, Cushman & Flint, 1928

This autobiography contains at p. 241 a letter from Riley to John Philip Sousa, dated August 4, 1904, beginning: *The promised box of medicine is received most gratefully;* uncollected.

THE LADY OF THE LIMBERLOST: THE LIFE AND LETTERS OF GENE STRATTON-PORTER. By Jeannette Porter Meehan. Garden City, N. Y., Doubleday, Doran & Co., Inc., 1928

Contains at p. 312, a letter to Mrs. Porter, dated October 19, 1915, beginning: *I am particularly glad that you set forth the creed of wholesomeness and cheer;* uncollected.

# 1929

JAMES WHITCOMB RILEY: MAN OF LETTERS. [By Julian Wetzel]. Indianapolis, Keystone Press, 1929

Wrappers. Contains a letter from Riley to Mr. and Mrs. Perry Rule, June 8, 1908, beginning: *In naming your three fine children you have greatly honored me;* uncollected. (The Rule triplets were named James, Whitcomb and Riley.) This letter had appeared in the *Indianapolis Star,* March 25, 1923.

JOAQUIN MILLER AND HIS OTHER SELF. By Harr Wagner. San Francisco, Calif., Wagner Publishing Co. [1929]

Contains at p. 163 Riley's introduction of Joaquin Miller at Plymouth Church, Indianapolis, beginning: *Enthusiastic love and pride for one's own country is, of course, natural to the citizen of any nation.* Contains also a letter to Joaquin Miller dated January 23, 1897, at p. 154, which begins: *Your good word of yesterday almost takes away a fellow's breath;* and another, at p. 220, dated July 18, 1903, beginning: *Your cheery ahoy is here, but not the book you say you sent me;* uncollected.

# 1935

SELECT WORKS OF YOUNG E. ALLISON. Louisville, Ky., 1935

Contains, at p. 25 of Part I (which is a biography of Young E. Allison written by J. Christian Bay) a parody of Allison's "The Derelict." The parody, beginning, *Fifteen men on the dead man's chest*, was written by Riley in a book which he presented to Allison, and appeared in *The Phoenix*, June, 1915. It appeared also in the *Boston Evening Transcript*, October 25, 1924. Uncollected.

# 1939

BLATCHLEYANA II. A Supplementary List of the Published Writings of W[illis] S[tanley] Blatchley. Indianapolis, Nature Publishing Co., 1939

Wrappers. Contains, at p. 41, a letter to Blatchley, in facsimile, dated January 31, 1916, beginning: *Thank you heartily for your good letter.* The poem, "Nessmuk," printed herein, had been published previously. A 4-line inscription by Riley in a book given to Blatchley is reproduced in facsimile.

# Undated

[A leaflet, 6½″ x 5⅛″; endorsements of Myra Churchill Holmes as a reader; n.p., n.d.]

Contains, on the second page, Riley's tribute to Myra Churchill Holmes, in facsimile, undated, beginning: *The endowments of Miss Holmes as an interpreter of real life-character is unusual in this day of many readers of high gifts;* uncollected.

[A card, 5¼″ x 3⅝″, n.p., Brooklyn, Ind.?, n.d.]

Bears the poem, "Jap Miller," on one side, an advertisement of Jap Miller's lectures on the other. Mr. Miller gave his lectures over a number of years and the date of this card cannot be established beyond the fact that it appeared not earlier than 1889. The Riley poem was frequently used by Jap Miller in similar ways.

REPRINT EDITIONS

# Books and Pamphlets

THE FOLLOWING is a representative selection of books and pamphlets by James Whitcomb Riley which contain no first edition material. Some are first separate printings in book form of poems previously collected; these are so identified.

ALL THE YEAR ROUND.
Indianapolis, Bobbs-Merrill [1912]

Illustrations by Gustave Baumann. First separate reprint of "A Hoosier Calendar"; title changed. Earliest binding blue cloth with white shelfback; later full blue cloth.

Issued also with an inserted leaf bearing Riley's speech at a luncheon held by the Jovian League, Hotel Severin, Indianapolis, August 3, 1914; it begins: *It was stipulated when I accepted the invitation to come here, that in deference to my health a speech would not be required of me.* Printed with the speech is a poem beginning, *Season halest of the year*, which is Part II of "Time of Clearer Twitterings."

Copies of *All the Year Round* were given by the club's Indianapolis members to 3,000 members of the Rotary Club present at a convention in Cincinnati, June, 1916. These bear the Rotary Club, Indianapolis, emblem gilt-stamped on the front cover. Inserted in each copy is a facsimile of a typewritten letter by Riley, dated June 21, 1916, addressed *To The Rotarians*. The letter appears in the *Indiana Daily Times*, July 25, 1916, and is reprinted in *Gems from Indiana-Rotary's Literary Belt* [n.d., June, 1920].

The book has been found with yet another insertion: a leaf bearing a printed Christmas greeting, signed in facsimile, *Bert A. Boyd*, and dated 1916. Below it is printed in facsimile Riley's poem beginning: *O Brother mine of birth divine* (stanza 2 of "Child's Christmas Carol"), apparently reprinted from Riley's Christmas greetings of 1914 and 1915.

AWAY.
Indianapolis, Bobbs-Merrill [1913]
Decorations by Emily Hall Chamberlain. *Riley Booklet, No. 6.*
Boards; and, ooze leather. First known separate reprint of the poem
"Away."

BABY BALLADS.
Indianapolis, Bobbs-Merrill [1914]
Wrappers. Reissue of *The Riley Baby Book* (1913).

THE BEST LOVED HOME BALLADS OF JAMES WHITCOMB RILEY.
New York, Blue Ribbon Books [1931]

THE BEST LOVED POEMS AND BALLADS OF JAMES WHITCOMB RILEY.
New York, Blue Ribbon Books [1934]
Illustrations by Ethel Franklin Betts. Omnibus edition, a one-
volume reissue of *The Best Loved Poems of James Whitcomb Riley* and
*The Best Loved Home Ballads of James Whitcomb Riley.*

THE BEST LOVED POEMS OF JAMES WHITCOMB RILEY.
New York, Blue Ribbon Books [1920]
Illustrations by Ethel Franklin Betts.

THE BOY LIVES ON OUR FARM.
Indianapolis, Bobbs-Merrill [1908, *i.e.* 1911]
Illustrations by Ethel Franklin Betts. Reissue of part of *The
Orphant Annie Book* (1908). Copyright page bears the final date
1908; actually issued in 1911.

THE COMPLETE POETICAL WORKS OF JAMES WHITCOMB RILEY. Preface
by Donald Culross Peattie.
Indianapolis, Bobbs-Merrill [1937]
A one-volume reprint of the *Memorial Edition.* The preface,
"Riley as a Nature Poet," is new.

CONTENTMENT.*
Indianapolis, Bobbs-Merrill [1914]
Decorations by Emily Hall Chamberlain. *Riley Booklet, No. 8.*
Boards; and, ooze leather. Contains poem, "Contentment" (previ-
ously published as "Kneeling with Herrick") and "Just to Be
Good."

---

*Published September, 1914. Some copies were apparently issued later as
Valentine and Easter greetings, with the dust wrappers so marked.

THE DAYS GONE BY.*
  Indianapolis, Bobbs-Merrill [1914]
  Decorations by Emily Hall Chamberlain. *Riley Booklet*, No. [?].
  Boards; and, ooze leather. Contains "The Days Gone By," the last
  2 stanzas of "Be Our Fortunes As They May" and the first stanza
  of "Who Bides His Time." Not to be confused with the book of
  the same title, published 1895, *q.v.*

DIALECT IN LITERATURE.
  Indianapolis, Bowen-Merrill, 1896
  Wrappers. With, and without, gilt top. Printed from the standing
  type of the 1895 edition of *Neghborly Poems*. First separate reprint.

A DISCOURAGING MODEL.
  Indianapolis, Bobbs-Merrill [1914]
  Illustrations by Howard Chandler Christy, decorations by Franklin Booth. Boards, cloth shelfback. First separate reprint of the
  poem; a reissue of part of *Riley Roses* (1909).

DO THEY MISS ME.
  Indianapolis, Bobbs-Merrill [1913]
  Decorations by Emily Hall Chamberlain. *Riley Booklet*, No. 7.
  Boards; and, ooze leather. First separate reprint of "A Old Played-
  Out Song"; title changed.

DOWN AROUND THE RIVER AND OTHER POEMS.
  Indianapolis, Bobbs-Merrill [1911]
  Boards, cloth shelfback; and, full cloth. One of the illustrated
  series of six books named by the publishers, "Brandywine Books."

ECCENTRIC MR. CLARK.
  New York, The New York Book Co., 1913.
  Eight prose sketches reprinted from earlier Riley books.

FAVORITE POEMS OF JAMES WHITCOMB RILEY CHOSEN BY WILLIAM
LYON PHELPS.
  See: *Selected Poems . . . Chosen by William Lyon Phelps*.

FLOWERS AND FRUIT FROM RILEY.
  New York, Cupples & Leon Co. [1909]

---

*See note *ante*.

GEMS FROM RILEY.
>Boston, De Wolfe, Fiske & Co. [1904]
>Also: *New York*, Cupples & Leon Co. [190–?]

THE GIRL I LOVED.
>Indianapolis, Bobbs-Merrill [1910]

>Illustrations by Howard Chandler Christy, decorations by Margaret Armstrong. First separate reprint of "Farmer Whipple— Bachelor"; title changed. Occurs in various states, of which the earliest is bound in green cloth with decorations on front cover similar to *An Old Sweetheart of Mine* (1902) and *Out to Old Aunt Mary's* (1904).

THE GLAD SWEET FACE OF HER.
>Indianapolis, Bobbs-Merrill [1914]

>Decorations by Emily Hall Chamberlain. *Riley Booklet, No.* [?]. Boards; and, ooze leather. First separate reprint of "Ike Walton's Prayer"; title changed.

GOOD-BYE, JIM.
>Indianapolis, Bobbs-Merrill [1913]

>Illustrations by Howard Chandler Christy, decorations by Bertha Stuart. First separate printing of "The Old Man and Jim"; title changed.

HE AND I.
>Indianapolis, Bobbs-Merrill [1913]

>Decorations by Emily Hall Chamberlain. *Riley Booklet, No. 2.* Boards; and, ooze leather. First separate reprint.

HER BEAUTIFUL EYES.
>Indianapolis, Bobbs-Merrill [1913]

>Decorations by Emily Hall Chamberlain. *Riley Booklet, No. 5.* Boards; and, ooze leather. First separate reprint in book form; published earlier in sheet music form (see p. 212).

HOME AGAIN WITH ME.
>Indianapolis, Bobbs-Merrill [1908]

>Illustrations by Howard Chandler Christy, decorations by Franklin Booth. First separate reprint of "Home Ag'in"; title changed. Similar in format to *An Old Sweetheart of Mine* (1902).

A HOOSIER ROMANCE.
New York, Century, 1910.

Illustrations by John Wolcott Adams. First separate reprint of "Squire Hawkins's Story"; title changed. The Bobbs-Merrill reprint, 1912, occurs in various states; some copies were used in 1922 as souvenirs of the Riley Birthday Luncheon, at the time of the dedication of the James Whitcomb Riley Hospital for Children, in Indianapolis.

A HOST OF CHILDREN.
Indianapolis, Bobbs-Merrill [1920]

Illustrations by Ethel Franklin Betts.

A JAMES WHITCOMB RILEY CALENDAR [for] 1912.
Indianapolis, Bobbs-Merrill [1911]

Illustrations by Ethel Franklin Betts. Reissued in 1912 as the calendar for 1913. An earlier calendar appeared under the title: THE RILEY CALENDAR . . . 1911.

THE JAMES WHITCOMB RILEY READER. Selected, graded, and with suggestions for the observance of Riley Day, by Charity Dye.
Indianapolis, Bobbs-Merrill [1915]

JAMES WHITCOMB RILEY'S CHILDHOOD POEMS.
Racine, Wis., Whitman Publishing Co. [1940]

Illustrations by Ethel Bonney Taylor.

JEWELS FROM JAMES WHITCOMB RILEY.
Buffalo, N. Y., Berger Publishing Co. [1907]

JUST BE GLAD.
Indianapolis, Bobbs-Merrill [1914]

Decorations by Emily Hall Chamberlain. *Riley Booklet, No.* [?]. Boards; and, ooze leather. Contains the poem, "Just Be Glad" (previously published as "Kissing the Rod") and "A Song," beginning: *There is ever a song somewhere, my dear.*

KNEE-DEEP IN JUNE AND OTHER POEMS.
Indianapolis, Bobbs-Merrill [1912]

One of the "Brandywine Books" series.

LITTLE ORPHAN ANNIE.
Indianapolis, Bobbs-Merrill [1908, *i.e.* 1910]

Illustrations by Ethel Franklin Betts. Reissue of *The Orphant Annie Book*, with same number of pages but a different arrangement of the latter part of the text. Although the copyright page bears the final date 1908, this book did not appear until 1910.

LITTLE ORPHAN ANNIE. (Cover title: EF YOU DON'T WATCH OUT).
Indianapolis, Bobbs-Merrill [1908, *i.e.* 1911]

Illustrations by Ethel Franklin Betts. Reissue of part of *The Orphant Annie Book*. The copyright page bears the final date 1908, but not issued until 1911.

MRS. MILLER.
Indianapolis, Bobbs-Merrill [1911]

In a boxed set of 12 volumes by Indiana authors, uniformly bound in red cloth, issued by The Indiana Society of Chicago and presented to members at the seventh annual dinner, December, 1911. In 1912 the society offered for sale a special edition of 100 sets bound in green ooze leather. The book contains two reprinted prose sketches: "Mrs. Miller" and "Jamesy."

THE NAME OF OLD GLORY; POEMS OF PATRIOTISM.
Indianapolis, Bobbs-Merrill [1917]

Frontispiece by Howard Chandler Christy. Appreciation by Booth Tarkington.

NEW SUBURBAN TRAIN SERVICE ON THE BALTIMORE & OHIO SOUTH-WESTERN R. R.
[Cincinnati, A. H. Pugh Printing Co., n.d., 1896? 1897?] (Cover title: OUR NEW SUBURBAN TRAINS)

Wrappers. Presented with the compliments of the Passenger Department of the Baltimore & Ohio Railroad Company in 1896 or 1897, as nearly as the date can be established by this company. The Riley poem, "The Sooburbs," first collected in *Neghborly Poems* (1891) under the title, "Town and Country," appears here with the introduction, "Benj. F. Johnson of Boone Again Heard From," as in the *Indianapolis Journal*, April 10, 1891.

OLD-FASHIONED ROSES.
Indianapolis, Bobbs-Merrill [1909, *i.e.* 1914]

Illustrations by Howard Chandler Christy, decorations by Franklin Booth. Boards, cloth shelfback. First separate reprint of the poem; a reissue of part of *Riley Roses* (1909). Although the final copyright date is stated as 1909, the book was not published until 1914; the second state has the date 1914 on the copyright page.

OLD SCHOOL DAY ROMANCES.
Indianapolis, Bobbs-Merrill [1909]

Illustrations and decorations by E. Stetson Crawford. First separate reprint of "Friday Afternoon"; title changed. First state binding has a decorative panel by Crawford, measuring 6⅜" x 5", inlaid on the front cover; the second issue,* has a larger inlay, 8½" x 5¹³⁄₁₆", done by Worth Brehm.

AN OLD SWEETHEART.
Indianapolis, Bowen-Merrill, 1891

13 lithographed plates, 7⁹⁄₁₆" x 9¹¹⁄₁₆", by Armstrong & Co., Boston, on heavy white bristol boards hinged on linen, bound in a variety of colors and patterns of cloth. This is the first separate reprint of the poem. See *An Old Sweetheart of Mine* (1902) for the extended version, with first edition material.

THE OLD SWIMMIN'-HOLE AND OTHER POEMS.
Indianapolis, Bobbs-Merrill [1912]

One of the "Brandywine Books" series.

THE OLD TIMES.
Indianapolis, Bobbs-Merrill [1915]

OUT TO OLD AUNT MARY'S (facsimile manuscript edition—see p. 99)

POEMS.
London, Gay & Hancock, Ltd., 1913

The *Publishers' Note*, p. [v], states: "His [Riley's] poems deserve to be better known in this country, and so, with the approval of the Author and American publishers, we issue this popular volume."

THE PRAYER PERFECT AND OTHER POEMS.
Indianapolis, Bobbs-Merrill [1912]

One of the "Brandywine Books" series.

THE RILEY CALENDAR COMPILED FROM THE WORKS OF JAMES WHITCOMB RILEY 1911. [n.p., 1910]

Other Riley calendars are listed under the title: A JAMES WHITCOMB RILEY CALENDAR.

---

*Advertised as a "new edition," October 7, 1911, in the *Indianapolis News*.

RILEY CHILD-RHYMES.

Indianapolis, Bowen-Merrill, 1899 [*i.e.* 1898]

Illustrations by Will Vawter. Occurred in several states before the Bobbs-Merrill imprint replaced the Bowen-Merrill, some of the distinguishing features being as follows: *State* 1, front matter printed wholly in black; copyright page without printers' slug; pp. xv and xvii without decoration; no marginal line drawings. *State* 2, front matter partly in red; decorative headings on pp. xv and xvii; illustration and heading changed at top of p. 51; contents rearranged and both tables of contents and illustrations reset. *State* 3, same as State 2 but with Braunworth & Co.'s slug on the copyright page, and line drawings added on margins and elsewhere.

The proem, untitled, consists of the last ten lines of "The Hoosier Folk-Child."

RILEY CHILD VERSE.

Indianapolis, Bobbs-Merrill [1906, *i.e.* 1908]

Illustrations by Ethel Franklin Betts. Reprint of part of *While the Heart Beats Young*. Final date on the copyright page 1906; actually published 1908.

RILEY FAIRY TALES.

Indianapolis, Bobbs-Merrill [1923]

Illustrations by Will Vawter.

RILEY FARM-RHYMES.

Indianapolis, Bowen-Merrill [1901]

Illustrations by Will Vawter.

RILEY FAVORITES.

Indianapolis, Bobbs-Merrill [1914?]

A one-volume collection of seven of the "Riley Booklets": A SONG OF LONG AGO; HE AND I; WHEN MY DREAMS COME TRUE; THE ROSE; AWAY; HER BEAUTIFUL EYES; DO THEY MISS ME. The copyright dates 1913 and 1914 appear.

RILEY HOOSIER STORIES.

Indianapolis, Bobbs-Merrill [1917]

Illustrations by Will Vawter. Reprint of six prose sketches.

RILEY ROSES.
Indianapolis, Bobbs-Merrill [1909]

Illustrations by Howard Chandler Christy. *State* 1, green cloth. *State* 2, rose-colored cloth; text and illustrations rearranged. Contains three poems: "A Discouraging Model," "Old-Fashioned Roses" and "The Rose," later issued as three separate books.

RILEY SONGS OF HOME.
Indianapolis, Bobbs-Merrill [1910]

Illustrations by Will Vawter.

THE ROSE.
Indianapolis, Bobbs-Merrill [1913]

Decorations by Emily Hall Chamberlain. *Riley Booklet, No. 4.* Boards; and, ooze leather. First separate reprint of the poem.

With illustrations by Howard Chandler Christy, *Indianapolis,* Bobbs-Merrill, 1914 (from the plates of *Riley Roses* [1909]).

THE RUNAWAY BOY.
Indianapolis, Bobbs-Merrill [1906, *i.e.* 1908]

Illustrations by Ethel Franklin Betts. Reprint of part of *While the Heart Beats Young* (1906).

SELECTED POEMS BY JAMES WHITCOMB RILEY CHOSEN BY WILLIAM LYON PHELPS.
Indianapolis, Bobbs-Merrill [1931]

Reprinted, New York, Triangle Books [1938], under the title: *Favorite Poems of James Whitcomb Riley Chosen by William Lyon Phelps.*

SKETCHES IN PROSE AND OCCASIONAL VERSES.
Indianapolis, Bowen-Merrill, 1891

A reissue of *The Boss Girl* (1886). The title of the prose sketch, "The Boss Girl," is here changed to "Jamesy." In 1901 the book was recopyrighted under the title, *Sketches in Prose with Interluding Verses,* but with no first edition material added.

A SONG OF LONG AGO.
Indianapolis, Bobbs-Merrill [1913]

Decorations by Emily Hall Chamberlain. *Riley Booklet No. 1.* Boards; and, ooze leather. First separate reprint of the poem.

A SUMMER'S DAY AND OTHER POEMS.
>   Indianapolis, Bobbs-Merrill [1911]
>
>   Boards, cloth shelfback; and, full cloth. One of the "Brandywine Books" series.

TO MY FRIEND.
>   Indianapolis, Bobbs-Merrill [1914]
>
>   Decorations by Emily Hall Chamberlain. *Riley Booklet No. 11.* Boards; and, ooze leather. First separate reprint of the poem, "To My Old Friend, William Leachman"; title changed.

WESLEY COTTERL OF THE GENUS CHECKER PLAYER. A Conception of James Whitcomb Riley Revised and Illustrated by Samuel Severn, Publisher of the Sammie Checker Book.
[n.p., n.d., not before 1917]
>   Wrappers. The first separate printing of Riley's prose sketch, "The Champion Checker-Player of Ameriky"; title changed. The text is unrevised; illustrations are added.

WHEN MY DREAMS COME TRUE.
>   Indianapolis, Bobbs-Merrill [1913]
>
>   Decorations by Emily Hall Chamberlain. *Riley Booklet No. 3.* Boards; and, ooze leather. First separate reprint of the poem.

WHEN SHE COMES HOME.*
>   Indianapolis, Bobbs-Merrill [1914]
>
>   Decorations by Emily Hall Chamberlain. *Riley Booklet No. 10.* Boards; and, ooze leather. Contains the poem, "When She Comes Home" which had no earlier separate appearance except in the form of sheet music; also contains the first 4 stanzas of "Her Beautiful Hands."

WHEN SHE WAS ABOUT SIXTEEN.
>   Indianapolis, Bobbs-Merrill [1911]
>
>   Illustrations by Howard Chandler Christy. Cloth; and, full red leather. First separate reprint of "His Pa's Romance," under a changed title.

---

*Published September, 1914. Some copies were apparently issued later as Valentine and Easter greetings, with the dust wrappers so marked.

WHEN THE FROST IS ON THE PUNKIN AND OTHER POEMS.
  Indianapolis, Bobbs-Merrill [1911]
    Boards, cloth shelfback; and, full cloth. One of the "Brandywine
Books" series.

WILD ROSES FROM RILEY.
  New York, Hayes Lithographing Co. [1910]

    NOTES: Riley's poems have been published in many forms other
than those described in the foregoing pages. There have appeared innumerable post cards with selections from Riley, entire poems or ex-
tracts from them. These are not first appearances, although they may be
first separate publications. The Scofield-Pierson Company, Indianapolis,
issued a post card, copyrighted 1906, illustrated, bearing the last two
lines of "Thoughts fer the Discuraged Farmer." In 1907 the same firm
advertised a series of ten Riley post cards (see the *Indianapolis News*,
November 15, 1907). The Prince Publishing Company, Buffalo, N.Y.,
copyrighted a post card in 1908 which bears part of "Wet-Weather
Talk," under the title, "Philosophy." In 1912 the Majestic Publishing
Company, Indianapolis, issued a series of fourteen or more Riley cards
(Series No. 503). The imprint of the H. R. Pierson Company, Indianapolis, occurs on two or more cards similar to some in the Majestic
Publishing Company series. A series of eight Riley post cards was
published by the Hoover-Watson Printing Company, Indianapolis.
The last five lines of "Kissing the Rod" occur on a white post card
with an orange border, no imprint. No doubt other post cards have
been issued.
    A number of poems appeared in the form of Christmas greetings,
used by Riley, his publishers and others. Riley's Christmas greeting for
1912 consisted of his poem, "Child's Christmas Carol," signed (in facsimile) and dated, printed within ornamental borders on a sheet of heavy
paper, 8⅝" x 7". His Christmas greeting for 1913 was a card bearing
the words, "In the words of Tiny Tim Cratchit 'God Bless us Every
One.' " In 1914 he used the second stanza of "Child's Christmas Carol,"
without the title, beginning: "O Brother mine of birth Divine," in a
leaflet with poinsettias on the first page; undated. The year following,
his Christmas greeting consisted of the same stanza with a printed spray
of holly, on a white card, 4" x 5⅞"; undated.
    The Bobbs-Merrill Company issued Christmas leaflets with ex-
cerpts from Riley's poems. One contains an illustration by Will Vawter,
from *A Defective Santa Claus* (1904), with the last stanza of "A Christmas
Glee," untitled, beginning: "With a hey! and a hi! and a hey-ho-ho!"

Another bears a different illustration, from the same book, and the poem, "Christmas Afterthought," untitled, beginning: "After a thoughtful, almost painful pause." A third one has an illustration which shows Santa Claus in his sleigh above the treetops, and the last stanza of "Who Santy Claus Wuz," untitled, beginning: "Wisht that yarn wuz true about him, as it 'peared to be."

This last-named poem, in its entirety, was used in a holiday greeting issued by Mr. and Mrs. Joseph James White, Chicago, 1926, bound in pictorial boards.

The poem, "Just As of Old," appeared on a Christmas greeting issued in December, 1940, captioned: "A Remembrance from the Birthplace of the Beloved Hoosier Poet James Whitcomb Riley." This same poem, under the title, "Envoy," had been used in 1933 in a leaflet issued by the Strobridge Lithographing Company, Cincinnati, advertising Linweave papers, printed in blue and decorated in gilt.

"Das Krist Kindel" has been noted on a Christmas greeting issued by the advertising firm of William G. Schnellé, 248 Lexington Avenue, New York City, 1936.

Part III of "A Time of Clearer Twitterings," beginning: "Season halest of the year," was printed on a card of greetings, 5⅛" x 4⅛", issued at the time of Riley's birthday, October 7, 1915; the same part was mounted on the box containing the Birthday Dinner Edition of *Poems Here at Home*, October 7, 1915.

The Seymour-Riley Panels consist of a collection of six broadsides on cream-colored Florentine cardboard, hand-lettered and colored, 10" x 7¼", issued in 1905 in a cardboard box; also, in mailing envelopes. On the box appears the following: The | Seymour-Riley Panels | Six Poems by | James Whitcomb Riley | Lettered and decorated | by | Ralph Fletcher Seymour | and printed separately | as panels | The Bobbs-Merrill Company | Publishers, Indianapolis   All of the poems had been collected previously; most of them had appeared with the Seymour decorations in *The Reader Magazine* in 1904–1905. The titles are: "As Created"; "God Bless Us Every One"; "Ike Walton's Prayer"; "Kissing the Rod"; "The Prayer-Perfect"; "Wet Weather Talk." "The Prayer-Perfect," printed in green on cream-colored, coated paper, with the Seymour decorations, as in *The Reader Magazine*, November, 1904, was used as a souvenir by Bobbs-Merrill; it bears a notice of their sixty-seventh holiday opening, November 25, 1904. Copies of the same panel were given as premiums for renewed subscriptions to *The Home Magazine*, published by Bobbs-Merrill, in 1906 or 1907.

"Hymn Exultant | For Easter" appeared on a white card, 7⅛" x 5⅜", decorated with yellow and purple, dated 1909. Possibly this is the card referred to in the *Indianapolis News*, April 6, 1917, as printed "seven years ago" for the Indianapolis Orphan Asylum's annual flower sale.

In 1901 "The Name of Old Glory" was printed on a broadside, 14″ x 5⅛″, headed: "Indiana Day" | Pan-American Exposition | Saturday, September 14, 1901 | Poem by "The Hoosier Poet."

A book mark was issued on October 7, 1914, bearing three stanzas of "On the Sunny Side."

"Just Be Glad" (collected under the title, "Kissing the Rod") was printed in an illuminated leaflet, undated but undoubtedly after 1900.

Under the heading, "Boosters' Creed," the poem, "Let Something Good Be Said," appeared on a sheet of white coated paper, 9″ x 12″, printed within a red decorative border by P. C. Darrow, Chicago; undated, probably after 1900.

"The Fishing Party" has been noted on a white card, 5″ x 3⅛″, printed in blue at the left of a column of figures, 1 to 10. Above the poem is printed: "Kindness of Mr. J. N. and Mrs. Emma Foster. Compliments of J. B. Wilson, W. M. Mills." A date, *Dec. 4, '90*, appears below the poem.

On February 8, 1914, the First Unitarian Church of San Diego, California, held a James Whitcomb Riley service. On the program distributed at the time appears a greeting from Riley: "To my friends in San Diego | Hale and hearty greetings | and tidings of good cheer" followed by the last two lines of "Thoughts fer the Discuraged Farmer."

The preceding list is representative of the countless occasional publications, ephemeral in nature, containing material by Riley. When they occur it is important to check original appearances in order to determine bibliographical status. Particular attention must be paid to the possibility of changed titles.

# Sheet Music

~~~~~~~~~~~~~~~~~~~~~~~~~~~~~~~~~~~~~~~~~~~~~~~~~~~

THE FOLLOWING is a representative list of the Riley poems set to music and published. The list is undoubtedly far from complete but suggests the extent of the appearance of his poems in such form. No attempt has been made to indicate the various keys in which they have been issued.

In every case but one, the first listed piece of sheet music is the first known separate printing of the poem; the exception is "An Old Sweetheart of Mine" which had appeared earlier as a separate book (see p. 90). Six pieces of sheet music are printings before collection in a Riley book and are collated in the first editions section: "The Messiah of Nations," "Baby Bye," "Leonainie," "A Song of the Road," "A Christmas Glee," "Say Farewell and Let Me Go."

All of James Whitcomb Riley's poems are Ascap-controlled.

AMERICA (see: "The Messiah of Nations," p. 162)

BABY BYE (see p. 148)

BABYHOOD (see "Heigh-ho! Babyhood")

THE BEE-BAG. Composer: Fritz Krull. Indianapolis, Fritz Krull, 1913. Reissued in: *Four Songs from the Poems of James Whitcomb Riley* by Fritz Krull (see p. 220)

BILLY AND HIS DRUM. Composer: Gerrit Smith. Boston, A. P. Schmidt, 1906.

BILLY GOODIN. In: *A Riley Album* by Rupert Hughes (see p. 219) and *Ten Songs of Childhood* by Archie A. Mumma (see p. 219)

THE BOY PATRIOT. In: *The Ward-Stephens Musical Settings of Selected Poems by James Whitcomb Riley* (see p. 220)

THE BROOK SONG. Composer: Harriet Kendall. (Recitation with musical accompaniment.) London, Reynolds & Co., 1920.

CHILDHOOD. Composer: Ida Leigh Hilton. New York, Carl Fischer, 1905. (Poem previously collected under the title, "Babe Herrick.")

A CHRISTMAS GLEE (see p. 164)

CHRISTINE'S SONG (Up in Tentoleena Land). In: *The Ward-Stephens Musical Settings of Selected Poems by James Whitcomb Riley* (see p. 220)

COFFEE LIKE HIS MOTHER USED TO MAKE. In: *A Riley Album* by Rupert Hughes (see p. 219)

CRADLE SONG (see "Baby Bye," p. 149)

THE DARING PRINCE. In: *The Daring Prince and Nine Other Piano Pieces* by Angela Diller (see p. 220)

THE DARING PRINCE AND NINE OTHER PIANO PIECES by Angela Diller (see p. 220)

THE DAYS GONE BY. Composer: Homer N. Bartlett. Boston, Oliver Ditson Co., 1895.
   Also set to music by Elizabeth J. Cotton, arrangement by Barclay Walker; Indianapolis, Elizabeth J. Cotton, 1916.

THE DEAD LOVER. In: *A Riley Album* by Rupert Hughes (see p. 219)

THE DEAD WIFE. Composer: Fritz Krull. Indianapolis, Fritz Krull, 1914. (The poem beginning, "Always I see her in a saintly guise.")

DEARTH. Composer: Fritz Krull. Indianapolis, Fritz Krull, 1914.

THE DINERS IN THE KITCHEN. In: *The Daring Prince and Nine Other Piano Pieces* by Angela Diller (see p. 220)

DON'T CRY (see "A Life-Lesson")

A DREAM OF AUTUMN. Composer: Harry C. Eldridge. Cincinnati, Geo. B. Jennings Co., 1899.

DWAINIE—A SPRITE SONG. In: *Ten Songs of Childhood* by Archie A. Mumma (see p. 219)

EVER A SONG SOMEWHERE (see "A Song")

EXTREMES. Composer: Marshall Bartholomew, in: *The Music Hour in the Kindergarten and First Grade* (see p. 221). Also in: *The Daring Prince and Nine Other Piano Pieces* by Angela Diller (see p. 220)

THE FIRST BLUEBIRD. Composer: John Carlyle Davis. New York, G. Schirmer, Inc., 1925.

FOOL YOUNGENS.*

---

*For record of a musical setting see *Biographical Edition*, Vol. 6, p. 462.

THE FUNNY LITTLE FELLOW. In: *Churchill-Grindell Song Book No. 1* (see p. 221)

THE GOBBLE-UNS'LL GIT YOU EF YOU DON'T WATCH OUT! Composer: Everard Jack Appleton. Cincinnati, George B. Jennings Co., 1892. (The first separate printing of the poem, "Little Orphant Annie." Its first known appearance in a musical setting is in *The Franklin Square Song Collection, No. 6* selected by J. P. McCaskey; New York, Harper & Bros., 1889. Among later musical settings are the following:)

LITTLE ORPHANT ANNIE. Composer: Alicia Adélaide Needham. London & New York, Boosey & Co., 1899.

LITTLE ORPHANT ANNIE. Composer: B. Margaret Hoberg. New York [etc.], M. Witmark & Sons, 1911.

LITTLE ORPHANT ANNIE. Composer: Clayton Thomas. Boston, Arthur P. Schmidt, 1913.

LITTLE ORPHANT ANNIE. Composer: Fritz Krull. Indianapolis, Fritz Krull, 1913. (Reissued in *Four Songs from the Poems of James Whitcomb Riley* by Fritz Krull; see p. 220)

LITTLE ORPHANT ANNIE. In: *The Ward-Stephens Musical Settings of Selected Poems by James Whitcomb Riley* (see p. 220)

LITTLE ORPHANT ANNIE. Composer: Barclay Walker. Indianapolis, Beardsley-Woods Publishing Co., 1916. (This contains Riley's letter to George Ade, introducing Barclay Walker; in facsimile on inside front cover; also in Walker's musical setting of "Out to Old Aunt Mary's," 1916.)

GOOD-BY ER HOWDY-DO. Composer: Hubbard Taylor-Smith. Washington, D. C., John F. Ellis & Co., 1889.

Later set to music by T. G. L[ansden]. [n.p.], Lake Publishing Co., 1911.

GRANNY'S COME TO OUR HOUSE. In: *A Riley Album* by Rupert Hughes (see p. 219)

GRIGGSBY'S STATION. In: *A Riley Album* by Rupert Hughes (see p. 219)

HEIGH-HO! BABYHOOD. Composer: Florence O'Neill. Arranged by Charles M. Couch. Allegheny, Pa., Couch & Holden, 1894; deposited for copyright July 20, 1894. (Poem previously collected under the title, "Babyhood.")

Also, BABYHOOD. Composer: R. I. José. Boston, White-Smith Music Publishing Co., 1894; deposited for copyright October 3, 1894.

HER BEAUTIFUL EYES. Composer: Carl Hahn. Cincinnati, John Church Co., 1897.

Also set to music and published by Edgar Dwight Johnston, Los Angeles, 1941 (chorale, 1942).

HER BEAUTIFUL HANDS. Composer: Ward-Stephens. New York, Chappell & Co., Ltd., 1915.

Also in *The Ward-Stephens Musical Settings of Selected Poems by James Whitcomb Riley* (see p. 220)

A HUMBLE SINGER. Composer: Lulu Maye Lockwood. Boston, C. W. Thompson & Co., 1912.

I WANT TO BE A SOLDIER. Composer: Bertha M. Jackson. Cincinnati, Willis Music Co., 1917. (Poem previously collected under the title, "The Boy Patriot.")

I WILL WALK WITH YOU, MY LAD (see "A Song of the Road," p. 159)

IF I KNEW WHAT POETS KNOW. Composer: William D. Armstrong. Philadelphia, Hatch Music Co., 1901.

AN IMPETUOUS RESOLVE. In: *A Riley Album* by Rupert Hughes (see p. 219)

This appeared later in *Churchill-Grindell Song Book No. 1*, Platteville, Churchill-Grindell Co., 1905.

Also, in sheet music, composer: Carrie B. Adams; Dayton, Lorenz Publishing Co., 1911.

Also, in *The Daring Prince and Nine Other Piano Pieces* by Angela Diller (see p. 220)

IN THE ORCHARD WHERE THE CHILDREN USED TO PLAY. Composer: Barclay Walker. New York, Jos. W. Stern & Co., 1909. (Poem previously collected under the title, "Where the Children Used to Play.")

IT. In: *The Daring Prince and Nine Other Piano Pieces* by Angela Diller (see p. 220)

THE JOLLY MILLER; RESTORED ROMAUNT. Composer: Fritz Krull. Indianapolis, Fritz Krull, 1914.

THE KINGDOM OF A CHILD. Composer: Martha Mendenhall Rippell. Buffalo, N. Y., Deux-Arts Studio, 1936.

(The words are the same as the proem in *Riley Child-Rhymes*, 1899: consisting of the last ten lines of "The Hoosier Folk-Child.")

LAST NIGHT AND THIS. Composer: Laura Dye Carpenter. New York, Globe Music Co., 1905.

A LEAVE-TAKING. Composer: Fritz Krull. Indianapolis, Fritz Krull, 1914.

LEONAINIE (see p. 147)

A LIFE-LESSON. Composer: Jules Jordan. Boston, A. P. Schmidt & Co., 1889. Deposited for copyright April 29, 1889. Also set to music by Edward Campion, published Cleveland, J. H. Rogers, 1889, under the title, "There, Little Girl, Don't Cry," deposited for copyright November 29, 1889. A third composition was published the same year, under the latter title, with music by P. A. Schnecker, New York, G. Schirmer Co., deposited for copyright December 11, 1889.

Among later musical settings are the following:

DON'T CRY. Composer: Mary Knight Wood. Boston, Oliver Ditson Co., 1893.

THERE LITTLE GIRL, DON'T CRY. Composer: Homer A. Norris. Philadelphia, Theo. Presser Co., 1893.

THERE, LITTLE GIRL, DON'T CRY. Composer: Alvah Glover Salmon. Boston, Louis H. Ross & Co., 1893.

THERE LITTLE GIRL, DON'T CRY. Composer: Henry B. Vincent. Philadelphia, Theo. Presser Co., 1896.

THERE! LITTLE GIRL, DON'T CRY. Composer: Carl Sobeski. Boston, Oliver Ditson Co., 1898.

A LIFE LESSON. Composer: Ethelbert Nevin. Boston, Boston Music Co., G. Schirmer, Jr., 1898.

THERE LITTLE GIRL; DON'T CRY. Composer: Clarence Forsyth. Indianapolis, Wulschner & Son, 1900.

A LIFE'S LESSON. Composer: William D. Armstrong. Philadelphia, Hatch Music Co., 1901.

LITTLE GIRL, DON'T CRY. Composer: P. A. Tirindelli. Cincinnati, John Church Co., 1901.

THERE LITTLE GIRL DON'T CRY. Composer: George Chadwick Stock. New York, Wm. A. Pond & Co., 1902.

THERE! LITTLE GIRL, DON'T CRY. Composer: Caro Roma. New York, M. Witmark & Sons, 1903.

THE SILVER LINING. Composer: Charles Willeby. Cincinnati, John Church Co., 1905.

THERE, LITTLE GIRL, DON'T CRY. Composer: Edward Campion. New York, G. Schirmer, 1906 (reissue of 1889 edition).

THERE, LITTLE GIRL, DON'T CRY. Composer: Ernest Newton. London, Leonard & Co., 1909.

A LIFE LESSON. Composer: Claude Kilworth. Columbus, O., Claude Kilworth, 1912.

THERE! LITTLE GIRL; DON'T CRY! In: *Ten Songs of Childhood* by Archie A. Mumma (see p. 219)

A LIFE-LESSON. Composer: Fritz Krull. Indianapolis, Fritz Krull, 1913. Reissued in *Four Songs from the Poems of James Whitcomb Riley* by Fritz Krull (see p. 220)

THERE LITTLE GIRL DON'T CRY. Composer: Hallett Gilberté. Boston, C. W. Thompson & Co., 1915.

THERE! LITTLE GIRL; DON'T CRY (A LIFE-LESSON). Composer: Ward-Stephens. New York, Chappell & Co., Ltd., 1915. (Also in *The Ward-Stephens Musical Settings of Selected Poems by James Whitcomb Riley* [1915].)

THERE, LITTLE GIRL, DON'T CRY. Composer: Liza Lehmann. London, Chappell & Co., Ltd., 1916.

THERE LITTLE GIRL DON'T CRY. Composer: William T. Pierson. Hartford, C. C. Church & Co., 1919.

THERE, LITTLE GIRL, DON'T CRY. Composer: Elizabeth Wood Vance. Adapted by John Winter Thompson. [n.p.], 1942.

LIGHT OF LOVE. Composer: E. L. Fentress. Washington, H. Kirkus Dugdale Co., Inc., 1912.

LITTLE GIRLY-GIRL. In: *Ten Songs of Childhood* by Archie A. Mumma (see p. 219)

 Also: LITTLE GIRLIE-GIRL. Composer: Elizabeth J. Cotton. Arranged by Barclay Walker. Indianapolis, Elizabeth J. Cotton, 1916.

 Also: LITTLE GIRLY-GIRL. Composer: Linn Seiler. New York, G. Schirmer, Inc., 1918.

LITTLE ORPHANT ANNIE (see "The Gobble-Uns'll Git You Ef You Don't Watch Out")

THE LITTLE RED APPLE TREE. Composer: Carrie B. Adams. Terre Haute, C. B. Adams Music Co., 1912.

 Also: THE LITTLE-RED-APPLE TREE. Composer: Elizabeth J. Cotton. Arranged by Barclay Walker. Indianapolis, Elizabeth J. Cotton, 1916.

THE LITTLE RED RIBBON (see "The Ribbon, the Ring and the Rose")

THE LITTLE TINY KICKSHAW. In: *A Riley Album* by Rupert Hughes (see p. 219)

LOCKERBIE STREET. Composer: Elizabeth J. Cotton. Indianapolis, Elizabeth J. Cotton, 1915.

THE LOST LOVER. Composer: Eleanor Kent. New York, M. Witmark & Sons, 1909. (Poem previously collected under the title, "A Lost Love.")

LULLABY (see "Baby Bye," p. 148)

MAKE ME A SONG. Composer: Henry Hadley. New York, G. Schirmer, 1916. (Poem previously collected under the title, "An Order for a Song.")

THE MAN IN THE MOON. In: *The Ward-Stephens Musical Settings of Selected Poems by James Whitcomb Riley* (see p. 220)
Also: THE MAN IN THE MOON. Composer: Will A. Harding. Chicago, Clayton F. Summy Co., 1932.

MAX AND JIM. In: *Ten Songs of Childhood* by Archie A. Mumma (see p. 219)

MAYMIE'S STORY OF RED-RIDING-HOOD. Incidental music by George Edwards. Cincinnati, Willis Music Company, 1913.

THE MESSIAH OF NATIONS (see p. 162)

MR. HAMMOND'S PARABLE. In: *Churchill-Grindell Song Book No. 1* (see p. 221)

A MOTHER SONG. Composer: John H. Densmore. Boston, Boston Music Co., 1913.
Also: A MOTHER-SONG. Composer: Elizabeth J. Cotton. Arranged by Barclay Walker. Indianapolis, Elizabeth J. Cotton, 1916.
Also: A MOTHER-SONG. Composer: Ruggero Vené. New York, G. Ricordi & Co., 1943.

MY FIDDLE. Composer: H. O. Wheeler. Kansas City, Mo., J. R. Bell, 1891.

MY MARY. Composer: Armsby Sutherland. Pittsburgh, C. C. Mellor Co., 1908.

O HEART OF MINE. Composer: Tod B. Galloway. Philadelphia, Theo. Presser Co., 1905. (Previously collected under the title, "Kissing the Rod.")

O, I WILL WALK WITH YOU, MY LAD (see "A Song of the Road," p. 159)

AN OLD SWEETHEART OF MINE. Composer: A. J. Goodrich. New York, Edgar S. Werner & Co., 1906.
Also: AN OLD SWEETHEART OF MINE. Composer: Fritz Krull. Indianapolis, Fritz Krull, 1913.
Also: AN OLD SWEETHEART OF MINE. Composer: Paul Th. Miersch. New York, G. Schirmer, Inc., 1921.

THE OLD TRUNDLE BED. Composer: H. N. Bartlett. Boston, Oliver Ditson Co., 1895.

OUR OWN—A CHANT. In: *A Riley Album* by Rupert Hughes (see p. 219)

OUT TO OLD AUNT MARY'S. Composer: Robert Atkinson. Boston, Oliver Ditson Co., 1897.

Also: OUT TO OLD AUNT MARY'S. Composer: John E. Fancher. [Indianapolis], Carlin Music Co., 1905.

OUT TO OLD AUNT MARY'S. Composer: Barclay Walker. Indianapolis, Beardsley-Woods Publishing Co., 1916. (Note: This contains, on the inside front cover, an undated letter from Riley to George Ade, in facsimile, beginning: "My friend for many years, Mr. Barclay Walker, is going to New York, and it is my personal hope that this line may make you two acquainted"; also in Walker's musical setting of "Little Orphant Annie," 1916.)

PANSIES. Composer: W. Ralph Cox. Boston, Oliver Ditson Co., 1912. Later in: *Something to Sing,* compiled by W. J. Baltzell (1915).

Also set to music by Annabel Morris Buchanan. New York, H. W. Gray Co., 1920.

PARENTAL CHRISTMAS PRESENTS. In: *The Daring Prince and Nine Other Piano Pieces* by Angela Diller (see p. 220)

A PET OF UNCLE SIDNEY'S. In: *The Daring Prince and Nine Other Piano Pieces* by Angela Diller (see p. 220)

THE PIXY PEOPLE. Composer: Frances McCollin. New York, G. Schirmer, Inc., 1943.

THE PRAYER PERFECT. Composer: Teresa Del Riego. London & New York, Chappell & Co., Ltd., 1908.

Also: THE PRAYER PERFECT. Composer: Alexander Russell. Cincinnati, John Church Co., 1912.

THE PRAYER PERFECT. Composer: Ervine J. Srenson. Cleveland, Sam Fox Publishing Co., 1916.

PRAYER PERFECT. Composer: Ivy Ash. Pierre, S. D., 1917.

THE PRAYER PERFECT. Composer: Oley Speaks. New York, G. Schirmer, 1930.

THE PRAYER PERFECT. Composer: C. W. Dieckmann. Boston, White-Smith Publishing Co., 1931.

Note: There was evidently an earlier musical setting than any of the above, so far unlocated but reported in the *Saturday Evening Spectator* (*Minneapolis*), May 9, 1891: "James Whitcomb Riley's 'Prayer' has been set to music by Prof. Colville, and is published by J. W. Dyer & Bro."

A PRIMROSE. Composer: Grace Lee Brown. Philadelphia, Theo. Presser Co., 1900. (Poem previously collected under the title, "The Lovely Child.")

THE RAGGEDY MAN. Composer: Fritz Krull. Boston, The Boston Music Co., 1908.

Also: THE RAGGEDY MAN. Composer: Carrie B. Adams. Terre Haute, Ind., C. B. Adams Music Co., 1912.

THE RAGGEDY MAN. In: *Ten Songs of Childhood* by Archie A. Mumma (see p. 219)

THE RIBBON, THE RING AND THE ROSE. Composer: Charles Willeby. Cincinnati, John Church Co., 1909. (The poem previously collected under the title "The Little Red Ribbon.")

Also: THE LITTLE RED RIBBON. Composer: Hallett Gilberté. New York, Carl Fischer, 1914.

A RILEY ALBUM by Rupert Hughes (see p. 219)

THE RILEY HOME SONGS (series title for 5 songs with music by Elizabeth J. Cotton: "The Days Gone By," "The Little-Red-Apple Tree," "Little Girlie-Girl," "Lockerbie Street," "A Mother Song")

SAY FAREWELL AND LET ME GO (see p. 155)

A SCRAWL. In: *A Riley Album* by Rupert Hughes (see p. 219)

A SEA SONG FROM THE SHORE. Composer: E. E. Starr. Boston, Oliver Ditson Co., 1897. ("C. E. Starr" appears on the cover, but the copyright was registered in name of E. E. Starr.)

Also: A SEA SONG FROM THE SHORE. Composer: E. Harold Davies. London, Novello & Co., Ltd. 1912 (in a collection of *Five Songs of Childhood*, of which only this one title is Riley's).

SHE "DISPLAINS" IT. In: *Ten Songs of Childhood* by Archie A. Mumma (see p. 219)

THE SILVER LINING (see "A Life-Lesson")

SOME SCATTERING REMARKS OF BUB'S. In: *The Daring Prince and Nine Other Piano Pieces* by Angela Diller (see p. 220)

A SONG (beginning: "There is ever a song somewhere, my dear"). Composer: Sidney C. Durst. Cleveland, J. H. Rogers; Chicago, Lyon & Healy, 1892.

Also: THERE IS EVER A SONG SOMEWHERE. Composer: W. H. Pontius. Logansport, Ind., Home Music Co., 1895.

THERE IS EVER A SONG SOMEWHERE, MY DEAR! Composer: John Hyatt Brewer. Boston, A. P. Schmidt, 1897.

A SONG. Composer: Fritz Krull. Indianapolis, Fritz Krull, 1913. Reissued in: *Four Songs from the Poems of James Whitcomb Riley*, by Fritz Krull (see p. 220)

A SONG (THERE'S EVER A SONG SOMEWHERE). In: *The Ward-Stephens Musical Settings of Selected Poems by James Whitcomb Riley* (1915).

THERE IS EVER A SONG. Composer: Platon Brounoff. Philadelphia, Theo. Presser Co., 1917.

Note: Under the title, "Ever a Song Somewhere," this appeared in *Moods: A Series of Songs Composed by E. L. Ashford* (1903).

A SONG AND A SMILE (see "The Weather")

A SONG OF THE ROAD (see p. 158)

TEN SONGS OF CHILDHOOD by Archie A. Mumma (see p. 219)

THERE IS EVER A SONG SOMEWHERE (see "A Song")

THERE, LITTLE GIRL, DON'T CRY (see "A Life-Lesson")

THE TREE TOAD. Composer: Mary Wyman Williams. Chicago, Clayton F. Summy Co., 1922.

UNCLE SIDNEY. In: *A Riley Album* by Rupert Hughes (see p. 219)

UNCLE SIDNEY SAYS. In: *The Daring Prince and Nine Other Piano Pieces* by Angela Diller (see p. 220)

UNCLE SIDNEY'S LOGIC. In: *Ten Songs of Childhood* by Archie A. Mumma (see p. 219)

A VERY YOUTHFUL AFFAIR. Composer: John Barnes Wells. Cincinnati, John Church Co., 1911.

THE WARD-STEPHENS MUSICAL SETTINGS OF SELECTED POEMS BY JAMES WHITCOMB RILEY (see p. 220)

THE WEATHER. Composer: Elizabeth L. Skinner. New York, G. Schirmer, 1908. Poem previously collected under the title, "Says He" and "Whatever the Weather May Be." It appeared as "A Song and a Smile," with music by Russell M. Dodge, in *Folk Songs and Art Songs for Intermediate Grades, Book II*, compiled by M. Teresa Armitage, published by C. C. Birchard & Co., Boston, 1924.

WHEN EVENING SHADOWS FALL. Composer: Edward Strubel. [Chicago?], 1924. A single sheet of paper, printed on one side only, 10¼″ x 7″. Awarded first prize in the contest for American Folk Songs by the Vereinigte Männerchöre of Chicago, June, 1924.

WHEN OUR BABY DIED. In: *Ten Songs of Childhood* by Archie A. Mumma (see p. 219)

WHEN SHE COMES HOME AGAIN. Composer: Herbert J. Wrightson. New York, Wm. Maxwell Music Co., 1913.

Also: WHEN SHE COMES HOME. Composer: Fritz Krull. Indianapolis, Fritz Krull, 1914.

WHEN THE FROST IS ON THE PUNKIN. In: *Churchill-Grindell Song Book No. 1* (see p. 221)

 Also, with music by Victor Herbert, in *Junior Laurel Songs*, compiled by M. Teresa Armitage, published Boston, C. C. Birchard & Co., 1915; reissued 1917.

WHERE SHALL WE LAND. Composer: Fritz Krull. Indianapolis, Fritz Krull, 1914.

WIND OF THE SEA. Composer: Clayton Johns. Boston, C. C. Birchard & Co., 1906. (Poem previously collected as Part IV of "Some Songs after Master-Singers.")

"WINKY-TOODEN" SONG. In: *The Daring Prince and Nine Other Piano Pieces* by Angela Diller (see p. 220)

## *NOTES*

Several Riley albums have been published, some of which contain first musical settings of the poems:

A RILEY ALBUM. Music by Rupert Hughes. New York & London, Edward Schuberth & Co., 1902. Contains ten songs, all first musical settings:

 Billy Goodin
 The Dead Lover
 Granny's Come to Our House (collected under the title "Granny")
 Griggsby's Station
 An Impetuous Resolve
 Coffee Like His Mother Used to Make (collected under the title, "Like His Mother Used to Make")
 The Little Tiny Kickshaw
 Our Own—A Chant
 A Scrawl
 Uncle Sidney

TEN SONGS OF CHILDHOOD. Music by Archie A. Mumma. Dayton (Ohio), Archie A. Mumma & Co., 1913. Six of these songs are first musical settings:

 Dwainie—A Sprite Song
 Little Girly-Girl
 Max and Jim
 She "Displains" It
 Uncle Sidney's Logic
 When Our Baby Died

The other four songs had earlier musical settings: "Cradle Song"; "The Raggedy Man"; "There! Little Girl; Don't Cry"; "Billy Goodin."

THE DARING PRINCE AND NINE OTHER PIANO PIECES. Music by Angela Diller. New York, G. Schirmer, Inc., 1940. Eight of the songs herein are first musical settings:

The Daring Prince*
The Diners in the Kitchen*
It*
A Pet of Uncle Sidney's*
"Winky-Tooden" Song*
Uncle Sidney Says*
Parental Christmas Presents†
Some Scattering Remarks of Bub's
The song "Extremes" had previously appeared with a musical setting by Marshall Bartholomew, in *The Music Hour in the Kindergarten and First Grade* (see p. 221); "An Impetuous Resolve" had earlier musical settings.

THE WARD-STEPHENS MUSICAL SETTINGS OF SELECTED POEMS BY JAMES WHITCOMB RILEY. New York, Chappell & Co., Ltd., 1915. A collection of eight songs of which four are first musical settings:

The Boy Patriot
Her Beautiful Hands§
The Man in the Moon
Christine's Song (Up in Tentoleena Land)
The other four songs had earlier musical settings: "A Song (There's Ever a Song Somewhere)"; "A Life-lesson (There! little girl; don't cry!)"§; "America"; "Little Orphant Annie"§.

FOUR SONGS FROM THE POEMS OF JAMES WHITCOMB RILEY. Music by Fritz Krull. Indianapolis, T. V. Krull Co., 1916. Contains: "The Bee-Bag"; "Little Orphant Annie"; "A Life-Lesson"; "A Song"; published separately in 1913.

---

*Previously collected as part of "A Session with Uncle Sidney." In the *Biographical Edition*, " 'Winky-Tooden' Song" appears as Part V of "A Session with Uncle Sidney," captioned: "Sings a 'Winky-Tooden' Song"; "Uncle Sidney Says" appears as Part II captioned "Uncle Brightens Up."

†In the *Biographical Edition* this appears as Part III of "Some Christmas Youngsters."

§Noted in separate, sheet music form: "Her Beautiful Hands," 1915, stamped: *Professional copy. Not to be sold;* "There! Little Girl; Don't Cry! (A Life-Lesson)," 1915; "Little Orphant Annie," 1916, stamped: *With the Publishers' Compliments.*

The following song books contain first known musical settings of Riley's poems:

THE FRANKLIN SQUARE SONG COLLECTION, No. 6. Selected by J. P. McCaskey. New York, Harper & Brothers, 1889. Contains "Little Orphant Annie," p. 143; composer unknown.

CHURCHILL-GRINDELL SONG BOOK No. 1. By F. F. Grindell and Clara Grindell. Platteville, Wis., Churchill-Grindell Co., 1905. Contains first musical settings of: "The Funny Little Fellow"; "Mr. Hammond's Parable"; "When the Frost Is on the Punkin." The other Riley poems herein set to music had earlier appearances ("An Impetuous Resolve"; "Little Orphant Annie").

THE MUSIC HOUR IN THE KINDERGARTEN AND FIRST GRADE. New York, Silver, Burdett & Co., 1929. Contains "Extremes," pp. 162–163, with music by Marshall Bartholomew.

\* \* \*

Of the nine recordings made of Riley's own recitations of his poems,\* only four were issued, by the Victor Talking Machine Company: "Out to Old Aunt Mary's"; "Little Orphant Annie"; "The Happy Little Cripple"; "The Raggedy Man." Other recordings of Riley's poems have appeared but only those named were made by him.

---

\*See accounts in the *Indianapolis Star* and *Indianapolis News* of July 6, 1912. The five which were apparently not put on the market are: "Good-Bye, Jim"; "When the Frost Is on the Punkin"; "An Old Sweetheart of Mine"; "On the Banks of Deer Crick"; "The Rain." Riley wrote a number of "rain" poems; it is unknown which one he recorded.

# Collected Works

~~~~~~~~~~~~~~~~~~~~~~~~~~~~~~~~~~~~

## 1897–1914

### THE HOMESTEAD EDITION

*16 Volumes*

THE POEMS AND PROSE SKETCHES OF JAMES WHITCOMB RILEY
New York, Charles Scribner's Sons, 1897–1914

Vol. I—*Neghborly Poems*—1897
Vol. II—*Sketches in Prose*—1897
Vol. III—*Afterwhiles*—1898
Vol. IV—*Pipes o' Pan at Zekesbury*—1898
Vol. V—*Rhymes of Childhood*—1898
Vol. VI—*The Flying Islands of the Night*—1898
Vol. VII—*Green Fields and Running Brooks*—1898
Vol. VIII—*Poems Here at Home*—1898
Vol. IX—*Armazindy*—1898
Vol. X—*A Child-World*—1898
Vol. XI—*Rubáiyát of Doc Sifers and Home-Folks*—1902
Vol. XII—*The Book of Joyous Children*—1902
Vol. XIII—*His Pa's Romance*—1908
Vol. XIV—*Morning*—1908
Vol. XV—*Early Poems*—1914
Vol. XVI—*Fugitive Pieces*—1914 (with index of the set)

These volumes bear the titles of earlier Riley books (with the exception of Vols. XV and XVI, which contain material reprinted from the *Biographical Edition*) but have omissions and additions. Some of the additions in seven of the volumes consist of first edition matter, hence these volumes: III, IV, V, VI, XI, XII and XIII are collated in Section I of this bibliography. For description of bindings, etc., see pp. 71, 72. There were revisions later within the *Homestead Edition* itself but none of these constitute first appearances.

# 1900–1916

## *THE GREENFIELD EDITION*

### *14 Volumes*

**THE GREENFIELD EDITION**

Indianapolis, The Bowen-Merrill Company [1900]; The Bobbs-Merrill Company [1905, 1908, 1916]

Bowen-Merrill:

10 volumes (1900): *Neghborly Poems, Sketches in Prose, Afterwhiles, Pipes o' Pan at Zekesbury, Rhymes of Childhood, The Flying Islands of the Night, Green Fields and Running Brooks, Armazindy, A Child-World, Home-Folks*

Bobbs-Merrill:

11th volume: *His Pa's Romance* (1905)
12th volume: *Morning* (1908)
13th and 14th volumes: *The Old Soldier's Story, The Old Times* (1916)

Volumes unnumbered, bound uniformly in green cloth with gilt-stamped stalks of grain on the spine; top edge gilt, other edges untrimmed; also issued in half-calf. The set was offered in 1916 in full leather. None of the volumes contain first edition material.

# 1913

## *BIOGRAPHICAL EDITION*

### *6 Volumes*

THE COMPLETE WORKS OF JAMES WHITCOMB RILEY. Collected and Edited by Edmund Henry Eitel. Indianapolis, The Bobbs-Merrill Company [1913]

Contains a life sketch of Riley, bibliographic notes and indexes. The poems are not only indexed by title and first line, but also by subject. All six volumes contain some first edition material and are collated in Section I of this bibliography. For details regarding binding, etc., see pp. 123, 124.

# 1915

## ELIZABETH MARINE RILEY EDITION
### 6 Volumes

THE COMPLETE WORKS OF JAMES WHITCOMB RILEY. Collected and Edited by Edmund Henry Eitel. New Castle, Pa., C. B. Randall [1913, *i.e. ca.* 1915]

Subscription set printed from the plates of the *Biographical Edition*, on laid paper, with wide margins, in a limited edition of 140 sets (150? The limitation notice states that "there have been printed and bound CXL sets, each registered in Roman letters from I to CL"). Throughout the volumes are inserted leaves with added material. These insertions vary with the sets, and consist chiefly of original water-color illustrations by Glenn Henshaw, J. Alfred Seaford, H. Rex Cotton, Mary McAuley and others. Some of the inserts are mounted sheets bearing Riley poems. The poem, "George A. Carr," first collected in *The Old Soldier's Story* (1915), is present on an inserted leaf in Mr. Edmund H. Eitel's set. His set also contains insertion of a poem apparently uncollected, entitled, "For Mrs. Lizbeth Sewell Foster," beginning: *Lizbeth she ist* laughs, *an'* sings; also a poem, "For—Mrs. Ovid B. Jameson," beginning, *Jevver watch a primrose 'bout* which is part of "Armazindy." "The Apology," an uncollected poem by Riley beginning: *What thought I scantly trust ye can* is inserted in Vol. II of Mr. Curt H. Reisinger's set.* An uncollected poem, without title, beginning: *THE OLD FRIENDS! Be they sung* has been noted in two of the sets. Some of the inserted poems are late appearances. Bindings vary as well as insertions.

---

*"The Apology" was copyrighted by Mr. Reisinger, 1915; printed on a single sheet of J. Whatman hand-made paper, 8½" x 6¾"; verso blank. At the foot is the statement: "Hitherto unpublished in any form, and only printed for the Author's(!) set of the Elizabeth Marine Riley edition."

# 1916

## *MEMORIAL EDITION*

### *10 Volumes*

MEMORIAL EDITION | JAMES WHITCOMB RILEY'S COMPLETE WORKS . . . Indianapolis, The Bobbs-Merrill Company, 1916

This is an extended reissue of the *Biographical Edition* with the sketch of Riley's life somewhat altered. It was issued later, 1917, with Harper & Brothers imprint and title rephrased: *Memorial Edition The Complete Works of James Whitcomb Riley in Ten Volumes*. . . . The Collier edition is still later, 1931. Volumes V, VII and IX contain first edition material and are collated in Section I. For further description see p. 140.

# 1937

## *THE COMPLETE POETICAL WORKS OF JAMES WHITCOMB RILEY*

THE COMPLETE POETICAL WORKS OF JAMES WHITCOMB RILEY. Preface by Donald Culross Peattie. Indianapolis, The Bobbs-Merrill Company [1937]

A one-volume reprint based on the *Memorial Edition;* contains no first edition Riley material. The preface by Peattie is entitled, "Riley as a Nature Poet." The book has appeared frequently since 1937 with various imprints.

\* \* \*

In addition to the above collections there have been published *The Lockerbie Book* (1911) and *The Hoosier Book* (1916), companion volumes, collated in Section I (pp. 119, 138); and, several series of Riley books:

THE DEER CREEK ILLUSTRATED EDITION, so named in the publishers' lists but not in the books themselves; issued 1898 to 1917 in more or less similar bindings:

*Riley Child-Rhymes* (1899)—reprint
*Riley Love-Lyrics* (1899)—collated, p. 80
*Riley Farm-Rhymes* (1901)—reprint
*Riley Songs o' Cheer* (1905)—collated, p. 101
*Riley Songs of Summer* (1908)—collated, p. 117
*Riley Songs of Home* (1910)—reprint
*Riley Songs of Friendship* (1915)—collated, p. 134
*Riley Hoosier Stories* (1917)—reprint

Four of these books contain first edition material and are collated in Section I, at pages indicated above. The other four are reprints.

THE CHRISTY-RILEY BOOKS, named by the publishers for the illustrator, Howard Chandler Christy:

*An Old Sweetheart of Mine* (1902)—collated, p. 90
*Out to Old Aunt Mary's* (1904)—collated, p. 98
*Home Again with Me* (1908)—reprint
*Riley Roses* (1909)—reprint
*The Girl I Loved* (1910)—reprint
*When She Was about Sixteen* (1911)—reprint
*Good-Bye, Jim* (1913)—reprint
*A Discouraging Model* (1914)—reprint
*Old-Fashioned Roses* (1909, *i.e.* 1914)—reprint
*The Rose* (1914)—reprint

Two of these books contain first edition material and are collated in Section I, at pages indicated above. The other eight are reprints.

THE RILEY-BETTS BOOKS, named by the publishers for the illustrator, Ethel Franklin Betts:

*While the Heart Beats Young* (1906)—collated, p. 103
*The Raggedy Man* (1907)—reprint
*Riley Child Verse* (1908)—reprint
*The Runaway Boy* (1908)—reprint
*The Orphant Annie Book* (1908)—collated, p. 113
  *Little Orphan Annie* (1908, *i.e.* 1910); *Little Orphan Annie* (cover title: *Ef You Don't Watch Out;* 1908, *i.e.* 1911); *The Boy Lives on Our Farm* (1908, *i.e.* 1911) are all reprints, wholly or in part, of *The Orphant Annie Book.*

Two of these books contain first edition material and are collated in Section I, at pages indicated above. The others are reprints.

BRANDYWINE BOOKS, illustrated by Will Vawter and others, all reprints:

*Down around the River and Other Poems* (1911)
*A Summer's Day and Other Poems* (1911)
*When the Frost Is on the Punkin and Other Poems* (1911)
*Knee-Deep in June and Other Poems* (1912)
*The Old Swimmin'-Hole and Other Poems* (1912)
*The Prayer Perfect and Other Poems* (1912)

THE RILEY BOOKLETS, decorated by Emily Hall Chamberlain:

*A Song of Long Ago* (1913)—reprint, first separate
*He and I* (1913)—reprint, first separate
*When My Dreams Come True* (1913)—reprint, first separate
*The Rose* (1913)—reprint, first separate
*Her Beautiful Eyes* (1913)—reprint, first separate in book form*
*Away* (1913)—reprint, first separate
*Do They Miss Me* (1913)—reprint, first separate
*Contentment* (1914)—reprint
*The Days Gone By* (1914)—reprint
*When She Comes Home* (1914)—reprint
*To My Friend* (1914)—reprint, first separate
*The Glad Sweet Face of Her* (1914)—reprint, first separate
*Just Be Glad* (1914)—reprint

Issued in boards with cloth shelfback, in envelopes bearing a stanza from the booklet's contents. Also issued in ooze leather, boxed, with title and number printed on the box.

---

*Earlier in sheet music form; see p. 212

# ATTRIBUTIONS

# Attributions

~~~~~~~~~~~~~~~~~~~~~~~~~~~~~~~~~~~~~~~~~~~~~~~~~~~

## NOT BY RILEY

"The Autobiography of James Whitcomb Riley" (written by Edgar Wilson ["Bill"] Nye; see p. 170)

"Cost of a Song" (written by James Riley; in *New England Magazine*, May, 1900, indexed in *Readers' Guide* as by James Whitcomb Riley)

"The Evangelist" (written by B. F. Phemister; Riley's name was signed to it by mistake; for story see *Indianapolis News*, November 26, 1914)

"A Hand on the Shoulder" (written by Frank L. Stanton? Not by Riley according to a statement by Edmund H. Eitel's secretary; see *Indianapolis News*, May 14, 1918; it had appeared under Riley's name in the *Lynchburg [Virginia] News*, September 28, 1913)

"Jeannette" (written by Charles G. Halpine. Gene Stratton-Porter ascribed it to Riley; see the *Indianapolis News*, July 5, 1922)

"The King" (beginning, "Where e'er the sun is shining,")  In the *Indianapolis News*, December 26, 1916, with a statement that the poem had been written "thirty-two years ago this Christmas day" by Riley in a Bible owned by Manson U. Davis of Greenfield, and that the Bible had been presented to the Greenfield Public Library. The Greenfield Public Library does not have the book, and the whole matter may be dismissed as a hoax, modeled after "Leonainie." The real author of the poem (name unknown), according to authoritative information, concocted the story, including the name "Manson U. Davis," in an attempt to prove that he could write poetry which would be accepted as Riley's. He did not receive the satisfaction of notoriety by exposure, but was completely ignored. So far as known, the poem is elsewhere unpublished.

"The Little Maiden" (written by James Riley? Published in *Dick's Recitations and Readings*, No. 14 [1882] as by James W. Riley)

"O, Pinching-Bug!" (written by the "Poet of the Waste-Basket"; not Riley's, according to a penciled note in Lee Burns' copy of *The Days Gone By* [1895], *q.v.*)

231

"Our Two Opinions" (written by Eugene Field; in *Indianapolis Journal*, April 20, 1890 under name of James Whitcomb Riley)

"A Sog of Subber" (written by Lee O. Harris; reprinted from the *Anderson Democrat* in *Riley's First Poems* [1901], *q.v.*)

"Tague Farrell" (written by James Riley; in *Current Literature*, July, 1902; indexed in *Readers' Guide* as by James Whitcomb Riley)

"A Thank-Ye Ma'am" (written by Tudor Jenks; published in the *Century Magazine*, March, 1889 with a preface: "The kind of poetry that makes James Whitcomb Riley"; reprinted in the *Post Express Rochester, N. Y.*, May 16, 1889, over Riley's name)

"A Wholesale Poet" (an anecdote of Riley, not by him; published in *The Days Gone By* [1895], *q.v.*)

## OTHER ATTRIBUTIONS

"After Death" (beginning: "'Tis after death—the mortal struggle done") A spirit message to Mrs. Brunn (Elizabeth Kahle); see p. 144

"Apple Time" (beginning: "Shower-time, flower-time—") Published anonymously in the *Greenfield News*, *ca.* 1875; written by Riley according to William Ross Hartpence, in *Early Recollections of James Whitcomb Riley*, by *Major Ridgeway* (1902).

"A Comparison" (beginning: "I'd ruther lay out here among the trees,") In *Judge*, July 28, 1888, signed *James Whitcomb Riley;* reprinted frequently in newspapers. The *Sun* (*New York*), July 14, 1890, contains an article that seems to prove that Riley was not the author of the poem.

"How Silly 'Twould Be" (beginning: "'You have heard,' said a youth to his sweetheart, who stood,") In *Bulletin of Pharmacy*, Parke, Davis & Co., Detroit, Michigan, July, 1891, under caption: "Posthumous Poems of James Whitcomb Riley." The other "posthumous" poetry printed with it consists of "Dot Leedle Boy of Mine," which is Riley's. There are no known records indicating Riley's authorship of "How Silly 'Twould Be" and Parke, Davis & Company can shed no light on its publication.

"I Wood Not Be a Drummer" (beginning: "I wood not be a drummer, no,") In the *Saturday Review* (*Indianapolis*), August 19, 1882, signed with Riley's pseudonym: "Benj. F. Johnson, of Boone." Before Riley's identity was disclosed, several persons claimed to be the rural poet, "Benj. F. Johnson."* So far as known, Riley did not

---

*See *New Castle* (*Ind.*) *Courier*, August 11, 1882, for account of a Henry County resident who was said to have written some, but not all, of the Benj. F. Johnson poems.

disclaim authorship of this poem in print, but neither did he make public denial of any poems attributed to him but not written by him.

"The Jay-Bird—A Genuine American" (beginning: "A-leanin' on a bar post an' a-thinkin' fer a minit") In "*Greeley*," *A Journal of Natural Science*, January, 1889, signed *James Whitcomb Riley*. This is in no way similar to Riley's poem, "The Jaybird," which begins: "The Jaybird he's my favorite," and there is no record that he wrote it; it was reprinted in an unidentified newspaper under the title, "A Good Word for the Jay-Bird."

"Oh Yes He Would" (beginning: "We must revise our estimate") In *Long Beach* (*California*) *Press-Telegram*, June 10, 1938, together with another poem entitled "To the First Fly" (beginning: "Hail pioneer of all the buzzing host"). Both, it was claimed, were written by Riley and found in an old trunk by George B. Hayes, a relative of Riley's. The *Hancock Democrat* (*Greenfield, Ind.*), August 4, 1938, stated that Mr. Hayes was not a relative of the poet and that Riley was not the author of the poems.

"The Passing of the Backhouse" (beginning: "When memory keeps me company and moves to smiles and tears") Printed in broadside, leaflet and pamphlet form, under various titles: "The Country Privy," "The Passing of the Old Back-House," *etc*. It also appeared in a pamphlet entitled, *Suppressed Poems by James Whitcomb Riley and Eugene Field* [n.d.]. One of the printings, a leaflet, carries the following statement: "An Unpublished Poem by James Whitcomb Riley found among his manuscripts after his death." Thus far no such manuscript has been located. Riley's close friends and relatives say that Riley did not write the poem. It is significant that nowhere in his correspondence or in any publications before his death has there been found any reference to it.

In response to a query regarding Riley's possible authorship of this poem, William Lyon Phelps, editor of *The Letters of James Whitcomb Riley* (1930), stated, in a letter dated May 6, 1943, "I have never found any proof whatever that he wrote it."

George Ade, in his convocation address on James Whitcomb Riley delivered at Purdue University, October 5, 1922, said: "He [Riley] never wrote anything which had to be circulated privately, and if any one tells you that he ever wrote anything which needed expurgating, you are hereby commissioned to nail the statement as a falsehood."*

---

*In *Bulletin of Purdue University*, January, 1923, p. 6.

"When the Booze Is in the Bottle" (first line same as title) In *Bruno's Weekly*, July 29, 1916 (reprinted from the issue of October 30, 1915*) with a circumstantial story that Riley composed it during a drinking bout with a Chicago newspaperman, "20 years ago," but never wanted to see it written down.

A 4-line poem without title, beginning: "He was a sawyer—blind from birth," included in a letter to Clara E. Laughlin, published in *Reminiscences of James Whitcomb Riley*, by Clara E. Laughlin (1916), p. 32. Riley asks if she recalls "the inspired blind wood-sawyer's lines." Miss Laughlin quotes the poem again in her autobiography, *Traveling through Life* (1934), p. 71, and attributes it to Riley. Whether or not Riley actually wrote these lines is not known. However, it is an adaptation from "The Blind Wood-Sawyer," by Josiah F. Kimball (see *Poets and Poetry of Printerdom* . . . edited by Oscar H. Harpel, Cincinnati, 1875, p. 254).

*Poem without title, beginning:* "If you should see a fellow man with trouble's flag unfurled" (reprinted from the *Anderson Democrat* in *Riley's First Poems* [1901], *q.v.*)

*Poem without title, beginning:* "This world at best is but a hash of pleasure and of pain" (reprinted from the *Anderson Democrat* in *Riley's First Poems* [1901], *q.v.*; reprinted under titles: "Cheer Your Fellow-Man" and "God Will Sprinkle Sunshine.")

"The pressure of long engaged work will, for an indefinite time, hold Mr. Riley from all other engagements." This statement is printed on a white card measuring 3⅜" x 6¼" issued from the office of James Whitcomb Riley, The Union Trust Company, Indianapolis. Undated; possibly *ca.* 1905.

## NOTES

Prose in the *Anderson Democrat*, 1877, attributed to Riley by Marcus Dickey (in *The Youth of James Whitcomb Riley* [1919], pp. 339 and 355) include the following titles: "The Anderson Mystery"; "The Duck Creek Jabberwock"; "Over the Hills to the Poor House." On p. 35 in this same book, Mr. Dickey mentions an article by Riley, "To Parents and Preceptors," which may have appeared also in the *Anderson Democrat*.

Prose in the *Indianapolis Journal*, July 16, 27 and 30, 1881, respectively, attributed to Riley by Marcus Dickey (in *The Maturity of James Whitcomb Riley* [1922], pp. 70 and 74) include the following: "The Giant on the Show-Bills"; "The Way We Walk"; "Every Editor His Own Humorist" (beginning: "It has been kindly suggested by many hundred readers that the Journal really ought occasionally to have its columns embellished with some 'funny business' ").

---

*Not seen.

# RILEYANA

# Books, Pamphlets, Leaflets, Broadsides

~~~~~~~~~~~~~~~~~~~~~~~~~~~~~~~~~~~~~~~~~~~~~~

WHERE no page references are given, the books contain an index providing ready reference to the Riley material. Encyclopedias have been omitted. Also omitted are innumerable ephemeral pieces such as handbills and programs for Riley's appearances on the lecture platform, programs of celebrations honoring his birthday, material issued in connection with the James Whitcomb Riley Hospital for Children, etc. The most important biographies of Riley are Edmund Henry Eitel's sketch published in the *Complete Works of James Whitcomb Riley: Biographical Edition* (1913); Meredith Nicholson's "James Whitcomb Riley," in his book, *The Man in the Street* (1921), reprinted from the *Atlantic Monthly*, October, 1916; and Marcus Dickey's: *The Youth of James Whitcomb Riley* (1919) and *The Maturity of James Whitcomb Riley* (1922). Minnie Belle Mitchell's *Hoosier Boy: James Whitcomb Riley* (1942) is drawn from her own acquaintance with the poet and the recollections of other Greenfield people. Other books and pamphlets devoted wholly to Riley appear in the list below (note particularly Carman, Daggett, Hartpence, Hitt, Howland, Laughlin, Nolan, Wetzel). The *Letters of James Whitcomb Riley*, edited by William Lyon Phelps (1930) are revealing as to Riley's personality and friendships.

A selective list of biographical references in magazines appears at pp. 248–260; lack of space prevents listing of the

237

thousands of sketches, including interviews, published in newspapers.

ABERNETHY, Julian W. American Literature. New York, Maynard, Merrill, 1902. p. 463

ADAMS, George Matthew (comp.). Uncle Walt [Walt Mason]: The Poet Philosopher. Chicago, 1910. *Contains a tribute to Riley by Walt Mason, p. 34.*

ADE, George. Convocation Address, Purdue University, October 5, 1922. *Broadside. (See Bulletin of Purdue University, listed on p. 250)*

ALEY, Robert Judson & ALEY, Max. The Story of Indiana and Its People. Chicago, O. P. Barnes [1912]. pp. 281–282

[ALLISON] Select Works of Young E. Allison. Louisville, Ky., 1935. *Part I contains much material relating to Riley.*

AMERICAN ACADEMY OF ARTS AND LETTERS. In Memoriam. A Book of Record Concerning Former Members. March, 1922, p. 215. *Academy Publication No. 83: "Catalogue 1934–1935 of the Museum of the American Academy of Arts and Letters," lists two Riley items. For another Academy publication, see* GARLAND, *Hamlin.*

AUSLANDER, Joseph. Five American Immortals. Worcester, Achille St. Onge, 1940. pp. 21–26. *Contains a specimen of the 10c U. S. postage stamp in the "Famous Americans" issue, 1940.*

AUTOBIOGRAPHY OF JAMES WHITCOMB RILEY. [By Bill Nye] *See p. 170*

AVARY, Myrta Lockett. Joel Chandler Harris and His Home. [Atlanta, Uncle Remus Memorial Association, 1913]. p. 18

BALLOU, Jenny. Period Piece. Ella Wheeler Wilcox and Her Times. Boston, Houghton Mifflin, 1940

BARNES, Walter. The Children's Poets. Yonkers-on-Hudson, N. Y., World Book Co., 1924. pp. 176–96

BARR, James (comp.). Humour of America. New York, Scribner, 1894. p. 456

BATES, Katherine Lee. American Literature. New York, Macmillan, 1898. p. 204

BEERS, Henry Augustin. Studies in American Letters. Meadville, Pa., Flood & Vincent, 1895. pp. 210–212

BEERS, Henry Augustin. The Connecticut Wits and Other Essays. New Haven, Yale University Press, 1920. pp. 31–43

BEESON, R[ebecca] Katherine. Literary Indiana. Indianapolis, Bobbs-Merrill [1925]. *Wrappers.* p. 16

BENÉT, William Rose (comp.). Poems for Youth. New York, Dutton [1925]

BEVERIDGE, Albert J. The Meaning of the Times. Indianapolis, Bobbs-Merrill [1908]. pp. 254–259

BINFORD, John H. History of Hancock County, Indiana. Greenfield, Ind., King & Binford, 1882. p. 493

BLAIR, Ed. Sunflower Siftings. New York, Gorham Press, 1914

BLATCHLEY, Willis S. Blatchleyana II.—A Supplementary List of the Published Writings of W. S. Blatchley. Indianapolis, Nature Publishing Co., 1939. *Wrappers*. pp. 32–42

[BLOUËT, Paul] A Frenchman in America. By Max O'Rell [pseudonym]. New York, Cassell [1891]. pp. 307–308

BOWMAN, Heath. Hoosier. Indianapolis, Bobbs-Merrill [1941]

BURDETTE, Clara B. (ed.). Robert J. Burdette: His Message. Pasadena, Cal., Clara Vista Press [1922]. pp. 163–186

CARMAN, Bliss. Poetry of Life. Boston, L. C. Page & Co. [1905]. pp. 159–176

CARMAN, Bliss. James Whitcomb Riley: An Essay. New York, privately printed [1918]

CARMAN, Bliss & HOVEY, Richard. Last Songs from Vagabondia. Cambridge, Small, Maynard, 1901. p. 54. *Boards. Contains a poem to James Whitcomb Riley by Richard Hovey.*

CASTLE, Henry A. The Army Mule and Other War Sketches. Indianapolis & Kansas City, Bowen-Merrill, 1898. *Contains Russel M. Seeds' interview with Riley, entitled: "James Whitcomb Riley's Stories of the Humorist, Edgar Wilson Nye [Bill Nye]," pp. 259–269.*

CAWEIN, Madison. The Cup of Comus. New York, Cameo Press 1915. p. 81. *Contains a sonnet to Riley on his birthday, October 7, 1912. For another poem by Cawein to Riley see* ROTHERT, *The Story of a Poet (1921)*

CLEMENS, Samuel L. How to Tell a Story and Other Essays by Mark Twain. New York, Harper, 1897. pp. 5–8

COLEMAN, McAlister. Eugene V. Debs. New York, Greenberg [1930]

CONTEMPORARY CLUB OF INDIANAPOLIS: [History of the] 1890–1940. [Indianapolis, 1940]. *Wrappers*. pp. 9, 12

COOPER, Mrs. George (Lotta M. Bottsford). Clara Louise: An Idyll; and Other Offerings. [n.p., 1937]. *Wrappers*. pp. 9–21

COTTMAN, George S. Indiana; Its History, Constitution and Present Government. Indianapolis, Bobbs-Merrill [1925]. pp. 225–227

COTTMAN, George S. & HYMAN, Max R. Centennial History and Handbook of Indiana. Indianapolis, Max R. Hyman, 1915

DAGGETT, Mabel Potter. In Lockerbie Street; A Little Appreciation of James Whitcomb Riley. New York, B. W. Dodge & Co., 1909. *Boards.*

DEBS, Eugene V.   Riley, Nye & Field; Personal Notes . . . Reprinted from *National Magazine* [*ca.* October, 1915]. *Pamphlet.*

DEBS, Eugene V. Pastels of Men. New York, 1919. *Wrappers.* pp. 7–20

DEBS: His Life, Writings and Speeches. Girard, Kansas, Appeal to Reason, 1908. p. 67. *For other references to friendship between Riley and Debs see:* COLEMAN, *Eugene V. Debs; and* KARSNER, *Debs: His Authorized Life*

DENNIS, Charles H. Eugene Field's Creative Years. Garden City, N. Y., Doubleday, Page, 1924

DICKEY, Marcus. The Youth of James Whitcomb Riley. Indianapolis, Bobbs-Merrill [1919]

DICKEY, Marcus. The Maturity of James Whitcomb Riley. Indianapolis, Bobbs-Merrill [1922]

DOWNING, Olive Inez. Indiana's Poet of the Wildwood. Marion, Ind., News Publishing Co. [1941]. *Contains a poem to James Whitcomb Riley by Sarah T. Bolton, p. 88*

DUNN, Jacob P. Indiana and Indianans. 5 vols. Chicago & New York, American Historical Society, 1919

DYE, Charity. The James Whitcomb Riley Reader. Indianapolis, Bobbs-Merrill [1915]. *Contains selections from Riley with introduction by Charity Dye.*

EITEL, Edmund Henry (ed.). The Complete Works of James Whitcomb Riley. Biographical Edition. 6 vols. Indianapolis, Bobbs-Merrill [1913]. *Biographical sketch, Vol. 1, pp. 367–387*

ELLIS, Horace. A Day with Riley in Indiana: Programs and Materials. Indianapolis, 1917. *Wrappers.*

ELLSWORTH, William Webster. A Golden Age of Authors. Boston, Houghton Mifflin [1919]. p. 34

ESAREY, Logan. A History of Indiana from 1850 to the Present. Indianapolis, B. F. Bowen, 1918. Vol. 2, pp. 1136–1141.

FIELD, Eugene. Hoosier Lyrics. Chicago, M. A. Donohue & Co. [1905]. *Contains "Hoosier Lyrics Paraphrased," paraphrases of Riley's poem by Field, done at the time of the Harrison campaign, 1888.*

FORD, Robert. American Humorists, Recent and Living. London, A. Gardner, 1897. pp. 295–304

FRENCH, Joseph L. (ed.). Sixty Years of American Humor. Boston, Little, Brown, 1925. *A brief note on Riley precedes his "Champion Checker-Player," p. 83.*

FULLERTON, B[radford] M. Selective Bibliography of American Literature, 1775–1900. New York, Payson, 1932. pp. 229–230

GARLAND, Hamlin. Commemorative Tribute to James Whitcomb Riley. American Academy of Arts and Letters, 1922. *Wrappers.*

GARLAND, Hamlin. Roadside Meetings. New York, Macmillan, 1930. pp. 224–239

GARLAND, Hamlin. James Whitcomb Riley. In: Human Documents, Portraits and Biographies of Eminent Men. New York, S. S. McClure, 1895. p. [152]

GREATHOUSE, C. A. Suggestions and Materials, Riley Day Programs. Indianapolis, 1915. *Wrappers.*

GUEST, Edgar Albert. James Whitcomb Riley (poem). [Chicago], Reilley & Britton, 1917. *Broadside.*

GUGLER, Julius. Wie's die Stunde Gab. Milwaukee, Julius Gugler, 1910. pp. 135–139

HADLEY, Almira Harvey. A Brief History of Mooresville and Its Vicinity. [n.p., 1918]. *Wrappers.*

*Hancock Democrat*, Greenfield, Ind., Art Supplement: "The Hoosier Poet at His Old Home." March 16, 1899. *Pamphlet.*

*Hancock Democrat*, Greenfield, Ind., The Riley Old Home Souvenir Edition, September 23, 1937. *Pamphlet.*

HARRIS, Julia Collier. The Life and Letters of Joel Chandler Harris. Boston, Houghton Mifflin, 1918

[HARTPENCE, W. Ross]. Early Recollections of James Whitcomb Riley by Major Ridgeway (pseudonym). Harrison, Ohio, 1922. *Wrappers.*

HAWHORNE, Julian, *et al.* The Literature of All Nations and All Ages. Chicago [*etc.*], E. R. DuMont, 1902. Vol. 10, p. 358. *Brief sketch, with selections from Riley.*

HITT, George C. Riley Loved Children. [Indianapolis], Indianapolis Public Library, 1937. *Pamphlet.*

THE HOOSIER ALMANACK AND FAMILY MAGAZINE. Indiana Society of Chicago, 1912. *Wrappers. Contains poem to Riley by William Dudley Foulke, p. 26.*

THE HOOSIER CLUB OF GREATER KANSAS CITY. *Leaflet*, pertaining to its organization on November 30, 1897.

HOWLAND, John A. James Whitcomb Riley in Prose and Picture. Chicago, Handy & Higgins, 1903.

HUDSON, Thomas Howard. A Tribute to James Whitcomb Riley, and Other Poems. Kansas City, Mo., Burton Publishing Co. [1917].

[HUTTON] From the Books of Laurence Hutton. New York, Harper, 1892.

IN HONOR OF JAMES WHITCOMB RILEY. A Meeting of the Indiana State Teachers' Association, Dec. 28, 1905. Indianapolis [1906]. *Wrappers*.

INDIANA SOCIETY OF CHICAGO. A Record of the Speeches and Other Proceedings of a Centennial Dinner, 1916. *Pamphlet*. pp. 15–22

INDIANA SOCIETY OF CHICAGO. An Account of the Proceedings Had on the occasion of the 21st Annual Dinner; Dec. 5, 1925. *Wrappers*. pp. 23–27

INDIANA SOCIETY OF CHICAGO. Services in Memory of the Late James Whitcomb Riley. The Rev. William Chalmers Covert, D. D., Minister. Chicago, Oct. 29, 1916. *Wrappers*.

INDIANAPOLIS PUBLIC SCHOOLS. Some Suggestions for the Observance of Riley Day, October 6 [7]. Prepared by a group of Supervising Principals. [1911]. *Wrappers*.

INTERNATIONAL STEREOTYPERS AND ELECTROTYPERS' UNION. The Hoosier Souvenir. 1916. *Booklet*.

JOHNSON, J. H., *et al*. Laughter Library, Indianapolis, M. Droke [1936]. (Anecdote #725)

JOHNSON, Merle. American First Editions. Revised by Jacob Blanck, New York, Bowker, 1942.

JOHNSON, Merle. You Know These Lines! A Bibliography of the Most Quoted Verses in American Poetry. New York, Baker, 1935

KARSNER, David. Debs: His Authorized Life and Letters from Woodstock Prison to Atlanta. New York, Boni & Liveright [1919]. pp. 209–212

KENDALL, Ezra. The Vinegar Buyer. Sharp Sayings of Sharp People. Founded on James Whitcomb Riley's Poem, "Jap Miller." Cleveland, O., Cleveland News Co., 1909

KREYMBORG, Alfred. Our Singing Strength. An Outline of American Poetry. New York, Coward-McCann, Inc., 1929. pp. 242–243

LAUGHLIN, Clara E. Reminiscences of James Whitcomb Riley. New York, Fleming H. Revell [1916]

LAUGHLIN, Clara E. Traveling through Life. Boston, Houghton Mifflin, 1934.

LAWTON, William Cranston. Introduction to the Study of American Literature. New York, Globe School Book Co., 1902. pp. 329–330

LEVERING, Julia Henderson. Historic Indiana. New York, Putnam, 1909

LUCAS, Harriet M. (ed.). Prose and Poetry of Today; Regional America. Syracuse, N. Y., L. W. Singer Co. [1941]. *Contains Wilbur D. Nesbit's poem to James Whitcomb Riley.*

MACDOUGALL, Curtis D. Hoaxes. New York, Macmillan, 1940. p. 53

McFEE, Inez N. Studies in American and British Literature. Chicago, A. Flanagan Co. [1905]. pp. 165–177

McLAUGHLIN, Robert. Little Orphan Annie. A Comedy-Drama . . . from the Poems and Stories of James Whitcomb Riley. New York, Samuel French, 1935. *Wrappers.*

MARDEN, Orison Swett (ed.). How They Succeeded; Life Stories of Successful Men Told by Themselves. Boston, Lothrop Publishing Co. [1901]. pp. 357–365

MARDEN, Orison Swett (ed.). Little Visits with Great Americans. New York, Success Co., 1904. pp. 252–262

MARSH, Daniel L. The Faith of the People's Poet, James Whitcomb Riley. Indianapolis, Bobbs-Merrill [1920]

MASON, Harriet L. American Literature—A Laboratory Method. Philadelphia, John Wanamaker, 1901. pp. 47, 54

MATTHEWS, Brander. Introduction to American Literature. New York, American Book Co. [1918]. pp. 233–237

THE MEDAL [1916]. *Pamphlet, accompanying the medal designed by Lorado Taft, commemorating the Riley birthday dinner held October 7, 1915.*

MICHAUD, Regis. Panorama de la Littérature Americaine. 2nd edn. Paris [1926]. *Wrappers.* pp. 126, 182

[MILLER] Jap Miller. [n.p., n.d.] *Leaflet. Contains poem signed "G" entitled: "It's Up to James Whitcomb to Do Us Another Turn, Will You, Jim?"*

MITCHELL, Minnie Belle. Greenfield: the Historic Birthplace of the Nation's Poet, James Whitcomb Riley. Greenfield, Mitchell Co. [°1925–1926]. *Wrappers.*

MITCHELL, Minnie Belle. Hoosier Boy: James Whitcomb Riley. Indianapolis, Bobbs-Merrill [1942]

MOTHER GOOSE FOR ALL. [Indianapolis Flower Mission] November, 1898. *Wrappers. Contains "An Appreciation of Riley," by Chas. W. Moores, p. 8.*

NATIONAL CASH REGISTER COMPANY, DAYTON, OHIO. Pleasant Afternoons at the National Cash Register Factory. #11. *Leaflet. Program of Dec. 11, 1898. Contains Riley's poem, "A Life-Lesson," and photograph of "Mr. Riley in the Kindergarten" with note regarding his visit there.*

NICHOLSON, Meredith.* Address by Meredith Nicholson at Manual Training High School, Indianapolis, Oct. 6, 1911. *Wrappers.*

NICHOLSON, Meredith. A Hoosier Chronicle. Boston, Houghton Mifflin, 1912. p. 194

NICHOLSON, Meredith. The Hoosiers. New York, Macmillan, 1900.

NICHOLSON, Meredith. The Man in the Street. New York, Scribner's, 1921. pp. 26–64

NICHOLSON, Meredith. Old Familiar Faces. Indianapolis, Bobbs-Merrill [1929]. pp. 109–112

NICHOLSON, Meredith. Poems. Indianapolis, Bobbs-Merrill [1906]. *Contains a dedicatory poem to Riley.*

NICHOLSON, Meredith. See also: *Riverside Readers*, Fifth Reader

NOBLE, Charles. Studies in American Literature. New York, Macmillan, 1898. p. 357

NOLAN, Jeannette Covert. James Whitcomb Riley, Hoosier Poet. New York, J. Messner Inc. [1941]

NYE, Edgar Wilson. A Guest at the Ludlow. Indianapolis, Bowen-Merrill, 1897. *Contains a reprint from Godey's Magazine of "The Ambrosia of James Whitcomb Riley," by "Chelifer," pp. 264–272.*

[NYE] Bill Nye: His Own Life Story. Continuity by Frank Wilson Nye. New York, Century [1926]

ONDERDONK, James L. History of American Verse. Chicago, A. C. McClurg & Co., 1901. p. 351

O'RELL, Max. *See:* BLOUËT, *Paul*

PARKER, Benj. S. Hoosier Bards. Chicago, Charles H. Kerr & Co., 1891. *Contains a sonnet to Riley, p. 27.*

PARKER, Benj. S. & HEINEY, Enos B. Poets and Poetry of Indiana. New York, Silver, Burdett & Co. [1900]

PATTEE, Fred Lewis. History of American Literature since 1870. New York, Century, 1915. pp. 324–329

PATTEE, Fred Lewis. The New American Literature, 1890–1930. New York, Century [1930].

PAYNE, Leonidas Warren, Jr. (ed.). American Literary Readings with Introductory History of American Literature. Chicago & New York, Rand McNally & Co. [1918]. p. 512

---

*Meredith Nicholson's *The Poet* (1914), fictional, is based on the life and character of Riley.

PETERSON, Edward S. "Riley": An Appreciation. [n.p., n.d., 1905?]. *Pamphlet.*

PHELPS, William Lyon. The Advance of English Poetry in the Twentieth Century. New York, Dodd, Mead, 1918

PHELPS, William Lyon (ed.). Letters of James Whitcomb Riley. Indianapolis, Bobbs-Merrill [1930]. *With foreword and afterword by the editor.*

[PHELPS] WILLIAM LYON PHELPS AUTOBIOGRAPHY WITH LETTERS. New York, London [*etc.*], Oxford University Press, 1939. pp. 405–411

POND, Major J. B. Eccentricities of Genius. New York, G. W. Dillingham Co. [1900]. pp. 241–246

PRATT, Mrs. S[arah] S[mith]. The Old Crop in Indiana. Indianapolis, Pratt Poster Co., 1928. pp. 212–224

RANDALL, Ada M. & REELY, Mary K. Through Golden Windows; Children's Poets and Story Tellers. Chicago, Albert Whitman & Co., 1934. pp. 87–94

RICE, Alonzo (ed.). Some Indiana Writers and Poets. Marion, Ind., Teachers Journal Printing Co., 1908. *Wrappers.*

RICHMAN, George J. History of Hancock County, Indiana. Greenfield, Ind., William Mitchell Printing Co. (or: Indianapolis, Federal Publishing Co., Inc.), 1916. pp. 427–430

RIDGEWAY, Major. See: HARTPENCE, W. Ross

RILEY, James Whitcomb. The Days Gone By. Chicago, E. A. Weeks & Co. [1895]. *Contains material on Riley by Robert J. Burdette, Frank Preston Smart and William W. Pfrimmer.*

RILEY, James Whitcomb. Love Letters of the Bachelor Poet, James Whitcomb Riley to Miss Elizabeth Kahle. Boston, Bibliophile Society, 1922. *Boards, cloth back.*

RILEY, James Whitcomb. The Name of Old Glory. Indianapolis, Bobbs-Merrill [1917]. *Contains an appreciation of Riley by Booth Tarkington, p. 7.*

RING, Paulene Foster. The Children's Poets; Dramatic Readings. Boston, Richard G. Badger [1929]. pp. 51, 56

RIVERSIDE READERS. Fifth Reader. Boston, Houghton Mifflin [1912]. *Contains a biographical sketch of Riley by Meredith Nicholson.*

ROLL, Charles. Indiana; One Hundred and Fifty Years of American Development. Chicago, Lewis Publishing Co., 1931. Vol. 2, pp. 303, 306, 491

ROTHERT, Otto A. The Story of a Poet: Madison Cawein. Louisville, Ky., Filson Club Publication No. 30, 1921. pp. 246, 406

RUOFF, Henry W. (ed.). Leaders of Men or Types and Principles of Success as Illustrated in the Lives and Careers of Famous Americans of the Present Day. Springfield, Mass., King-Richardson Co., 1903. Chap. XXII

RUSSELL, Charles Edward. An Hour of American Poetry. Philadelphia, Lippincott, 1929. pp. 145–148

RUTHERFORD, Mildred Lewis. American Authors. Atlanta, Ga., Franklin Printing & Publishing Co., 1894. pp. 615–618

SHANKLE, George Earlie. American Nicknames. New York, Wilson, 1937. p. 446

SHEDD, George C. Miniatures. Lincoln, Nebraska, 1900. *Wrappers. Contains an essay on James Whitcomb Riley.*

SHERLEY, George Douglass. A Spray of Kentucky Pine Placed at the Feet of the Dead Poet, James Whitcomb Riley. Lexington, Ky., 1916. *Wrappers. Limited edition of 500 copies.*

SIMONDS, Arthur Beaman (ed.). American Song. New York, Putnam, 1894. pp. 284–285

SKINNER, Otis. Footlights and Spotlights. Indianapolis, Bobbs-Merrill [1924]. pp. 292–294

SMILEY, Amanda Jane. Literary Appreciations: Little Life Stories. Lafayette, Ind., Central Editorial Bureau, 1908. pp. 89–92

SMITH, William Henry. The History of the State of Indiana. Indianapolis, B. L. Blair Co., 1897. Vol. 2, pp. 844–848

STEDMAN, Edmund Clarence. Poets of America. Boston, Houghton Mifflin; Cambridge, Riverside Press, 1885. p. 455

STEDMAN, Edmund Clarence & HUTCHINSON, Ellen Mackay (comp.). A Library of American Literature. New York, C. L. Webster & Co., 1890. Vol. 11, p. 576

STEDMAN, Edmund Clarence. An American Anthology. Boston & New York, Houghton Mifflin, 1900. *Biographical notes, p. 818.*

STOKER, Bram. Personal Reminiscences of Henry Irving. New York, Macmillan, 1906. Vol. 2, pp. 112–113, 160

TRIBUTES TO THE LIFE AND MEMORY OF JAMES WHITCOMB RILEY. [n.p., n.d.]. *Pamphlet.*

UNTERMEYER, Louis. Including Horace. New York, Harcourt, Brace & Howe, 1919. *Contains a parody: "James Whitcomb Riley Makes an Indiana 'Neighborly [sic] Poem' out of It," p. 25.*

WAGNER, Charles L. Seeing Stars. New York, Putnam [1942]. pp. 21, 31, 60

WALLACE, Alfred Russel. Edgar Allan Poe; a series of seventeen letters concerning Poe's scientific erudition in Eureka and his authorship of Leonainie. New York, privately printed [1930]. *Limited edition of 500 copies.*

WARNER, Charles Dudley (ed.). Library of the World's Best Literature. New York, R. S. Peale & J. A. Hill [1897]. Vol. 21, p. 12265

WEBB, Mary Griffin (ed.). Famous Living Americans. Greencastle, Ind., Chas. Webb & Co., 1915. *Contains "James Whitcomb Riley," by Anna Nicholas, pp. 387–399*

WEGNER, Laura Christine. Riley Readings with Living Pictures. Chicago, T. S. Denison & Co., [n.d., 1921?]. *Wrappers.*

WESTERN ASSOCIATION OF WRITERS. Program for banquet tendered James Whitcomb Riley by the Western Association of Writers and other friends, October 18, 1888. *Wrappers. The W. A. W. published souvenir books of their 4th, 5th and 6th annual meetings held 1889–1891. Riley was present at the 4th and 5th meetings and the books mention his name, but contain no discussion of his life or work.*

[WETZEL, Julian]. James Whitcomb Riley, Man of Letters. Indianapolis, Keystone Press [1929]. *Wrappers.*

WHITCOMB, Selden Lincoln. Chronological Outlines of American Literature. New York, Macmillan, 1894. p. 271

WILCOX, Ella Wheeler. The Worlds and I. New York, Doran [1918]. pp. 55–59

WILDER, Marshall P. The Sunny Side of the Street. New York & London, Funk & Wagnalls, 1905. pp. 139, 159

[WILSON, Carroll A.] First Appearance in Print of Some Four Hundred Familiar Quotations. Middletown, Conn., Olin Memorial Library, Wesleyan University, 1935 [Exhibition, February 24 to March 23, 1935. See also JOHNSON, M., *You Know These Lines!*]

WILSON, William E. The Wabash. [Rivers of America series]. New York, Farrar & Rinehart [1940].

WYATT, Edith. Great Companions. New York, Appleton, 1917. pp. 182–190

YOUNG, Art. On My Way: Being the Book of Art Young in Text and Picture. New York, Horace Liveright, 1928. pp. 221–223

YOUNG, Arthur. Authors' Readings. New York, Frederick A. Stokes Co. [1897]. p. 167

# Periodicals

THE ACADEMY (London)
    1888, October 20, p. 250. "Old-Fashioned Roses" (review of, by
        Richard Le Gallienne)
    1898, September 17, p. 272. "James Whitcomb Riley's Poetry" by
        Bliss Carman
        December 17, p. 472. "Hoosier Poet"

THE AMERICAN REVIEW OF REVIEWS
    1916, September, p. 327. "James Whitcomb Riley" (unsigned;
        tributes by Bliss Carman, Don Marquis, Mary Riley Smith
        quoted and story of "Leonainie" retold)

THE ARENA
    1897, June, p. 1121. "James Whitcomb Riley" (review of *A Child-*
        *World;* unsigned, probably by John Clark Ridpath)
    1907, November, p. 588. "Morning" (review of)
        December, p. 670. "A Poetical Gem by James Whitcomb
        Riley" (comment on *Morning*)
    1908, January, p. 126. "The Boys of the Old Glee Club" (review of)

THE ATLANTIC MONTHLY
    1898, September, p. 424. "Mr. Riley's Poetry" by Bliss Carman
    1902, October, p. 555. (Criticism of poetry of the commonplace,
        by H. W. Boynton)
    1916, October, p. 503. "James Whitcomb Riley" by Meredith
        Nicholson

THE BELLMAN
    1911, December 9, p. 746. "A Message and Some Memories" (by
        E. C. Edgar?)
    1916, August 12, p. 265. "Cawein and Riley: Poets of America" by
        Henry Adams Bellows
    1917, May 12, p. 521. "The Riley Medal"

THE BOOK BUYER
    1888, April, p. 96. "James Whitcomb Riley" by D. L. Paine

1898, October, p. 181. "James Whitcomb Riley as a Poet of Childhood" by Clara E. Laughlin

1902, December, p. [477]. "High Tide in Juvenile Literature" by Tudor Jenks (review of *The Book of Joyous Children*)

BOOK NEWS

1892, February, p. 278. "James Whitcomb Riley" by John Clark Ridpath

THE BOOK NEWS MONTHLY

1907, March, *Riley Number*. "James Whitcomb Riley as a Person" by Henry van Dyke; "A Typical Indianian: Riley as a Representative Hoosier" by Elizabeth Miller; "Riley—Poet of the People" by Bliss Carman; "Riley the Humorist" by H. H. Howland; "More about the Riley Humor" by Samuel D. McCoy; "Mr. Riley as a Public Reader" by George C. Hitt; "Riley Books of Every Description."

1910, December, p. 246. "Precious Riley Books. The Remarkable Darlington Collection" by D. Laurance Chambers

BOOK NOTES

1899, November, p. 251. "James Whitcomb Riley" by Lee Burns

THE BOOKMAN

1897, June, p. 282. (Comments on *A Child-World*)

1898, September, p. [13]. (Statement that Riley is *not* writing a comic opera in collaboration with Paul Laurence Dunbar)

1901, May, p. 280. (Comment on *Home-Folks*)

1903, December, p. [349]. (Poem to Riley by Joe S. Miller and caricature by George Brehm)

1904, September, p. [18]. "James Whitcomb Riley on a Country Newspaper" by Louise Parks Richards. (Reprinted in same periodical, September, 1916)

1911, March, p. [67]. "How Riley Came into His Own" by Hewitt Hanson Howland

1912, August, p. 637. " 'Jim' Riley (An Appreciation)" by Charles Virgil Tevis

1913, October, p. 163. "James Whitcomb Riley's Complete Works" by Herbert R. Hyman. (Review of the *Biographical Edition*)

1914, February, p. 598. "Kipling and Riley" (story of their friendship retold from the *Biographical Edition*)

1916, September, p. [22]. "Memories and the Last Meeting" by Charles Virgil Tevis

October, p. 158. "A Riley Tribute" (review of Clara E. Laughlin's tribute in *Ladies' Home Journal*, September, 1916)

1920, March, p. 93. "A Riley Biography" by Margaret Emerson Bailey. (Review of Marcus Dickey's *The Youth of James Whitcomb Riley*)

1923, May, p. 379. (Reminiscences of Riley, by Margaret M. Scott)

1923, June, p. 488. (Anecdote, relating to "Leonainie," by Nellie L. Claybaugh)

1929, November, p. 256. "Roadside Meetings of a Literary Nomad" by Hamlin Garland

1931, January, p. 552. "Letters of James Whitcomb Riley. Edited by William Lyon Phelps" (review of, by Margaret Wallace)

BRUNO'S WEEKLY

1916, July 29. "To James Whitcomb Riley" (poem, by William Lightfoot Visscher)

BULLETIN OF PURDUE UNIVERSITY

1923, January. "James Whitcomb Riley." The Convocation Address Delivered by Mr. George Ade, Purdue University, Oct. 5, 1922.*

THE CATHOLIC SCHOOL JOURNAL

1912, June, p. 102. "James Whitcomb Riley" by Elsie May Smith

THE CENTURY MAGAZINE

1884, July, p. 467. "Recent American Poetry" by Charles S. Robinson

1888, July, p. 479. "To J. W. R." (poem) by Patty Caryl

1888, November, p. 159. "O You Fellers in th' City" (poem to James Whitcomb Riley) by Richard D. Lang

1888, December, p. 320. "To James Whitcomb Riley on Attaining Popularity" (poem) by C. H. Crandall

1889, March, p. [800]. "A Thank-Ye-Ma'am: The Sort of Verse That Makes James Whitcomb 'Riley' " by Tudor Jenks

1889, April, p. 959. "That Poet of the Future" (poem) by Charles Henry Webb

1903, April, p. 961. "A Po'try Note to James Whitcomb Riley" (poem) by Charles McIlvaine

1927, October, p. 704. "James Whitcomb Riley: A Sketch of His Life and an Appraisal of His Work" by Edgar Lee Masters

CHRISTIAN LEADER

1928, November 10, p. 1414. "The Gospel according to Riley" by Frank Durward Adams

THE CHRISTIAN UNION

1892, June 4, p. 1088. "The Hoosier Poet" by George D. Black

---

*Also noted in broadside form, reprinted from the *Bulletin*.

COLLIER'S
>    1915, October 9, p. 23. "Riley and the Kids" by Edmund H. Eitel
>    December 25, p. [3]. "A Poet Came out of Tailholt" by William Allen White
>    1916, December 30, p. [3]. "Mr. Riley" by Booth Tarkington
>    1923, March 10, p. 22. "When Riley Discovered Tarkington" by Fred C. Kelly

THE CONTINENT
>    1912, December 5, p. 1736. "When Poet Riley Was a Boy" by Thomas Kane

CORONET
>    1940, April, p. 107. "Poe of the Midlands"

THE CRITERION (New York)
>    1902, December, p. 40. (Review of *The Book of Joyous Children*)

THE CRITIC
>    1887, December 10, p. 299. (Lowell's tribute to Riley at Authors' Readings, New York, quoted from and commented on)
>    1891, February 1, p. 67. "Riley's *Rhymes of Childhood*" (review of)
>    September 19, p. 142. (On Riley's reception in London)
>    September 26, p. 155. (Regarding *The Flying Islands of the Night;* Riley's repudiation of reports concerning it)
>    October 17, p. 197. (Review of second edition of *Old-Fashioned Roses*)
>    December 5, p. 315. (Review of *An Old Sweetheart of Mine*)
>    1892, February 13, p. 98. (Review of *The Flying Islands of the Night*)
>    April 9, p. 220. (Account of a reception for Riley given by President Harrison at the White House)
>    1893, April 15, p. 233. (Review of *Green Fields and Running Brooks*)
>    November 4, p. 284. (Review of *Poems Here at Home*)
>    1894, September 29, p. 208. (Comments on Riley with quotation from *Cincinnati Commercial Gazette*)
>    December 1, p. 369. (Review of *Armazindy*)
>    1896, November 14, p. 294. "*A Child-World*" (review of)
>    1897, December 18, p. 380. "*The Rubáiyát of Doc Sifers*" (review of)
>    1898, December, p. 460. "The Poetry of James Whitcomb Riley" by Maurice Thompson
>    1902, July, p. 91. "*Riley Farm Rhymes*" (review of)
>    1903, March, p. 234. "*The Book of Joyous Children*" (review of) by Clinton Scollard
>    1904, August, p. 155. (Review of *His Pa's Romance*, by Ridgely Torrence)

CURRENT LITERATURE

1897, March, p. 254. "Selections from *A Child-World* by James Whitcomb Riley" (brief review)

1898, September, p. 208. "American Poets of To-day: James Whitcomb Riley" by F. M. Hopkins

1900, April, p. 44. (Account, reprinted from *Chicago Times-Herald*, of Riley's literary beginnings)

October, p. 415. (Sketch of Riley's career and notice of the *Greenfield Edition*)

1904, April, p. 470; 478. "Dr. James Whitcomb Riley" (poem to Riley reprinted from the *Hartford Courant*); "Home Folks" (poem to Riley reprinted from *National Magazine*)

1906, August, p. 160. "The Much Loved Personality of James Whitcomb Riley" (with quotation from Bliss Carman's article on Riley in *New York Times Saturday Review*)

CURRENT OPINION

1916, February, p. 128. "To J. W. R." (poem) by Rudyard Kipling; "Lockerbie Street" (poem) by Bliss Carman

September, p. 196. "Estimates of the Genius of 'The Poet of America's Youth' "

December, p. 418. "The Last of the Hoosiers" (poem) by John Finley (reprinted from *Outlook*)

THE DAILY TATLER

1896, November 7, p. 5. "W. D. Howells Reviews James Whitcomb Riley's New Book, *A Child-World*"

THE DAWN (published by Indianapolis High School #1, now Shortridge High School)

1893, October 26, James Whitcomb Riley Number. (Quotations from, and articles about, Riley)

THE DELINEATOR

1908, September, p. 391. "In Lockerbie Street Where James Whitcomb Riley, the 'Hoosier Poet,' Lives As Just One of the Folks" by Mabel Potter Daggett

THE ETHICAL RECORD

1903, January, p. 73. "*The Book of Joyous Children*" (review of, signed M. S. M.)

EXPRESSION

1895, June, p. 29. "James Whitcomb Riley" by Daniel J. Cosgro

FARM AND FIRESIDE

1916, August 19, p. 8. "James Whitcomb Riley" (editorial)

1923, October, p. 10. "The True Story of James Whitcomb Riley's 'Little Orphan Annie' " by Marcus Dickey

1924, October, p. 14. "An Unpublished Story by James Whitcomb Riley—The Binder That Found Itself" by Marcus Dickey

1925, October, p. 4. "What James Whitcomb Riley Thought of Farming" by Marcus Dickey

FARM LIFE (Spencer, Indiana)

1922, March, p. 10. "Did He 'Come Down' to Farming?" by Marcus Dickey

1924, November, p. 43. "James Whitcomb Riley" by Jacob F. Weintz

THE FORTNIGHTLY REVIEW

1896, September 1, p. 391. "Some Notes on Poetry for Children" by E. V. Lucas

FORWARD (Philadelphia)

1925, June 13, p. 186. "Jack-of-All-Trades, and Master of One" by Beulah Dimmick

THE GENTLEMAN'S MAGAZINE

1897, March, p. 311. "The Hoosier Poet" by Sylvanus Urban (pseudonym for Joseph Knight?) (Review of *A Child-World*)

GODEY'S MAGAZINE

1896, March, p. 319. "The Ambrosia of James Whitcomb Riley" by Chelifer

GOOD HOUSEKEEPING

1912, October, p. 456. "The Best Beloved Poet" by Mrs. Riley M. Fletcher-Berry

HARPER'S MAGAZINE

1891, May, p. 965. (Review of *Rhymes of Childhood*, by W. D. Howells)

1917, December, p. [1]. "A Poet and His Child Friends; James Whitcomb Riley's Letters to Children" arranged with comment by Edmund H. Eitel

1918, February, p. [313]. "The Letters of James Whitcomb Riley; the Poet in the Making" arranged with comment by Edmund H. Eitel

May, p. [840]. "The Letters of James Whitcomb Riley; Realizing Success—1883-90" edited with comment by Edmund H. Eitel

1919, March, p. [473]. "Letters of Riley and Bill Nye" arranged with comment by Edmund H. Eitel

HARPER'S WEEKLY
> 1892, January 9, p. 27. (Tribute to Riley as an actor)
> 1904, July 16, p. 1099. (An estimate of James Whitcomb Riley, by James MacArthur)

HEARST'S INTERNATIONAL—COSMOPOLITAN
> 1927, November, p. 76. "Riley: the Most Lovable Hoosier" by George Ade

THE HIGH SCHOOL BUDGET (Greenfield, Indiana)
> 1899, June, p. 12. "Riley's Versatility" by Mrs. W. S. Montgomery

THE HOOSIER (published by The Writers' Club of Indiana University, Bloomington, Indiana)
> 1916, December, Riley Memorial Number. "Personal Reminiscences" by Meredith Nicholson; "Our Own Poet" by Gene Stratton-Porter, etc.

HOOSIER FARMER
> 1933, October, p. 11. "James Whitcomb Riley" (poem) by B. A. Casmire

THE HOUSEKEEPER (Minneapolis, Minn.)
> 1903, January, p. 11. "Riley and His River" by Pearl Howard Campbell

HUMAN LIFE
> 1909, October, p. 7. "James Whitcomb Riley, the Sign Painter Who Became the Widest Known and Most Loved Poet in America" by Earl Derr Biggers

THE ILLINOIS
> 1903, March, p. 135. "James Whitcomb Riley at Home" by Helen M. Crane

ILLINOIS CENTRAL MAGAZINE
> 1931, June, p. 9. "Poet Riley Arcola's Friend"

THE INDEPENDENT
> 1900, December 6, p. 1. "Home Folks" (review of)
> 1916, August 7, p. [208]. "James Whitcomb Riley—the People's Poet"
> August 14, p. 209. "James Whitcomb Riley" (poem) by Herbert Kaufman

INDIANA FARMER'S GUIDE
> 1935, December 7, p. 11. "Among Indiana Authors James Whitcomb Riley, Known as the Children's Poet, Is Also Beloved by Adults" by George A. Schumacher

INDIANA MAGAZINE OF HISTORY
> 1905, Fourth quarter, p. [163]. "Folk-Speech in Indiana" by Paul
> L. Haworth and O. G. S. (with comments on Riley's dialect)
>
> 1912, December, p. 190. "To James Whitcomb Riley" (poem) by
> Sarah T. Bolton
>
> 1913, March, p. 23. "Concerning the Hoosier" by Charles M.
> Walker (with comments on Riley)
>
> 1918, June, p. [99]. "Some Reminiscences of James Whitcomb
> Riley" by George S. Cottman
>
> 1936, September, p. [189]. "James Whitcomb Riley" by George C.
> Hitt
>
> 1939, June, p. [129]. "James Whitcomb Riley in 1876" by Robert
> Price

INDIANA UNIVERSITY ALUMNI QUARTERLY
> 1931, January, p. 13. "Letters of James Whitcomb Riley (William
> Lyon Phelps, Editor)" reviewed by Kate Milner Rabb

INDIANA STATE NEWS BULLETIN
> 1928, November 1, p. [1]. (Brief facts concerning Riley's life and
> work)

THE INDIANAPOLIS MEDICAL JOURNAL
> 1911, May, p. 207. (On Riley's tribute to the medical profession,
> by Dr. A. W. Brayton)

THE INTERIOR
> 1897, December 9, p. 1603. (Discussion of *The Rubáiyát of Doc
> Sifers*)
>
> 1899, December 14, p. 1588. (Brief review of *Riley Love-Lyrics*)
>
> 1900, November 22, p. 1456. (Review of *Home-Folks*)

JOURNAL OF EDUCATION
> 1916, August 24, p. 149. "The 'Hoosier Poet' " by Jane A. Stewart
> September 28, p. 298. " 'Riley Day' (October 7)"
> November 2, p. 432. "James Whitcomb Riley Memorial
> Park" by George A. Brennan
> November 30, p. 559. "James Whitcomb Riley" (poem) by
> Wilbur D. Nesbit

THE JOURNAL OF THE NATIONAL EDUCATION ASSOCIATION
> 1925, April, p. 135. "The Capital of Indiana" by Christopher B.
> Coleman

JUDGE
> 1889, August 10, p. 291. "James and William" (poem to Riley and
> Nye)

1890, February 15, p. 313. "An Indiana Hymn" (parody of "Little Orphant Annie")

September 20, p. 390. (Another parody of "Little Orphant Annie")

1891, Christmas number, p. 23. "The Gigglety Girl; An Adult Rileyism" by Philander Johnson

LADIES' HOME JOURNAL

1896, March, p. 22. "A 'Riley' Entertainment"

1902, January, p. 7. "James Whitcomb Riley's 'Home Folks' " by John F. Mitchell, Jr.

1915, November, p. 54. "The Real 'Orphant Annie.' The Living Answer to James Whitcomb Riley's 'Where Is Mary Alice Smith?' Comes out of Hiding" by Edmund H. Eitel

1916, September, p. 15. "What James Whitcomb Riley Did for Me" by Clara E. Laughlin

THE LAMP

1903, May, p. 289. "An Interview with James Whitcomb Riley" by M. C. Chomel

LIFE

1916, August 10, p. 237. "James Whitcomb Riley, 1853–1916" (poem) by Christopher Morley

LIPPINCOTT'S MONTHLY MAGAZINE

1891, October, p. 511. "*Rhymes of Childhood*" (review of) by R. M. Johnston

1893, September, p. 384. "Men of the Day" by M. Crofton

THE LITERARY DIGEST

1912, October 26, p. 728. "To James Whitcomb Riley" (poem) by Wilbur D. Nesbit

1913, October 25, p. 782. "When Riley Reached Sixty-Four" by Strickland Gillilan

1915, October 2, p. 730. "Riley Day and Riley"

1916, June 10, p. 1724. "The Call of the Hoosiers"

August 5, p. [304]. "Colleges Blamed for Our Lack of Authors" (with Riley as one of the American literary "immortals who had no college education")

August 19, p. [408]. "James Whitcomb Riley" (tributes by Don Marquis and others)

LITERARY WORLD

1900, May, p. 104. "An Open Letter to James Whitcomb Riley" (poem) by Nellie Frances Milburn

McClure's Magazine
  1894, February, p. [219]. "A Dialogue between James Whitcomb
      Riley and Hamlin Garland" recorded by Mr. Garland
Men and Women
  1904, June, p. 15. "A Little Chat about James Whitcomb Riley" by
      Edgar Allen Forbes
Mentor
  1916, July 15, p. 6. "American Poets of the Soil" by Burges Johnson
  1921, June, p. 33. (On Riley's profits from *An Old Sweetheart of Mine*)
Methodist Review
  1906, November, p. 908. "A Prophet of Good Cheer" by Fred
      Winslow Adams
Munsey's Magazine
  1895, July, p. 380. "The Hoosier Poet" by Rufus R. Wilson
  1898, May, p. 278. "James Whitcomb Riley"
The Nassau Literary Magazine
  1892, June, p. 82. "A Short Study of James Whitcomb Riley" by
      Newton Booth Tarkington
The Nation
  1894, December 20, p. 468. (Review of *Armazindy*)
  1901, March 7, p. 198. (Review of *Home-Folks*)
  1902, December 11, p. 466. (Review of *The Book of Joyous Children*)
  1913, October 16, p. 352. "The Hoosier Poet"
  1915, October 14, p. 454. "Indiana's Sentimental Bard"
The National Magazine
  1899, January, p. 322. "The Hoosier Poet at His Old Home" by
      Joe Mitchell Chapple
  1901, December, p. 270. "Whitcomb Riley's Favorite Poem"
Nature Study
  1918, November, p. 327. "Riley's Gift of Bird Song" by A. S. Ninman
The New Age Magazine
  1904, August-September, p. [265]. "A Poet and His Town" by
      Emma Look Scott
The New Republic
  1916, August 19, p. 71. "James Whitcomb Riley" by Edith Wyatt
The North American Review
  1899, May, p. 588. "The New Poetry" by W. D. Howells
  1916, September, p. [421]. "In Memoriam: James Whitcomb Riley"
      (address by George Harvey; foreword by Joe Mitchell
      Chapple)

THE OUTLOOK
    1915, September 29, p. 249. "A Hoosier Celebration"
    October 20, p. 396. "A Poet's Birthday"
    1916, October 25, p. 422. "The Last of the Hoosiers" by John Finley
    August 2, p. 778. "James Whitcomb Riley"
    1922, May 3, p. 8. "The Riley Memorial"
    1924, November 19, p. 436. "Riley Remembered"

OVERLAND MONTHLY
    1905, March, p. [256]. "Answering James Whitcomb Riley, When the Frost Is on the Punkin" (poem) by Dan. W. Graybill

THE PHOENIX
    1915, December. "Our Best Loved Poet" by Michael Monahan
    1916, September. "James Whitcomb Riley; Some Intimate Memorials" by Michael Monahan

POETRY
    1916, September, p. 305. "James Whitcomb Riley" (editorial, by Harriet Monroe)

PRIMARY PLANS
    1913, October, p. 25. "October Birthday Story—James Whitcomb Riley" by Betty Blyton

THE READER
    1903, January, p. [281]. (Review of *The Book of Joyous Children* by Bliss Carman)
    1907, October, (advertising section). "Mr. Boyheart" by Laurance Chambers (review of *Morning*)

ST. NICHOLAS MAGAZINE
    1916, February, p. 358. "The Children's Poet" by Hildegarde Hawthorne
    1923, January, p. 268. "The Book-Plate of James Whitcomb Riley" by Jennie M. Elrod
    1924, December, p. 213. "In Memory of a Poet"
    1930, October, p. 906. "Poetic Justice" by Edgar Lee Maines

THE SATURDAY EVENING POST
    1899, December 23, p. 525. "Letters from Bill Nye, with Some Anecdotes" by Major James B. Pond
    1930, September 27, p. 8. "Riley and His Friends" by George Ade

THE SATURDAY REVIEW OF LITERATURE
    1931, January 17, p. 5. "Main Street, Old Style" by Fred Lewis Pattee (review of *Letters of James Whitcomb Riley*, edited by William Lyon Phelps)

1937, July 3, p. 10. "Riley as a Nature Poet" by Donald Culross Peattie

1938, December 17, p. 4. "Limestone, Corn, and Literature" by Richard A. Cordell

SAXBY'S MAGAZINE

1898, November, p. 7. "Reminiscences of James Whitcomb Riley" by Howard Saxby

THE SCOOP (published by the Press Club of Chicago)

1915, January 2, p. 8. "James Whitcomb Riley: a Personal and Literary Appreciation" by Walter Hurt

SCRIBNER'S MAGAZINE

1903, February, p. 156. "To James Whitcomb Riley, Gardener" (poem) by Henry van Dyke

1930, November, p. 546. "As I Like It" by William Lyon Phelps

THE SHIELD OF PHI KAPPA PSI

1899, October 16, 1899, p. [7]. "Phi Kappa Psi's Poet Laureate, James Whitcomb Riley"

1904, April, p. 515. (An account of Riley's presence at a banquet of Phi Kappa Psi)

THE SHORTHAND ADVOCATE (Indianapolis)

1893, August, Riley Number. "James Whitcomb Riley" by J. B. Roberts; "An Hour with Riley" by S. H. East

THE STRAND MAGAZINE

1915, June, p. 164. "How They 'Broke into Print'" by Francis Arthur Jones

SUCCESS

1898, December 29, p. 63. "James Whitcomb Riley, the 'Hoosier Poet,' Tells the Story of His Early Struggles, and of His Beginnings as a Bard" by Walden Fawcett

1901, February, p. 617. "The Fires That Feed Genius—James Whitcomb Riley" by George M. Anderson
August, p. 949. "The Literary Redemption of Indiana . . . Discussed by Lewis Wallace and James Whitcomb Riley" (interview by Caroline Brown)

1903, December, p. 720. "James Whitcomb Riley and His Children. The Opinions of a Family Man Without a Family" by Roger Galeshore (Zona Gale?*)

---

*Written by Zona Gale, according to the *Indianapolis News*, July 24, 1916, p. 10, where the article is reprinted.

1906, November, p. 746. (Anecdote, relating to Riley and "Wes" Burnett in article by George Ade, "The Funniest Stories I've Heard")

TALENT

1904, September, p. 22. "Riley as a Lyceum Man" by [Paul] M. Pearson

1906, October, p. 5. "James Whitcomb Riley" by Paul M. Pearson

THE TATLER (Des Moines, Iowa)

1897, October. "James Whitcomb Riley" (a thoroughly inaccurate biographical sketch)

THE TEMPLE REVIEW

1916, November 10, p. 3. (A sermon on Divine Substitution using James Whitcomb Riley as an example, by Russell H. Conwell)

THE WAVE (San Francisco, California)

1892, December 17, p. 36. "James Whitcomb Riley" (notice of his forthcoming appearance in Los Angeles)

THE WESTERN COLLEGE MAGAZINE (Chicago)

1902, February. "Riley and Riley's" by Louis V. Jefferson

THE WESTMINSTER CHAP BOOK (Franklin, Indiana)

1902, August. (Notice of honorary degree conferred on Riley by Yale)

WISCONSIN LITERARY MAGAZINE

1916, October. "James Whitcomb Riley—the Sign Painter Poet" by Louis Wann

THE WORLD'S WORK

1913, March, p. 565. "The Boy Who Was Born in Our Town" by Samuel McCoy

THE WRITER (Boston)

1915, October, pp. 145; 153. "To James Whitcomb Riley" (tributes); "Personal Gossip about Authors"

THE WRITER'S MAGAZINE

1913, August, p. 8. "To James Whitcomb Riley" by Kate Masterson

YALE REVIEW

1920, January, p. 395. "The Singer of the Old Swimmin' Hole" by Henry A. Beers

YOUNG PEOPLE'S WEEKLY (Elgin, Illinois)

1904, January 16, p. 6. "The Hoosier Poet"

# FIRST LINES

## NOT IN BIOGRAPHICAL EDITION

### (1913)

# First Lines

THE FOLLOWING do not appear in the index of first lines in the *Biographical Edition*, Vol. 6. To be used as a supplement to the index in the *Biographical Edition*.

FIRST LINE          TITLE OR REFERENCE

A carpenter up in Du Chien—In: Letter to Robert J. Burdette, 1881

A Chimpanzee, at the Zoo, once said—The Chimpanzee's Apology

A Crawfordsville freshman named Tweedle—What Our Bright College Boys Are Doing [first series]

A domineerin' feller, like 'at he—The Raggedy Man Observing

A fair summer just begun—A Happy Dream

A file of papers from a rack—In: *The Maturity of James Whitcomb Riley*, by Marcus Dickey, p. 69

A glowworm blinked at a child and said—In: *Indianapolis Star*, October 7, 1934

A grave University student—What Our Bright College Boys Are Doing [fourth series]

A hundred hearts beat happily; and when—[*Anderson Democrat* jingle]

A little, dingy, dusty room—["Crow's Nest"]

A little, warty, dried-up sort—A Black Hills Episode

A "Midnight oil"-student of Andover—What Our Bright College Boys Are Doing [third series]

A notable lady of letters was she—In: Letter to Clara E. Laughlin, beginning: "Thank you for the letters my Biographer wants"

A stately figure, rapt and awed—Transfigured

About a fellow that both of us knows—Joe Biggsby's Proposal

Afterwhile I promised to—In: *Chicago Tribune*, March 3, 1889

Afterwhile-the poet-man—In: Letter to Mrs. Rosaline E. Jones, November 9, 1887

Ain't a-goin' to worry any more—See: Haint a-goin' to worry any more

All the pleasures of home have been numbered and sung (Later: Many pleasures of Youth have been buoyantly sung)—As I Sit in the Silence

Although his worthy life-work never knew—Maurice Perkins

An old graduate of Moore's Hill—What Our Bright College Boys Are Doing [fifth series]

An under-graduate, at Greencastle—What Our Bright College Boys Are Doing [second series]

And hence the Muse was prone to balk—[*Anderson Democrat* jingle]

"And I know well," said the man o' brains—The Wise Man

And now the jolly Muse, with rosy lip—[*Anderson Democrat* jingle]

And so, in the face o' the sun by day—In: Letter to Clara E. Laughlin, beginning: "Truly you deserve all praise and worship"

And there was something in his tone—In: *The Maturity of James Whitcomb Riley*, by Marcus Dickey, p. 45

And there's 'Gene Debs-a man 'at stands—Part of: Regardin' Terry Hut

And they's still another idy 'at I ort to here append—Set Him There K-Sock

And this is how it happened some discrepancies befell—Part of: Thanksgiving Day at Hunchley's

And when she still insisted—[*Anderson Democrat* jingle]

As brown as dusk of death is brown—A Last Meeting. (Later: "They faced each other: Topaz-brown"; retitled: The Quarrel)

As "everything goes," gracious knows—Pa's Soliloquy

As little wondering Willie once—The Melancholy Source of Tears

At La Ker-bie, nor mirth nor wit—In: *The Maturity of James Whitcomb Riley*, by Marcus Dickey, p. 298

Backward, throw backward the curtain tonight—Now We Can Sleep, Mother

Be high or low, or rich or poor—In: Letter to William Mitchell, August 7, 1882

Being a Jimpsy-jumpsy boy—In: Letter to Dorian Medairy, December 14, 1905

Billy has to go to pasture—Billy and "Old Muley"

Brighter than all of the cluster of stars—The Dead Leader

Carpets coarse and carpets fine—In: *The Youth of James Whitcomb Riley*, by Marcus Dickey, p. 228

Cease your overtures to me—To Old Age-Greeting

Charley he's my little buther—"Uncle Bob's Boy"

Chaw! Chaw! Chaw!—In: The Irrepressible Man at Bay

Christmas!—"Old Santa" Wags His Beard Once More

Clang the harp in its wildest key—The Poet's Realm

Climb'd Olympus, 'tother night—My Visit to Olympus

Come to the sanctum board to-night—[*Anderson Democrat* jingle]

Das Deutsche Haus is the place, I guess—The German House

"Dear Cousin," she wrote in her rollicking style—The Breeze of the Lake

Dear Editor: Your Tribune's here—Where It Natchurly Belongs

Dear ever indulgent and generous Muse—[*Anderson Democrat* jingle]

Dear Friend, You want a letter—Untitled poem of 9 stanzas, uncollected save for final 3 stanzas later entitled: A Letter to a Friend

Dear Man-happy husband and rapturous father—To a Benedict Friend
Deft master of the most grotesque—Upon Valentine-Designs by D. S.
Dinah she aint pleased at all—Untitled. In: *The Riley Baby Book*
"Dis razah pull!" W'y wat you sayin'?—An Easy Shave
*Don't* disturve me, Mommy!-Say,—Untitled. In: *The Riley Baby Book*
Dory Ann-O friend of mine—In: *Harper's Monthly Magazine*, December, 1917, p. 8
Draw aside the drapery of gloom—Memorial Day

Ef little boys makes such a noise—A Romper's Logic
Eyes lit with luminous drips—A Ballade of Wine

Falstaff. I call him dog, forsooth, because he snarls—In: A Remarkable Man
Fame, says I, go 'way from *me*—In: Letter to Charles Holstein, February 2, 1894
Feller wants to jes' go slow—Portion of an untitled poem beginning: "F'r instance, now, when *some* folks gits" (in: "At Zekesbury")
Fer them 'at's here in airliest infant stages—Poem which precedes: Our Queer Old World
Fifteen men on the dead man's chest—[Parody of Young E. Allison's "The Derelict"]
Fine! FINE!! SUPERFINE!!!—In: *Early Recollections of James Whitcomb Riley*, by Major Ridgeway, p. 60
First the printer damns the scrawl—In: *Journalist* (*New York*), January 11, 1890
F'r instance, now, when *some* folks gits—Part of: Thoughts on a Pore Joke. Also in: At Zekesbury
Forever old, forever young—In: Souvenir of 32nd National Saengerfest, 1908
Forever the birds are there—In: "Home, Sweet Home"

Gadzooks! My dainty lady typewriter—In: Letter to Western Association of Writers, secretary of, October 15, 1888
Gilded bands and polished steel—[*Anderson Democrat* jingle]
Girls ain't 'feared o' burds with wings—Bats
*Given*-Name is 'Mancipation—Untitled. In: *The Riley Baby Book*
Glorious Easter, feast of flowers—Easter
Go, search the earth from end to end—Part of: Regardin' Terry Hut
Good-night! I'm glad an' sorry, too—In: *Indianapolis Star*, October 6, 1935
Grandpa's name ain't much comparison—In: *Indianapolis Star*, May 26, 1940
Greenfield barbers cut my hair—In: *The Youth of James Whitcomb Riley*, by Marcus Dickey, p. 196

Hail to your fifty years of toil and stress—In: *Chicago Tribune*, Golden Jubilee Section, June 10, 1897

Haint a-goin' to worry any more—In: *New York Morning World*, August 20, 1892

"Have I been ever wrecked at sea["]*—[The Lover's Peril]

He owns the bird-songs of the hills—Part of: The Hoosier Folk-Child

He sat in a seat in the smoking-car—All Alone

He took his pen in hand, and then—In: *Indianapolis Sentinel*, November 4, 1891 (see p. 155)

He was wicked, they say and hard-hearted—Tom

Her face knew a purer glory—In: *Indianapolis Star*, May 26, 1940

Here lies a young man—In: The Gilded Roll

Here on the balcony, a sign—[*Anderson Democrat* jingle]

Here's a Water-Kelpie's daughter—Untitled. In: *The Riley Baby Book*

Hickory, dickory, dock—[*Anderson Democrat* jingle]

His daily, nightly task is o'er—James B. Maynard

His world, you fancy, must be cold—Blind

Hit's mighty good news er new-Ol' Uncle Remus Rhymes—[Letter in rhyme to Joel Chandler Harris]

Hootsy-tootsy, I declare—[*Greenfield News* advertising jingle]

How many miles to Barley Bright—Make It?—Why, Cert.


I allus argy that a man—Part of: My Philosofy

"I always know," said the English dude—The Two Dudes

I asked my tailor for a suit—In: *The Maturity of James Whitcomb Riley*, by Marcus Dickey, p. 119

I cannot sing the old songs now—The Happy Couple—A Duet

I follow you forever on—Song. In: The Flying Islands of the Night

I had two devoted lovers—Flames and Ashes

I hail thee, thou regal profession—A Transient Dental Monody

I hain't none of yer lofty breed!—ner don't p'tend to be—Honest Old Sam Hungerford

I have ranged all revels through—In: *Indianapolis Star*, October 3, 1937

I lay my head down in the lap of night—A Sonnet

I look from the window. The smoke goes straight—The Dead Wife

I once thought myself quite a poet—In: *The Maturity of James Whitcomb Riley*, by Marcus Dickey, p. 135

I send you the shadowy ghost of a face—Lines in a Letter Enclosing a Picture

I washed my face and combed my hair—In: *The Youth of James Whitcomb Riley*, by Marcus Dickey, p. 196

"I will know the worst!" he said—Kismet

If one of the little Cherubim—Untitled. In: *The Riley Baby Book*

If thou dost bid thy girl farewell—Counsel

If you ever live to see—In: *The Youth of James Whitcomb Riley*, by Marcus Dickey, p. 196

---

*Anonymous; a parody of "The Lover's Peril" by James T. Fields.

If your imperious command—A Custom-Made Valentine
I'm a Papoosie, an' Muvver's a Squaw—Untitled. In: *The Riley Baby Book*
I'm a very *serious* baby—Untitled. In: *The Riley Baby Book*
I'm in love with my darling profession—In: Letter to Miss Tarkington (later Mrs. Ovid Butler Jameson), February 15, 1883
I'm ist a little too skeer'd to know—Untitled. In: *The Riley Baby Book*
I'm shut up in a primitive town—[Letter in rhyme to Lewis D. Hayes]
In jousts of old, with couchant quill—In: Letter to Clara E. Laughlin, December 26, 1898
In the back of the book—Lines on a Error
In the heyday of life and the fullness of health—In: *Indianapolis Journal*, September 10, 1881
In the old convent of Heisterbach—The Legend of Heisterbach
In this existence, dry and wet—Part of: Wet-Weather Talk
Is it "Good-night" or "Good-morning," Dear—Untitled. In: *The Riley Baby Book*
Is it hot enough for you—Hot!
Is it too fine for thee—The Chamber over the Gate
It is a dream he has. In some strange place—An Ideal
It is all fal-de-ral, this old notion, you know—The True Age of Wisdom
It is the lecture agent—In: Letter to Edgar Wilson Nye, *ca*. April 14, 1886
It was a summer evening—A Famous Victory
It was late last night when you retired—The Father, and His Girl, and Her Young Man
It was merely a flirtation—A Flirtation
It was the night, ere New Year's night—New Year's Greeting of the Carriers of the Indianapolis Daily Journal
"It's my opinion," said Farmer Gray—He Was Right
I've give you up! It hain't no use—I've Give You Up

Jes' my ortograph, you say—In: *The Maturity of James Whitcomb Riley*, by Marcus Dickey, p. 196
Jevver watch a primrose 'bout—For-Mrs. Ovid B. Jameson, Indianapolis, Oct., 1894
Just a servant-Philip Moore—Philip Moore-of Denison House
Just across the street—[*Anderson Democrat* jingle]

Kate Shane, the coquette iv all Dayton—In: Letter to Clara E. Laughlin, beginning: "Till this blessed minute I've not had the chanst to thank yez for the lavish bunch of papers."
Kept open house, O, yes my dear—Open House
Killed by the cars, they found him—Killed by the Cars
Kindly and warm and tender—The Poet's Love for the Children
"Ki-yi!" said Mr. Squincher—The Gruesome Ballad of Mr. Squincher

Lather me lightly, and speak to me low—Lines to my Barber
"Leoloony," angels called her—Leoloony
"Leonainie"-Riley named her—"Leonainie"
"Leventeen Hundered-an-full-er-flees."—[Letter in rhyme to Joel Chandler Harris]
Liquors that so strangely lubricate—[*Anderson Democrat* jingle]
Little Boy! Halloo!-halloo!—In: *A Defective Santa Claus* (dedicatory poem)
Little Injun boys, like me—In: *The Riley Baby Book*
"Little Miriam is dead!"—Little Miriam
Little Orphant Annie she knows riddles, rhymes and things!—In: *The Orphant Annie Book* (proem)
Little pen, that to and fro—Choice Verses for Autograph Albums [3rd verse]
Lizbeth she ist *laughs*, an' *sings*—For Mrs. Lizbeth Sewell Foster, Indianapolis, Ind., Feb. 9, 1893
Lo! the autumn leaves is falling—The Autumn Leaves Is Falling
Look so very—In: *The Riley Baby Book*

Ma says-Couldn't mucher prize—In: *The Riley Baby Book*
"Make way for Liberty!" (he said)—[*Anderson Democrat* jingle]
Mamie's naething but a chick—The Twa Puir Chicks
Marcellus, won't you tell us—Uncle Sidney to Marcellus
Me and my little old man fell out—[*Greenfield News* jingle]
Mild and gentle, as he was brave—Part of: Away
Miss Medairy Dory-Ann—In: Letter to Dorian Medairy, beginning: "One time an old middle-aged man—'"*
Moving up from high to higher—In: [Speech in response to toast, "Our Guest," at Commercial Club Dinner, Indianapolis, April 21, 1897]
My dear young friend, regaled with love—In: *The Youth of James Whitcomb Riley*, by Marcus Dickey, p. 287
My dear young friend whose glowing love—In: Loss of the Bright-est Jewel
My dears, do you know, but a short time ago—The Babes in the When
My dears, do you know, one short Christmas ago—A Christmas-Time Jingle
My religen is to jest—In: *Indianapolis Star*, October 6, 1929

Name! Name! Name!—See: Grandpa's name ain't much comparison
Neglected genius-truth be said—In: *The Youth of James Whitcomb Riley*, by Marcus Dickey, p. 241
No matter, then, how all is mixed—In: *Indianapolis Star*, April 11, 1916
Nobody ever saw it—Some Custom-Made Riddles [first riddle]
Not long ago, when an elegant gent—He Knew a Good Thing When He Had It

---

*In *Harper's Monthly Magazine*, December, 1917, p. [5]. In *Letters of James Whitcomb Riley*, edited by William Lyon Phelps (1930), p. 255, the same poem appears linked with a different letter to Dorian Medairy, dated September 25, 1901, beginning, "No use trying, for I just can't tell you how proud I am"

Now the Muses Nine are ten—A Classic Bard's Protest
Now things is thawed—Choice Verses for Autograph Albums [4th verse]

O Brother mine of birth Divine—Part of: Child's Christmas Carol
O Courteous Muse, you have served me so long—Invocation
O dear! What can the matter be?—How Doth He Do It?
O gentle death, bow down and sip—The Dream of Death
O he was a poet weird and sad—In: *The Youth of James Whitcomb Riley*, by
    Marcus Dickey, p. 238
O I am a poet weird and sad—The Stars Won't Wane and the Moon Won't
    Wax
O kind friendth and neighborth, come lithen unto me—Little Jack Wiseman
O laughter, in thy dear companionship—Laughter
O, leafless vines of tune—In: *Saturday Herald* (*Indianapolis*), September 14,
    1878 [included in Riley's own criticism of "The Flying Islands of the
    Night"]
O little Dollie Dimpleton she loved the English Sparrow!—Little Dollie
    and Her Friends
O make home attractive! be cheerful and free—Make Home Attractive

O Playmate of the far-away—George A. Carr / July 21, 1914. Greenfield.
O rare old drink, the oldest, strongest far—On Quitting California (Bour-
    bon)
O, Reed, thou oracle whose name—To the Bard; In: [Letter to George C.
    Harding]
O, singer, in these later times—New Year's Address for the Carriers of the
    Indianapolis Daily Journal. 1880
O, tell me no more—[*Greenfield News* jingle]
O the Park!-University Park!—University Park
O were I not a clod, intent—A Song by Uncle Sidney
O, what a joy to meet—In: *Indianapolis News*, July 24, 1916
O, what strange tragedy is this of mine—In: Tale of a Spider
O, where-tell me where—[*Greenfield News* jingle]
Of all the stores, the cheapest one—[*Greenfield News* jingle]
Oh, bright is gleaming morn on mountain height—Song / Imitated from
    Tennyson's Idyls of the King
Oh, Muse! Inspire our "Faber No. 2"—In: *The Youth of James Whitcomb
    Riley*, by Marcus Dickey, p. 167
Oh, the hobo's life is a roving life—A Hobo Voluntary
"Oh! you snow! you beautiful snow!"—In: *Mooresville* (*Indiana*) *Enter-
    prise*, May 8, 1873
"Old Santa Claus is coming!"—[*Greenfield News* jingle]
Once on a time, in a town called Rome—The Diplomatic Spirit and Delicate
    Finesse of the True Social Host
Onc't little Wesley Offut watch—Why?
One Christmas in the early din—What "Old Santa" Overheard

One frisky frosty morning—The Old Hoss in New Gears
One gloomy day in the early Fall—The Duck-Hunters of the Kankakee
One guides us thro' the watches of the night!—Part of: The Watches of
the Night
One time a little girl she got her Ma to write and tell—In: [Letter in rhyme
to Mabel Wessels, April 10, 1897]
One! Two!—In: *Indianapolis Journal*, March 1, 1891 (in advertisement for
The When)
Our fortunes! O we need not waste—Kismet
Our teacher Miss King—In: Letter to Dorian Medairy, September 25, 1901
Out on the margin of Moonshine Land—Part of: The Lugubrious Whing-
Whang

Pa's rigged hisse'f out like a bride!—Bubb's Back-Cap
Pare your corn in the gray of the morn—This Will Knock a Corn Silly
Peace kindo' sorto' suits my diet—Part of: Thoughts on the Late War
Pete Stanley, a youth from Van Buren—Police Poetry
Plain Bill Wilson was his name—In: *Indianapolis Journal*, April 5, 1885
Pleasant here, in this dim retreat—Cream for Two
Pride o' all Kentucky, sah!—"Ole Longfellow"
Pride of thy Westland, and Loved of the Nation!—Hendricks

Rain, rain, go away—In: *The Youth of James Whitcomb Riley*, by Marcus
Dickey, p. 138
Rain! Rain! Rain!—In: Letter to Lee O. Harris, October 26, 1876
Ring in the wind his wedding chimes—In: Mrs. Miller
Rude was the man in speech, and rude—In the City Streets

Saddles and harness! O musical words—In: *The Youth of James Whitcomb
Riley*, by Marcus Dickey, p. 140
Season halest of the year—Part of: Time of Clearer Twitterings
Season of myths and monster circuses—In: The Circus Season
She never knew what love was like, because—She Never Knew
She was sleeping, oh! so life-like!—A Mockery
Sing a song o' slick-pence—In: *Indianapolis Journal*, December 22, 1890
(in advertisement for The When)
Sing as you will, O singers all—Sing!
Sing for the Oak Tree—In: *The Youth of James Whitcomb Riley*, by Marcus
Dickey, p. 140
Sister, sister, come and see!—In: Letter to Dorian Medairy, September 9,
1905
Sitting by the glimmer—Something
So were I but a minstrel, deft—Part of: In the South
Sometimes it's all alone—Some Custom-Made Riddles [second riddle]
'Spect you think I'm "a tough old jay"—In: *The Riley Baby Book*
Strop his razor till it gleams—[*Anderson Democrat* jingle]

Such silence-after such glad merriment—To-Edgar Wilson Nye
Swallowed up in gulfs of tho't—A Character
Sweet as the tune that drips—A Tune
Sweet is the sound, when oft at evening's close—[*Greenfield News* jingle]
Swiftly and surely—A Fragment

The "Artist" knew enough to know—In: *Indianapolis Star*, October 6, 1935
The Babes in the Woods-ef they didn't die there—Reconcilement
The Baby Elephant goes round and round—In: Letter to Thomas Whitcomb
Hays
The Bookman he's a humming-bird—To Young E. Allison-Bookman
The boy behind the soda-fount—The Boy Behind the Soda-Fount
The boy stood on his burning head—Casabianca and His Pa
The burdened heart is lighter—In: *The Maturity of James Whitcomb Riley*, by
Marcus Dickey, p. 263
The deadnin' and the thicket's jes' a b'ilin' full o' June—Part of: Romancin'
The deepest ice that ever froze—[*Greenfield News* jingle]
The Devil's feelings e'en were spared—In: Letter to Wilbur D. Nesbit,
January 8, 1904
The farmer works his hired hand—In: *The Youth of James Whitcomb Riley*,
by Marcus Dickey, p. 228
The first book far too bad to go—In: Letter to Wilbur D. Nesbit, January 8,
1904
The Year goes on and on and on—In: *The Golden Year* (proem)
The flowers that blooms in Beauty's bower—Choice Verses for Autograph
Albums [5th verse]
The fodder shocks reeled as the train spun past—From a Car Window
The Guvner he once said to me—State House
The hands are as busy—In: *The Youth of James Whitcomb Riley*, by Marcus
Dickey, p. 257
The Kind Spider said—The Spider with the Kind Heart
The man that struck his crazy bone—His Crazy-Bone
The north wind doth blow—The Wind and the When
The Old Friends! Be they sung—In: Broadside mounted in Vol. 5 of a set
of the *Elizabeth Marine Riley Edition* (see p. 225)
The praise of the Grocery men—[*Anderson Democrat* jingle]
The Reporter! Honor to—The Reporter
The signs is bad when folks commence—Just Do Your Best
The way I hate her rests me so—A Woman's Hate
The wind blows over the hills of dawn—Yatesesque
The women came running—In: Letter to Edgar Wilson Nye, April 7,
1886
There all day long the bullfrog cheeps—In: *The Youth of James Whitcomb
Riley*, by Marcus Dickey, p. 139
There are Bracelets rare—[*Greenfield News* jingle]
There are four of us girls in the family—The Amiable Old Sister

"What boots it?" Shakespeare asks—[*Anderson Democrat* jingle]

What happiness we had—The Last Waltz

"What house is this?" asked Dory Ann—Court House

What poverty like this! to laugh and sing—In: *The Maturity of James Whitcomb Riley*, by Marcus Dickey, p. 111

What thought I scantly trust ye can—The Apology

What verse shall I write—In an Album

What words of greeting will be best—Grant-At Indianapolis, December 9, 1879

What you think I care fer Stile—In: *The Riley Baby Book*

Whecht! mon, an' dyv' ye ken him, sir—"Dyv' Ye Ken Burns the Poemer?"

When Baby played—When Baby Played

When Dickens first dawned on us . . . Hey! to wake—St. Lirriper

When Dory Ann she gave a tea—In: Letter to Dorian Medairy, September 19, 1903

When he first came courting me—All She Could Do

When I heer'd this tetchin' story of the feller and his gal—A Southern Reminiscence of a Bully Boy in Blue

When in our blithest youth we sing—Youth and Age

When it rains! Weary heart—Part of: When It Rains

When other lips and other hearts—Then You'll Remember-Us

When Shakespeare's voice was heard of old—In: *New York Morning Journal*, May 1, 1892

When that I was a little tiny boy—In: *Indianapolis Journal*, December 17, 1890 (precedes "The Wind and the When" in advertisement for *The When*)

When the chill night drops like an ax and chops—Owl Song

When the heart like a plummet resounds in the dumps—[*Anderson Democrat* jingle]

When they go from us who are dear—When They Go from Us

When weenty-teenty Baby slept—When Baby Slept

When weenty-teenty Baby woke—When Baby Woke

When winter winds begin to blow—My Topic Wiles

When you meet me, lift your hat—When You Meet Me

When your parents named you—To My Namesake, James Riley Matthews

Where art thou, Love, still lost to me—In: *The Youth of James Whitcomb Riley*, by Marcus Dickey, p. 249

Where smooth the Roycroft presses grind—In: Letter to Roycrofters, August 1, 1902

Where the goods are all new—[*Anderson Democrat* jingle]

Where's a heart as mellow—Part of: On the Sunny Side

Wherever blooms of health are blown—In: *The Youth of James Whitcomb Riley*, by Marcus Dickey, p. 130

Whiles only hafflins gane tae bed—James Whitcomb Riley to Joseph Roland Piatt

White fruited cocoa shown against the shell—Part of: An Empty Glove

Who but he could read a watch's pedigree—[*Anderson Democrat* jingle]

Whoop-ee! What has he done to me—Always Unexpectedly

Willow ware, rich and rare—[*Greenfield News* jingle]

With face a masquerade of all affection—The False Friend

With joy too great—A Valentine Supplement

With joy too great for pen to state—In: Letter to Dorian Medairy, September 19, 1903

"Write me a rhyme of the present time"—[*Greenfield News* jingle]

Wuz me and "Chewrick" Morningstar—As "Clog-Step Johnny" Tells It

Yet himself a child at play—In: *James Whitcomb Riley An Essay* by Bliss Carman, p. [31]

You critics! I ignore you graciously—Sonnet on the Intolerable Conceit of Critics

You may break-you may shatter the little—In: Letter to Eugene Debs, February 18, 1890

You see, it's like this, what his weaknesses is—Part of: Them Flowers (stanza 3)

You'll find true happiness just begun—[*Greenfield News* jingle]

You're a dear little Edgar Lee Maines—In: Letter to Edgar Lee Maines, June 8, 1884

You've wrought a miracle-you've made—Lines Penned on an Apollo / To Melville Clark-With Another Order

Young Pulitzer Floy—Young Pulitzer Floy and "Say"

Young Rory McMoore was brave as the dawn—Bold Rory McMoore

Your generous hands outheld and warmly spread—To My Fellows and My Foes and My Good Master

Your letter was almost as dear to me—In: *The Maturity of James Whitcomb Riley*, by Marcus Dickey, p. 111

Your ringin' ballad, a la "Fuzzy Wuzz,"—To Wiley Owen

Your roses are the phrase and word—Adapted from: Three Several Birds

# PERIODICALS

CONTAINING FIRST APPEARANCES

# Periodicals
# Containing First Appearances

AMERICA
  1888: May        12    To My Fellows and My Foes and My Good
                           Master*
  1891: January    29    My Visit to Olympus*
ANDERSON (Indiana) DEMOCRAT†
  1877: April          (?) [Prose beginning: In making my salam (*sic*) to
                           the Anderson public]
        May       4(?) A Man of Many Parts
                 11(?) Willie
        June       1(?) Craqueodoom
                       Decoration Poem
                   8   Invocation (*anon.*)*
        July      13(?) Benson Out-Bensoned (*anon.*)*
                 20(?) Harlie (*signed* R)
        August    17    The Poet Poe in Kokomo! (*anon.*)*

        NOTE: In addition to the above, the 1877 issues contained the
        following:        Maud Muller
                          The Frog
                          Police Poetry
                          Now We Can Sleep, Mother
                          Wash Lowry's Reminiscence
                          George Mullen's Confession
                          "Tired Out"
                          A Test of Love
                          A Wrangdillion (in a July issue evidently; a re-
                          print in the *Indianapolis Journal*, July 14,
                          1877, ascribed it to the *Anderson Democrat*)
ARENA
  1897: June            "O Life! O Beyond!"
        December        Santa Claus

---

*Uncollected
†In addition to the titles here listed, the *Anderson Democrat*, from April 27,
1877 to August 17, 1877, is said to contain numerous advertising jingles, locals
and prose sketches by Riley (see *The Youth of James Whitcomb Riley* by Marcus
Dickey [1919] for an account of them. See also this bibliography, p. 187)

ATLANTA (Georgia) CONSTITUTION
    1893: April      16    "How Did You Rest, Last Night?"
    1901: August     5    To Frank L. Stanton

ATLANTIC MONTHLY
    1898: September     The Sermon of the Rose
           December     The Name of Old Glory

BALTIMORE SUN (see SUN)

BELFORD'S MAGAZINE
    1888: August     The Wife

THE BOOK BUYER
    1888: December     Little Johnts's Chris'mus

BOSTON DAILY GLOBE
    1901: September 19    Even As a Child

BOSTON [EVENING] TRANSCRIPT
    1924: October    25    [Letters to Michael Monahan:
                         December 22, 1914;
                         June 26, 1915]*

BRUNO'S WEEKLY
    1916: July      29    [Letter to Guido Bruno, December 6, 1915]*

BUFFALO (New York) EVENING NEWS
    1898: October    31    To Wiley Owen (*signed* J. W. R.)*

CENTURY MAGAZINE
    1883: September       In Swimming-Time
    1887: June            When She Comes Home
           August          Nothin' to Say
    1888: January        The Old Man and Jim
           February       At "The Literary"
           May             The Absence of Little Wesley
           July             Gladness
           November      'Mongst the Hills o' Somerset
           December      "Last Christmas Was a Year Ago"
    1889: January        The Poet of the Future
           February       The All-Kind Mother
           March          Down to the Capital
    1890: January        Thoughts on the Late War
           February       The Old Band
           April            "The Little Man in the Tin-Shop"
           November      Bereaved
           December      The Raggedy Man
                          A Boy's Mother
                          The Fishing-Party

---

*Uncollected.

CENTURY MAGAZINE—*continued*

| | |
|---|---|
| 1890: December | The Boy Lives on Our Farm |
| | The Runaway |
| | Our Hired Girl |
| 1891: January | Uncle William's Picture |
| February | Back from Town |
| 1892: November | The Poems Here at Home |
| December | Home Again |
| | The Spoiled Child |
| | The Doodle-Bugs's Charm |
| | Little Cousin Jasper |
| | The Bee-Bag |
| | The Truly Marvelous |
| 1894: August | "Home Ag'in" |
| 1895: August | The Green Grass av Owld Ireland |
| November | His Dancin' Days |
| 1896: December | "Them Old Cheery Words" |
| 1897: November | Rubáiyát of Doc Sifers |
| December | Rubáiyát of Doc Sifers—*Concluded* |
| 1900: February | The Penalty of Genius |
| | In Fervent Praise of Picnics |
| | A Pet of Uncle Sidney's |
| | Old Man Whiskery-Whee-Kum-Wheeze |
| | The Little Girl That Was Two Little Girls |
| | The Parent Reprimanded |
| October | The Bed |
| 1902: January | A Diverted Tragedy |
| | Thomas the Pretender |
| | Fool-Youngens |
| | Billy and His Drum |
| | In the Kindergarten of Noble Song |
| | A Gustatory Memory |
| 1904: June | Hoosier Spring-Poetry |
| 1907: October | "Mother" |
| 1913: July | My Conscience |

CHICAGO CURRENT (see CURRENT)

CHICAGO EVENING POST
1901: November 30    America, September 14, 1901. O Thou,
America—Messiah of Nations!

CHICAGO ILLUSTRATED GRAPHIC NEWS (see ILLUSTRATED GRAPHIC NEWS)

CHICAGO MORNING NEWS
1886: March    30    The Artemus of Michigan

CHICAGO TIMES
1891: October    9    The Common Patriot

CHICAGO TRIBUNE
    1889: March        3    [*Untitled poem beginning*: Afterwhile I promised
                                to]*
                            [*Untitled poem beginning*: This poor volume,
                                friends insist]*
    1897: June        10    [*Untitled poem beginning*: Hail to your fifty years
                                of toil and stress]*
          December 19       Christmas Times Along the Wires

CINCINNATI COMMERCIAL
    1877: November 5        [Letter to John M. Anderson, October 25, 1877]
          December  3       My Rose (*signed* J. N. Riley)

CINCINNATI ENQUIRER
    1901: March       15    Harrison's Home Tribute

CLEVELAND DAILY WORLD
    1902: January     12    James Whitcomb Riley to Joseph Roland Piatt*

COLLIER'S
    1903: February    28    A Simple Recipe
          September   26    The Old Man of the Sea
          December     5    The Old Days
    1904: February    27    Hanna: February 15, 1904*
          April        2    The Children of the Childless
          December     3    A Defective Santa Claus
    1905: March        4    General Lew Wallace
          April       15    Sis Rapalye
          October     28    Henry Irving
    1906: February    10    Lincoln—the Boy
    1907: March        2    Longfellow / 1807—February 27—1907
    1914: December    12    What "Old Santa" Overheard
    1915: April        3    When Baby Slept
                            When Baby Woke
          November    27    When Baby Played
          December    25    Something
    1916: April       22    Youth and Age
          August      19    Blind*
          September    2    Bats*
    1917: January     27    The Raggedy Man Observing*

COSMOPOLITAN
    1887: December           The Serenade
    1894: May                Up and Down Old Brandywine
    1904: December           What Little Saul Got, Christmas

CRITIC
    1888: November 24        To Robert Burns Wilson

---

*Uncollected.

CRITIC—*continued*

1893: January    7    Old Chums
1897: April    3    [Your Height Is Ours]

CURRENT (Chicago)

1884: April    19    Scotty
1886: April    24    A Waste of Genius at Zekesbury
1887: April    9    When My Dreams Come True

DANBURY (Conn.) NEWS

1874: February    25    At Last (*signed* Jay Whit)
      April    8    That Little Dorg (*signed* Jay Whit)
      May    23    My Jolly Friend's Secret (*signed* Jay Whit)
      July    11    A Summer Afternoon (*signed* Jay Whit)
         18    An Oriental Idyl (*signed* Jay Whit)
      August    8    A Poet's Wooing (*signed* Jay Whit)
         15    Private Theatricals (*signed* Jay Whit)

DAWN (Indianapolis High School, No. 1)

1893: May    6    To—"The J. W. R. Literary Club"
      October    26    After the Dark the Dawn

DAYTON (Ohio) DAILY HERALD

1903: December 19    [Letter to J. O. Hardesty, September 3, 1879]*
                       [Letter to Mrs. George McKeown, November 9, 1869]*

DEMOCRAT AND CHRONICLE (Rochester, N. Y.)

1894: May    4    [Letter to Rochester, N. Y., Art Club, May 1, 1894]*

DETROIT FREE PRESS

1901: December 21    The Quest of the Fathers

EARLHAMITE (Richmond, Indiana)

1877: February    Fame
      March    Dearth
      November    A Sonnet*

FORT SCOTT (Kansas) DAILY TRIBUNE

1893: April    25    The Rhymes of Ironquill

FORUM

1892: December    Dialect in Literature

FORTVILLE (Indiana) TRIBUNE

1895: December [19]    Where It Natchurly Belongs*

GALESBURG (Illinois) REPUBLICAN-REGISTER

1903: November 12    [Letter to F. E. Berquist, November 11, 1903]*

GREENFIELD (Indiana) COMMERCIAL

1870: September (?)    The Same Old Story Told Again (*signed* Edyrn)

---

*Uncollected.

GREENFIELD (Indiana) HIGH SCHOOL BUDGET (see HIGH SCHOOL BUDGET)
GREENFIELD (Indiana) NEWS*
    1874: February    28(?) Farmer Whipple—Bachelor
    1875 (?)                The Ancient Printerman (*signed* Jay Whit)
                            Leloine (*signed* Jay Whit)
HANCOCK DEMOCRAT (Greenfield, Indiana)
    1876: September  7  Dunbar (*signed* J. W. R.)
          December   7  Minnie
          February  10  "Johnson's Boy" (*signed* Jay Whit)
          November  23  [Over the Eyes of Gladness] (*signed* J. W. R.)
    1878: August     1  Memorial: Nellie M. Cooley (*signed* J. W. R.)†
    1879: March      13  Loss of the Bright-est Jewel (*signed* J. W. R.)§
          June       26  An Open Letter to the Public, and to Others
                            Whom It May Concern§
    1882: August     10  [Letter to William Mitchell, August 7, 1882]§
    1884: December   25  [A Golden Wedding]
    1895: December   24(?) To Almon Keefer
HARPER'S MAGAZINE
    1889: February        Waitin' fer the Cat to Die
    1917: December        [Letters to Dorian Medairy: September 25,
                            1901; September 19, 1903; September 9,
                            1905; December 14, 1905, October 16, 1906;
                            November 26, 1907; also 7 undated and un-
                            collected letters to same]
                          [Letter to Thomas Whitcomb Hays]§
                          [Letter to John Kern, Jr.]§
                          [Letter to Mrs. Medairy]§
                          [Letters to Edith M. Thomas]§
                          [Untitled poem beginning: Dory-Ann—O
                            friend of mine]§
                          The Canoe Club§
                          City Library§
                          Court House§
                          The German House§
                          State House§
                          University Park§
    1918: February        [Letters to John Riley: one undated, others of:
                            (July) 14, 1871; August 28, 1872; November,
                            1872; October 25, 1873]§
                          [Letters to John J. Skinner: September 14,
                            1875; October 7, 1875]

*See discussion under listing of *Early Recollections of James Whitcomb Riley*
(1902), p. 179 of this bibliography.
†Partially uncollected.
§Uncollected.

HARPER'S MAGAZINE—*continued*

1918: May            [Letter to Arthur Hooper Dodd, April 24, 1884]*
                     [Letter to Henry Eitel, November 30, 1887]*
                     [Letters to Dr. James Newton Matthews: November 23, 1887; October 12, 1888]*
                     [Letter to John Riley, February 17, 1890]*
                     [Letter to Alonzo Hilton Davis, April 16, 1885]
                     [Letter to Robert Browning, March 17, 1885]
                     [Letter to George C. Hitt, March 6, 1886]
                     [Letter to Mrs. Rosaline E. Jones, November 9, 1887; another, uncollected, of November 15, 1883]
                     [Letter to Howard Taylor, November 2, 1883]
                     [Letters to Edgar Wilson Nye: November 11, 1887; November 21, 1887; October 23, 1888; August 5, 1889]
1919: March          [Letter to Edgar Wilson Nye, *ca.* April 14, 1886; another, uncollected, of February 7, 1888]

HEARTH AND HOME
1875: April       10   A Destiny

HIGH SCHOOL BUDGET (Greenfield, Indiana)
1899: June           [Letter to Helen Downing, December 12, 1898]*
                     The Old Times Were the Best

HOME MAGAZINE
1888: November       Rest

ILLUSTRATED GRAPHIC NEWS (Chicago)
1886: August       7   Chairley Burke's in Town
      October      9   In Bohemia

INDEPENDENT (New York)
1888: December    6   His Mother
1891: November   26   The Watches of the Night (complete; see *Indianapolis Journal*, April 5, 1891)

INDIANAPOLIS JOURNAL
1877: January     10   Song of the New Year
      February      7   An Empty Nest
                   16   A Remarkable Man
                   24   A Whisper
      March        12   An Old Sweetheart of Mine
                   16   In the Dark
      April        19   Orlie Wilde
                   21   [Letter from Riley in answer to a criticism of "Orlie Wilde"]*

---

*Uncollected.

INDIANAPOLIS JOURNAL—*continued*

| | | | |
|---|---|---|---|
| 1877: | April | 27 | My Little Woman |
| | May | 22 | Dead Selves |
| | June | 1 | A Dream of Long Ago |
| | August | 5 | Say Something to Me |
| | | 14 | August |
| | | 30 | [Letter to the public, August 28, 1877] |
| | September | 22 | A Country Pathway |
| | November | 2 | Morton |
| | | 24 | The Rainy Morning |
| | December | 14 | We Are Not Always Glad When We Smile |
| | | 21 | A Summer Sunrise |
| | | 25 | A Dream of Christmas |
| 1878: | January | 1 | A New Year's Plaint |
| | February | 16 | "Dream" |
| | March | 16 | Ylladmar |
| | April | 23 | An Adjustable Lunatic |
| | June | 14 | Bryant |
| | July | 13 | The Iron Horse |
| | August | 29 | The Vision of Rabbi Ben Isaac |
| | October | 6 | The Lost Path |
| | | 13 | My Bride That Is to Be |
| | | 20 | Lullaby |
| | | 27 | The Romaunt of King Valdemere |
| | | | An Old Settler's Story |
| | November | 3 | An Old Settler's Story—*Concluded* |
| | | 10 | The Song I Never Sing |
| | | 24 | Unspoken |
| | December | 1 | Thanksgiving Day at Hunchley's |
| | | 8 | Apart |
| | | 15 | Toil |
| | | 29 | The Boss Girl |
| 1879: | January | 12 | My Room |
| | February | 4 | Of the Whole World, Mine |
| | | | Song |
| | April | 19 | The Shower |
| | May | 13 | Tale of a Spider |
| | November | 1 | Death |
| | | 8 | To Gambrinus |
| | | 24 | Lines to an Onsettled Young Man (*anon.*) |
| | | | Stanzas for New Song (*anon.*) |
| | | 27 | Hoagerty's Thanksgiving* |
| | | 29 | Lawyer and Child (*anon.*) |
| | | | Plantation Hymn (*anon.*) |

*Uncollected.

INDIANAPOLIS JOURNAL—*continued*

| | | |
|---|---|---|
| 1879: December | 2 | The Lost Kiss |
| | 3 | Trillpipe's Boy (*anon.*) |
| | 5 | The Father, and His Girl, and Her Young Man (*anon.*)* |
| | | Lines to My Barber (*anon.*)* |
| | 9 | Grant—At Indianapolis, December 9, 1879 (*anon.*)* |
| | 15 | Michael Flynn and the Baby (*anon.*) |
| 1880: January | 4 | Guinevere |
| | 6 | My Ghoul |
| | 8 | Opium |
| | 9 | An Idiot (*anon.*) |
| | 11 | The Gruesome Ballad of Mr. Squincher (*anon.*) |
| | 18 | An Order for a Song |
| | 21 | The Conqueror |
| | 23 | After Death: A Fancy (*anon.*) |
| | 25 | The Mad Lover |
| | 27 | To Robert Burns |
| February | 1 | [The Lover's Peril] (*Parody of James T. Fields' poem of this title; anon.*)* |
| March | 7 | Songs Tuneless |
| | 10 | Sister Jones's Confession |
| | 19 | The Dead Joke and the Funny Man |
| | 21 | Sleep |
| | 24 | One Angel |
| April | 3 | Laughter |
| | 4 | An Invocation |
| | 5 | From Below |
| | 11 | Glamour |
| | 18 | Just a Fiddler |
| | 30 | A Rough Sketch |
| May | 2 | My Laddie Wi' the Bashfu' Grace |
| | 9 | The Circus Parade (*anon.*) |
| | | A Tress of Hair |
| | 14 | In a Box |
| | 16 | An Old-Timer |
| | 18 | Yrsule |
| | 20 | O Her Beauty |
| | 23 | Ez (*anon.*) |
| | | Song of Parting |
| | 24 | The Same Old Friends* |
| | 28 | The Wandering Jew |
| | 30 | To Old Age—Greeting* |

*Uncollected.

INDIANAPOLIS JOURNAL—*continued*

| | | |
|---|---|---|
| 1880: June | 3 | The Used-to-Be |
| | 4 | Slumber-Song |
| | 7 | A Parting Pang* |
| | 13 | June |
| | 17 | Kissing the Rod |
| | 20 | Song |
| | 23 | The Old Hand-Organ |
| | 26 | Home at Night |
| | 27 | A Dream of Inspiration |
| | 30 | The Breeze of the Lake* |
| July | 1 | The Piper's Son |
| | 4 | A Variation |
| | 5 | There Is a Need |
| | 7 | To a Skull |
| | 9 | Voices |
| | 11 | Love's as Broad as Long |
| | 12 | Lockerbie Street |
| | 14 | The Old Wish |
| | 18 | Sleep, Little Brother! |
| | 20 | Little Dollie and Her Friends (*anon.*)* |
| | 25 | A Life-Lesson |
| | 30 | A Bit of Nature |
| | 31 | Unknown Friends |
| August | 1 | A Black Hills Episode |
| | | Yesterday |
| | 6 | An End |
| | 9 | Her Choice |
| | 13 | Our Own |
| | 16 | A Case in Pint |
| | 19 | Ole Bull |
| | 22 | A Wraith of Summer-time |
| | 27 | A Bad Boy's Version of "Jack the Giant-Killer" |
| | 28 | Requiescat |
| | 29 | At Sea |
| September | 5 | The Champion Checker-Player of Ameriky |
| | 10 | A Discouraging Model |
| | 12 | Blind |
| | 19 | Just as of Old |
| | 20 | Amen |
| | 26 | A Phantom |
| | 29 | Redress |
| October | 17 | Let Us Forget |
| | 18 | The Shoemaker |

*Uncollected.

INDIANAPOLIS JOURNAL—*continued*

| | | | |
|---|---|---|---|
| 1880: | October | 22 | The Sphinx |
| | | 29 | In the Corridor |
| | | 31 | Suspense |
| | November | 1 | Louella Wainie |
| | | 7 | For You |
| | | 8 | My First Spectacles |
| | | 14 | A Woman's Hate* |
| | | 15 | The Text |
| | | 21 | Tired |
| | | 25 | Thanksgiving |
| | | 28 | William Brown |
| | | 29 | A Mood |
| | December | 5 | The Touch of Loving Hands |
| | | | Why |
| | | | Nightmare |
| | | 6 | Tears |
| | | 9 | Tom* |
| | | 12 | A Cup of Tea |
| | | 13 | The Serenade |
| | | 18 | What a Dead Man Said |
| | | 19 | A Test |
| | | 25 | A Song for Christmas |
| 1881: | January | 1 | The Old Year and the New |
| | | 3 | Good-By, Old Year |
| | | | Open House (*signed* R)* |
| | | 14 | The Human Heart |
| | | 20 | Someday |
| | | 22 | False and True |
| | | 23 | When de Folks Is Gone (*signed* John C. Walker) |
| | | | A Ballad from April |
| | | 26 | The Twins |
| | | 30 | The Orchard Lands of Long Ago |
| | February | 4 | Deformed |
| | | 6 | While the Musician Played |
| | | 15 | Faith |
| | | 16 | The New Friend |
| | | 23 | A Hint of Spring |
| | | 27 | Last Night—and This |
| | March | 2 | Little Girly-Girl |
| | | 6 | Close the Book |
| | | 20 | Reach Your Hand to Me |
| | | | The Lost Thrill |

*Uncollected.

INDIANAPOLIS JOURNAL—*continued*

| | | | |
|---|---|---|---|
| 1881: March | 27 | Der Heimgang | |
| April | 8 | Mabel | |
| | 10 | At Dusk | |
| | 16 | Another Ride from Ghent to Aix | |
| | 17 | The Ripest Peach | |
| | 24 | Bedouin | |
| | 30 | Summertime | |
| May | 7 | Laughter* | |
| | 14 | The Circus Season (*signed* R) | |
| | 21 | Cream for Two* | |
| | 28 | Sun and Rain | |
| June | 25 | In the Heart of June | |
| | 30 | Science and Poetry | |
| July | 2 | My Boy | |
| | 9 | Because | |
| | 12 | Pansies | |
| | 16 | Baby's Dying | |
| | 19 | An Empty Glove | |
| | 21 | Sonnet—to the Cricket | |
| | 26 | The Old-Fashioned Bible | |
| | | The Dead Wife | |
| August | 3 | An Easy Shave* | |
| | 8 | Enough | |
| | 13 | A Lounger | |
| | 20 | Mr. What's-His-Name | |
| | | The Old Fiddler (*anon.*) | |
| | 22 | The Cross-Eyed Girl | |
| | 23 | Uncomforted | |
| | 27 | Homesickness | |
| September | 1 | A Hod Story (*anon.*)* | |
| | 3 | Mr. Trillpipe's Poem (*anon.*)* | |
| | 10 | [*Untitled poem beginning*: In the heyday of life and the fullness of health]* | |
| | | Mr. Trillpipe at Home (*anon.*) | |
| | | [He and I] | |
| | | [My White Bread] | |
| | 12 | From a Balloon | |
| | 15 | Trillpipe on Puns (*anon.*) | |
| | 17 | A Rondel | |
| October | 22 | After the Frost | |
| | | From a Car Window* | |
| | | What They Said | |
| November | 5 | The Legend of Heisterbach* | |

*Uncollected.

INDIANAPOLIS JOURNAL—*continued*

| | | |
|---|---|---|
| 1881: November | 7 | C. H. P. (*signed* J. W. R.) |
| | 12 | The False Friend* |
| | 19 | When It Rains |
| | 23 | The Assassin |
| December | 3 | Best of All |
| | 17 | The Jew Father |
| | 24 | Our Fortunes |
| 1882: January | 21 | Burdette at Home* |
| | | John Boyle O'Reilly* |
| | | Eros |
| | 28 | The Quiet Lodger |
| February | 4 | The Brook |
| | 25 | His Crazy-Bone |
| April | 22 | Bin a-Fishin' |
| | | Uncle Dan'l in Town over Sunday |
| | 29 | An Hour with Longfellow* |
| | | Emerson |
| May | 6 | The Eccentric Mr. Clark |
| | 20 | Your Violin |
| | 24 | [Soldiers Here To-day] |
| June | 3 | A Nest-Egg |
| | | A Windy Day |
| | 10 | The Boy from Xenia |
| | | Shadow and Shine |
| | 17 | The Old Swimmin'-Hole (*signed* Benj. F. Johnson) |
| | 24 | Thoughts fer the Discuraged Farmer (*signed* Benj. F. Johnson) |
| | | Some Other Evening |
| July | 1 | A Summer's Day (*signed* Benj. F. Johnson) |
| | 8 | A Hymb of Faith (*signed* Benj. F. Johnson) |
| | 20 | At Broad Ripple |
| | 21 | The Editor |
| | 22 | A Song of the Cruise |
| | | Worter-melon Time (*signed* Benj. F. Johnson of Boone) |
| | 29 | When Age Comes On |
| | | Mr. Johnson of Boone Philosophizes (*signed* Benj. F. Johnson) |
| August | 5 | When the Frost Is on the Punkin (*signed* Benj. F. Johnson) |
| | | That Night |
| | 12 | The Bat |

*Uncollected.

*Uncollected.

INDIANAPOLIS JOURNAL—*continued*

| | | | |
|---|---|---|---|
| 1883: | June | 2 | Jack-in-the-Box |
| | | 16 | To a Benedict Friend |
| | | | My Mary |
| | | | Two Sonnets to the June-Bug |
| | | 23 | A Transient Dental Monody |
| | | | The Assassin |
| | | | One Afternoon |
| | | 27 | A Famous Victory* |
| | | 30 | The Beautiful City |
| | | | A Life Term |
| | | | The Boy Behind the Soda-Fount (*anon*)* |
| | July | 5 | McFeeters' Fourth |
| | | 7 | At Ninety in the Shade |
| | | 14 | A Sudden Shower |
| | | 16 | Good-by er Howdy-do |
| | | 21 | With the Current |
| | | 28 | Wet-Weather Talk |
| | August | 4 | A Poor Man's Wealth |
| | | 18 | A Mere Outline |
| | September | 8 | The Best Is Good Enough for Me |
| | | 15 | A Dream of Autumn |
| | | 22 | He Called Her In |
| | October | 13 | Give Me the Baby |
| | | 22 | An Autumnal Tonic |
| | December | 15 | "Home, Sweet Home"* |
| | | 22 | Out of the Hitherwhere |
| 1884: | January | 12 | A Tinkle of Bells |
| | February | 20 | The Old Man |
| | March | 5 | Our Kind of a Man |
| | | 8 | The Little Coat |
| | | 29 | Me and Mary |
| | | | An Impromptu on Roller Skates |
| | April | 5 | "Cordaroy" Poetry | Never Talk Back |
| | | | Written in Bunner's "Airs from Arcady" |
| | | | Song |
| | | 12 | Nonsense Jingles |
| | | | The Little Fat Doctor |
| | | | My Friend |
| | | 19 | On the Sunny Side |
| | | 26 | The Harper |
| | May | 10 | The Blossoms on the Trees |
| | | | Laughter Holding Both His Sides |
| | | 17 | In State |

*Uncollected.

INDIANAPOLIS JOURNAL—*continued*

| 1885: April | 5 | [Untitled poem beginning: Plain Bill Wilson was his name]* |
| | 12 | To an Importunate Ghost |
| | | Lord Bacon (*signed* Amos J. Walker) |
| | | His First Womern |
| | | The Quest |
| | | Who Bides His Time |
| | 19 | At Noon—and Midnight |
| | | In "Smithses Settlement"* |
| | | When June Is Here |
| | | At Rev. McIntyre's* |
| | 26 | Song |
| | | Art and Love |
| | | Spirits at Home |
| May | 3 | The Willow |
| | | Pap's Old Sayin' |
| | 10 | Becalmed |
| | | Granny |
| | 17 | Back Where They Used to Be |
| | 31 | Fessler's Bees |
| June | 7 | Had a Hare-Lip |
| | 14 | Long About Knee Deep in June |
| | 21 | Song |
| | 28 | The Law of the Perverse |
| July | 12 | Out of Nazareth |
| | | The Smell of Bruised Grass |
| | 26 | Ike Walton's Prayer |
| | | The Dead Leader |
| August | 2 | "Curly Locks" |
| | | The Way It Wuz |
| | 9 | Grant |
| | 16 | On the Banks o' Deer Crick |
| September | 13 | The Way that Billy Could Ride |
| | 27 | Dave Field |
| October | 11 | M. C. R. |
| | 18 | Josh Billings |
| | 25 | The Land of Thus-and-So |
| November | 1 | The Hoss (*signed* Benj. F. Johnson of Boone) |
| | 8 | Lines on a' Old Played-Out Song (*signed* Benj. F. Johnson of Boone) |
| | 15 | The Elf Child |
| | 22 | A Dose't of Blues (*signed* Benj. F. Johnson) |
| December | 20 | The Train-Misser |

*Uncollected.

INDIANAPOLIS JOURNAL—*continued*

| | | | |
|---|---|---|---|
| 1886: | January | 17 | The Plaint Human |
| | | 31 | Which Ane |
| | February | 14 | In the City Streets* |
| | | 21 | The Amiable Old Sister |
| | | 28 | Regardin' Terry Hut |
| | March | 7 | A Tale of the Airly Days (*signed* Benj. F. Johnson) |
| | | 28 | The Rossville Lectur' Course |
| | April | 4 | Her Beautiful Eyes |
| | | | To a Jilted Swain |
| | | | A Prayer for Content with Simple Store |
| | | | Want to Be Whur Mother Is |
| | | | To a Babe Sleeping |
| | | 11 | In the South |
| | May | 23 | Has She Forgotten |
| | July | 18 | Wait for the Morning |
| | | 25 | Illileo |
| | August | 22 | He Cometh in Sweet Sense |
| | September | 5 | The Earthquake: Charleston |
| | | | When the World Bu'sts Through |
| | | | A Fall-Crick View of the Earthquake |
| | | 12 | The Old Retired Sea-Captain |
| | | 26 | Jim |
| | October | 24 | Sompin' Strange About October |
| | | 31 | Judith |
| | November | 14 | The Legend Glorified |
| | December | 12 | Written in John Boyle O'Reilly's "In Bohemia" |
| | | 19 | Old Man's Nursery Rhyme |
| | | 30 | Lewis D. Hayes |
| 1887: | January | 30 | A Local Politician from Away Back |
| | February | 6 | The Mute Singer |
| | March | 6 | Philip Moore—of Denison House* |
| | | 13 | The Cyclone |
| | | 20 | In Days to Come |
| | | 27 | The Stepmother |
| | April | 24 | The Chant of the Cross-Bearing Child |
| | May | 14 | The Dicktown "Wonder"* |
| | | 15 | Three Dead Friends |
| | August | 7 | When Old Jack Died |
| | | | Luther A. Todd |
| | | 14 | When the Hearse Comes Back |
| | | 21 | A Character |
| | | 28 | Back from a Two-Years' Sentence |

*Uncollected.

INDIANAPOLIS JOURNAL—*continued*

| | | | |
|---|---|---|---|
| 1888: | January | 17 | "Ole Longfellow"* |
| | | 22 | Our Old Friend Neverfail |
| | | | Dan O'Sullivan |
| | February | 26 | Dead, My Lords |
| | October | 19 | [Speech at Western Association of Writers Dinner, October 18, 1888]* |
| 1889: | August | 4 | Jap Miller |
| 1890: | January | 12 | [When Evening Shadows Fall] |
| | March | 2 | A Rose by Any Other Name |
| | May | 11 | A Southern Singer |
| | June | 8 | June at Woodruff |
| | July | 20 | Uncle Sidney's Views |
| | August | 10 | Maxinkuckee |
| | | 17 | John Boyle O'Reilly |
| | | 31 | Wilhelmina |
| | | | A Romper's Logic* |
| | | | The Boy's Friend |
| | | | Reconcilement* |
| | September | 7 | Meredith Nicholson |
| | | 14 | My Ruthers |
| | | 21 | [Monsieur le Secretaire] |
| | November | 6 | [Speech introducing Richard Malcolm Johnston]* |
| | December | 7 | Pa's Soliloquy (*advt.*; *anon.*)* |
| | | | Bubb's Back-Cap (*advt.*; *anon.*)* |
| | | 11 | The Sk-sk-skeme (*advt.*; *anon.*)* |
| | | 12 | The Very Tall Boy (*advt.*; *anon.*) |
| | | 13 | Song of the Bullet |
| | | | Young Pulitzer Floy and "Say" (*advt.*; *anon.*)* |
| | | 14 | The Babes in the When (*advt.*; *anon.*) |
| | | 15 | Then You'll Remember—Us (*advt.*; *anon.*)* |
| | | 16 | The Three Jolly Hunters (*advt.*; *anon.*) |
| | | 17 | The Wind and the When (*advt.*; *anon.*)* |
| | | 18 | The Two Dudes (*advt.*; *anon.*)* |
| | | | The Wise Man (*advt.*; *anon.*)* |
| | | 19 | Through Sleepy-Land (*advt.*; *anon.*) |
| | | 20 | Stanley (*advt.*; *anon.*) |
| | | 21 | A Classic Bard's Protest (*advt.*; *anon.*)* |
| | | 22 | [Untitled poem beginning: Sing a song o' slickpence] (*advt.*; *anon.*)* |
| | | 23 | Folks at Lonesomeville (*advt.*; *anon.*) |
| | | 25 | "Old Santa" Wags His Beard Once More (*advt.*; *anon.*)* |

*Uncollected.

INDIANAPOLIS JOURNAL—*continued*

| | | |
|---|---|---|
| 1890: December | 27 | This Will Knock a Corn Silly (*advt.*; *anon.*) |
| | | To Take off Freckles—Scotch Ones (*advt.*; *anon.*) |
| | 28 | A Sea-Song from the Shore (*advt.*; *anon.*) |
| | 29 | The King of Oo-Rinktum-Jing (*advt.*; *anon.*) |
| | 31 | Make It?—Why, Cert. (*advt.*; *anon.*)* |
| | | The Old Hoss in New Gears (*advt.*; *anon.*)* |
| 1891: January | 1 | Larry Noolan's New Year (*advt.*; *anon.*) |
| | 4 | Some Custom-Made Riddles (*advt.*; *anon.*) |
| | 11 | The Happy Couple—A Duet (*advt.*; *anon.*)* |
| | 25 | The When's Machine (*advt.*; *anon.*)* |
| February | 1 | The Melancholy Source of Tears (*advt.*; *anon.*)* |
| | 8 | The Spider with the Kind Heart (*advt.*; *anon.*)* |
| | 22 | Choice Verses for Autograph Albums (*advt.*; *anon.*; all but two of these verses are uncollected*) |
| March | 1 | [Untitled poem beginning: One! Two!] (*advt.*; *anon.*)* |
| | 15 | The Diplomatic Spirit and Delicate Finesse of the True Social Host (*advt.*; *anon.*)* |
| | 20 | Easter (*advt.*; *anon.*)* |
| | 22 | The Little Toy Penny-Dog (*advt.*; *anon.*) |
| | | The Trestle and the Buck-Saw (*advt.*; *anon.*) |
| April | 5 | The Doggy That Walked Round the World (*advt.*; *anon.*) |
| | | The Watches of the Night (one stanza only) (see *Independent* [*N. Y.*], 1891, November 26) |
| | 8 | [Speech introducing Nye and Burbank]* |
| | 10 | The Sooburbs (*signed* Benj. F. Johnson) |
| | 12 | He Knew a Good Thing When He Had It (*advt.*; *anon.*)* |
| | 19 | The Two Dreams (*advt.*; *anon.*) |
| | | The First Boone County Bluebird (*signed* Benj. F. Johnson) |
| May | 1 | Elizabeth Meredith Steele |
| | 3 | A Few of the Bird Family (*advt.*; *anon.*) |
| | 10 | The Twa Puir Chicks (*advt.*; *anon.*)* |
| September | 10 | Benj. F. Johnson on Skates |
| | 12 | Cuored o' Skeerin' |
| | 13 | Old Winters on the Farm |
| October | 11 | Owl Song (*advt.*; *anon.*)* |
| | 18 | Summer-Time and Winter-Time (*advt.*; *anon.*) |
| | 25 | Always Unexpectedly (*advt.*; *anon.*)* |
| | | How Doth He Do It? (*advt.*; *anon.*)* |

*Uncollected.

INDIANAPOLIS JOURNAL—*continued*

| | | |
|---|---|---|
| 1891: November | 1 | What Our Bright College Boys Are Doing, 1st Series (*advt.*; *anon.*)* |
| | 8 | What Our Bright College Boys Are Doing, 2d Series (*advt.*; *anon.*)* |
| | 22 | What Our Bright College Boys Are Doing, 3d Series (*advt.*; *anon.*)* |
| | 29 | What Our Bright College Boys Are Doing, 4th Series (*advt.*; *anon.*)* |
| December | 6 | The Yellow Bird (*advt.*; *anon.*) |
| | 12 | Oscar C. McCulloch |
| | 13 | A Child's Choice (*advt.*; *anon.*) |
| | 27 | Rabbit in the Cross-Ties (*advt.*; *anon.*) |
| | | Billy and "Old Muley" (*advt.*; *anon.*)* |
| 1892: January | 3 | What Our Bright College Boys Are Doing, 5th Series (*advt.*; *anon.*)* |
| February | 7 | The Chimpanzee's Apology (*advt.*; *anon.*)* |
| | | Right Here at Home |
| | 14 | Casabianca and His Pa (*advt.*; *anon.*)* |
| | 21 | A Noon Lull (*advt.*; *anon.*) |
| 1892: March | 13 | Little Marjorie |
| April | 16 | Kathleen Mavourneen |
| | 17 | Old John Henry |
| August | 7 | The Curse of the Wandering Foot |
| | 28 | As My Uncle Ust to Say |
| 1893: September | 5 | Armazindy: A Borned Soldier and Hero |
| November | 19 | To a Western Singer—James Newton Matthews |
| December | 3 | Master and First Song-Friend—Lee O. Harris |
| | 10 | The Clearer Hail—Benjamin S. Parker |
| 1895: May | 1 | The Silent Singer |
| September | 13 | A Peace-Hymn of the Republic |
| 1896: February | 23 | Edgar Wilson Nye: Obit. February 22, 1896; also: [Prose tribute to Edgar Wilson Nye] |
| 1897: April | 18 | Hymn Exultant |
| | 22 | [Speech at Commercial Club Dinner, Indianapolis, April 21, 1897]* |
| 1898: June | 25 | Frank L. Stanton |
| August | 30 | Claude Matthews |
| 1899: January | 31 | The Onward Trail |
| February | 19 | To Lesley (*anon.*) |
| December | 31 | Dr. Wickliffe Smith |
| 1900: February | 6 | The Home-Voyage |
| June | 28 | When They Go From Us (Mrs. William R. Hough: Obit.)* |

*Uncollected.

INDIANAPOLIS JOURNAL—*continued*

| | | | |
|---|---|---|---|
| 1900: October | 28 | Home-Folks |
| 1901: January | 17 | William Pinckney Fishback |
| | 18 | A Good Man: James A. Mount |
| | 25 | His Heart of Constant Youth: Major Charles L. Holstein |
| March | 14 | [Prose tribute to Benjamin Harrison]* |
| December | 18 | The Hoosier in Exile |
| | 29 | To the Mother |

INDIANAPOLIS NEWS

| | | | |
|---|---|---|---|
| 1879: August | 7 | Where Shall We Land |
| 1890: July | 5 | Iry and Billy and Jo |
| 1892: September | 7 | Whittier—At Newburyport |
| October | 1 | Rosamond C. Bailey |
| | 6 | Tennyson |
| | 25 | Mrs. Harrison |
| 1901: February | 15 | Maurice Thompson |
| 1902: May | 15 | The Soldier |
| 1904: January | 27 | Art and Poetry: Some of Wess's Views (*signed* J. W. R.) |
| August | 11 | [Prose reply to poem "Riley's Flat"; latter by unknown author]* |
| 1905: April | 3 | [Her Smile of Cheer and Voice of Song] |
| December | 22 | [Letter to Indiana Society of Chicago, December 14, 1905] |
| 1906: May | 12 | To Kin Hubbard—The Father of His Countryman, Abe Martin (*signed* J. W. R.) |
| November | 21 | [Speech at dedication of Herron Art Institute, Indianapolis]* |
| 1907: March | 23 | [Speech at Maennerchor Opening Banquet, March 22, 1907]* |
| September | 30 | William McKinley |
| 1908: October | 10 | Lines Penned on an Apollo |
| | 27 | The Tribute of His Home |
| 1911: April | 28 | [Letter to school children of Connersville, Indiana]* |
| 1914: November | 6 | [Letter to school children of Port Fulton]* |
| 1915: September | 28 | [Letter to Governor Samuel M. Ralston]* |
| October | 7 | [Letter to school children of Chicago]* |
| | 8 | [Letter to Mrs. Ona B. Talbot, October 7, 1915]* |
| | | [Speech at Riley Day Banquet, October 7, 1915]* |
| | | [Letter to DePauw University students]* |

*Uncollected.

INDIANAPOLIS NEWS—*continued*

1915: October   20   [Letter to school children of Longfellow School, Greenfield, October 19, 1915]*

1916: July     24   [Untitled poem beginning: O, what a joy to meet] (*signed* J. W. R.)*

             25   A Happy Dream
[Letter to Dr. S. Weir Mitchell, February 5, 1898]*

1935: July     6   [Letter to William Herschell]*

1943: July    17   [Letter to National Institute of Arts and Letters, January, 1912]*

INDIANAPOLIS PEOPLE (see PEOPLE)

INDIANAPOLIS PRESS

1894: December  9   A Motto

1901: January   21   [John Clark Ridpath]

INDIANAPOLIS SATURDAY EVENING MIRROR (see SATURDAY MIRROR)

INDIANAPOLIS SATURDAY HERALD (see SATURDAY HERALD)

INDIANAPOLIS SATURDAY MIRROR (see SATURDAY MIRROR)

INDIANAPOLIS SATURDAY REVIEW (see SATURDAY REVIEW)

INDIANAPOLIS SENTINEL

1876: January    9   The Old Guitar

             30   "Friday Afternoon"

    February   6   When Mother Combed My Hair (*anon.*)

             20   Her Beautiful Hands

    March     26   Lusus Naturae

1878: August    4   At Oakland, August 3, 1878

1885: February   1   A Leave-Taking

1890: July      2   Hendricks*

1891: November  4   [Untitled poem beginning: He took his pen in hand, and then]*

1898: February  16   [Speech at First Annual Banquet of the Hoosier Club of Greater Kansas City, February 14, 1898]*

1901: December  22   My Most Memorable Christmas*

1902: September  14   James B. Maynard

INDIANAPOLIS STAR

1906: December  29   [Speech introducing Dr. Henry van Dyke]*

1907: April     29   The Doctor

1909: December  27   Lee O. Harris | Christmas Day—1909

1911: March    15   To Benj. S. Parker

    October   6   [Letter to school children of Indianapolis, October 7, 1911]

---

*Uncollected.

INDIANAPOLIS STAR—*continued*

| | | | |
|---|---|---|---|
| 1912: | October | 7 | [Letter to school children, October 7, 1912] |
| | December | 3 | [Letter to Governor Hadley]* |
| 1913: | October | 9 | [Speech at Indiana University, October 8, 1913]* |
| 1914: | May | 28 | [Letter to Joseph E. Bell, May 25, 1914]* |
| | July | 22 | George A. Carr |
| | October | 7 | [Letter to school children of Indianapolis, October 6, 1914] |
| 1916: | February | 23 | [Letter to Atlanta Ad Men's Club]* |
| | April | 11 | [Untitled poem beginning: No matter, then, how all is mixed]* |
| 1923: | March | 25 | [Letter to Mr. and Mrs. Perry Rule, June 8, 1908]* |
| | | | [Letter to James, Whitcomb and Riley Rule]* |
| 1929: | May | 26 | [Letter to Drucilla Cravens, June 9, 1900]* |
| | July | 21 | [Letters to Harry S. New: August 14, 1893; September 9, 1904]* |
| | October | 6 | [Letter and two notes to George C. Smith]* |
| | | | [Untitled poem beginning: My Religen is to jest (*signed* Benj. F. Johnson)]* |
| 1930: | October | 5 | Mr. Locke Makes a Hit* |
| 1931: | October | 4 | [Letter to Cooley Family, October 28, 1877]* |
| | | | [Untitled poem beginning: Three fishers came walking out of the west]* |
| | | | [Letter to Mrs. Emma M. Cox, April 19, 1885]* |
| | | | [Letter to Haute Tarkington, February 15, 1883]* |
| 1934: | October | 7 | [Untitled poem beginning: Though haply you have played no part]* |
| | | | [Untitled poem beginning: A glowworm blinked at a child and said]* |
| 1935: | October | 6 | [Untitled poem beginning: Good-night! I'm glad an' sorry, too]* |
| | | | [Untitled poem beginning: The "Artist" knew enough to know]* |
| 1936: | October | 4 | [Letter to Mrs. Mary Riley Payne, March 25, 1889]* |
| 1937: | October | 3 | [Untitled poem beginning: I have ranged all revels through]* |
| 1938: | March | 27 | [Letter to Rue Carolyn Miller, March 31, 1897]* |
| 1939: | September | 24 | [Letter to Walter E. Evans, January 8, 1894]* |
| 1940: | May | 26 | [Untitled poem beginning: Grandpa's name ain't much comparison]* |

*Uncollected.

INDIANAPOLIS STAR—*continued*

   1940: May       26   [Untitled poem beginning: Her face knew a purer glory]*

   1943: September  8   [Untitled poem beginning: 'Twas a tender little poem]*

INDIANAPOLIS SUN

   1895: October   26   Maurice Perkins*

   1900: August    1   [Prose tribute to John Clark Ridpath]*

INDIANAPOLIS SUNDAY HERALD (see SUNDAY HERALD)

INDIANAPOLIS TIMES

   1935: October    7   [Letter to William Carey, January 21, 1894]

INTERIOR (Chicago)

   1894: December 13   The Christmas Long Ago

   1896: December 10   Little Mandy's Christmas-Tree

   1899: August    10   Billy Miller's Circus-Show

INTERNATIONAL-COSMOPOLITAN (HEARST'S)

   1927: November    [Letter to George Ade and John T. McCutcheon, November 30, 1903]

JOURNALIST (New York)

   1890: January   11   [Untitled poem beginning: First the printer damns the scrawl]*

JUDGE

   1887: Christmas Issue  Long Afore He Knowed Who Santy-Claus Wuz

   1888: Christmas Issue  John and Percilly

KOKOMO (Indiana) DISPATCH

   1877: August    2   Leonainie (*signed* E. A. P.)

        October   4   What the Wind Said

KOKOMO (Indiana) TRIBUNE

   1877: September  1   Leoloony (*anon.*)*

   1878: January   5   Luther Benson

        February  16   [Letter to citizens of Kokomo, February 15, 1878]*

        July      20   T. C. Philips

   1879: February  1   To Leonainie

        March    22   A Solemn Protest (*signed* John C. Walker)* (includes poem: Make Home Attractive)

        April     5   Use and Abuse of the Poetic Theme (*signed* John C. Walker)* (includes poem: The Chamber over the Gate)

                12   The Man Who Talks in Initials (*signed* J. C. Walker)*

---

*Uncollected.

Kokomo (Indiana) Tribune—*continued*

| | | |
|---|---|---|
| 1879: April | 19 | The Irrepressible Man at Bay (*signed* John C. Walker)* |
| May | 3 | A Bully Boy in Blue (*signed* John C. Walker)* |
| | 24 | Dreams (*signed* John C. Walker) |
| | 31 | Tom Johnson's Quit (*signed* John C. Walker) |
| June | 21 | Romancin' (*signed* John C. Walker) |
| July | 12 | A Full Harvest (*signed* John C. Walker) |
| August | 2 | This Man Jones (*signed* John C. Walker) |
| | | The Ballad of Smiles and Tears |
| | 16 | The Beetle |
| September | 6 | Marthy Ellen (*signed* John C. Walker) |
| November | 8 | The Ginoine Ar-Tickle (*signed* John C. Walker) |
| | 15 | Tired |
| December | 27 | John Golliher's Third Womern (*signed* John C. Walker) |
| | | The Singer |
| 1880: May | 1† | My Grandfather Squeers (*anon.*) |
| | 15 | His Grandpa (*anon.*) |
| | | Just with Your Hands |
| | 22 | The Summer-Time (*signed* John C. Walker) |
| | | The Elderly Squeers (*anon.*) |
| | 29 | Squeers the Ancient (*anon.*) |
| June | 12 | The Antique Squeers (*anon.*) |
| | 19 | The Rivals |
| July | 10 | My Henry (*signed* John C. Walker) |
| August | 7 | As "Clog-Step Johnny" Tells It (*signed* John C. Walker)* |
| October | 2 | A Lost Love |
| 1881: March | 19 | Kate Kennedy Philips (*signed* J. W. R.) |

Ladies' Home Journal

| | |
|---|---|
| 1891: January | His Vigil (with preface: In Prose and in Verse) |
| 1895: December | At the Gate |
| 1896: February | Little Maid-o'-Dreams |
| June | Cassander |
| August | While the Heart Beats Young |
| December | A Dubious "Old Kriss" |
| 1903: January | His Pa's Romance |
| March | Almost Beyond Endurance |
| | The Toy-Balloon |
| 1912: May | [Letter to Anna Jarvis, January 29, 1912]* |

---

*Uncollected.

†In addition to the titles here listed, jingles by Riley, called "Kick-Shaws," appeared in 1880 in the following issues: Jan. 31, Feb. 21, Mar. 6, Mar. 13, Mar. 27, Apr. 17, Apr. 24, May 1, May 5, May 8, May 15, May 22, June 5, June 12, June 19, July 3 and July 24.

LIFE
    1883: March    8    Judkins' Boy on Spiders (*anon.*)\*†
                          The Muskingum Valley
                          Serenade—To Nora
              15    Her Light Guitar
              29    Judkins' Boy on the Mud Turtle (*anon.*)
                        Says He Would Smile (*signed* J. W. R.)\*
        April    12    When Maimie Married
              19    Judkins' Boy (*anon.*)
        May    3    While Cigarettes to Ashes Turn
              17    When You Meet Me (*signed* J. W. R.)\*
                        Judkins' Boy (*anon.*)
              31    Judkins' Boy (*anon.*)
        June    7    Judkins' Boy (*anon.*)
              14    The Old Trundle-Bed
        July    12    A Ballade of Wine\*
        August    16    The Stars Won't Wane and the Moon Won't
                        Wax\*
    1884: May    8    All She Could Do\*
    1887: March    17    Kismet\*
    1895: Christmas Number    A Christmas Memory

LIPPINCOTT'S MONTHLY MAGAZINE
    1890: January    In the Evening
    1892: January    The Gudewife
          June    Being His Mother
    1899: July    A Song of the Road

LOCOMOTIVE FIREMEN'S MAGAZINE
    1887: November    Them Flowers

LOUISVILLE COURIER-JOURNAL
    1892: April    22    [Speech at Commercial Club Banquet, Louis-
                       ville, April 21, 1892]\*
    1906: December    9    Ours

LOUISVILLE HERALD
    1912: March    26    [Letter to Charles A. Lehmann, March, 1912]\*

MANHATTAN
    1883: August    Sonnet on the Intolerable Conceit of Critics\*

McCLURE'S MAGAZINE
    1897: August    Our Queer Old World

MODERN ART
    1894: October    1    The Schoolboy's Favorite

---

\*Uncollected.
†Possibly this had earlier appearance in the *Anderson Democrat*.

MOORESVILLE (Indiana) ENTERPRISE
    1873: May          8    [Letter to the editor, April 24, 1873 (*signed* Doc
                            Marigold)]*

MUNCIE (Indiana) MORNING STAR
    1906: December 30    What's the Matter with Newyears?*

NEW CASTLE (Indiana) MERCURY
    1876: June          1    [The Silent Victors] (*portion only*)
                        8    Scraps
            November 16    Three Sonnets to Autumn: Morning, Evening,
                            Night
            December    7    If I Knew What Poets Know
                        (?) The Funny Little Fellow
    1879: February    22    [Letter to citizens of New Castle, February 18,
                            1879]*

NEW YORK MORNING JOURNAL
    1892: May          1    [Untitled poem beginning: When Shakespeare's
                            voice was heard of old]*

NEW YORK SUN (see SUN)

NEW YORK TIMES
    1900: December 22    To Edmund Clarence Stedman
    1934: February    18    A Valentine Supplement*

NEW YORK TRIBUNE
    1889: December 24    Henry W. Grady

NEW YORK WORLD (see WORLD)

NORTH AMERICAN REVIEW
    1916: September        [Letter to Joe Mitchell Chapple, January 15,
                            1916]*

NORTHWESTERN MILLER (Minneapolis)
    1886: Christmas Number    Kingry's Mill
                                The Restored Romaunt of the "Jolly Miller"
    1887: Christmas Number    At the Old Home by the Mill
    1888: Christmas Number    That Air Youngen

OHIO STATE JOURNAL (Columbus)
    1899: April        23    To Oliver Davie—The Naturalist

OMAHA WORLD-HERALD
    1897: November 21    Thanksgiving*

PEOPLE (Indianapolis)
    1874: July        19    Job Work (*signed* Jay Whit)
    1876: January      1    Karl Schronz's Christmas Story (*signed* Jay Whit)

PHILISTINE
    1902: October          [Letter to the Roycrofters, August 1, 1902]*

---

*Uncollected.

PHOENIX
 1915: May     St. Lirriper
   June     [Parody of Young E. Allison's "The Derelict"]*
 1916: September  [Eight letters from Riley to Michael Monahan,
           January 26, 1915—April 4, 1916]*

PITTSBURGH BULLETIN
 1888: May 20 (not later than) How It Happened

PITTSBURGH COMMERCIAL GAZETTE
 1891: January  30 Our Kind of a Man

QUIET OBSERVER
 1900: May    3† To the Quiet Observer
          [Letter to Erasmus Wilson]

READER MAGAZINE
 1904: Christmas Number A Carol
 1905: March    On Reading Dr. Henry van Dyke's Latest
         Volume of Poems—Music
   April    Thinkin' Back
   July     The Voice of Peace
   September  I' Got to Face Mother To-Day!
   October   Imitations of Three Southern Singers (signed
         John Challing)
   November  Songs o' Cheer
   December  A Christmas Glee
 1906: May    Rabbit
 1907: November  The Boys of the Old Glee Club

ROCHESTER (New York) DEMOCRAT AND CHRONICLE (see DEMOCRAT
 AND CHRONICLE)

ST. NICHOLAS
 1880: November  A Nonsense Rhyme
 1888: February  She "Displains" It
 1889: January   Naughty Claude
 1890: October   The Little-Red-Apple Tree
 1895: December  Dream March of the Children
 1897: November  Mister Hop-Toad
 1923: January   [Letter to Jennie Elrod, November 9, 1906]*
 1930: October   [Letter to Edgar Lee Maines, June 8, 1884]*

SAN FRANCISCO EXAMINER
 1893: January  1 [Letter to the editor, December 17, 1892]*

SATURDAY EVENING CALL (Peoria, Illinois)
 ca. 1879: August  Roses

---

*Uncollected.
†The Princeton University Library copy, bearing this date, contains the following statement: "Several copies of this issue bear date of April 26, which was the original date for issue but which was changed to May 3."

SATURDAY HERALD (Indianapolis)

| 1875: | June | 26 | Red Riding-Hood (*signed* Jay Whit) |
|---|---|---|---|
| 1877: | September | 1 | [Parody of] "Leonainie" (*anon.*)* |
| | | 22 | Father William (*signed* Harrison Driley) |
| | November | 3 | An Autumnal Extravaganza |
| | | 17 | The Merman (*anon.*) |
| | December | 15 | My Topic Wiles* |
| 1878: | January | 12 | Ezra House |
| | | 26 | Schoolboy Silhouettes—No. I* |
| | February | 2 | Schoolboy Silhouettes—No. II* |
| | | 9 | Squire Hawkins's Story |
| | May | 11 | "Respectfully Declined" Papers of the Buzz Club [No. I] (*anon.*)† |
| | June | 15 | "Respectfully Declined" Papers of the Buzz Club, No. II (*anon.*)† |
| | July | 6 | "Respectfully Declined" Papers of the Buzz Club, No. III (*anon.*)† |
| | August | 24 | "Respectfully Declined" Papers of the Buzz Club, No. IV (*anon.*)† |
| | September | 14 | [Untitled prose regarding "The Flying Islands of the Night"] (*anon.*)* |
| | | | To My Friend, Dan Paine |
| | | 28 | "Respectfully Declined" Papers of the Buzz Club, No. V (*anon.*)† |
| | | | [Letter to George C. Harding]* |
| | November | 16 | "Respectfully Declined" Papers of the Buzz Club, No. VI (*anon.*)† |
| 1879: | May | 31 | The Little Tiny Kickshaw (*anon.*) |
| | June | 7 | The True Philosopher (*anon.*)* |
| | | | The Little Dead Man (*anon.*) |
| | | 14 | Old-Fashioned Roses (*anon.*) |
| | | | The Liar (*anon.*)* |
| | | 21 | The Empty Song (*anon.*) |
| | | | Counsel (*anon.*)* |
| | | | A Rose in October (*anon.*) |
| | | 28 | The Little Old Poem That Nobody Reads (*anon.*) |
| | | | Lullaby (*anon.*) |
| | | | Mirage (*anon.*) |
| | | | Night (*anon.*) |
| | July | 5 | Pan (*anon.*) |
| | | | Lines \| On Hearing a Cow Bawl. . . (*anon.*) |
| | | | Glimpse (*anon.*) |
| | | | Lines \| On Receiving a Present from an Unknown Friend (*anon.*) |

---

*Uncollected.
†Partially uncollected.

SATURDAY HERALD (Indianapolis)—*continued*
1879: July        12    The Rain (*anon.*)
                        To H. S. T. (*anon.*)
                        My Bachelor Chum (*anon.*)
                        When our Baby Died (*anon.*)
                  19    "Uncle Bob's Boy" (*anon.*)*
                        Little Tommy Smith (*anon.*)
                        Eternity (*anon.*)
                        An Old Friend
                  26    At Bay (*anon.*)
                        God Bless Us Every One (*anon.*)
                        To a Worn-Out Pencil (*anon.*)
                        Last Words (*anon.*)
      August      2     The Witch of Erkmurden (*anon.*)
                        Song (*anon.*)
                        A Treat Ode (*anon.*)
                  9     Wait (*anon.*)
                        A Dream of Autumn (*anon.*)
                  16    The Serenade (*anon.*)
                        Since My Mother Died (*anon.*)
                  23    Sleep (*anon.*)
                  30    Her Valentine (*anon.*)
      September   6     Delilah (*anon.*)
                  13    The Little Town o' Tailholt (*anon.*)
                  27    Hope (*anon.*)
1880: July        3     In Memoriam: John W. Love
1885: April       18    As We Read Burns
                        [A Letter to a Friend]
      May         30    To the Judge
      October     31    Dyv' Ye Ken Burns the Poemer?*
      November    21    Par Nobile Fratrum (*signed* J. W. R.)
      December    19    A Last Meeting

SATURDAY MIRROR (Indianapolis)
1872: March       30    Man's Devotion (*signed* Jay White [*sic.*])
      April       13    A Mockery (*signed* Jay Whit)*
                  20    Flames and Ashes (*signed* Jay Whit)*
      May         11    A Ballad/ With a Serious Conclusion (*anon.*)
                  25    Johnny (*signed* Jay Whit)*

SATURDAY REVIEW (Indianapolis)
1880: October     30    The True Age of Wisdom
1881: February    12    The Traveling Man
      May         14    [Prose tribute to George C. Harding]*
      June        25    She Never Knew*

---

*Uncollected.

SATURDAY REVIEW (Indianapolis)—*continued*
    1881: July          16    Hot!*
    1882: October      28    Little Miriam*

SCOOP (Chicago)
    1915: January       2    To My Namesake, James Riley Matthews
                             (*signed* J. W. R.)*
                             [Untitled poem beginning: Thish-here's a
                             present-book I send]*
                             The Girl Who Sewed the Button on for Me*
                             [Letter to Dr. William C. Cooper, April 16,
                             1897]

SCRIBNER'S MAGAZINE
    1897: December          On a Youthful Portrait of Robert Louis
                             Stevenson
    1899: July              The Enduring
    1916: December          Grandfather*

SHIELD OF PHI KAPPA PSI
    1902: January      15    [Speech at Phi Kappa Psi banquet, November 27,
                             1901]*

SOUTH BEND (Indiana) SUNDAY NEWS
    1902: January      19    [Letter to Timothy E. Howard, January 12,
                             1902]* [Note: *Toward* for *Howard* in
                             heading]

SUCCESS
    1903: December          It's *Got* to Be

SUN (Baltimore)
    1892: April         6    [Letter to D. M. Henderson, March 31, 1892]*

SUN (New York)
    1880: April        11    Silence
                       18    Puck
                       25    The Skeptic's Prayer
              June     13    My Old Friend
                       20    Something Good
            August     15    The Drum
                       29    Somep'n Common-Like

SUNDAY HERALD (Indianapolis)
    1873: May          31    A Flirtation (*signed* Jay Whit)*
    1875: January      24    I Smoke My Pipe (*signed* Jay Whit)

TOPEKA STATE JOURNAL
    1899: September 15       On Reading Eugene Ware's "Old Kansas
                             Veteran"

---

*Uncollected.

UNCLE REMUS'S MAGAZINE
    1907: October        The Hired Man's Dog-Story

WAXAHACHIE (Texas) DAILY LIGHT
    1915: November 19    [Letter to the school children of Waxahachie,
                        Texas, October 26, 1915]*

WIDE AWAKE
    1881: June          Mother Goose
         August        The Land of Used-to-Be
    1882: August      The Circus-Day Parade
    1884: August      The Little Pixy People

WORLD (New York)
    1887: October   23    The Rain
         December 11    Doc Sifers
                      Robert Louis Stevenson
    1888: April     8    A Man by the Name of Bolus
         May     13    When the Green Gits Back in the Trees
    1890: December 25    Christmas Greetings
    1892: August   20    [Untitled poem beginning: Haint a-goin' to
                      worry any more]*
    1900: November 25    America's Thanksgiving: 1900

YOUTH'S COMPANION
    1903: February  26    Her Lonesomeness

---

*Uncollected.

# GENERAL INDEX

# General Index

NOTE: On pp. 329–333 of this general index, certain books are referred to merely
by the author's surname. These are:

   *Phelps* (Letters of James Whitcomb Riley, edited by William Lyon Phelps)
   *Dickey I* (The Youth of James Whitcomb Riley, by Marcus Dickey)
   *Dickey II* (The Maturity of James Whitcomb Riley, by Marcus Dickey)
   *Carman* (James Whitcomb Riley: An Essay, by Bliss Carman)
   *Laughlin* (Reminiscences of James Whitcomb Riley, by Clara E. Laughlin)